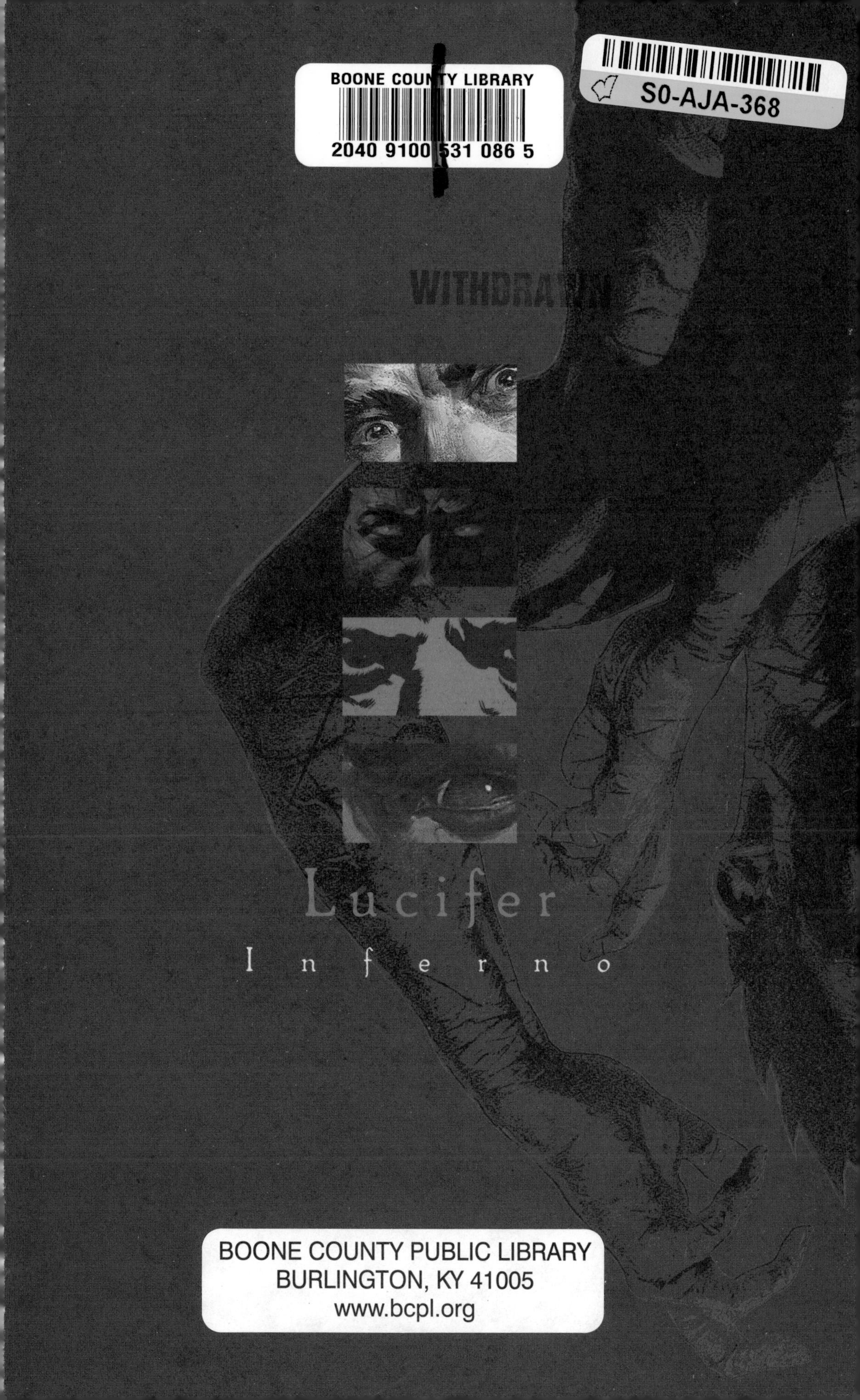
Lucifer
Inferno

Karen Berger VP-Executive Editor

Shelly Bond Editor-original series

Mariah Huehner Assistant Editor-original series

Scott Nybakken Editor-collected edition

Robbin Brosterman Senior Art Director

Paul Levitz President & Publisher

Georg Brewer VP-Design & Retail Product Development

Richard Bruning Senior VP-Creative Director

Patrick Caldon Senior VP-Finance & Operations

Chris Caramalis VP-Finance

Terri Cunningham VP-Managing Editor

Alison Gill VP-Manufacturing

Rich Johnson VP-Book Trade Sales

Hank Kanalz VP-General Manager, WildStorm

Lillian Laserson Senior VP & General Counsel

Jim Lee Editorial Director-WildStorm

David McKillips VP-Advertising & Custom Publishing

John Nee VP-Business Development

Gregory Noveck Senior VP-Creative Affairs

Cheryl Rubin Senior VP-Brand Management

Bob Wayne VP-Sales & Marketing

LUCIFER: INFERNO

Published by DC Comics.

Cover and compilation copyright © 2004 DC Comics.

All Rights Reserved.

Originally published in single magazine form as LUCIFER 29-35.

Copyright © 2002, 2003 DC Comics. All Rights Reserved.

All characters, their distinctive likenesses and related elements featured in this publication are trademarks of DC Comics. The stories, characters, and incidents featured in this publication are entirely fictional. DC Comics does not read or accept unsolicited submissions of ideas, stories or artwork.

DC Comics, 1700 Broadway, New York, NY 10019

A Warner Bros. Entertainment Company

Printed in Canada. Second Printing.

ISBN: 1-4012-0210-1

Cover illustrations by Christopher Moeller

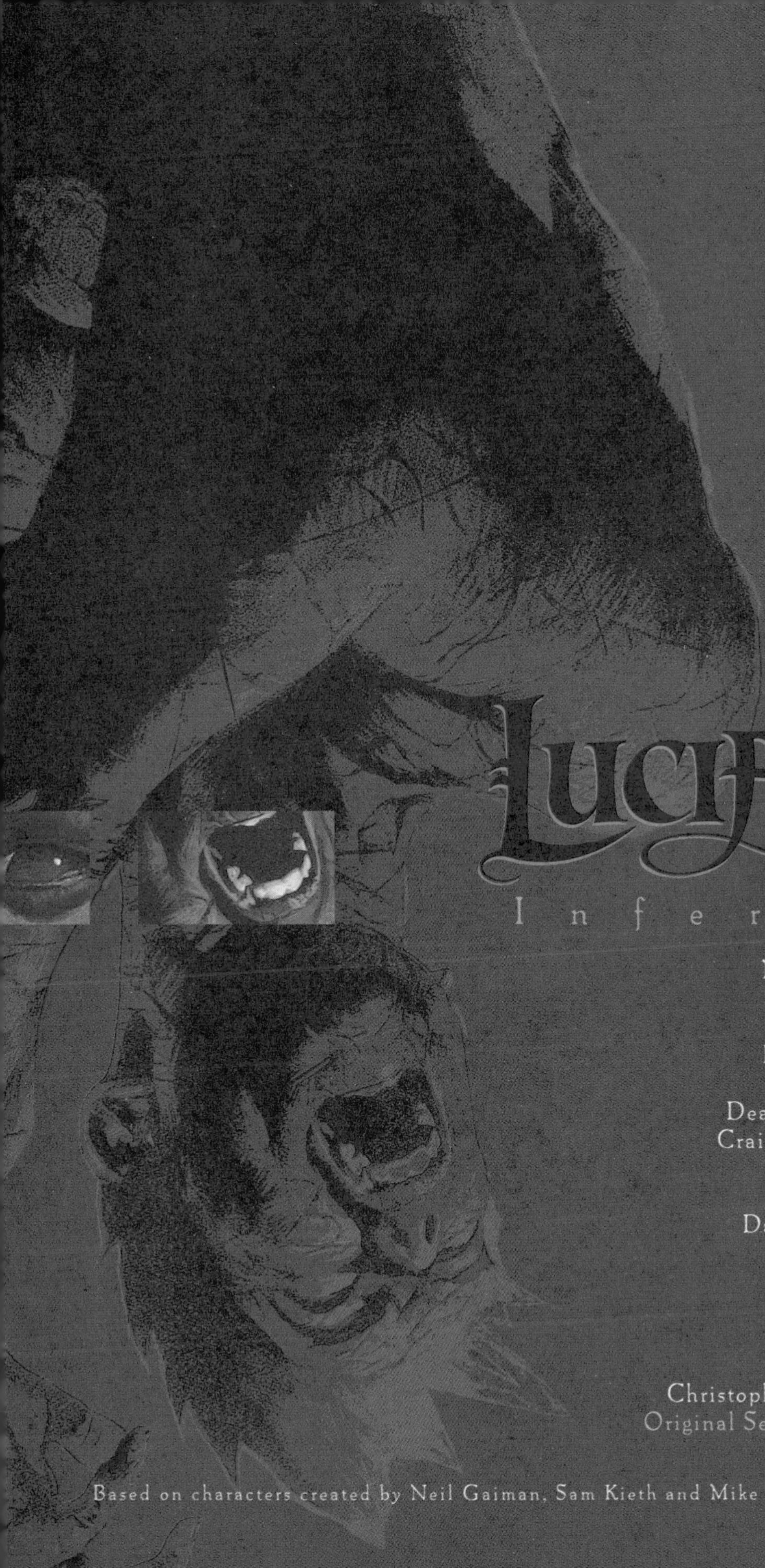

Lucifer

Inferno

Mike Carey
Writer

Peter Gross
Ryan Kelly
Dean Ormston
Craig Hamilton
Artists

Daniel Vozzo
Colorist

Comicraft
Letterer

Christopher Moeller
Original Series Covers

Based on characters created by Neil Gaiman, Sam Kieth and Mike Dringenberg

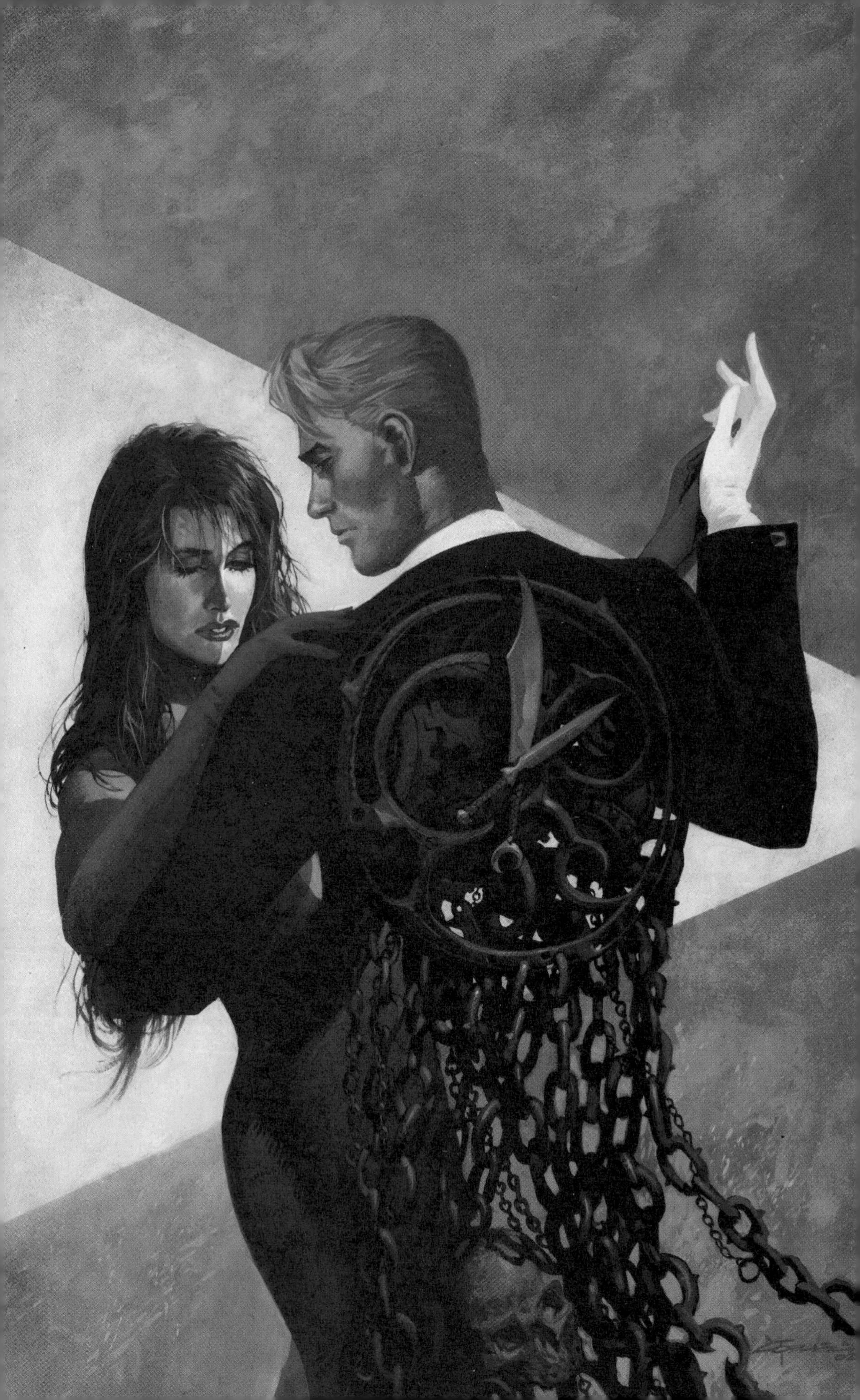

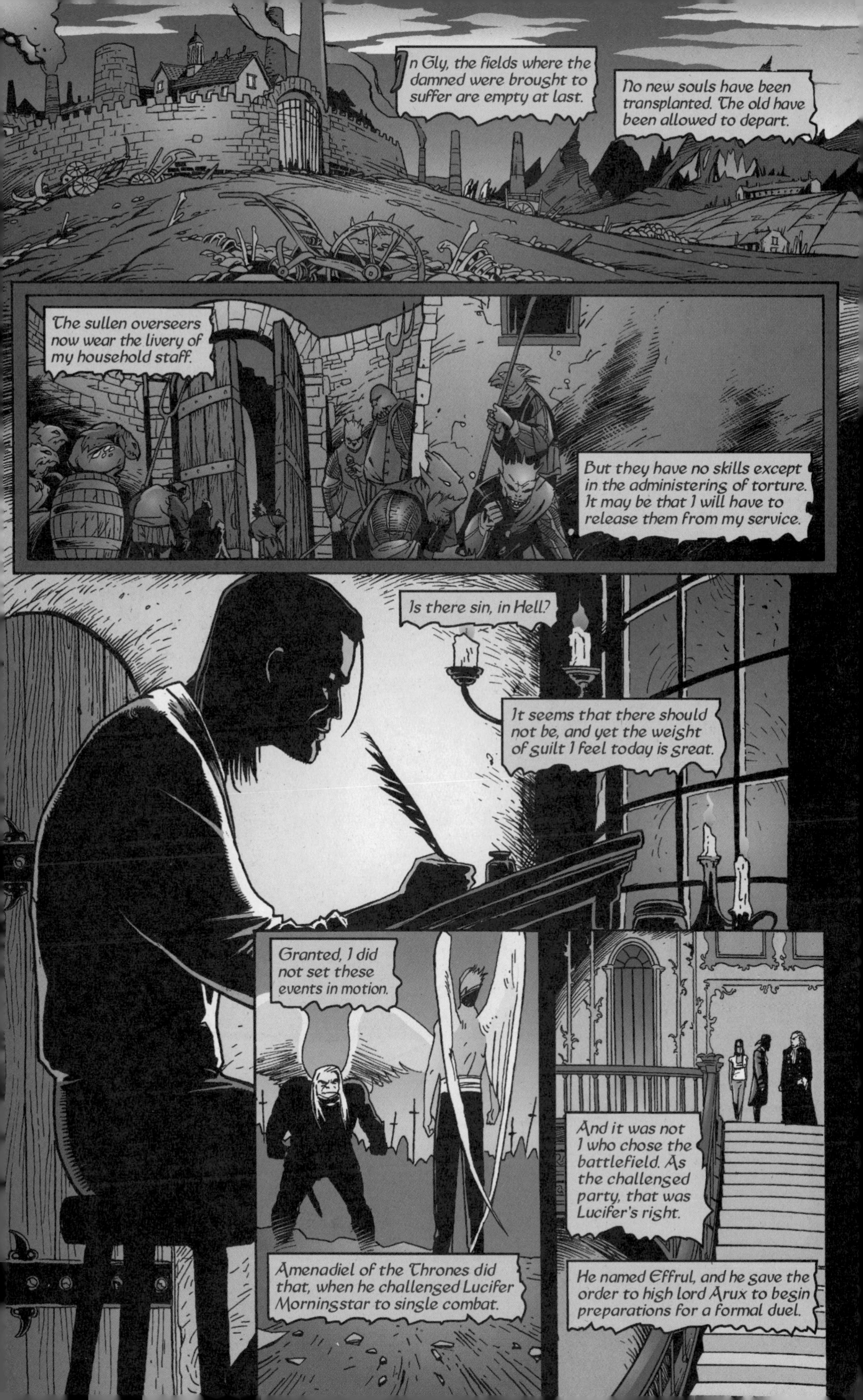
In Gly, the fields where the damned were brought to suffer are empty at last.
No new souls have been transplanted. The old have been allowed to depart.
The sullen overseers now wear the livery of my household staff.
But they have no skills except in the administering of torture. It may be that I will have to release them from my service.
Is there sin, in Hell?
It seems that there should not be, and yet the weight of guilt I feel today is great.
Granted, I did not set these events in motion.
Amenadiel of the Thrones did that, when he challenged Lucifer Morningstar to single combat.
And it was not I who chose the battlefield. As the challenged party, that was Lucifer's right.
He named Effrul, and he gave the order to high lord Arux to begin preparations for a formal duel.

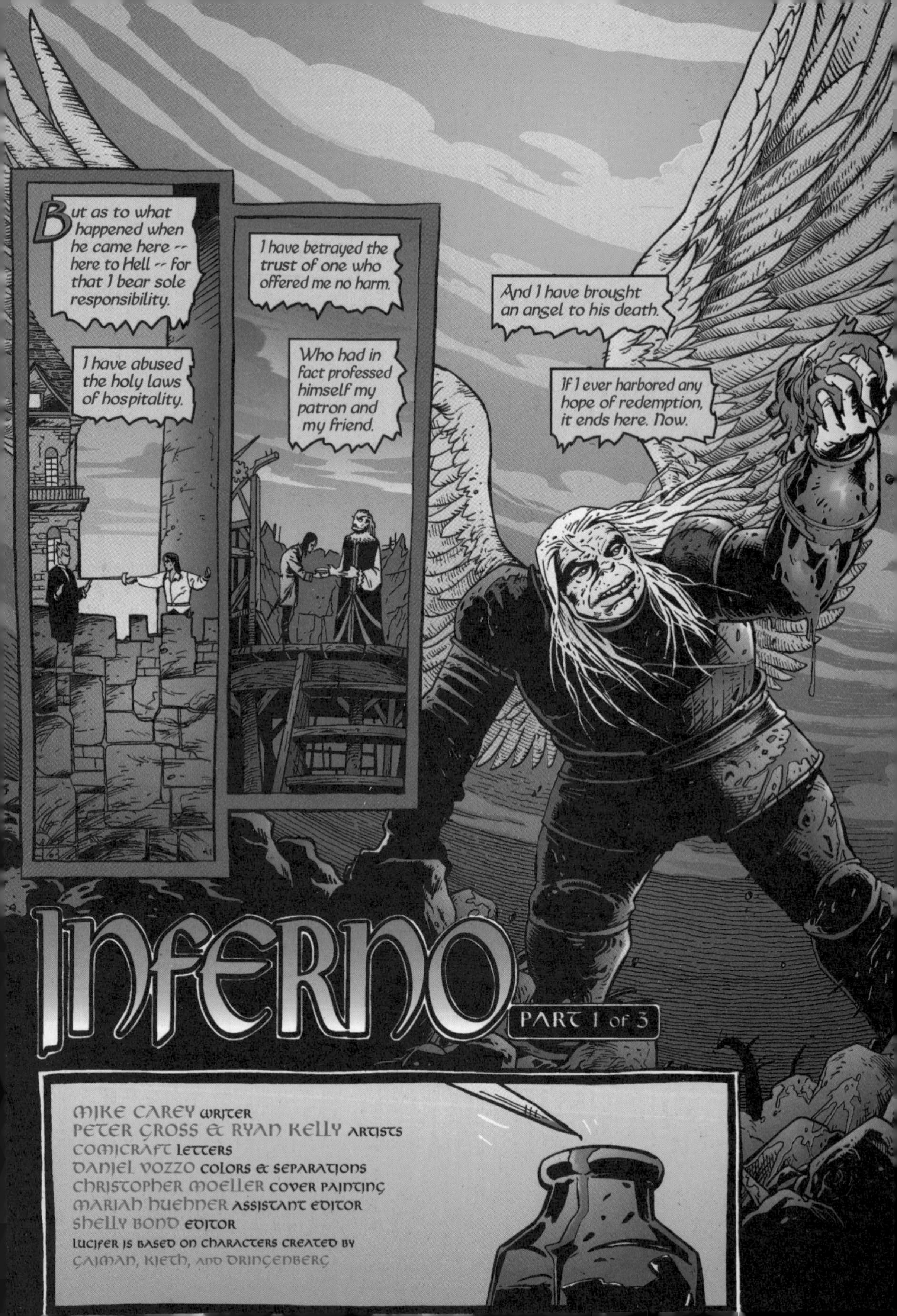
But as to what happened when he came here -- here to Hell -- for that I bear sole responsibility.
I have abused the holy laws of hospitality.
I have betrayed the trust of one who offered me no harm.
Who had in fact professed himself my patron and my friend.
And I have brought an angel to his death.
If I ever harbored any hope of redemption, it ends here. Now.
INFERNO
PART 1 of 3
MIKE CAREY writer
PETER GROSS & RYAN KELLY artists
COMICRAFT letters
DANIEL VOZZO colors & separations
CHRISTOPHER MOELLER cover painting
MARIAH HUEHNER assistant editor
SHELLY BOND editor
LUCIFER is based on characters created by
GAIMAN, KIETH, and DRINGENBERG

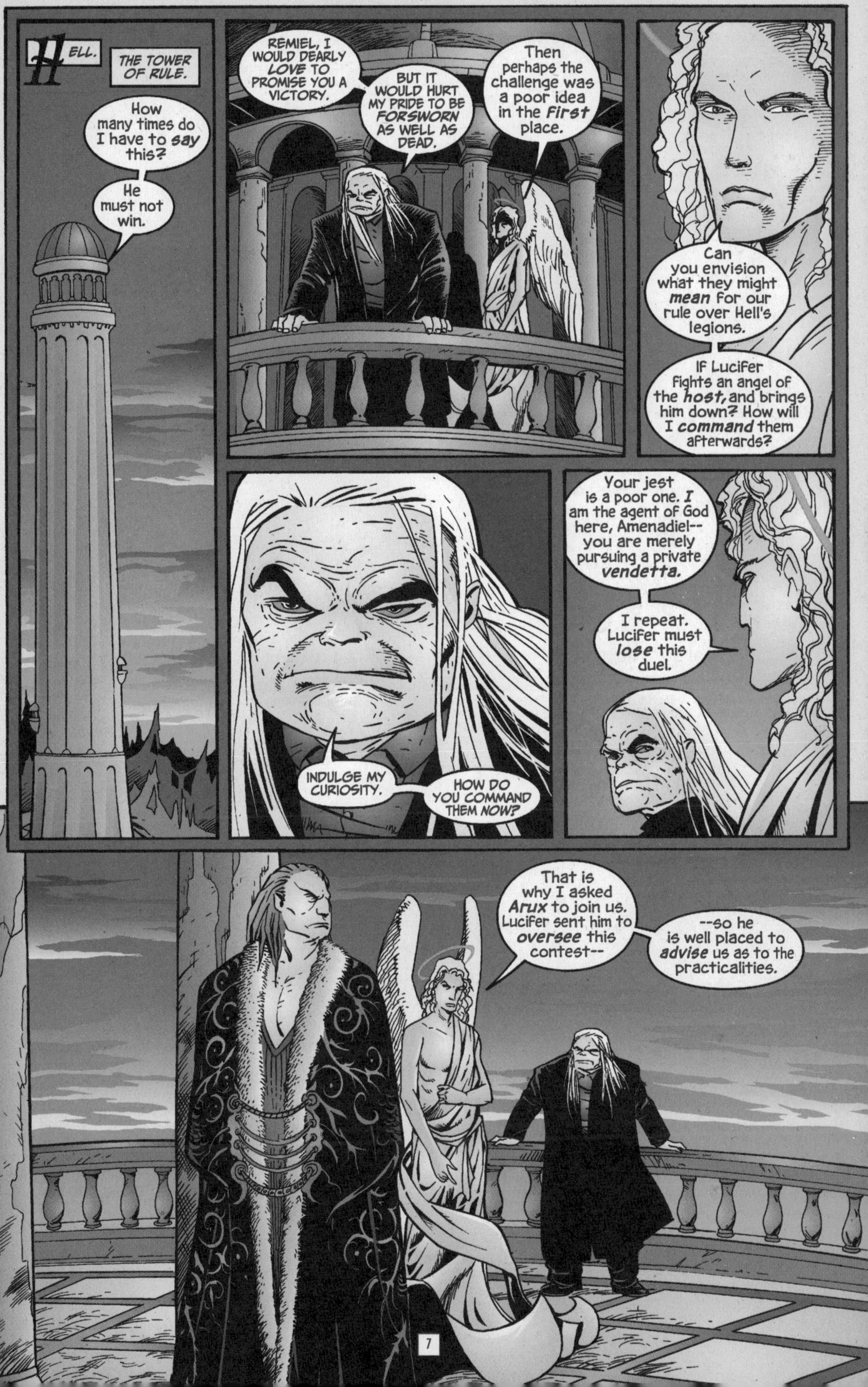
HELL.
THE TOWER OF RULE.
How many times do I have to say this?
He must not win.
REMIEL, I WOULD DEARLY LOVE TO PROMISE YOU A VICTORY.
BUT IT WOULD HURT MY PRIDE TO BE FORSWORN AS WELL AS DEAD.
Then perhaps the challenge was a poor idea in the first place.
Can you envision what they might mean for our rule over Hell's legions.
If Lucifer fights an angel of the host, and brings him down? How will I command them afterwards?
INDULGE MY CURIOSITY.
HOW DO YOU COMMAND THEM NOW?
Your jest is a poor one. I am the agent of God here, Amenadiel-- you are merely pursuing a private vendetta.
I repeat. Lucifer must lose this duel.
That is why I asked Arux to join us. Lucifer sent him to oversee this contest--
--so he is well placed to advise us as to the practicalities.

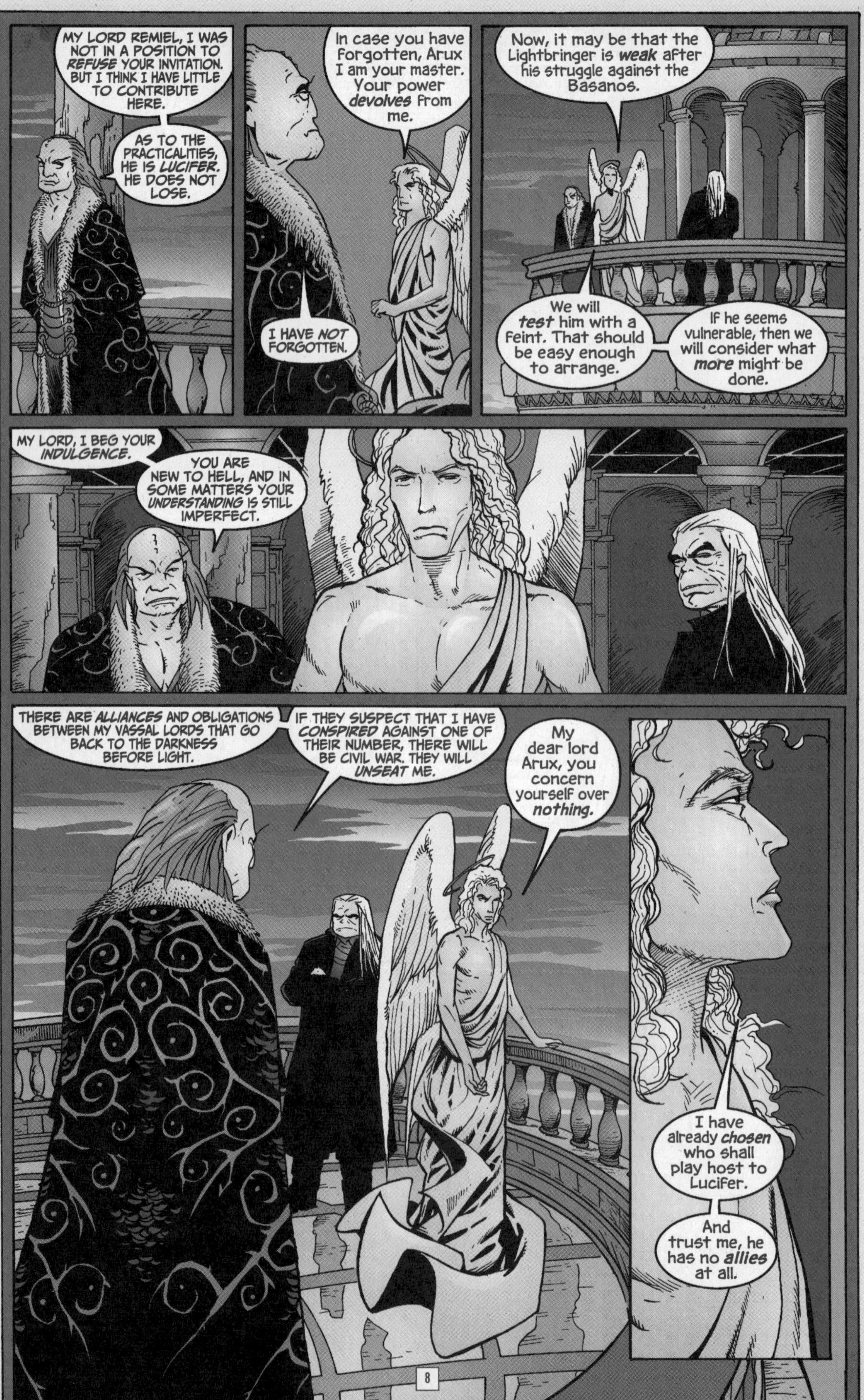
MY LORD REMIEL, I WAS NOT IN A POSITION TO REFUSE YOUR INVITATION. BUT I THINK I HAVE LITTLE TO CONTRIBUTE HERE.
AS TO THE PRACTICALITIES, HE IS LUCIFER. HE DOES NOT LOSE.
In case you have forgotten, Arux I am your master. Your power devolves from me.
I HAVE NOT FORGOTTEN.
Now, it may be that the Lightbringer is weak after his struggle against the Basanos.
We will test him with a feint. That should be easy enough to arrange.
If he seems vulnerable, then we will consider what more might be done.
MY LORD, I BEG YOUR INDULGENCE.
YOU ARE NEW TO HELL, AND IN SOME MATTERS YOUR UNDERSTANDING IS STILL IMPERFECT.
THERE ARE ALLIANCES AND OBLIGATIONS BETWEEN MY VASSAL LORDS THAT GO BACK TO THE DARKNESS BEFORE LIGHT.
IF THEY SUSPECT THAT I HAVE CONSPIRED AGAINST ONE OF THEIR NUMBER, THERE WILL BE CIVIL WAR. THEY WILL UNSEAT ME.
My dear lord Arux, you concern yourself over nothing.
I have already chosen who shall play host to Lucifer.
And trust me, he has no allies at all.

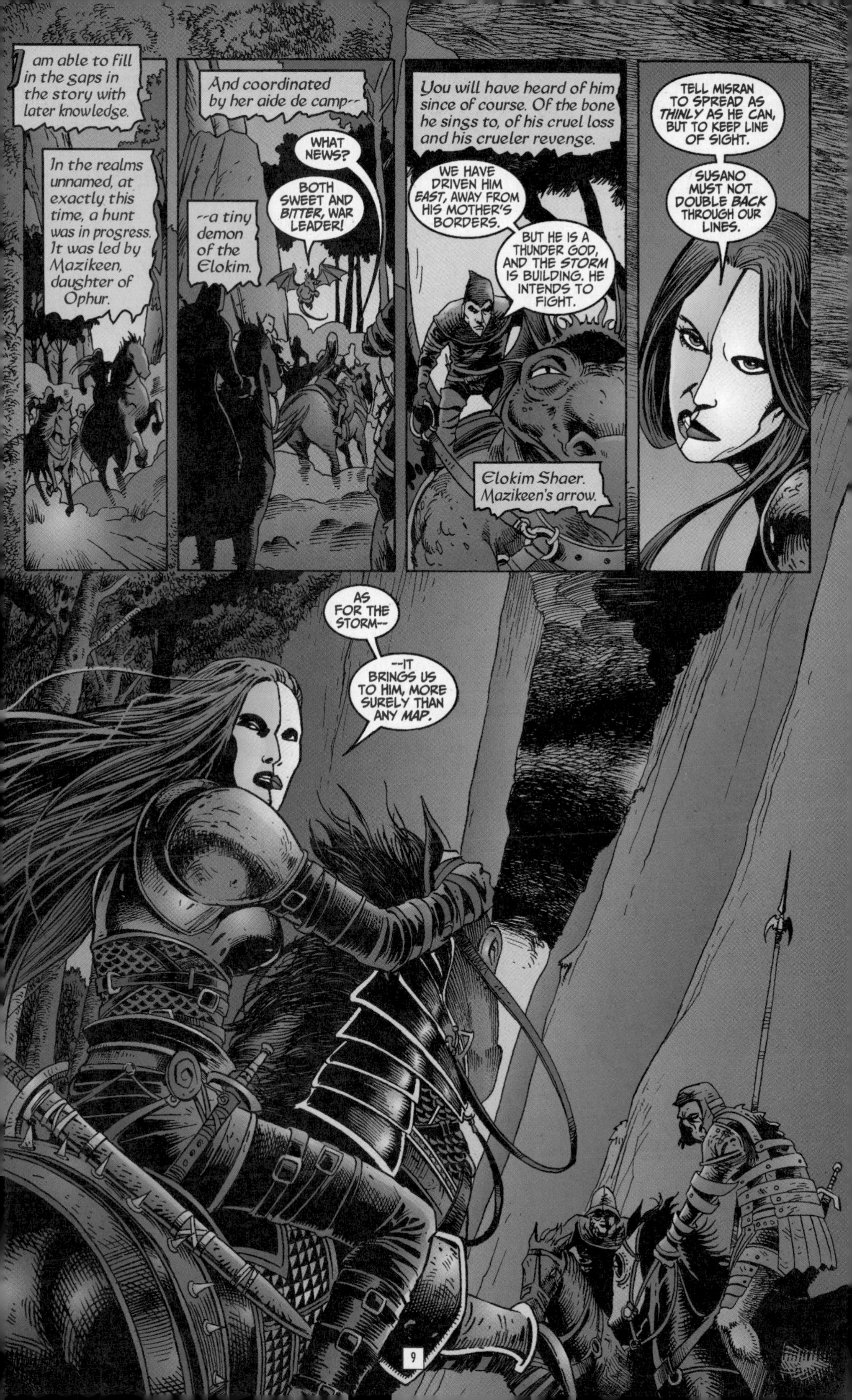
I am able to fill in the gaps in the story with later knowledge.
In the realms unnamed, at exactly this time, a hunt was in progress. It was led by Mazikeen, daughter of Ophur.
And coordinated by her aide de camp--
WHAT NEWS?
BOTH SWEET AND BITTER, WAR LEADER!
--a tiny demon of the Elokim.
You will have heard of him since of course. Of the bone he sings to, of his cruel loss and his crueler revenge.
WE HAVE DRIVEN HIM EAST, AWAY FROM HIS MOTHER'S BORDERS.
BUT HE IS A THUNDER GOD, AND THE STORM IS BUILDING. HE INTENDS TO FIGHT.
Elokim Shaer. Mazikeen's arrow.
TELL MISRAN TO SPREAD AS THINLY AS HE CAN, BUT TO KEEP LINE OF SIGHT.
SUSANO MUST NOT DOUBLE BACK THROUGH OUR LINES.
AS FOR THE STORM--
--IT BRINGS US TO HIM, MORE SURELY THAN ANY MAP.

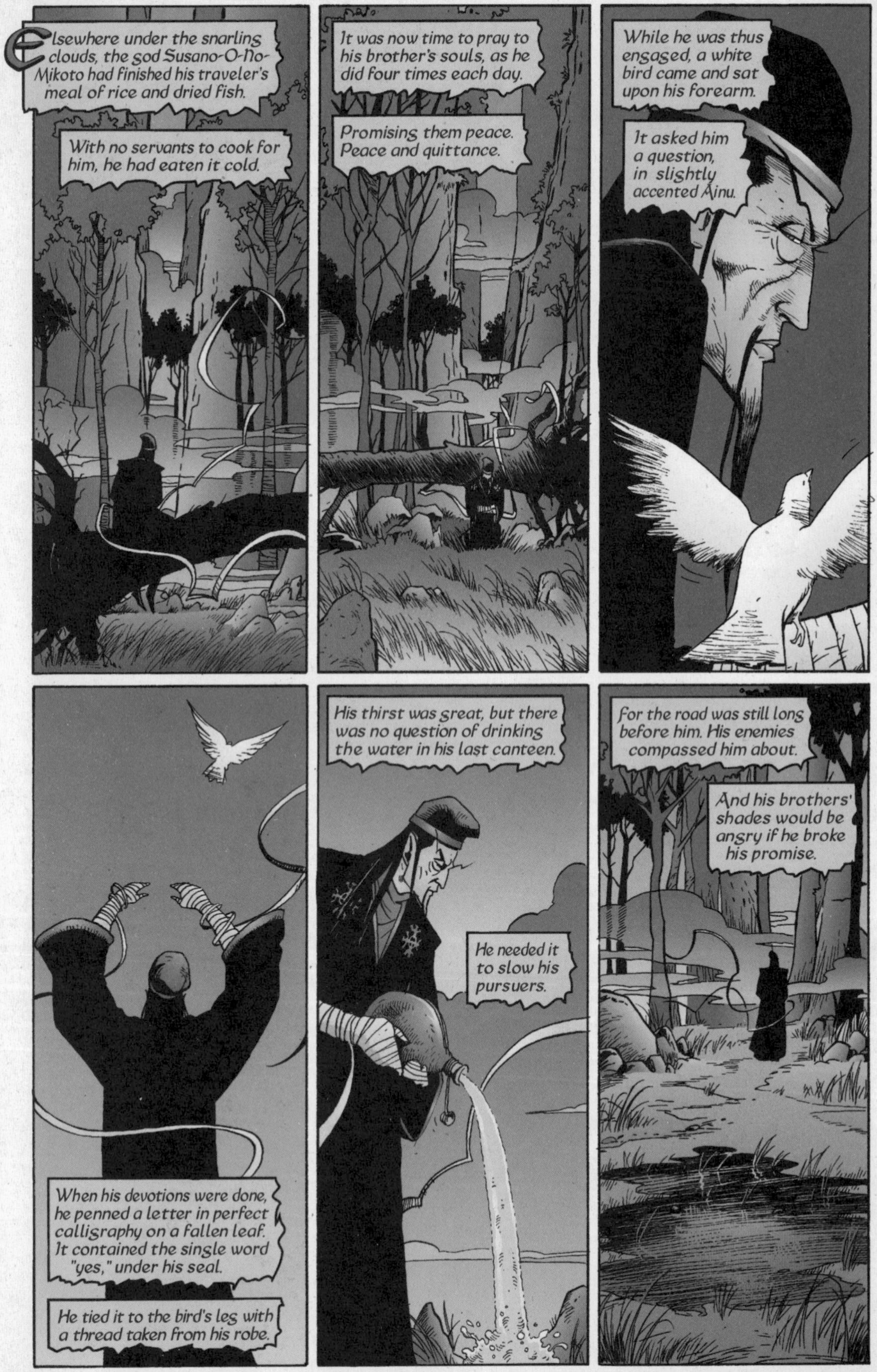
Elsewhere under the snarling clouds, the god Susano-O-No-Mikoto had finished his traveler's meal of rice and dried fish.
With no servants to cook for him, he had eaten it cold.
It was now time to pray to his brother's souls, as he did four times each day.
Promising them peace. Peace and quittance.
While he was thus engaged, a white bird came and sat upon his forearm.
It asked him a question, in slightly accented Ainu.
When his devotions were done, he penned a letter in perfect calligraphy on a fallen leaf. It contained the single word "yes," under his seal.
He tied it to the bird's leg with a thread taken from his robe.
His thirst was great, but there was no question of drinking the water in his last canteen.
He needed it to slow his pursuers.
for the road was still long before him. His enemies compassed him about.
And his brothers' shades would be angry if he broke his promise.

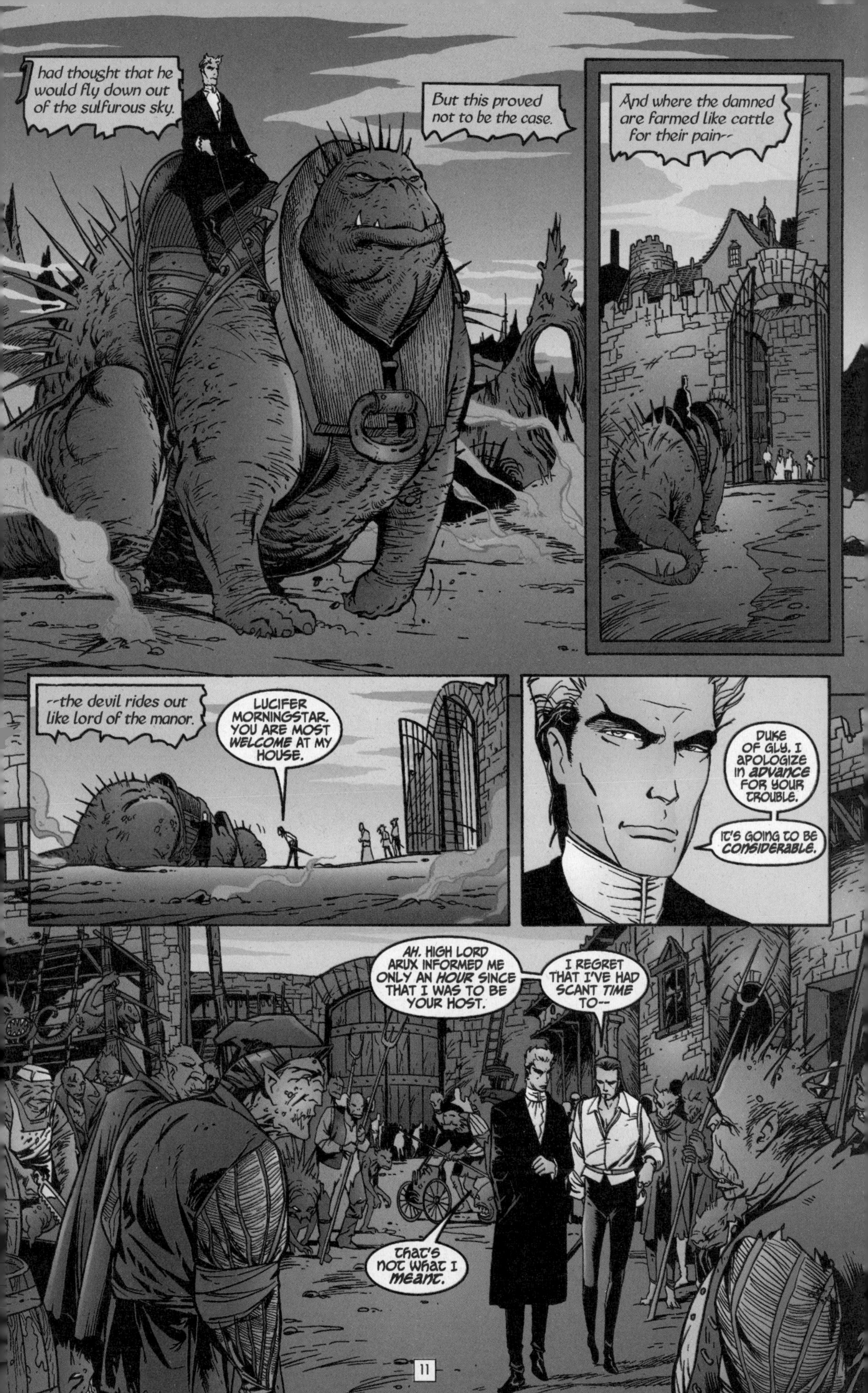
I had thought that he would fly down out of the sulfurous sky.
But this proved not to be the case.
And where the damned are farmed like cattle for their pain--
--the devil rides out like lord of the manor.
LUCIFER MORNINGSTAR. YOU ARE MOST WELCOME AT MY HOUSE.
DUKE OF GLY. I APOLOGIZE IN ADVANCE FOR YOUR TROUBLE.
IT'S GOING TO BE CONSIDERABLE.
AH. HIGH LORD ARUX INFORMED ME ONLY AN HOUR SINCE THAT I WAS TO BE YOUR HOST.
I REGRET THAT I'VE HAD SCANT TIME TO--
THAT'S NOT WHAT I MEANT.

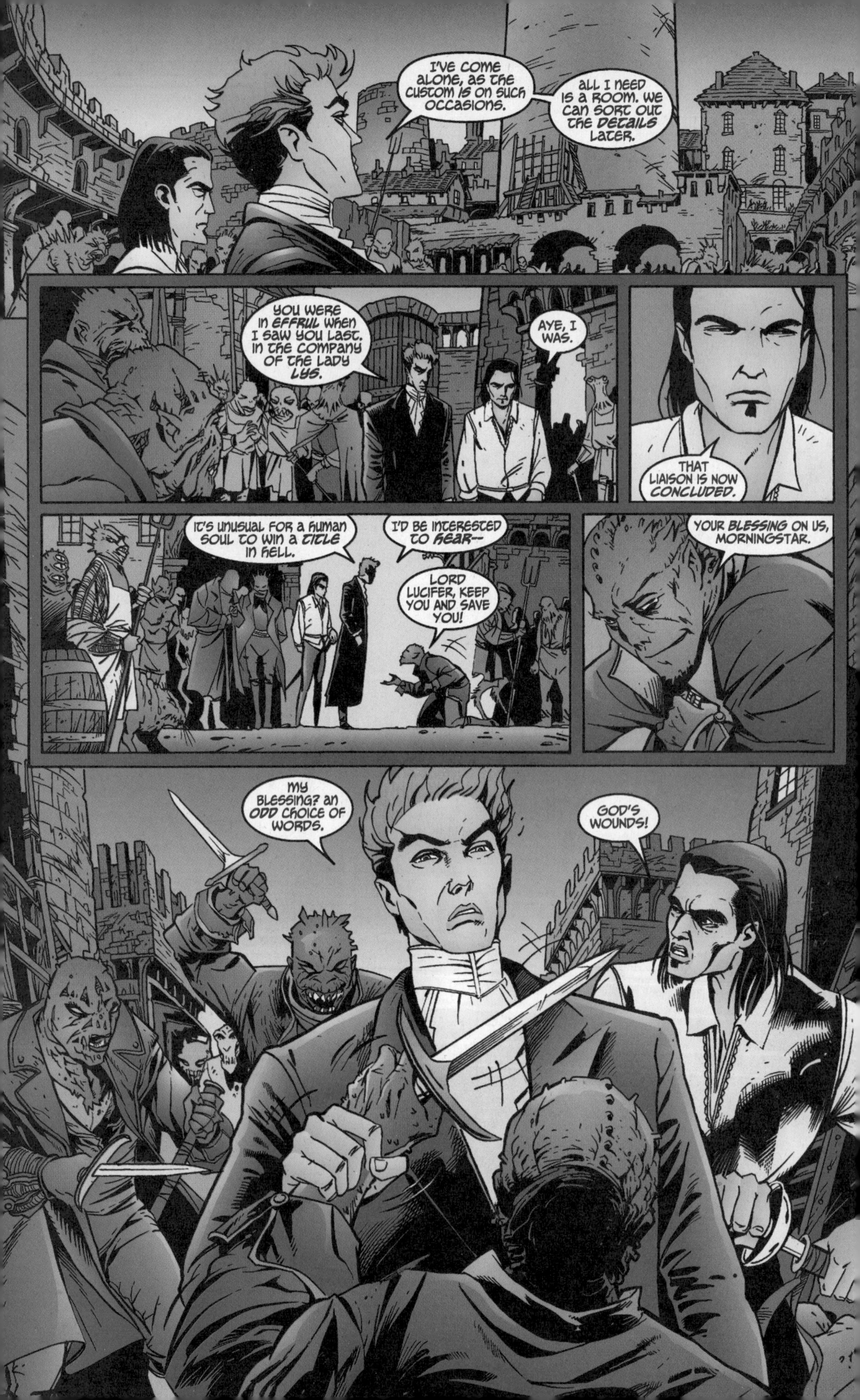
I'VE COME ALONE, AS THE CUSTOM IS ON SUCH OCCASIONS.
ALL I NEED IS A ROOM. WE CAN SORT OUT THE DETAILS LATER.
YOU WERE IN EFFRUL WHEN I SAW YOU LAST. IN THE COMPANY OF THE LADY LYS.
AYE, I WAS.
THAT LIAISON IS NOW CONCLUDED.
IT'S UNUSUAL FOR A HUMAN SOUL TO WIN A TITLE IN HELL.
I'D BE INTERESTED TO HEAR--
LORD LUCIFER, KEEP YOU AND SAVE YOU!
YOUR BLESSING ON US, MORNINGSTAR.
MY BLESSING? AN ODD CHOICE OF WORDS.
GOD'S WOUNDS!

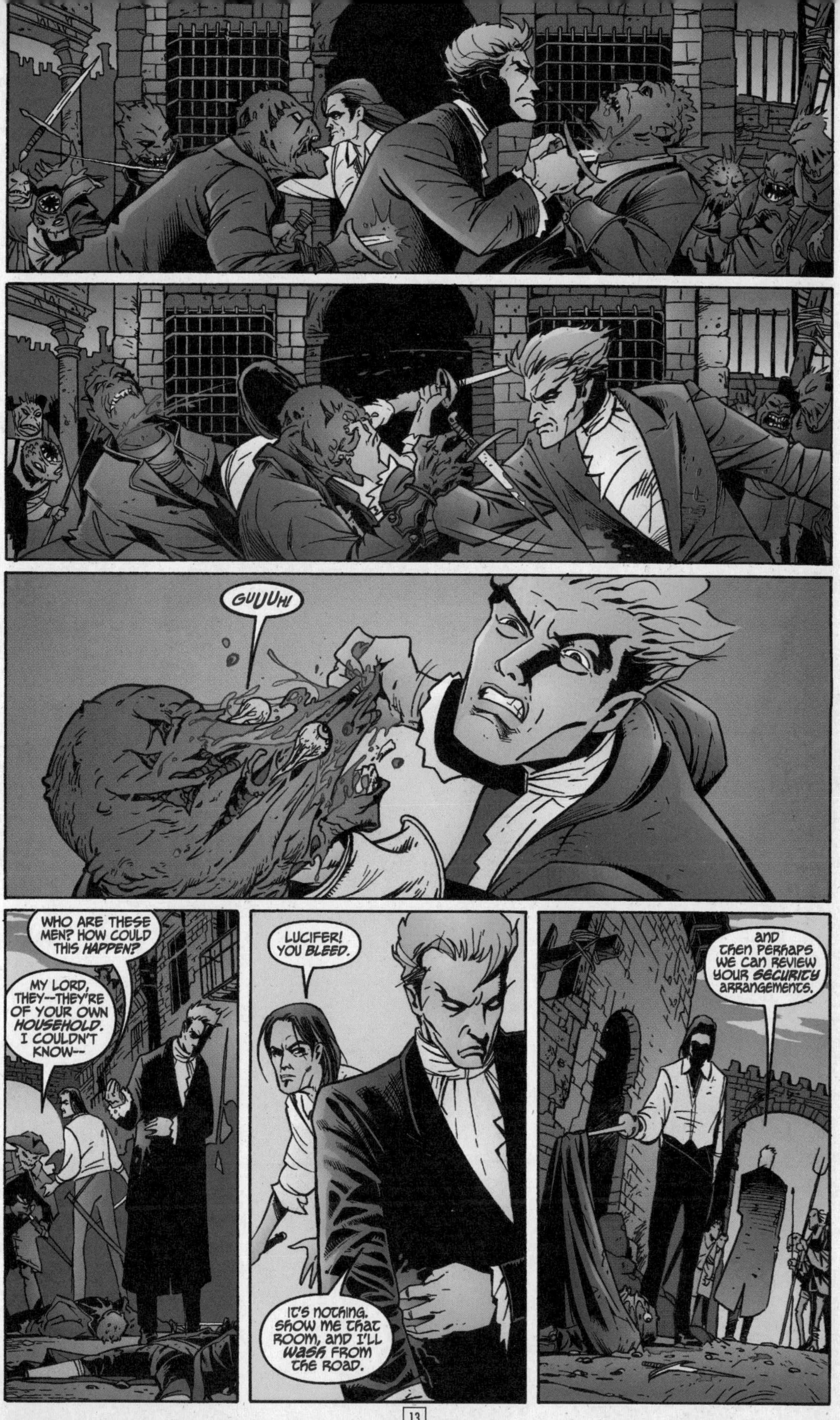
GUUUH!
WHO ARE THESE MEN? HOW COULD THIS HAPPEN?
MY LORD, THEY--THEY'RE OF YOUR OWN HOUSEHOLD. I COULDN'T KNOW--
LUCIFER! YOU BLEED.
IT'S NOTHING. SHOW ME THAT ROOM, AND I'LL WASH FROM THE ROAD.
AND THEN PERHAPS WE CAN REVIEW YOUR SECURITY ARRANGEMENTS.

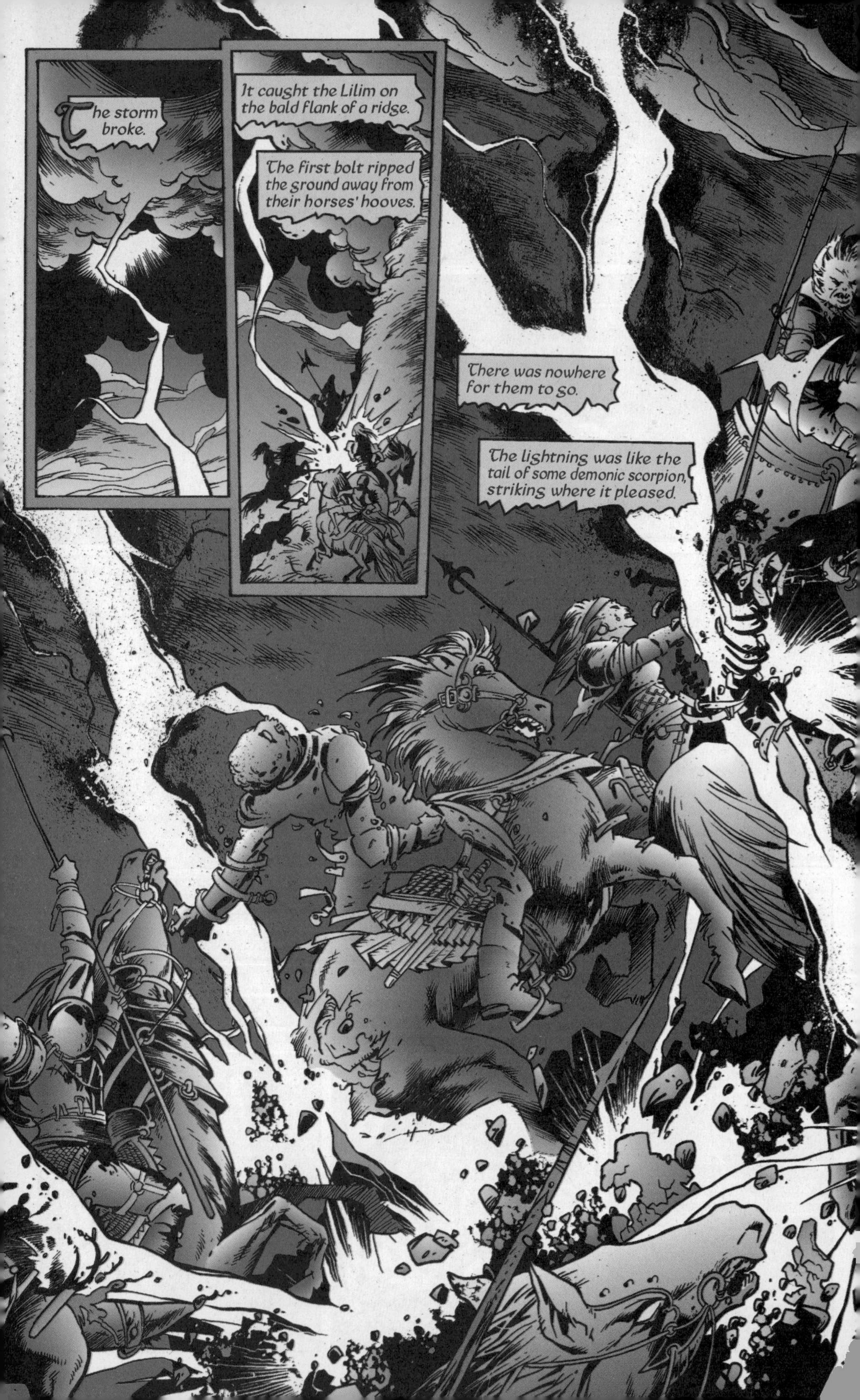
The storm broke.
It caught the Lilim on the bald flank of a ridge.
The first bolt ripped the ground away from their horses' hooves.
There was nowhere for them to go.
The lightning was like the tail of some demonic scorpion, striking where it pleased.

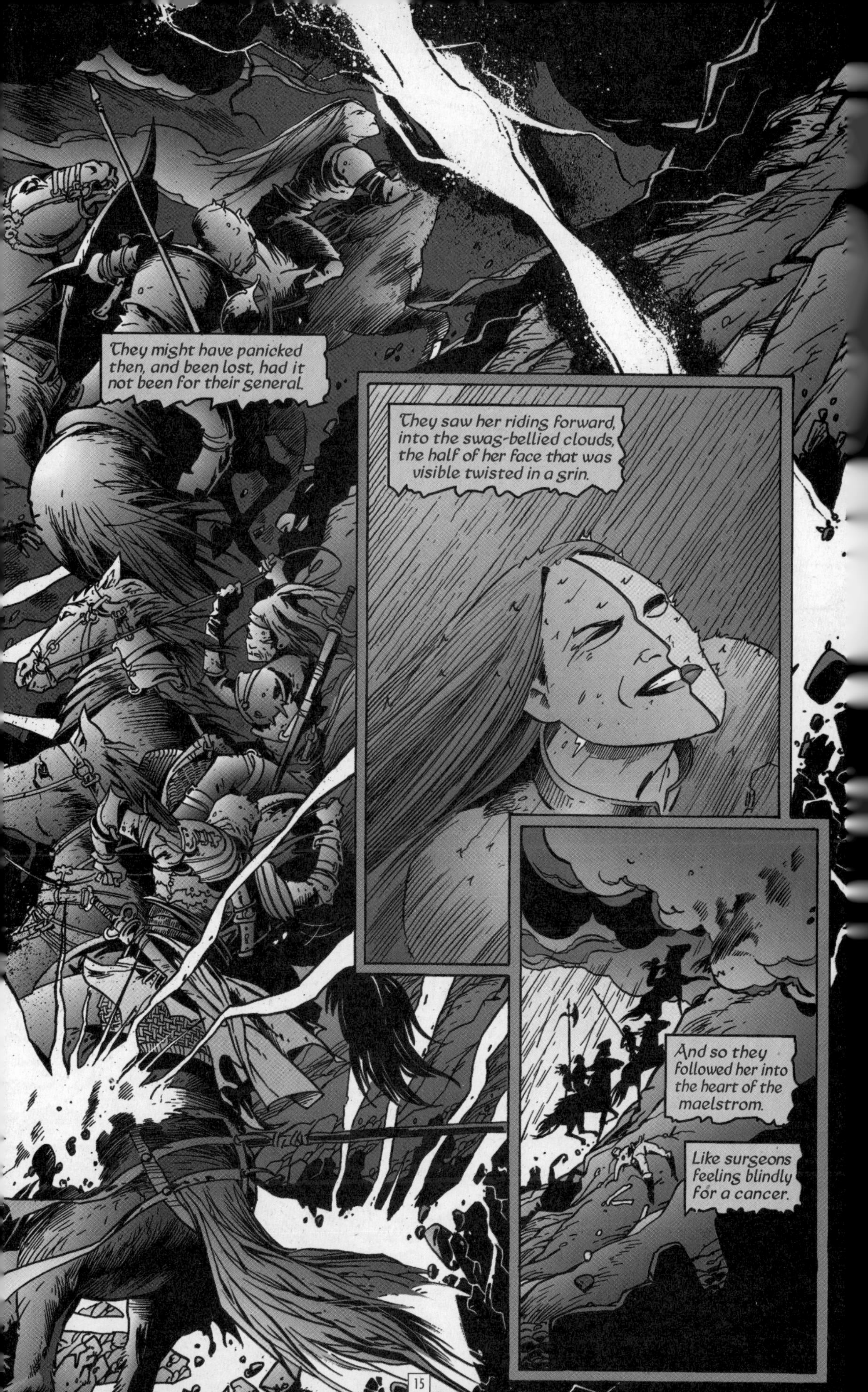
They might have panicked then, and been lost, had it not been for their general.
They saw her riding forward, into the swag-bellied clouds, the half of her face that was visible twisted in a grin.
And so they followed her into the heart of the maelstrom.
Like surgeons feeling blindly for a cancer.

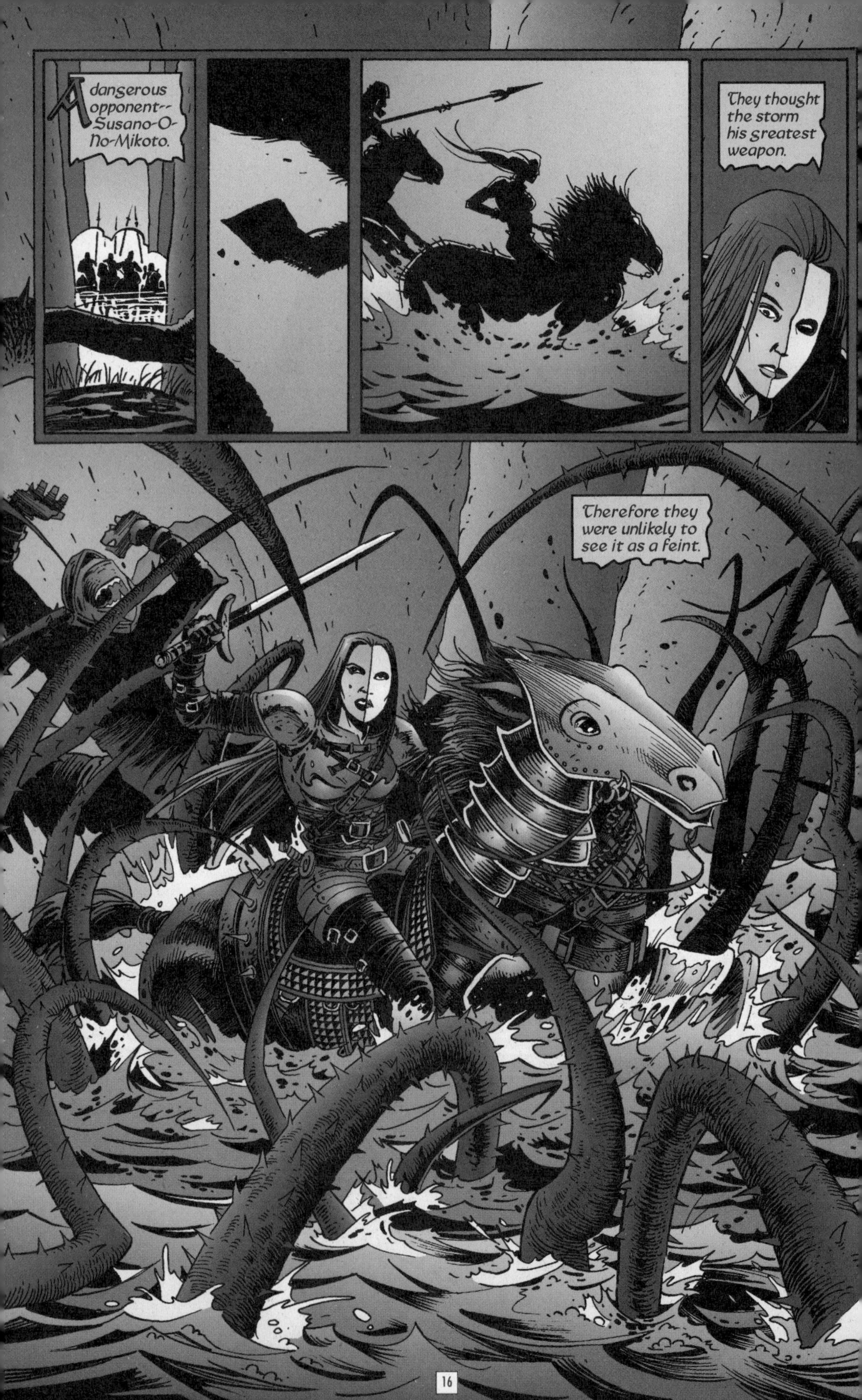
A dangerous opponent-- Susano-O-No-Mikoto.
They thought the storm his greatest weapon.
Therefore they were unlikely to see it as a feint.

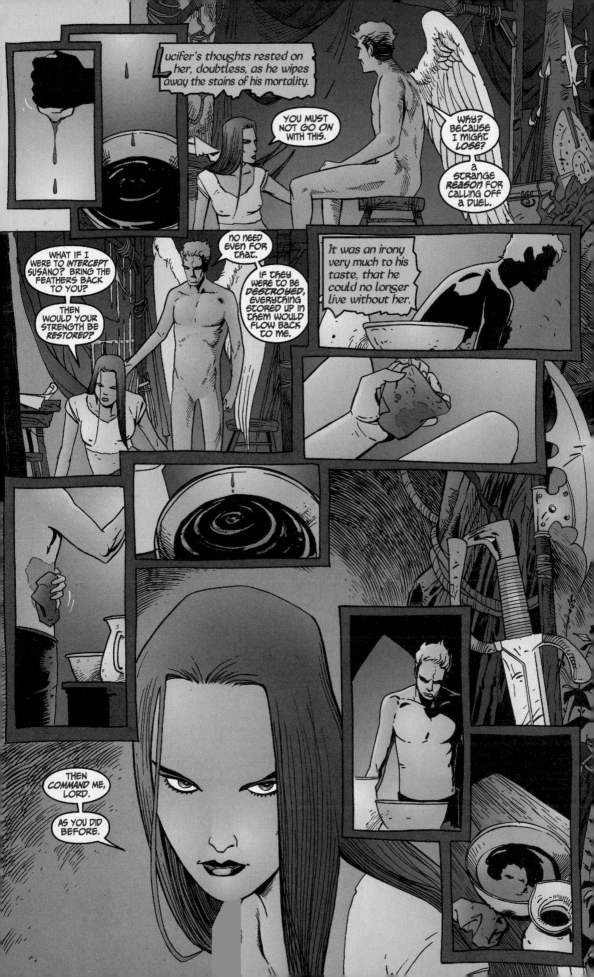

Lucifer's thoughts rested on her, doubtless, as he wipes away the stains of his mortality.

YOU MUST NOT GO ON WITH THIS.

WHY? BECAUSE I MIGHT LOSE?

A STRANGE REASON FOR CALLING OFF A DUEL.

WHAT IF I WERE TO *INTERCEPT* SUSANO? BRING THE FEATHERS BACK TO YOU?

THEN WOULD YOUR STRENGTH BE RESTORED?

NO NEED EVEN FOR THAT.

IF THEY WERE TO BE *DESTROYED,* EVERYTHING STORED UP IN THEM WOULD FLOW BACK TO ME.

It was an irony very much to his taste, that he could no longer live without her.

THEN *COMMAND* ME, LORD.

AS YOU DID BEFORE.

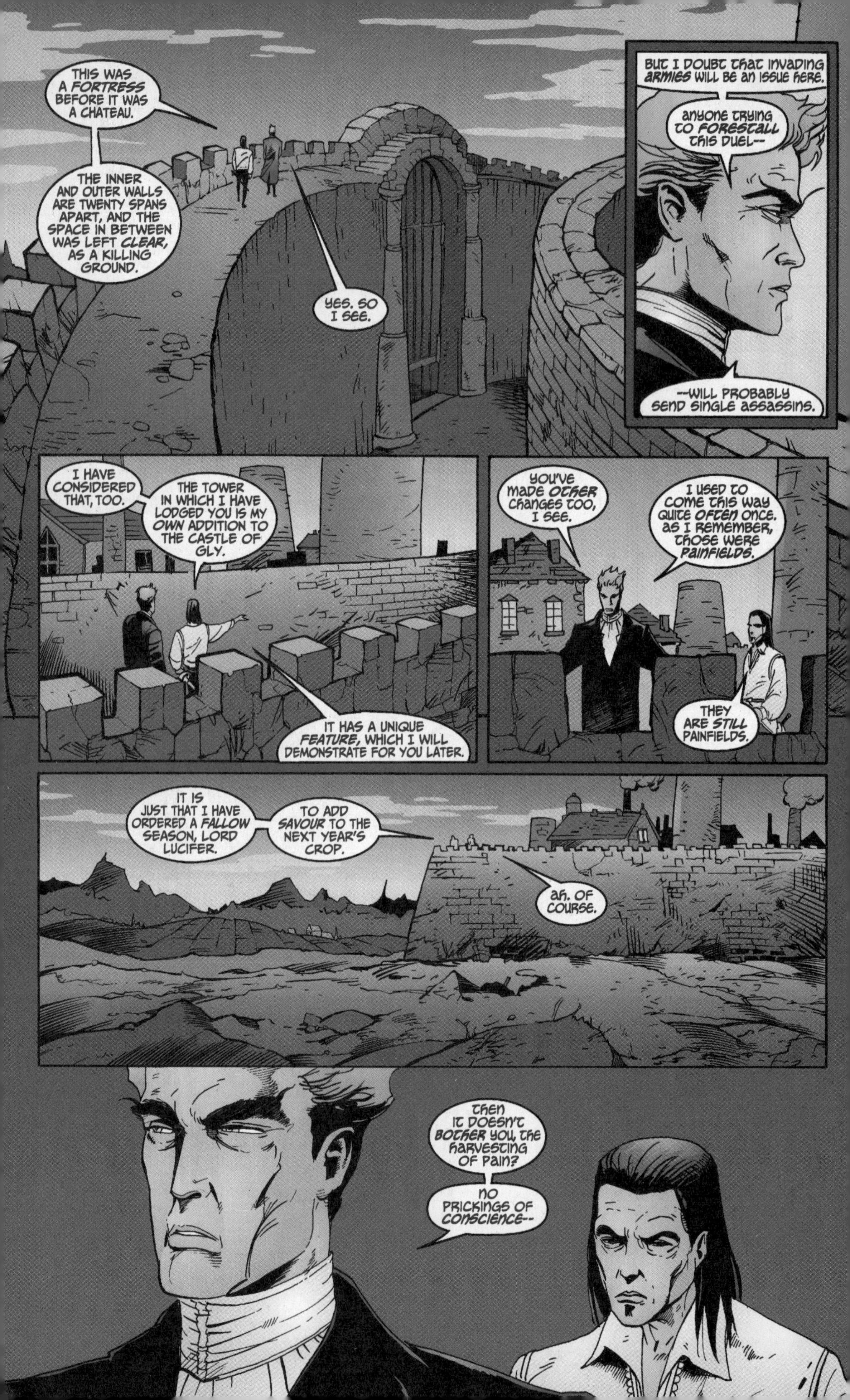
THIS WAS A FORTRESS BEFORE IT WAS A CHATEAU.
THE INNER AND OUTER WALLS ARE TWENTY SPANS APART, AND THE SPACE IN BETWEEN WAS LEFT CLEAR, AS A KILLING GROUND.
YES. SO I SEE.
BUT I DOUBT THAT INVADING ARMIES WILL BE AN ISSUE HERE.
ANYONE TRYING TO FORESTALL THIS DUEL--
--WILL PROBABLY SEND SINGLE ASSASSINS.
I HAVE CONSIDERED THAT, TOO.
THE TOWER IN WHICH I HAVE LODGED YOU IS MY OWN ADDITION TO THE CASTLE OF GLY.
IT HAS A UNIQUE FEATURE, WHICH I WILL DEMONSTRATE FOR YOU LATER.
YOU'VE MADE OTHER CHANGES TOO, I SEE.
I USED TO COME THIS WAY QUITE OFTEN ONCE. AS I REMEMBER, THOSE WERE PAINFIELDS.
THEY ARE STILL PAINFIELDS.
IT IS JUST THAT I HAVE ORDERED A FALLOW SEASON, LORD LUCIFER.
TO ADD SAVOUR TO THE NEXT YEAR'S CROP.
AH. OF COURSE.
THEN IT DOESN'T BOTHER YOU, THE HARVESTING OF PAIN?
NO PRICKINGS OF CONSCIENCE--

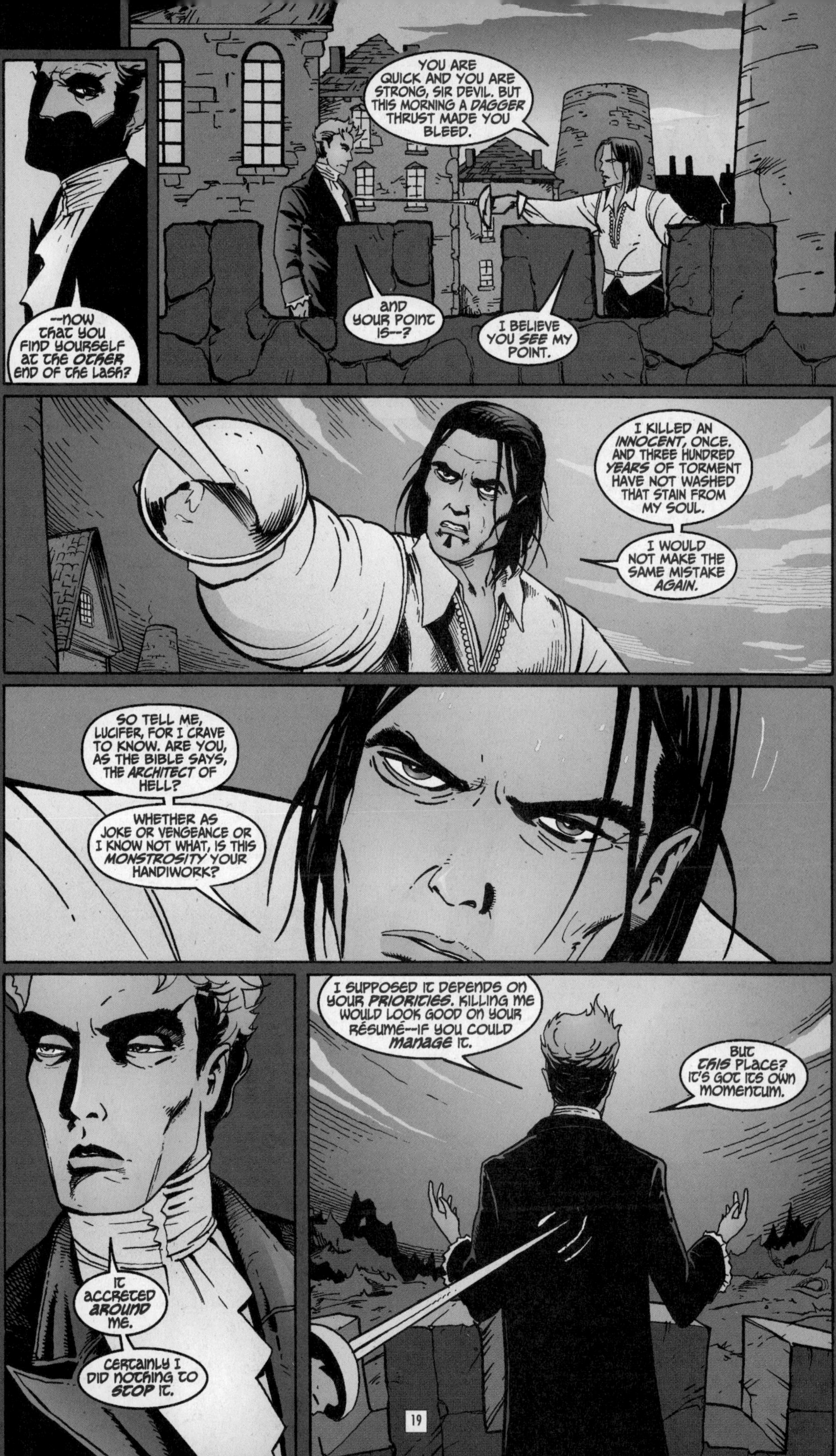
--NOW THAT YOU FIND YOURSELF AT THE OTHER END OF THE LASH?
YOU ARE QUICK AND YOU ARE STRONG, SIR DEVIL. BUT THIS MORNING A DAGGER THRUST MADE YOU BLEED.
AND YOUR POINT IS--?
I BELIEVE YOU SEE MY POINT.
I KILLED AN INNOCENT, ONCE. AND THREE HUNDRED YEARS OF TORMENT HAVE NOT WASHED THAT STAIN FROM MY SOUL.
I WOULD NOT MAKE THE SAME MISTAKE AGAIN.
SO TELL ME, LUCIFER, FOR I CRAVE TO KNOW. ARE YOU, AS THE BIBLE SAYS, THE ARCHITECT OF HELL?
WHETHER AS JOKE OR VENGEANCE OR I KNOW NOT WHAT, IS THIS MONSTROSITY YOUR HANDIWORK?
IT ACCRETED AROUND ME.
CERTAINLY I DID NOTHING TO STOP IT.
I SUPPOSED IT DEPENDS ON YOUR PRIORITIES. KILLING ME WOULD LOOK GOOD ON YOUR RÉSUMÉ--IF YOU COULD MANAGE IT.
BUT THIS PLACE? IT'S GOT ITS OWN MOMENTUM.

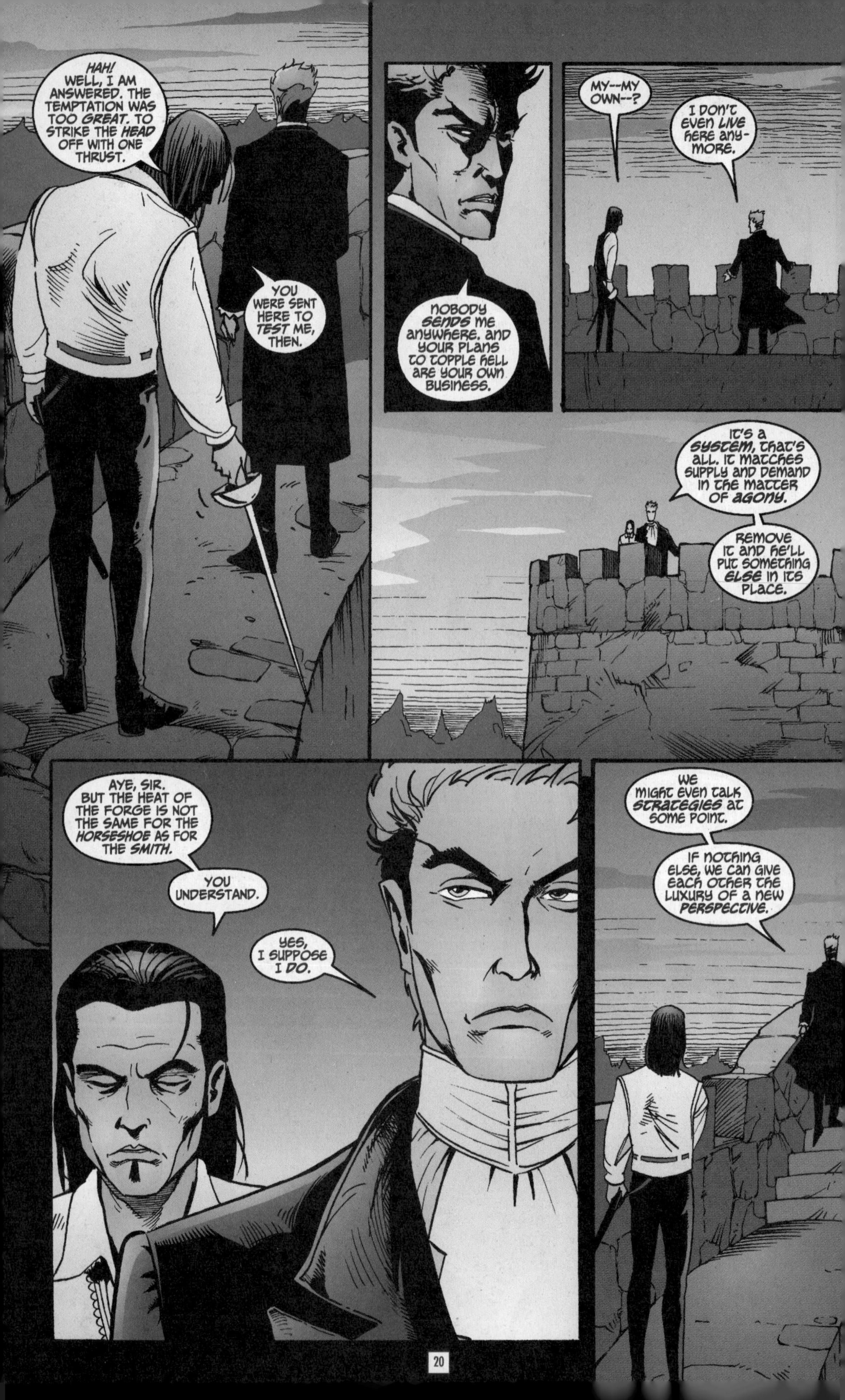
HAH! WELL, I AM ANSWERED. THE TEMPTATION WAS TOO GREAT. TO STRIKE THE HEAD OFF WITH ONE THRUST.
YOU WERE SENT HERE TO TEST ME, THEN.
NOBODY SENDS ME ANYWHERE. AND YOUR PLANS TO TOPPLE HELL ARE YOUR OWN BUSINESS.
MY--MY OWN--?
I DON'T EVEN LIVE HERE ANY-MORE.
IT'S A SYSTEM, THAT'S ALL. IT MATCHES SUPPLY AND DEMAND IN THE MATTER OF AGONY.
REMOVE IT AND HE'LL PUT SOMETHING ELSE IN ITS PLACE.
AYE, SIR. BUT THE HEAT OF THE FORGE IS NOT THE SAME FOR THE HORSESHOE AS FOR THE SMITH.
YOU UNDERSTAND.
YES, I SUPPOSE I DO.
WE MIGHT EVEN TALK STRATEGIES AT SOME POINT.
IF NOTHING ELSE, WE CAN GIVE EACH OTHER THE LUXURY OF A NEW PERSPECTIVE.

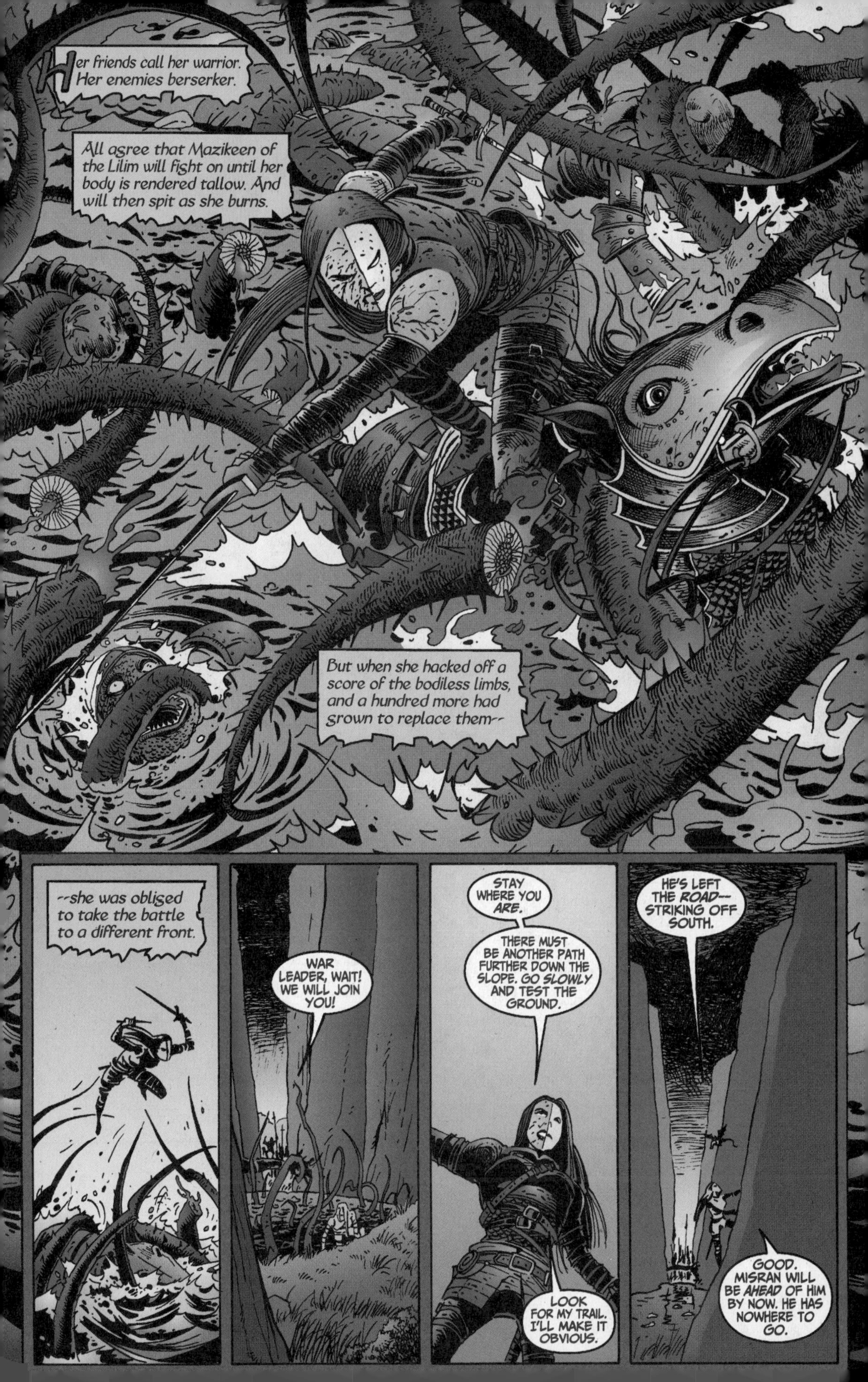

Her friends call her warrior. Her enemies berserker.
All agree that Mazikeen of the Lilim will fight on until her body is rendered tallow. And will then spit as she burns.
But when she hacked off a score of the bodiless limbs, and a hundred more had grown to replace them--
--she was obliged to take the battle to a different front.
WAR LEADER, WAIT! WE WILL JOIN YOU!
STAY WHERE YOU ARE.
THERE MUST BE ANOTHER PATH FURTHER DOWN THE SLOPE. GO SLOWLY AND TEST THE GROUND.
LOOK FOR MY TRAIL. I'LL MAKE IT OBVIOUS.
HE'S LEFT THE ROAD-- STRIKING OFF SOUTH.
GOOD. MISRAN WILL BE AHEAD OF HIM BY NOW. HE HAS NOWHERE TO GO.

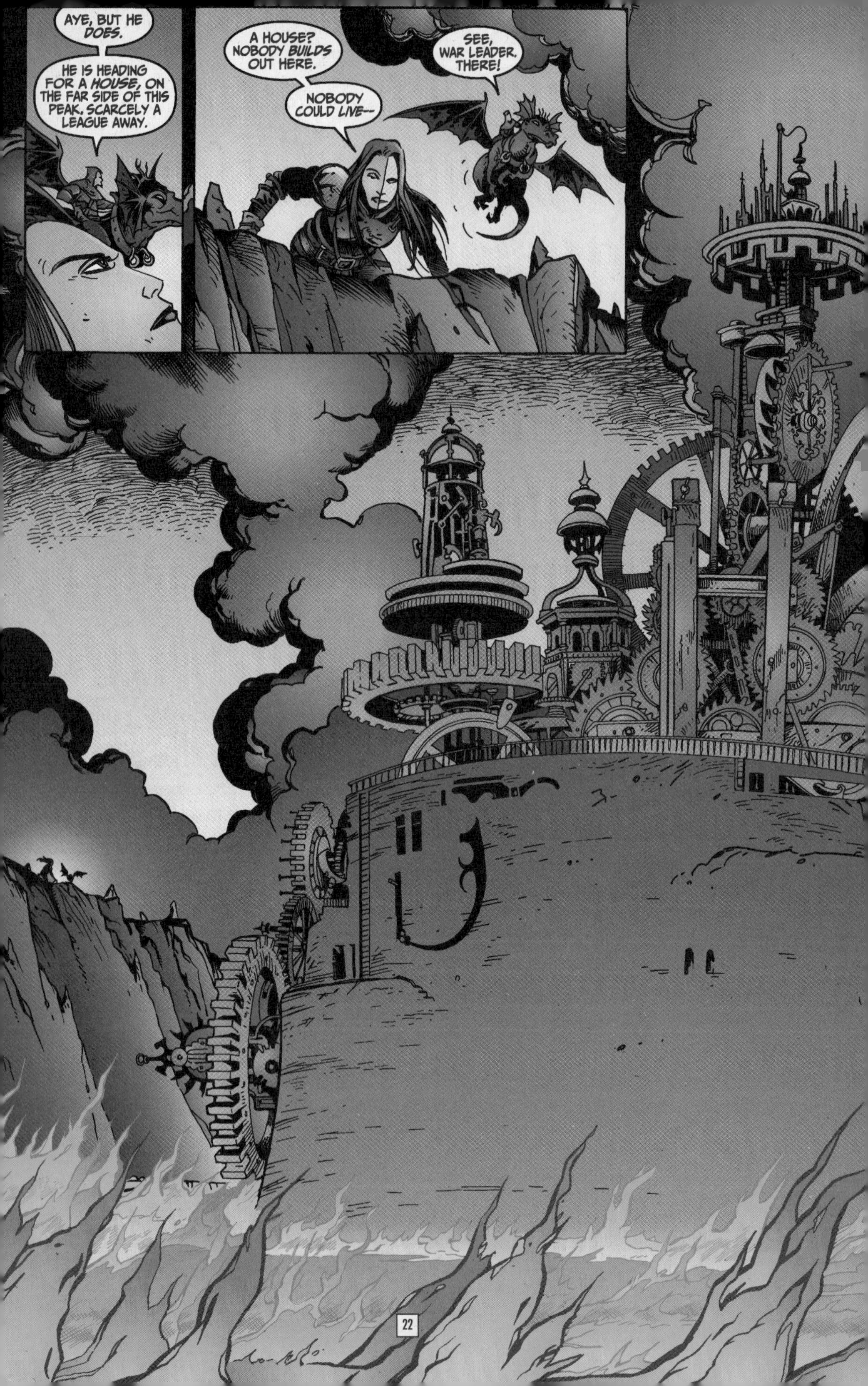
AYE, BUT HE DOES.
HE IS HEADING FOR A HOUSE, ON THE FAR SIDE OF THIS PEAK. SCARCELY A LEAGUE AWAY.
A HOUSE? NOBODY BUILDS OUT HERE.
NOBODY COULD LIVE--
SEE, WAR LEADER. THERE!

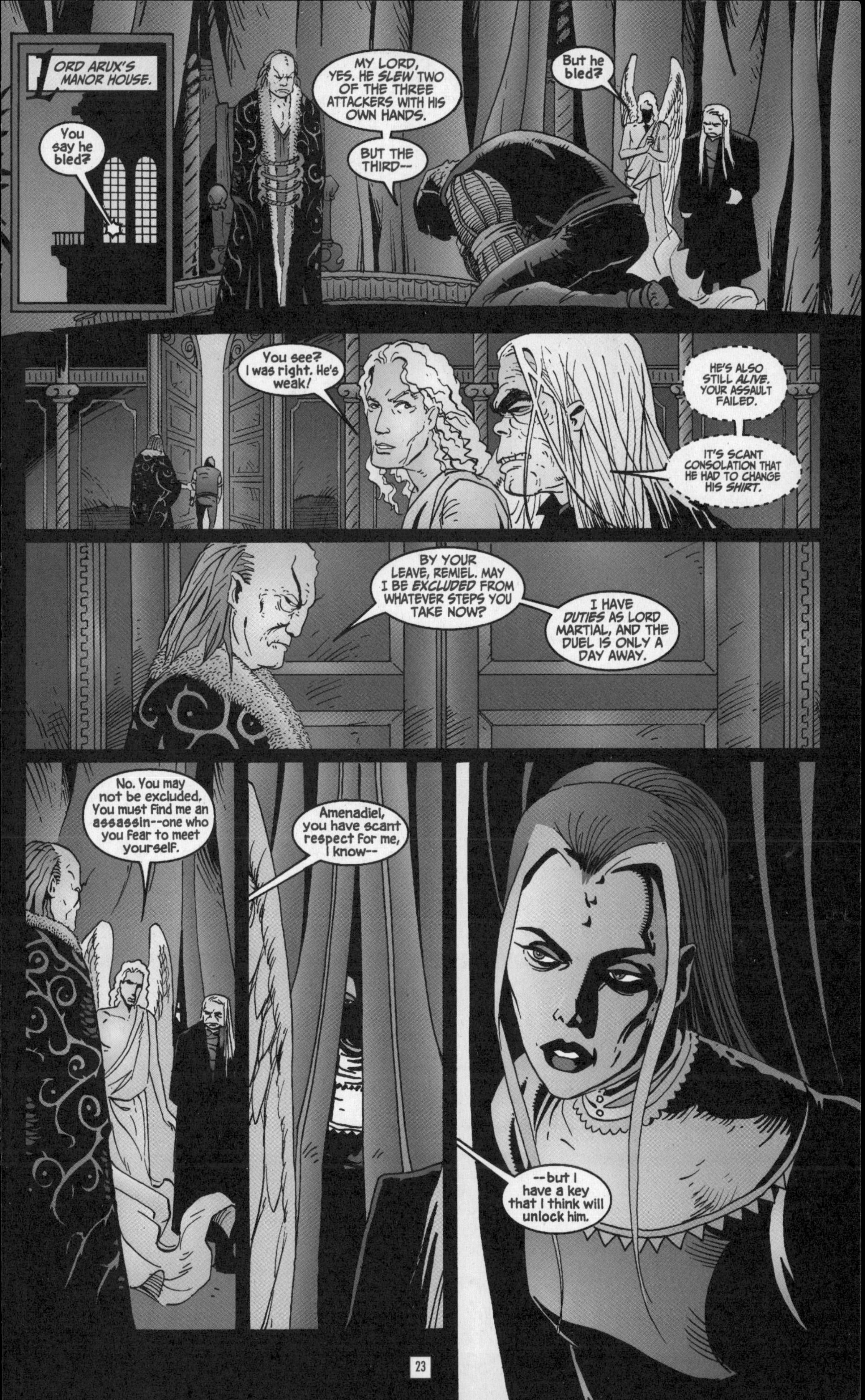
LORD ARUX'S MANOR HOUSE.
You say he bled?
MY LORD, YES. HE SLEW TWO OF THE THREE ATTACKERS WITH HIS OWN HANDS.
BUT THE THIRD--
But he bled?
You see? I was right. He's weak!
HE'S ALSO STILL ALIVE. YOUR ASSAULT FAILED.
IT'S SCANT CONSOLATION THAT HE HAD TO CHANGE HIS SHIRT.
BY YOUR LEAVE, REMIEL. MAY I BE EXCLUDED FROM WHATEVER STEPS YOU TAKE NOW?
I HAVE DUTIES AS LORD MARTIAL, AND THE DUEL IS ONLY A DAY AWAY.
No. You may not be excluded. You must find me an assassin--one who you fear to meet yourself.
Amenadiel, you have scant respect for me, I know--
--but I have a key that I think will unlock him.

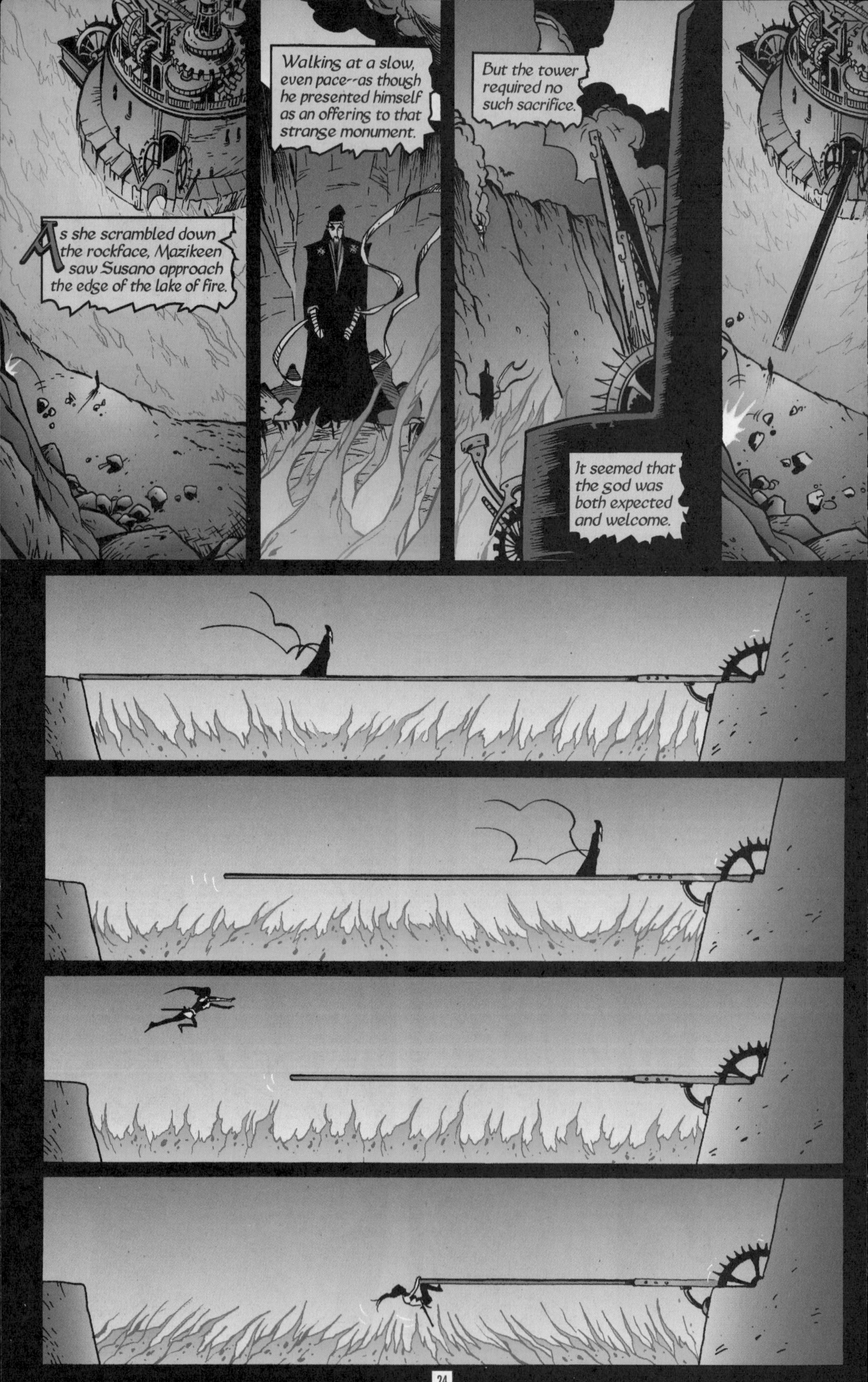
As she scrambled down the rockface, Mazikeen saw Susano approach the edge of the lake of fire.
Walking at a slow, even pace--as though he presented himself as an offering to that strange monument.
But the tower required no such sacrifice.
It seemed that the god was both expected and welcome.

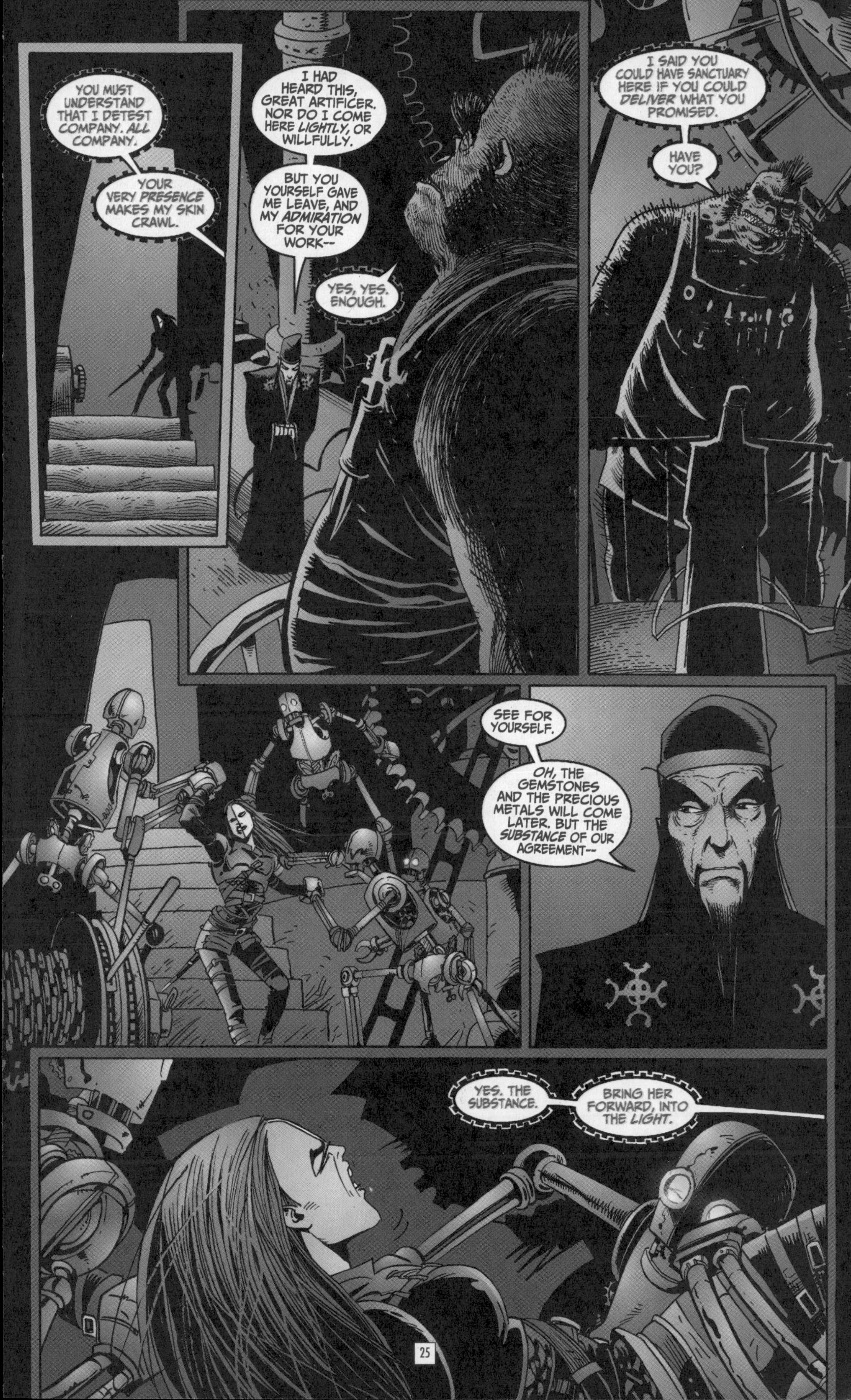
YOU MUST UNDERSTAND THAT I DETEST COMPANY. ALL COMPANY.
YOUR VERY PRESENCE MAKES MY SKIN CRAWL.
I HAD HEARD THIS, GREAT ARTIFICER. NOR DO I COME HERE LIGHTLY, OR WILLFULLY.
BUT YOU YOURSELF GAVE ME LEAVE, AND MY ADMIRATION FOR YOUR WORK--
YES, YES. ENOUGH.
I SAID YOU COULD HAVE SANCTUARY HERE IF YOU COULD DELIVER WHAT YOU PROMISED.
HAVE YOU?
SEE FOR YOURSELF.
OH, THE GEMSTONES AND THE PRECIOUS METALS WILL COME LATER. BUT THE SUBSTANCE OF OUR AGREEMENT--
YES. THE SUBSTANCE.
BRING HER FORWARD, INTO THE LIGHT.

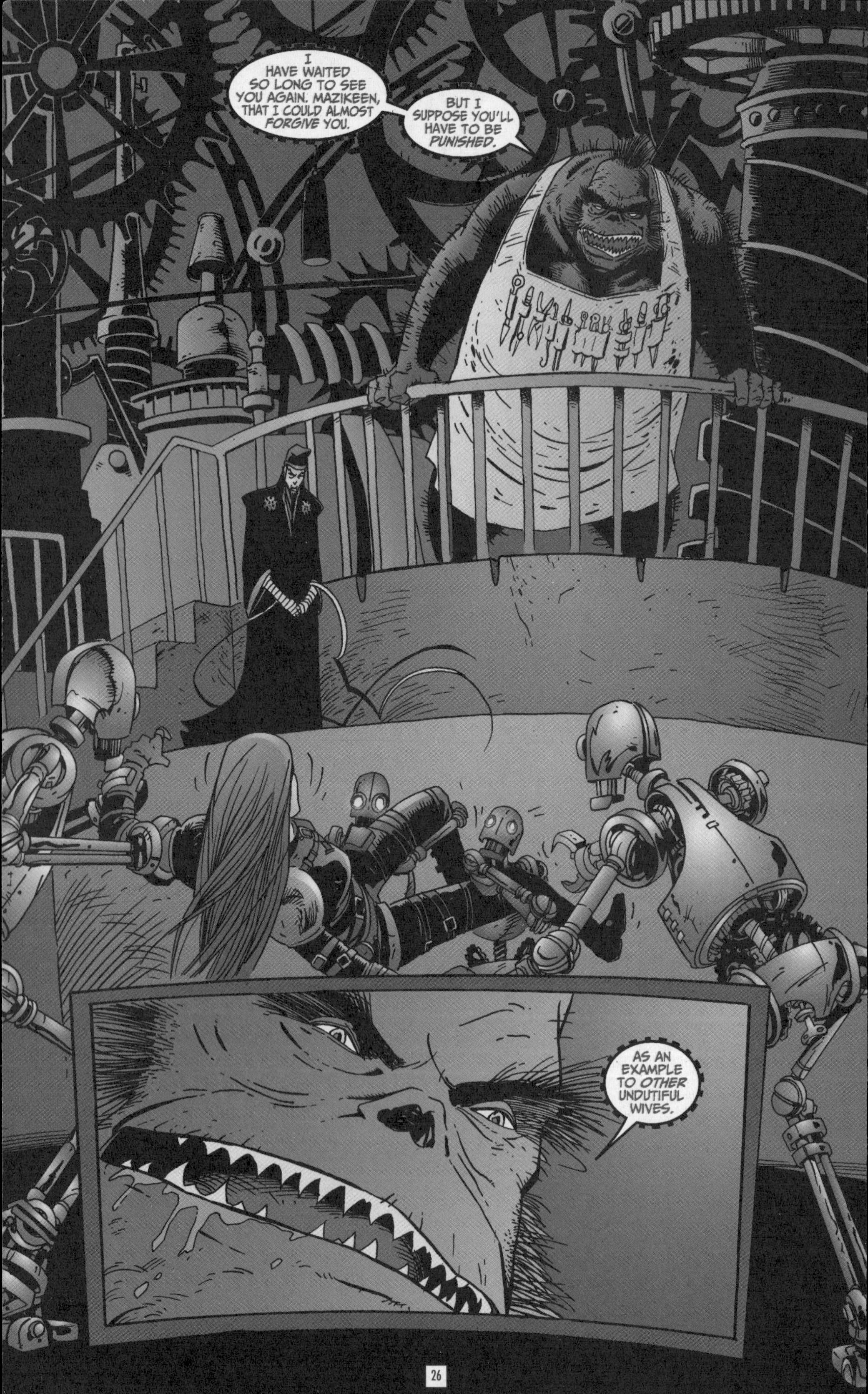
I HAVE WAITED SO LONG TO SEE YOU AGAIN, MAZIKEEN, THAT I COULD ALMOST FORGIVE YOU.
BUT I SUPPOSE YOU'LL HAVE TO BE PUNISHED.
AS AN EXAMPLE TO OTHER UNDUTIFUL WIVES.

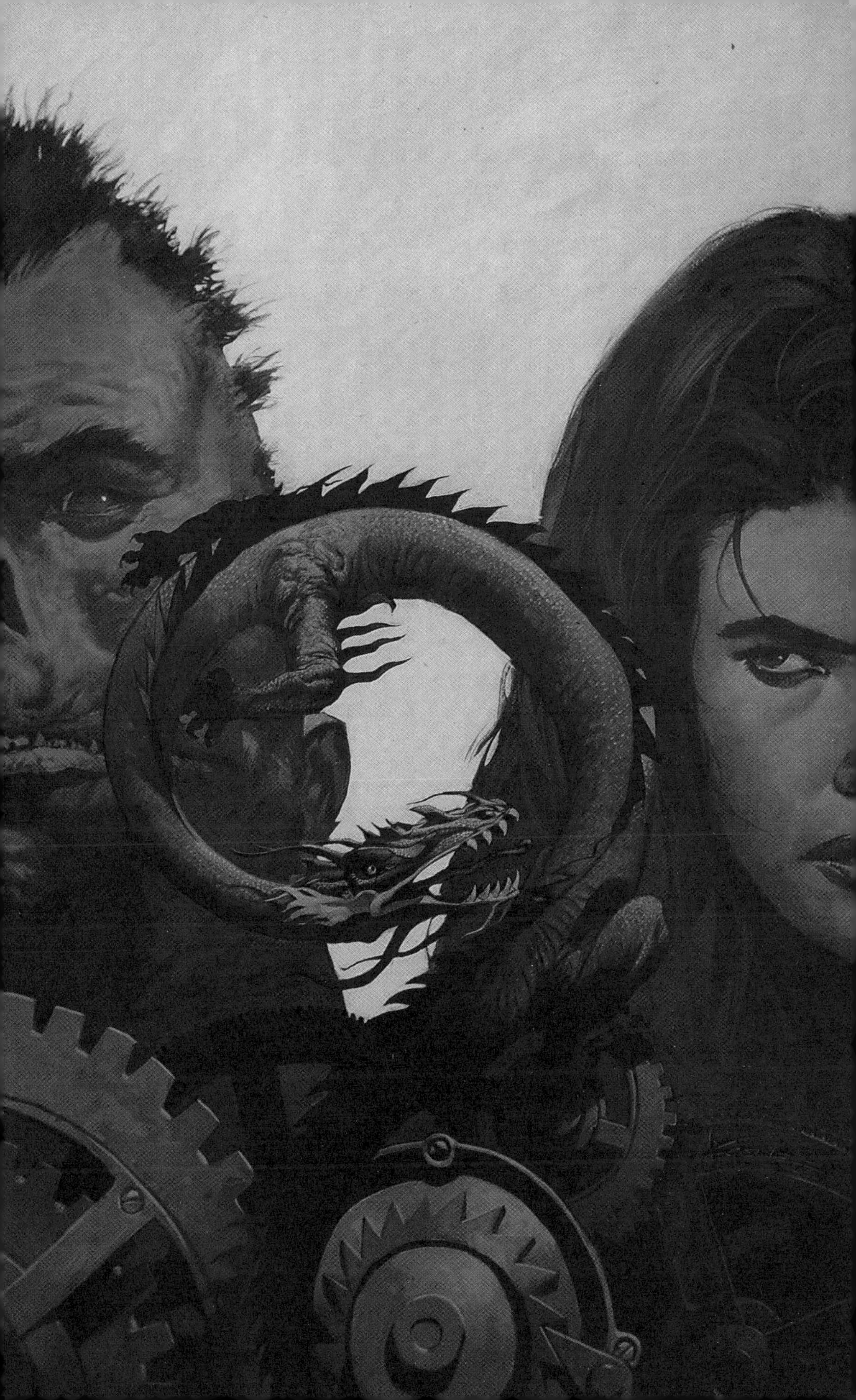

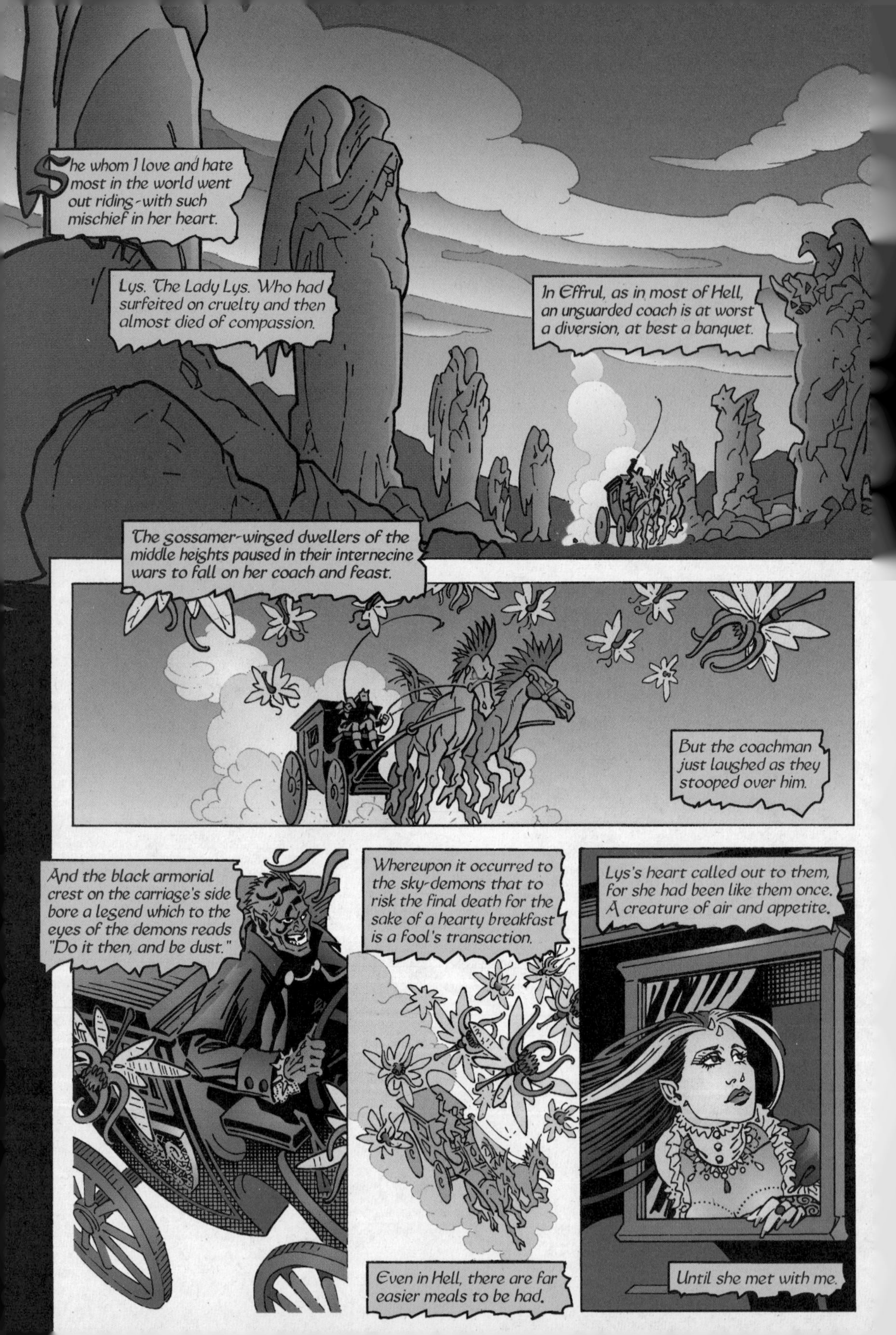
She whom I love and hate most in the world went out riding-with such mischief in her heart.
Lys. The Lady Lys. Who had surfeited on cruelty and then almost died of compassion.
In Effrul, as in most of Hell, an unguarded coach is at worst a diversion, at best a banquet.
The gossamer-winged dwellers of the middle heights paused in their internecine wars to fall on her coach and feast.
But the coachman just laughed as they stooped over him.
And the black armorial crest on the carriage's side bore a legend which to the eyes of the demons reads "Do it then, and be dust."
Whereupon it occurred to the sky-demons that to risk the final death for the sake of a hearty breakfast is a fool's transaction.
Even in Hell, there are far easier meals to be had.
Lys's heart called out to them, for she had been like them once. A creature of air and appetite.
Until she met with me.

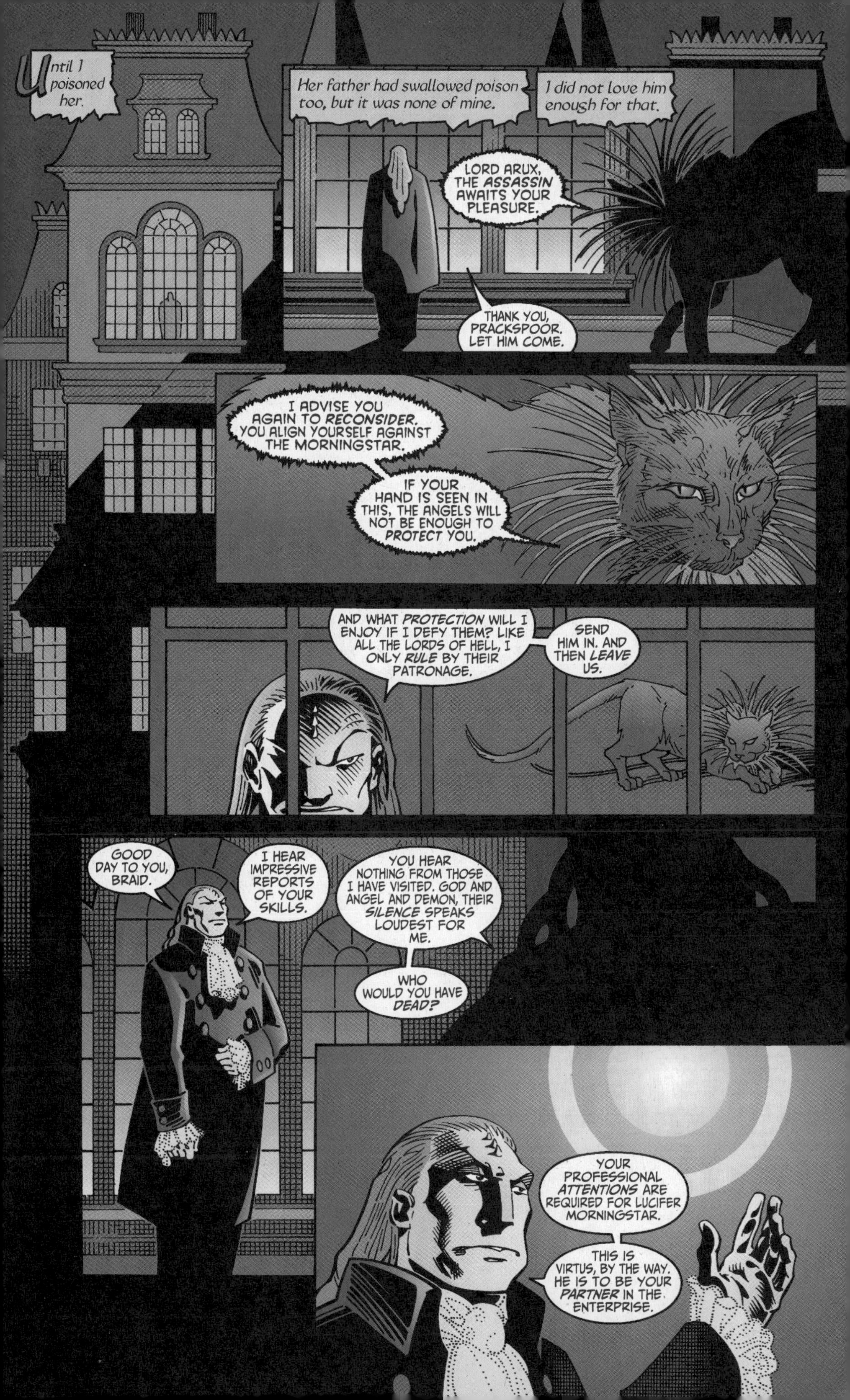
Until I poisoned her.
Her father had swallowed poison too, but it was none of mine.
I did not love him enough for that.
LORD ARUX, THE ASSASSIN AWAITS YOUR PLEASURE.
THANK YOU, PRACKSPOOR. LET HIM COME.
I ADVISE YOU AGAIN TO RECONSIDER. YOU ALIGN YOURSELF AGAINST THE MORNINGSTAR.
IF YOUR HAND IS SEEN IN THIS, THE ANGELS WILL NOT BE ENOUGH TO PROTECT YOU.
AND WHAT PROTECTION WILL I ENJOY IF I DEFY THEM? LIKE ALL THE LORDS OF HELL, I ONLY RULE BY THEIR PATRONAGE.
SEND HIM IN. AND THEN LEAVE US.
GOOD DAY TO YOU, BRAID.
I HEAR IMPRESSIVE REPORTS OF YOUR SKILLS.
YOU HEAR NOTHING FROM THOSE I HAVE VISITED. GOD AND ANGEL AND DEMON, THEIR SILENCE SPEAKS LOUDEST FOR ME.
WHO WOULD YOU HAVE DEAD?
YOUR PROFESSIONAL ATTENTIONS ARE REQUIRED FOR LUCIFER MORNINGSTAR.
THIS IS VIRTUS, BY THE WAY. HE IS TO BE YOUR PARTNER IN THE ENTERPRISE.

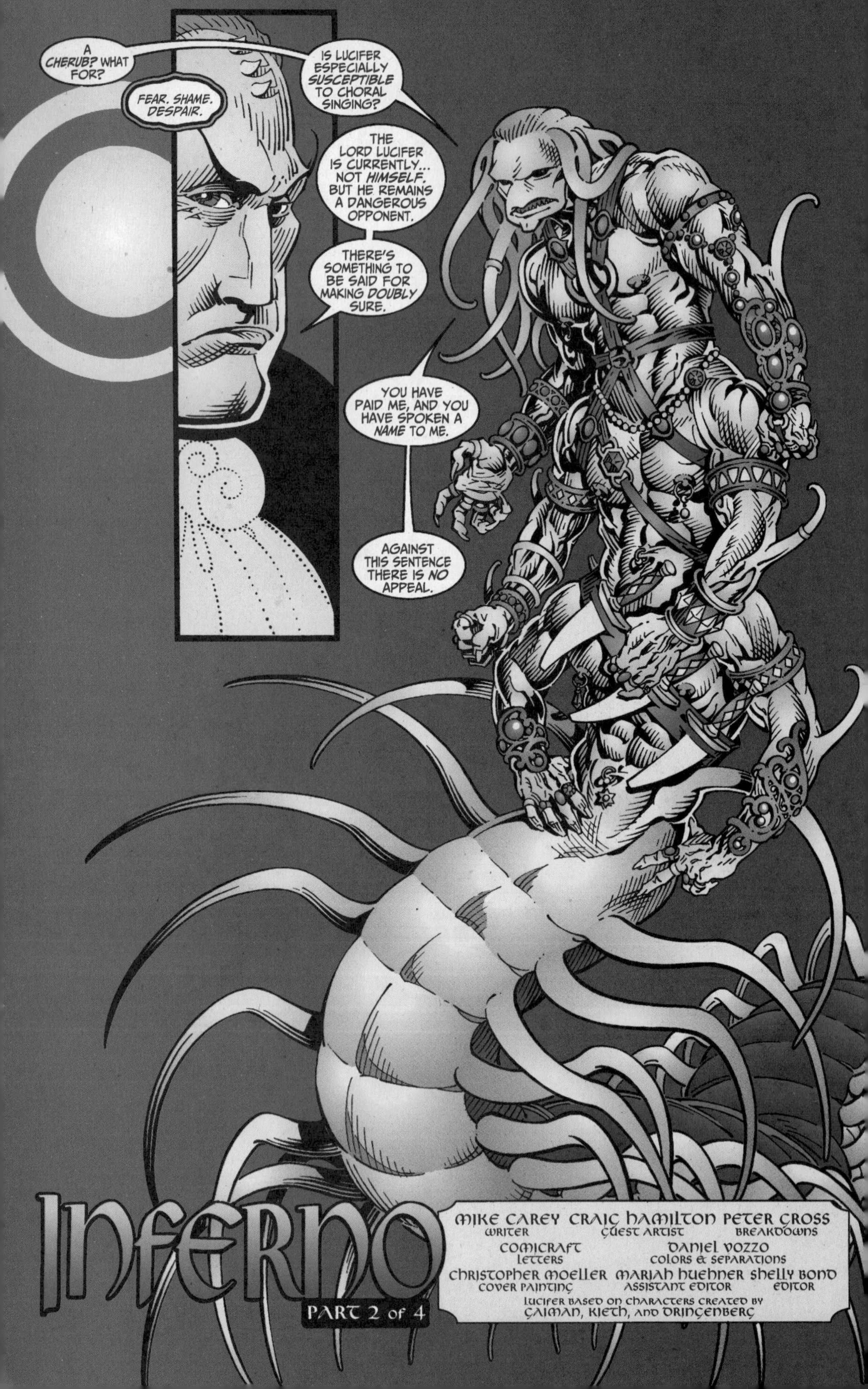
A CHERUB? WHAT FOR?
IS LUCIFER ESPECIALLY SUSCEPTIBLE TO CHORAL SINGING?
FEAR. SHAME. DESPAIR.
THE LORD LUCIFER IS CURRENTLY... NOT HIMSELF. BUT HE REMAINS A DANGEROUS OPPONENT.
THERE'S SOMETHING TO BE SAID FOR MAKING DOUBLY SURE.
YOU HAVE PAID ME, AND YOU HAVE SPOKEN A NAME TO ME.
AGAINST THIS SENTENCE THERE IS NO APPEAL.
INFERNO
PART 2 of 4
MIKE CAREY WRITER
CRAIG HAMILTON GUEST ARTIST
PETER GROSS BREAKDOWNS
COMICRAFT LETTERS
DANIEL VOZZO COLORS & SEPARATIONS
CHRISTOPHER MOELLER COVER PAINTING
MARIAH HUEHNER ASSISTANT EDITOR
SHELLY BOND EDITOR
LUCIFER BASED ON CHARACTERS CREATED BY GAIMAN, KIETH, AND DRINGENBERG

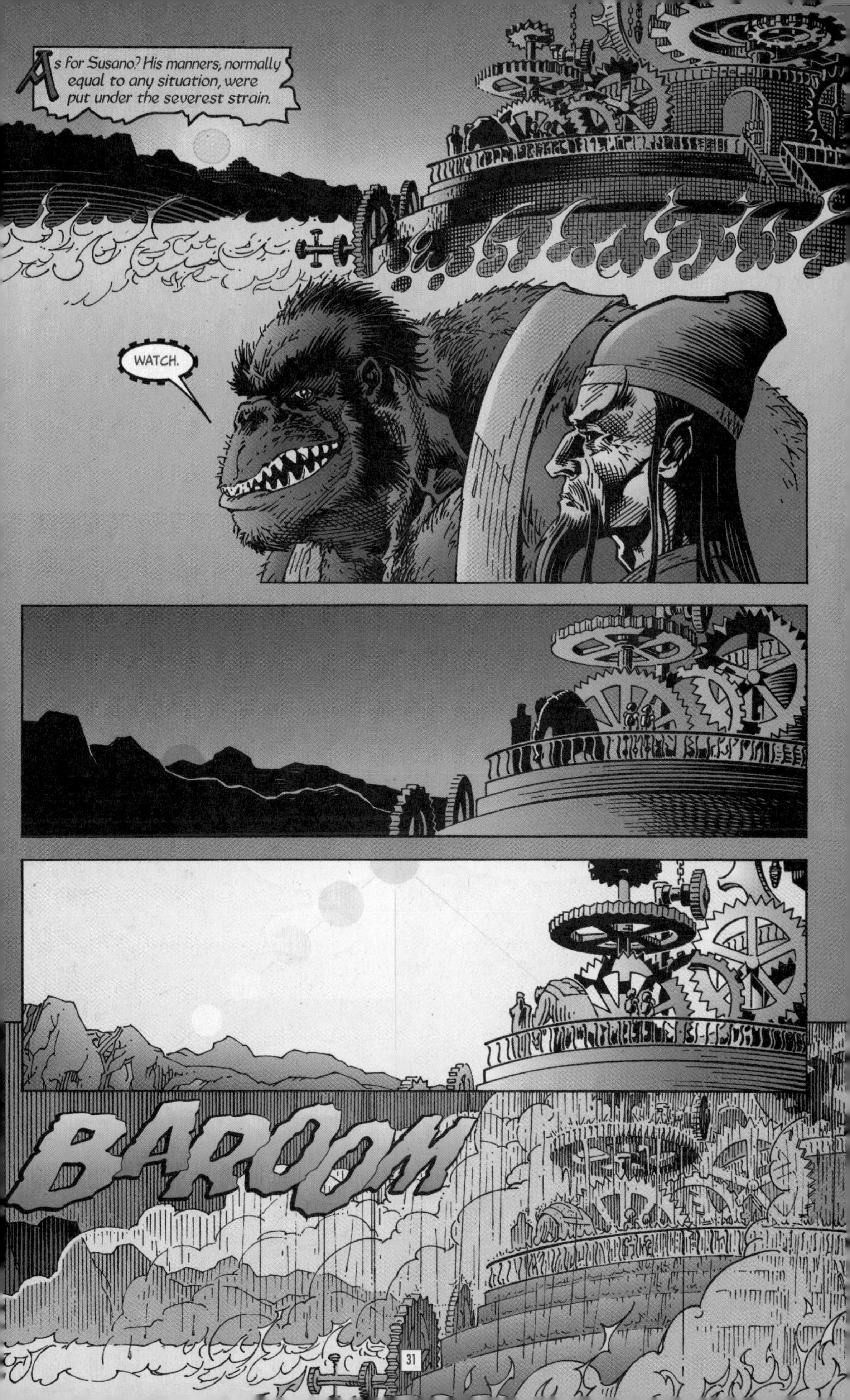
As for Susano? His manners, normally equal to any situation, were put under the severest strain.
WATCH.
BAROOM

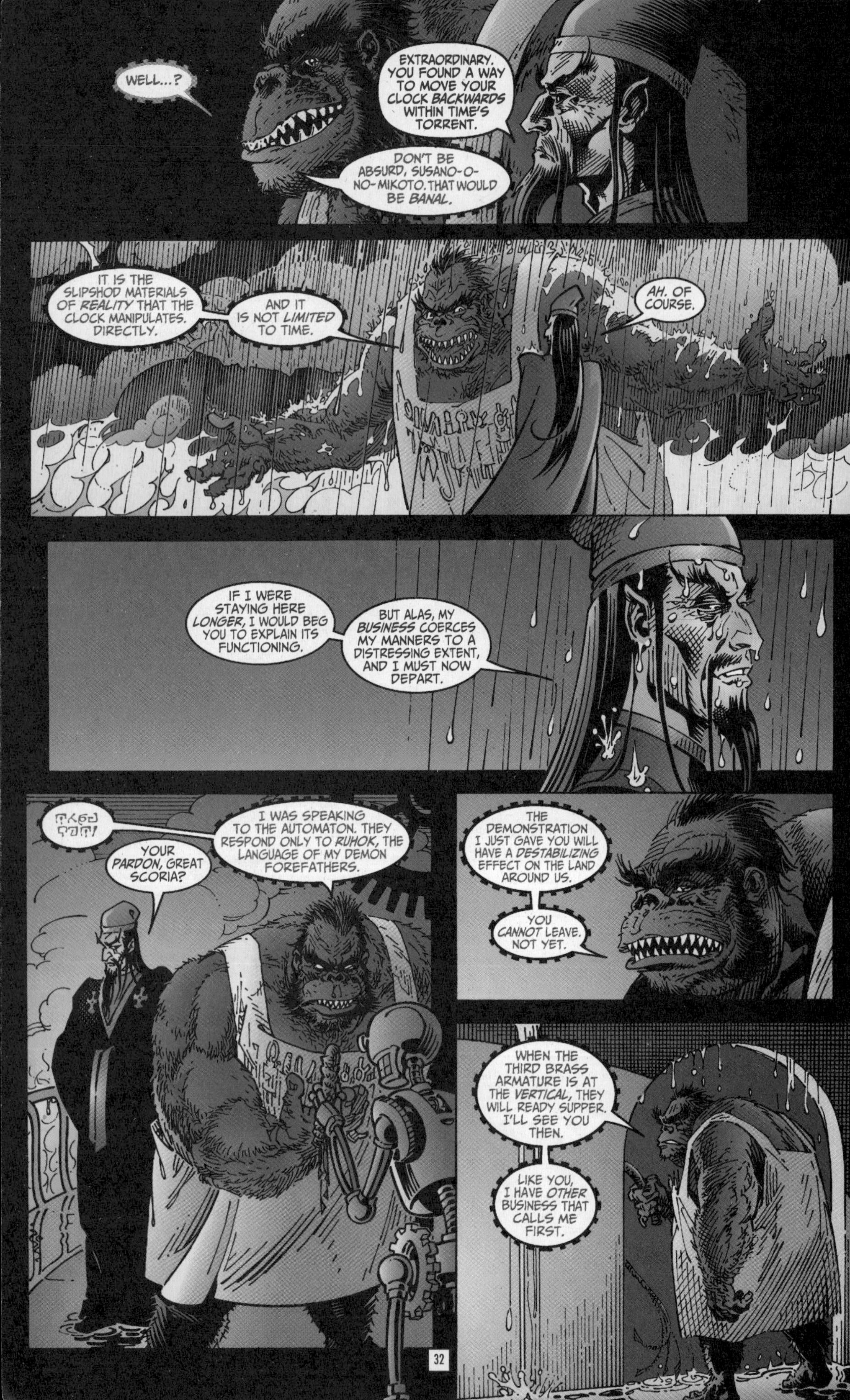
WELL...?
EXTRAORDINARY. YOU FOUND A WAY TO MOVE YOUR CLOCK BACKWARDS WITHIN TIME'S TORRENT.
DON'T BE ABSURD, SUSANO-O-NO-MIKOTO. THAT WOULD BE BANAL.
IT IS THE SLIPSHOD MATERIALS OF REALITY THAT THE CLOCK MANIPULATES. DIRECTLY.
AND IT IS NOT LIMITED TO TIME.
AH. OF COURSE.
IF I WERE STAYING HERE LONGER, I WOULD BEG YOU TO EXPLAIN ITS FUNCTIONING.
BUT ALAS, MY BUSINESS COERCES MY MANNERS TO A DISTRESSING EXTENT, AND I MUST NOW DEPART.
YOUR PARDON, GREAT SCORIA?
I WAS SPEAKING TO THE AUTOMATON. THEY RESPOND ONLY TO RUHOK, THE LANGUAGE OF MY DEMON FOREFATHERS.
THE DEMONSTRATION I JUST GAVE YOU WILL HAVE A DESTABILIZING EFFECT ON THE LAND AROUND US.
YOU CANNOT LEAVE. NOT YET.
WHEN THE THIRD BRASS ARMATURE IS AT THE VERTICAL, THEY WILL READY SUPPER. I'LL SEE YOU THEN.
LIKE YOU, I HAVE OTHER BUSINESS THAT CALLS ME FIRST.

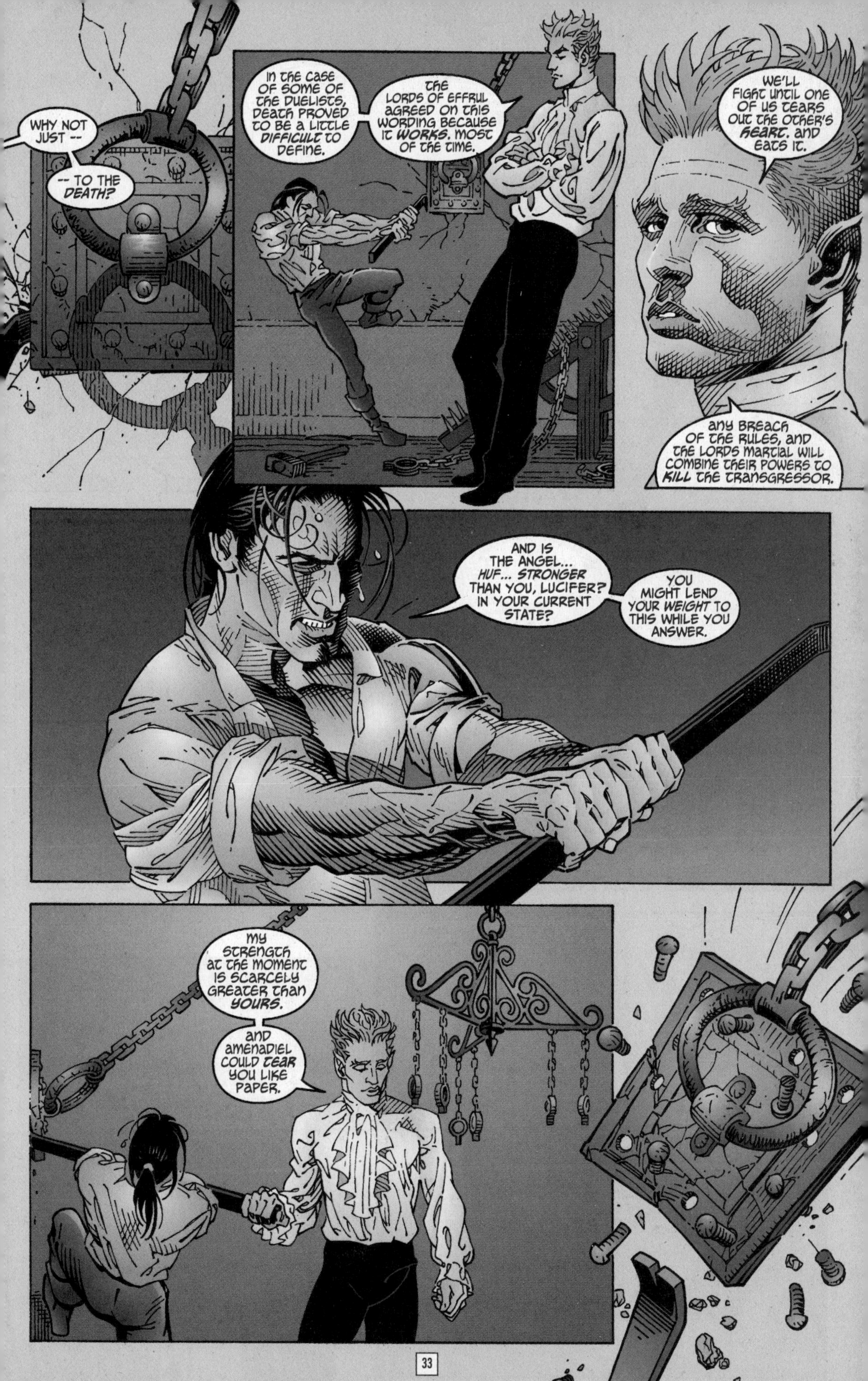
WHY NOT JUST --
-- TO THE DEATH?
IN THE CASE OF SOME OF THE DUELISTS, DEATH PROVED TO BE A LITTLE DIFFICULT TO DEFINE.
THE LORDS OF EFFRUL AGREED ON THIS WORDING BECAUSE IT WORKS. MOST OF THE TIME.
WE'LL FIGHT UNTIL ONE OF US TEARS OUT THE OTHER'S HEART, AND EATS IT.
ANY BREACH OF THE RULES, AND THE LORDS MARTIAL WILL COMBINE THEIR POWERS TO KILL THE TRANSGRESSOR.
AND IS THE ANGEL... HUF... STRONGER THAN YOU, LUCIFER? IN YOUR CURRENT STATE?
YOU MIGHT LEND YOUR WEIGHT TO THIS WHILE YOU ANSWER.
MY STRENGTH AT THE MOMENT IS SCARCELY GREATER THAN YOURS.
AND AMENADIEL COULD TEAR YOU LIKE PAPER.

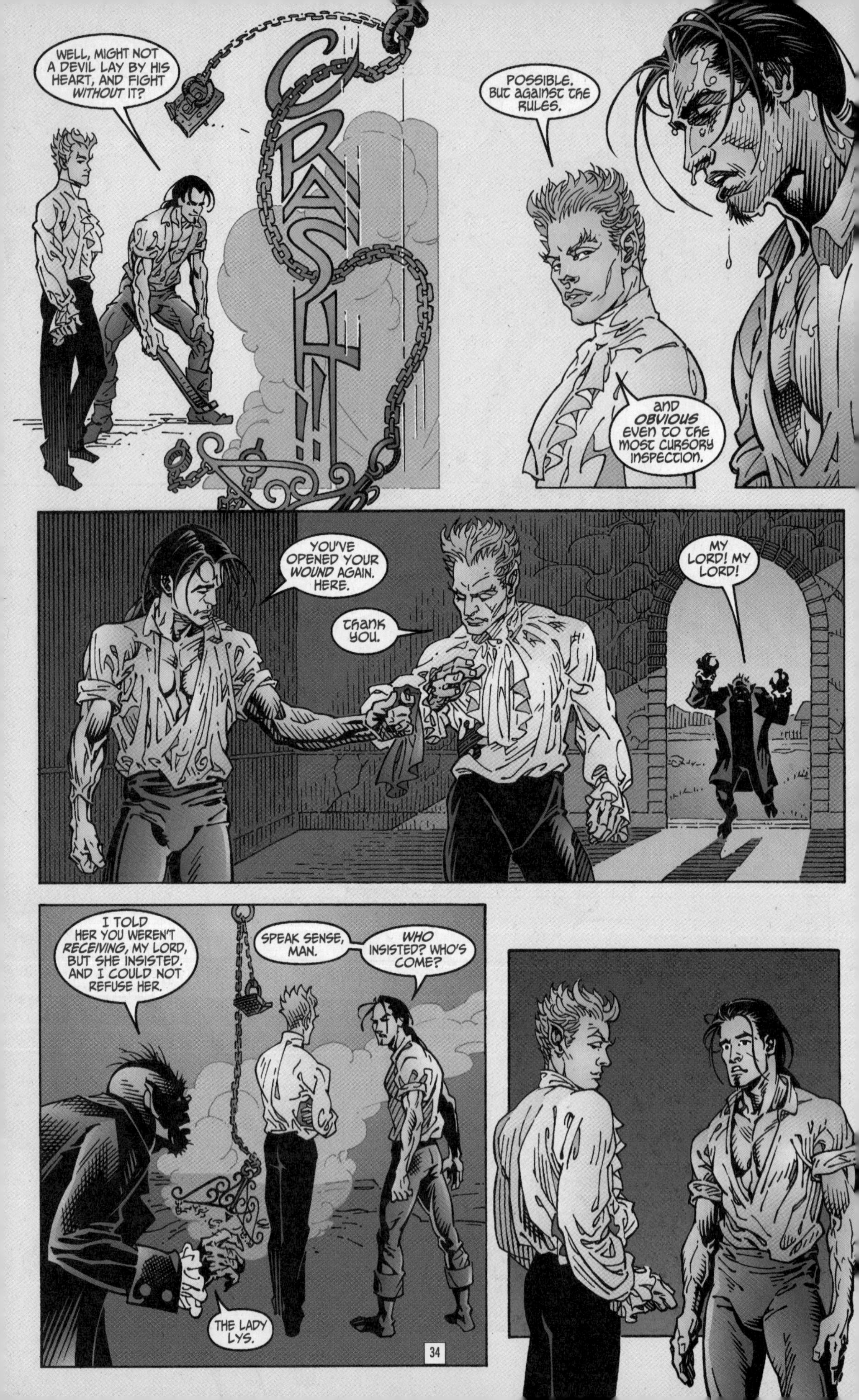
WELL, MIGHT NOT A DEVIL LAY BY HIS HEART, AND FIGHT WITHOUT IT?
CRASH!!
POSSIBLE. BUT AGAINST THE RULES.
AND OBVIOUS EVEN TO THE MOST CURSORY INSPECTION.
YOU'VE OPENED YOUR WOUND AGAIN. HERE.
THANK YOU.
MY LORD! MY LORD!
I TOLD HER YOU WEREN'T RECEIVING, MY LORD, BUT SHE INSISTED. AND I COULD NOT REFUSE HER.
SPEAK SENSE, MAN.
WHO INSISTED? WHO'S COME?
THE LADY LYS.
34

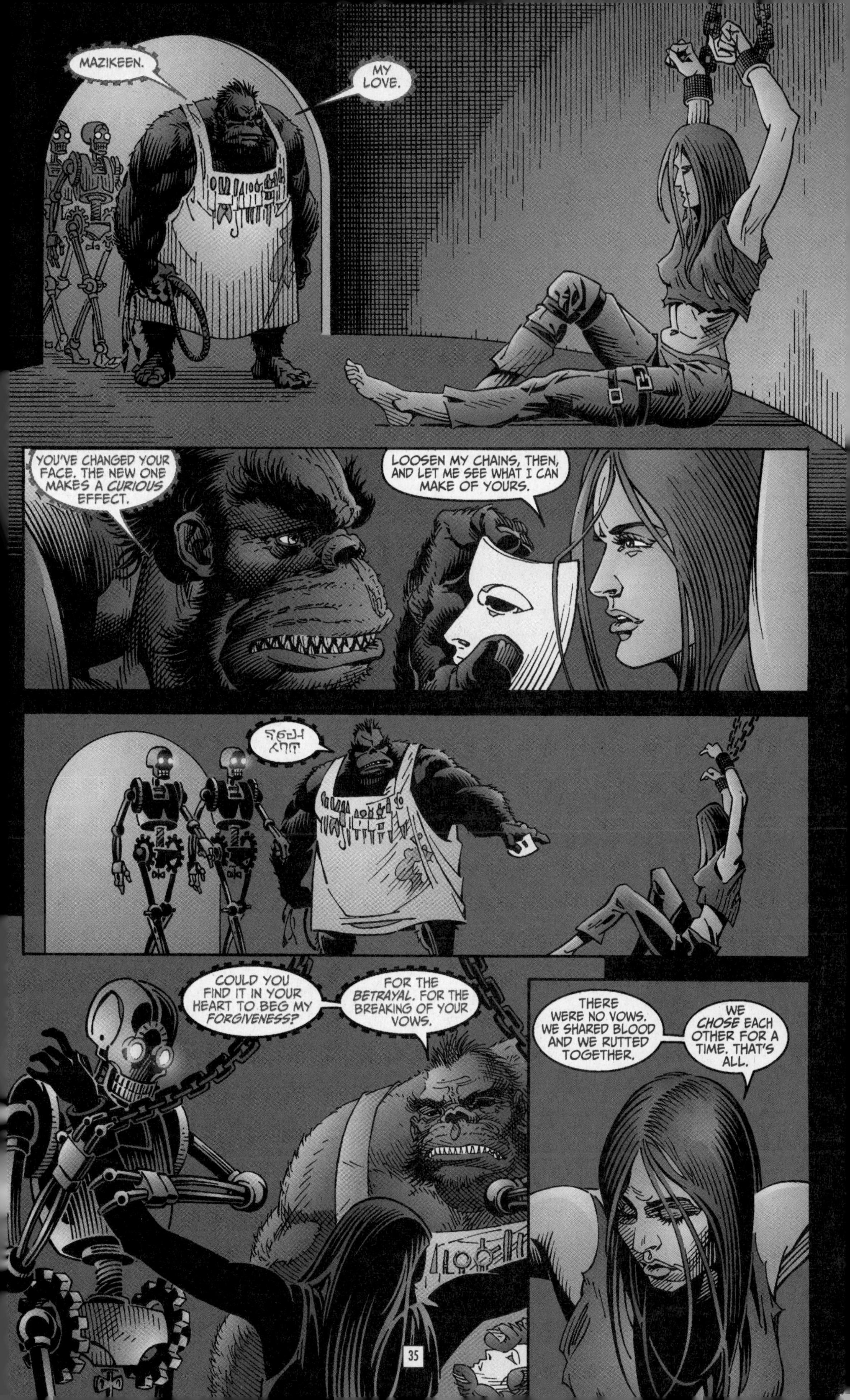
MAZIKEEN.
MY LOVE.
YOU'VE CHANGED YOUR FACE. THE NEW ONE MAKES A *CURIOUS* EFFECT.
LOOSEN MY CHAINS, THEN, AND LET ME SEE WHAT I CAN MAKE OF YOURS.
COULD YOU FIND IT IN YOUR HEART TO BEG MY *FORGIVENESS?*
FOR THE *BETRAYAL.* FOR THE BREAKING OF YOUR VOWS.
THERE WERE NO VOWS. WE SHARED BLOOD AND WE RUTTED TOGETHER.
WE *CHOSE* EACH OTHER FOR A TIME. THAT'S ALL.

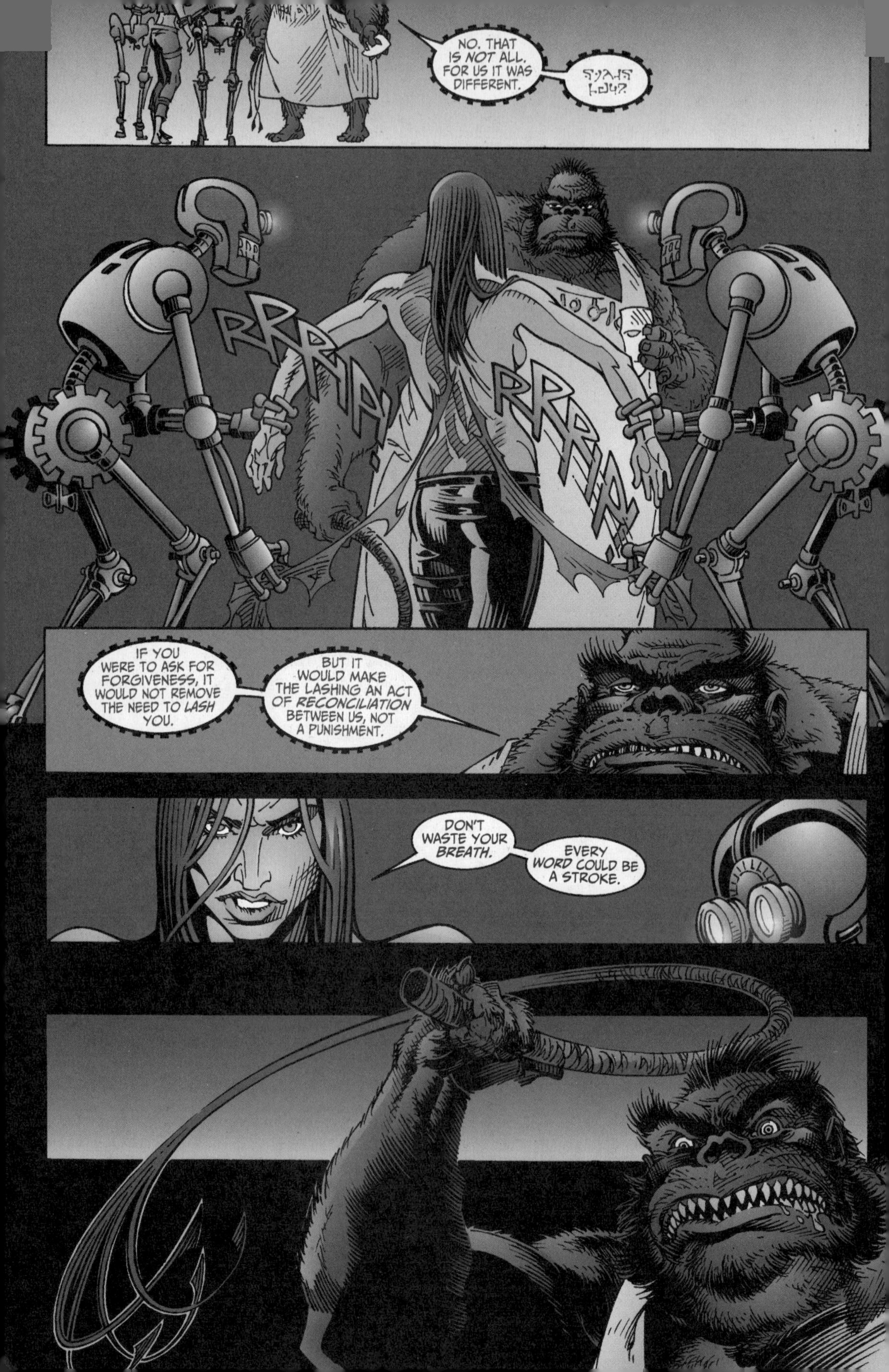

NO. THAT IS NOT ALL. FOR US IT WAS DIFFERENT.
RRRIP!
RRRIP!
IF YOU WERE TO ASK FOR FORGIVENESS, IT WOULD NOT REMOVE THE NEED TO LASH YOU.
BUT IT WOULD MAKE THE LASHING AN ACT OF RECONCILIATION BETWEEN US, NOT A PUNISHMENT.
DON'T WASTE YOUR BREATH.
EVERY WORD COULD BE A STROKE.

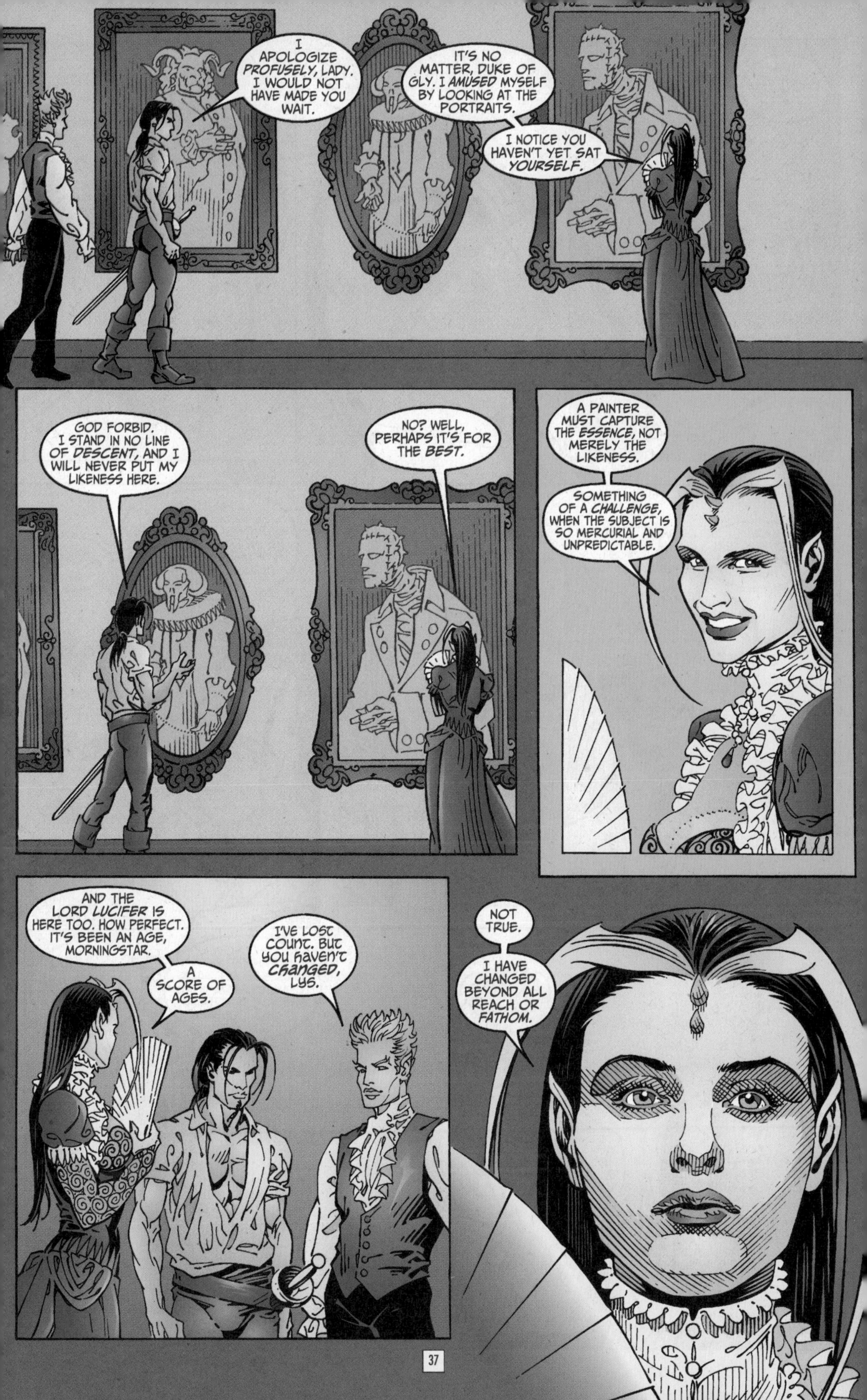
I APOLOGIZE PROFUSELY, LADY. I WOULD NOT HAVE MADE YOU WAIT.
IT'S NO MATTER, DUKE OF GLY. I AMUSED MYSELF BY LOOKING AT THE PORTRAITS.
I NOTICE YOU HAVEN'T YET SAT YOURSELF.
GOD FORBID. I STAND IN NO LINE OF DESCENT, AND I WILL NEVER PUT MY LIKENESS HERE.
NO? WELL, PERHAPS IT'S FOR THE BEST.
A PAINTER MUST CAPTURE THE ESSENCE, NOT MERELY THE LIKENESS.
SOMETHING OF A CHALLENGE, WHEN THE SUBJECT IS SO MERCURIAL AND UNPREDICTABLE.
AND THE LORD LUCIFER IS HERE TOO. HOW PERFECT. IT'S BEEN AN AGE, MORNINGSTAR.
A SCORE OF AGES.
I'VE LOST COUNT. BUT YOU HAVEN'T CHANGED, LYS.
NOT TRUE.
I HAVE CHANGED BEYOND ALL REACH OR FATHOM.

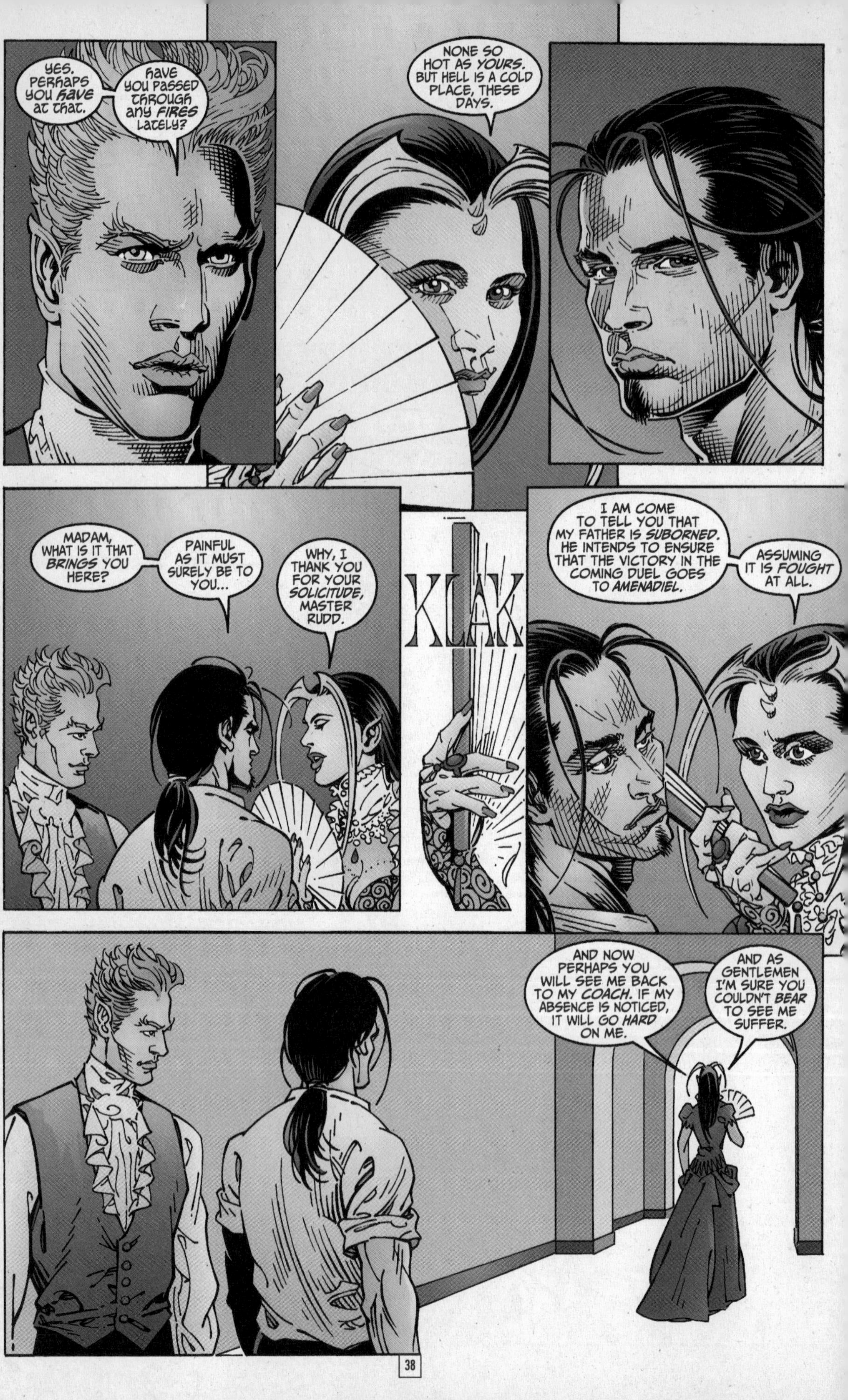

YES. PERHAPS YOU HAVE AT THAT.
HAVE YOU PASSED THROUGH ANY FIRES LATELY?
NONE SO HOT AS YOURS. BUT HELL IS A COLD PLACE, THESE DAYS.
MADAM, WHAT IS IT THAT BRINGS YOU HERE?
PAINFUL AS IT MUST SURELY BE TO YOU...
WHY, I THANK YOU FOR YOUR SOLICITUDE, MASTER RUDD.
KLAK
I AM COME TO TELL YOU THAT MY FATHER IS SUBORNED. HE INTENDS TO ENSURE THAT THE VICTORY IN THE COMING DUEL GOES TO AMENADIEL.
ASSUMING IT IS FOUGHT AT ALL.
AND NOW PERHAPS YOU WILL SEE ME BACK TO MY COACH. IF MY ABSENCE IS NOTICED, IT WILL GO HARD ON ME.
AND AS GENTLEMEN I'M SURE YOU COULDN'T BEAR TO SEE ME SUFFER.

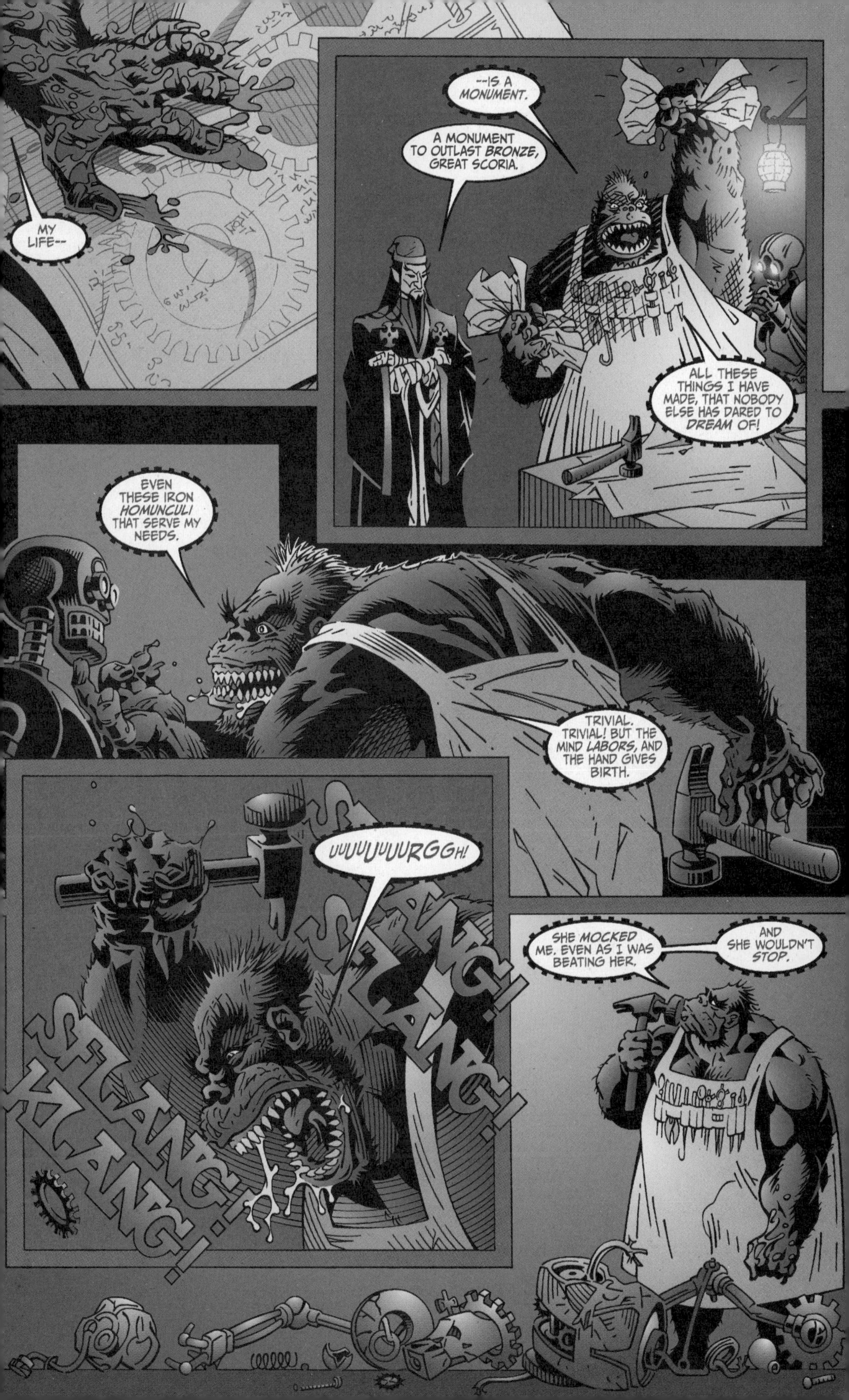

MY LIFE--
--IS A MONUMENT.
A MONUMENT TO OUTLAST BRONZE, GREAT SCORIA.
ALL THESE THINGS I HAVE MADE, THAT NOBODY ELSE HAS DARED TO DREAM OF!
EVEN THESE IRON HOMUNCULI THAT SERVE MY NEEDS.
TRIVIAL. TRIVIAL! BUT THE MIND LABORS, AND THE HAND GIVES BIRTH.
UUUUUUURGGH!
SKLANG! SKLANG! SKLANG! KLANG!
SHE MOCKED ME. EVEN AS I WAS BEATING HER.
AND SHE WOULDN'T STOP.

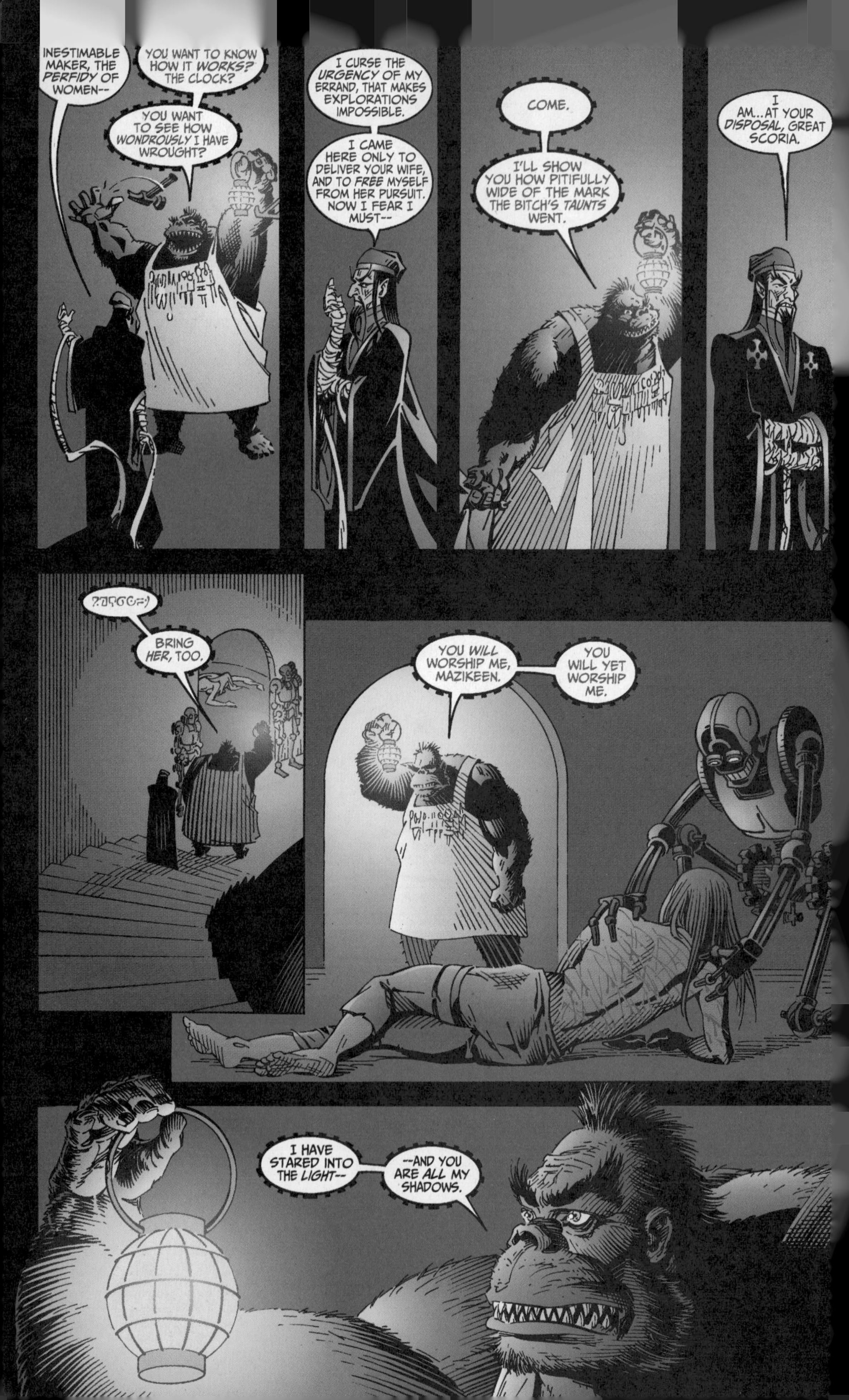

INESTIMABLE MAKER, THE PERFIDY OF WOMEN--
YOU WANT TO KNOW HOW IT WORKS? THE CLOCK?
YOU WANT TO SEE HOW WONDROUSLY I HAVE WROUGHT?
I CURSE THE URGENCY OF MY ERRAND, THAT MAKES EXPLORATIONS IMPOSSIBLE.
I CAME HERE ONLY TO DELIVER YOUR WIFE, AND TO FREE MYSELF FROM HER PURSUIT. NOW I FEAR I MUST--
COME.
I'LL SHOW YOU HOW PITIFULLY WIDE OF THE MARK THE BITCH'S TAUNTS WENT.
I AM...AT YOUR DISPOSAL, GREAT SCORIA.
BRING HER, TOO.
YOU WILL WORSHIP ME, MAZIKEEN.
YOU WILL YET WORSHIP ME.
I HAVE STARED INTO THE LIGHT--
--AND YOU ARE ALL MY SHADOWS.

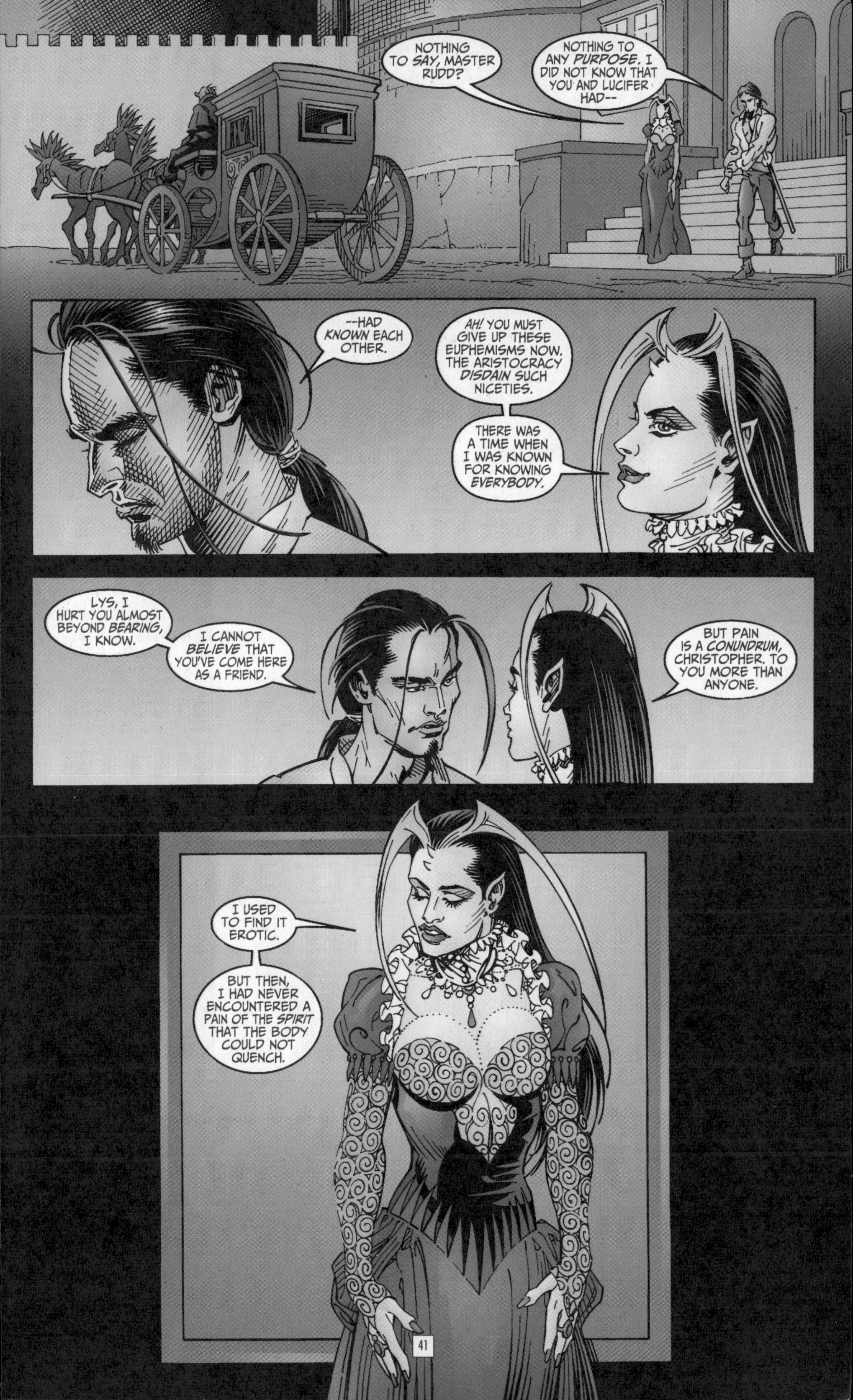
NOTHING TO SAY, MASTER RUDD?
NOTHING TO ANY PURPOSE. I DID NOT KNOW THAT YOU AND LUCIFER HAD--
--HAD KNOWN EACH OTHER.
AH! YOU MUST GIVE UP THESE EUPHEMISMS NOW. THE ARISTOCRACY DISDAIN SUCH NICETIES.
THERE WAS A TIME WHEN I WAS KNOWN FOR KNOWING EVERYBODY.
LYS, I HURT YOU ALMOST BEYOND BEARING, I KNOW.
I CANNOT BELIEVE THAT YOU'VE COME HERE AS A FRIEND.
BUT PAIN IS A CONUNDRUM, CHRISTOPHER. TO YOU MORE THAN ANYONE.
I USED TO FIND IT EROTIC.
BUT THEN, I HAD NEVER ENCOUNTERED A PAIN OF THE SPIRIT THAT THE BODY COULD NOT QUENCH.

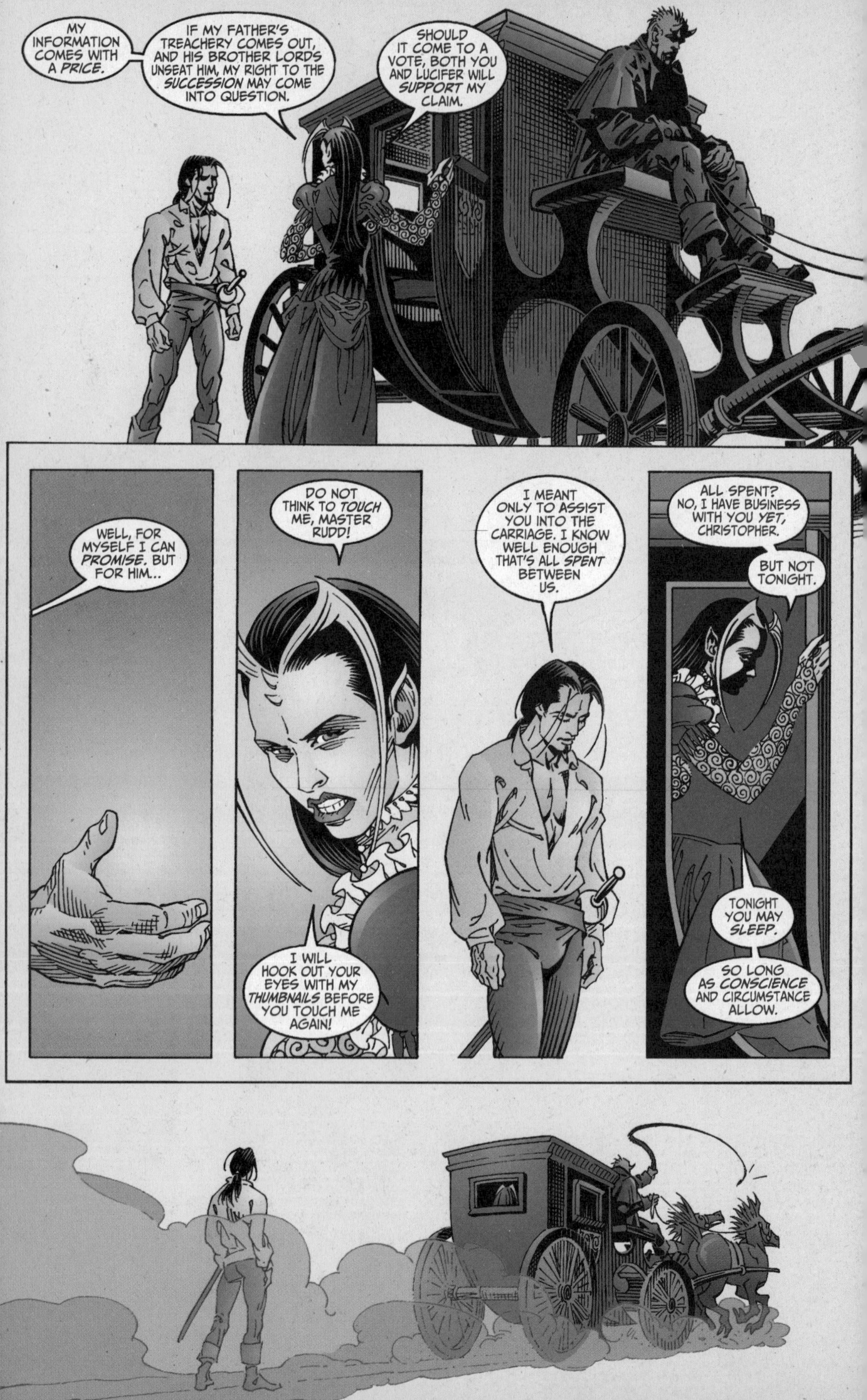
MY INFORMATION COMES WITH A *PRICE*.
IF MY FATHER'S TREACHERY COMES OUT, AND HIS BROTHER LORDS UNSEAT HIM, MY RIGHT TO THE *SUCCESSION* MAY COME INTO QUESTION.
SHOULD IT COME TO A VOTE, BOTH YOU AND LUCIFER WILL *SUPPORT* MY CLAIM.
WELL, FOR MYSELF I CAN *PROMISE*. BUT FOR HIM...
DO NOT THINK TO *TOUCH* ME, MASTER RUDD!
I WILL HOOK OUT YOUR EYES WITH MY *THUMBNAILS* BEFORE YOU TOUCH ME AGAIN!
I MEANT ONLY TO ASSIST YOU INTO THE CARRIAGE. I KNOW WELL ENOUGH THAT'S ALL *SPENT* BETWEEN US.
ALL SPENT? NO, I HAVE BUSINESS WITH YOU *YET*, CHRISTOPHER.
BUT NOT TONIGHT.
TONIGHT YOU MAY *SLEEP*.
SO LONG AS *CONSCIENCE* AND CIRCUMSTANCE ALLOW.

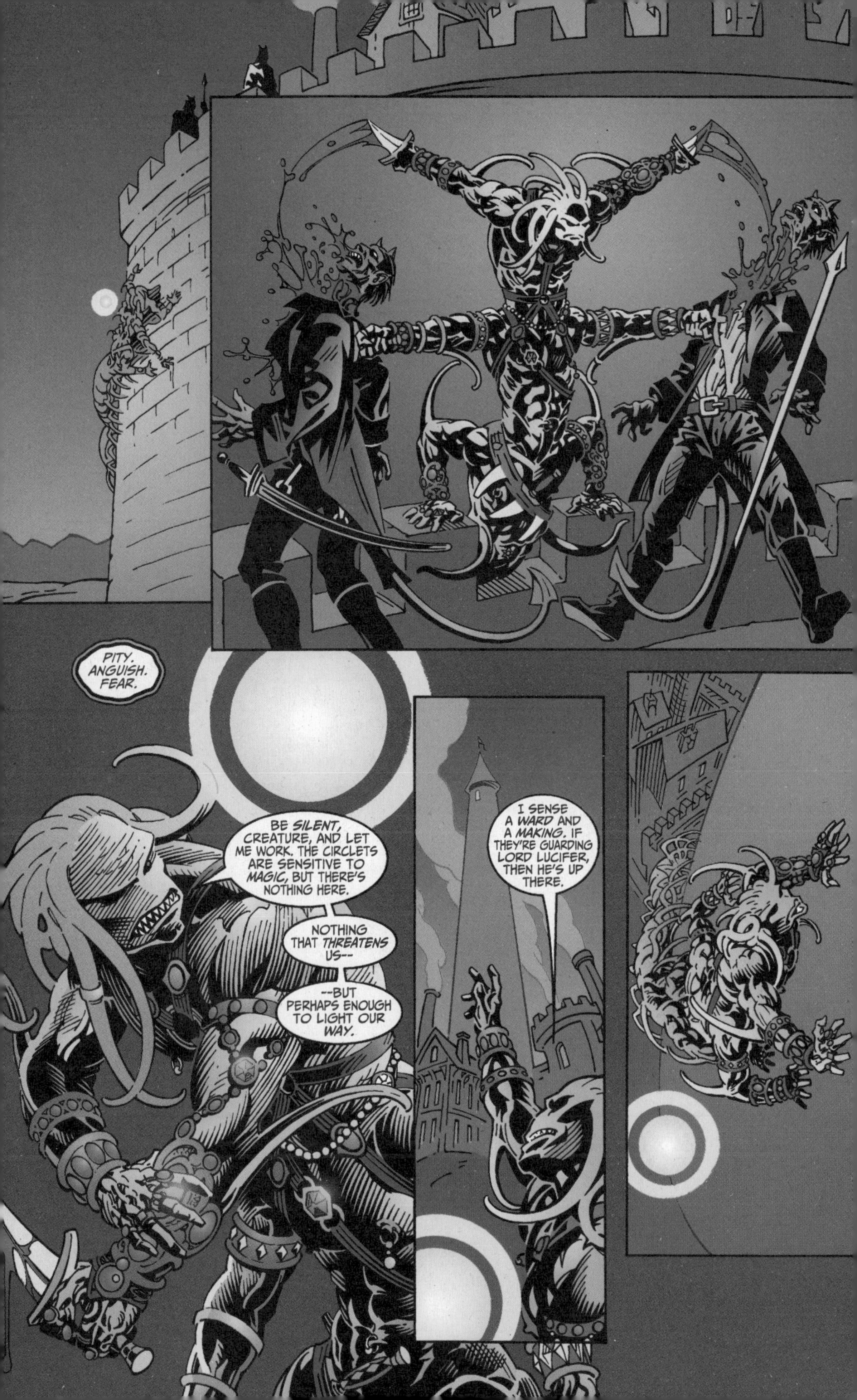
PITY. ANGUISH. FEAR.
BE SILENT, CREATURE, AND LET ME WORK. THE CIRCLETS ARE SENSITIVE TO MAGIC, BUT THERE'S NOTHING HERE.
NOTHING THAT THREATENS US--
--BUT PERHAPS ENOUGH TO LIGHT OUR WAY.
I SENSE A WARD AND A MAKING. IF THEY'RE GUARDING LORD LUCIFER, THEN HE'S UP THERE.

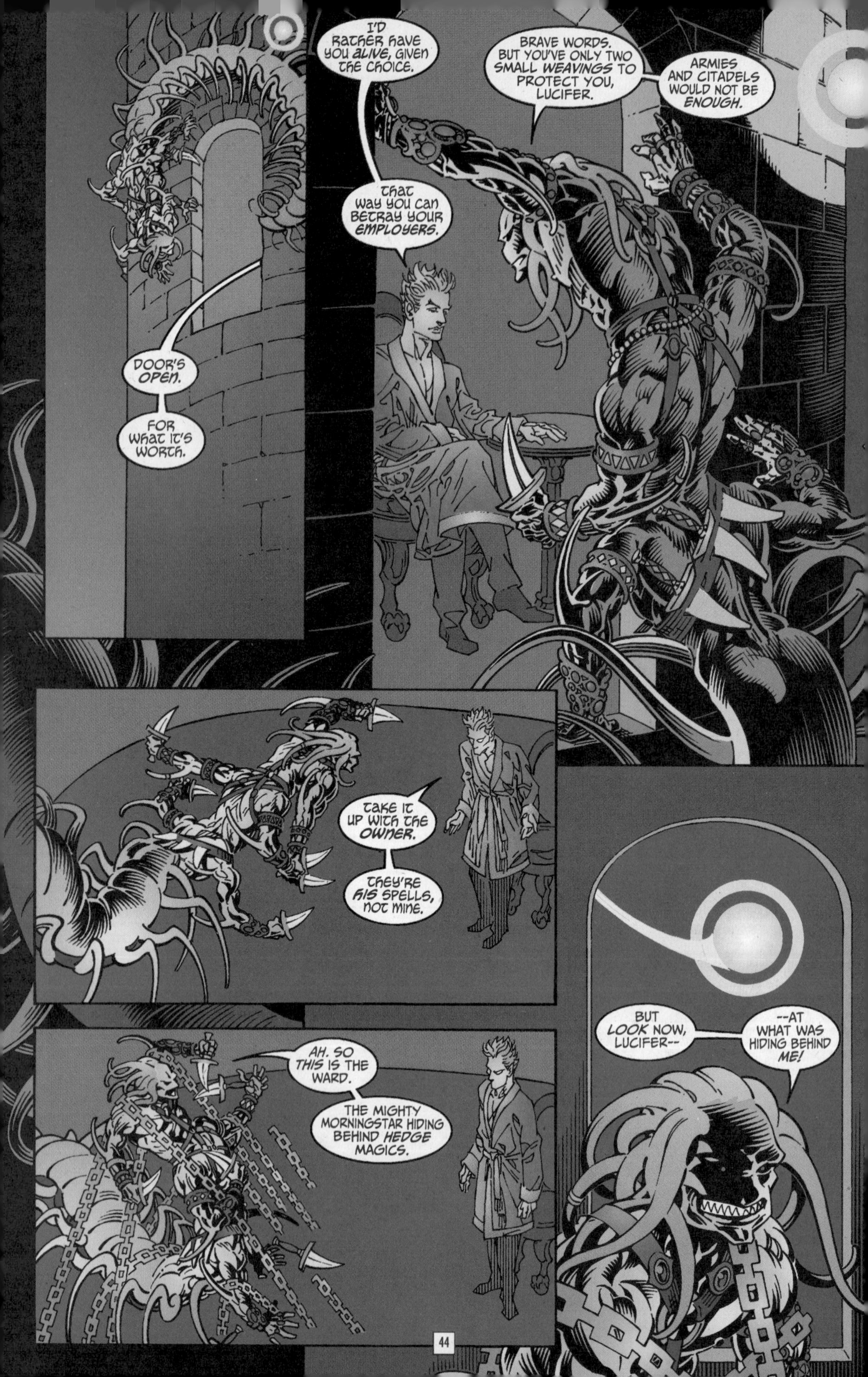
I'D RATHER HAVE YOU ALIVE, GIVEN THE CHOICE.
THAT WAY YOU CAN BETRAY YOUR EMPLOYERS.
BRAVE WORDS. BUT YOU'VE ONLY TWO SMALL WEAVINGS TO PROTECT YOU, LUCIFER.
ARMIES AND CITADELS WOULD NOT BE ENOUGH.
DOOR'S OPEN.
FOR WHAT IT'S WORTH.
TAKE IT UP WITH THE OWNER.
THEY'RE HIS SPELLS, NOT MINE.
AH. SO THIS IS THE WARD.
THE MIGHTY MORNINGSTAR HIDING BEHIND HEDGE MAGICS.
BUT LOOK NOW, LUCIFER--
--AT WHAT WAS HIDING BEHIND ME!

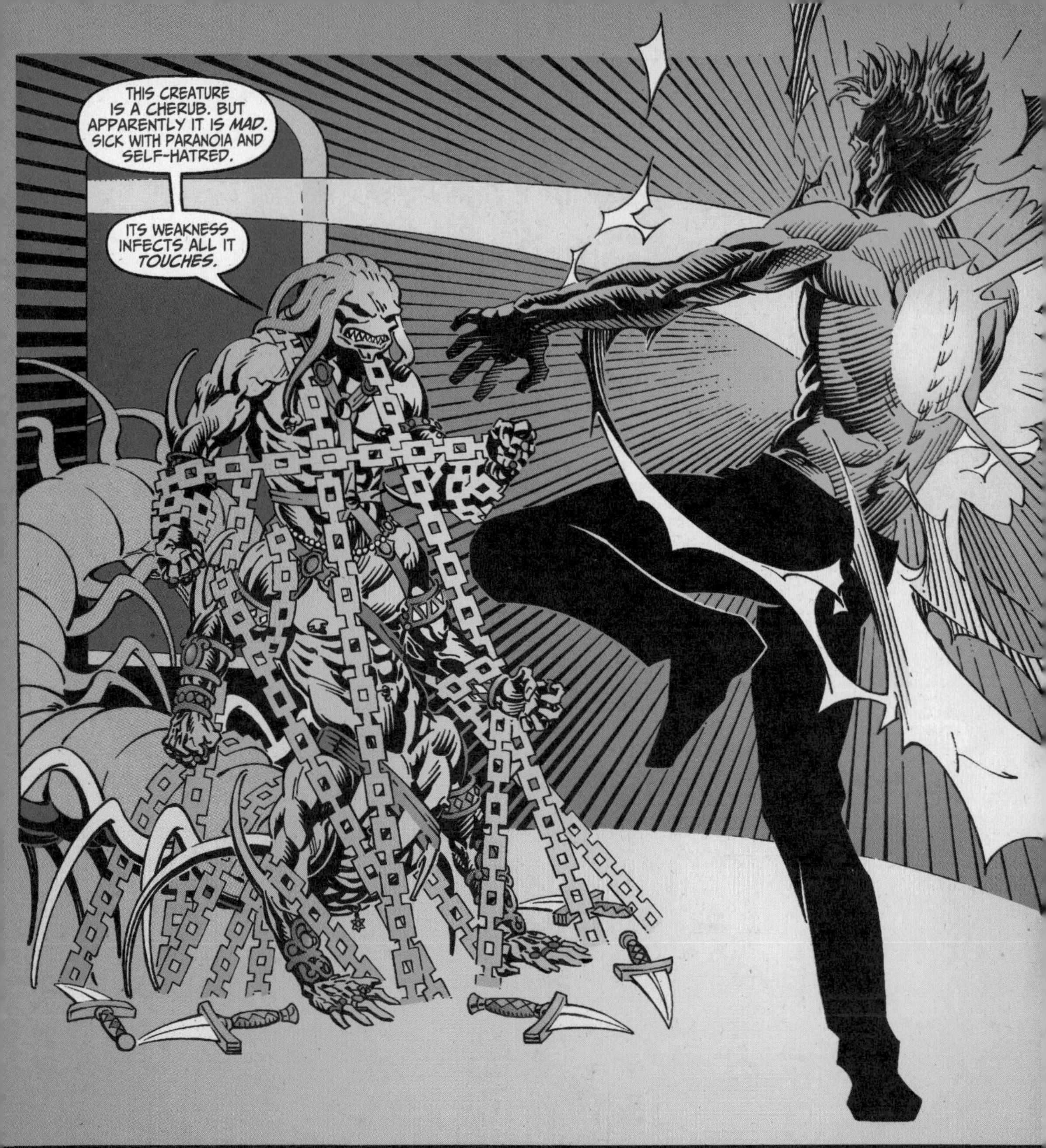
THIS CREATURE IS A CHERUB. BUT APPARENTLY IT IS *MAD*. SICK WITH PARANOIA AND SELF-HATRED.
ITS WEAKNESS INFECTS ALL IT *TOUCHES*.

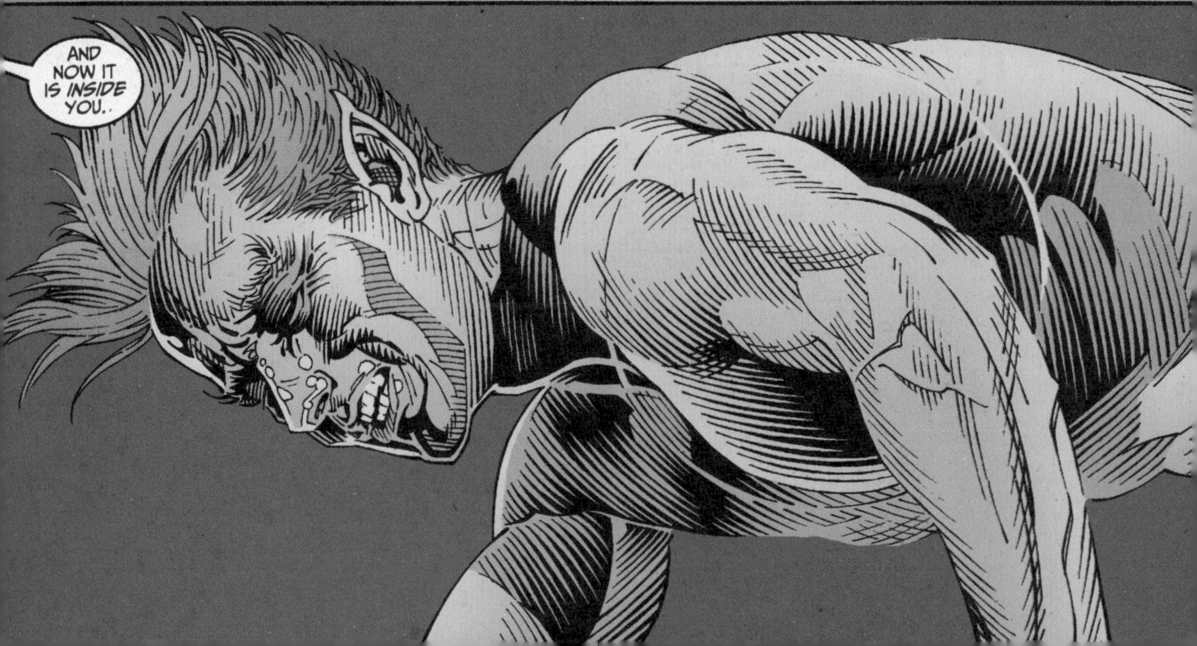
AND NOW IT IS *INSIDE* YOU..

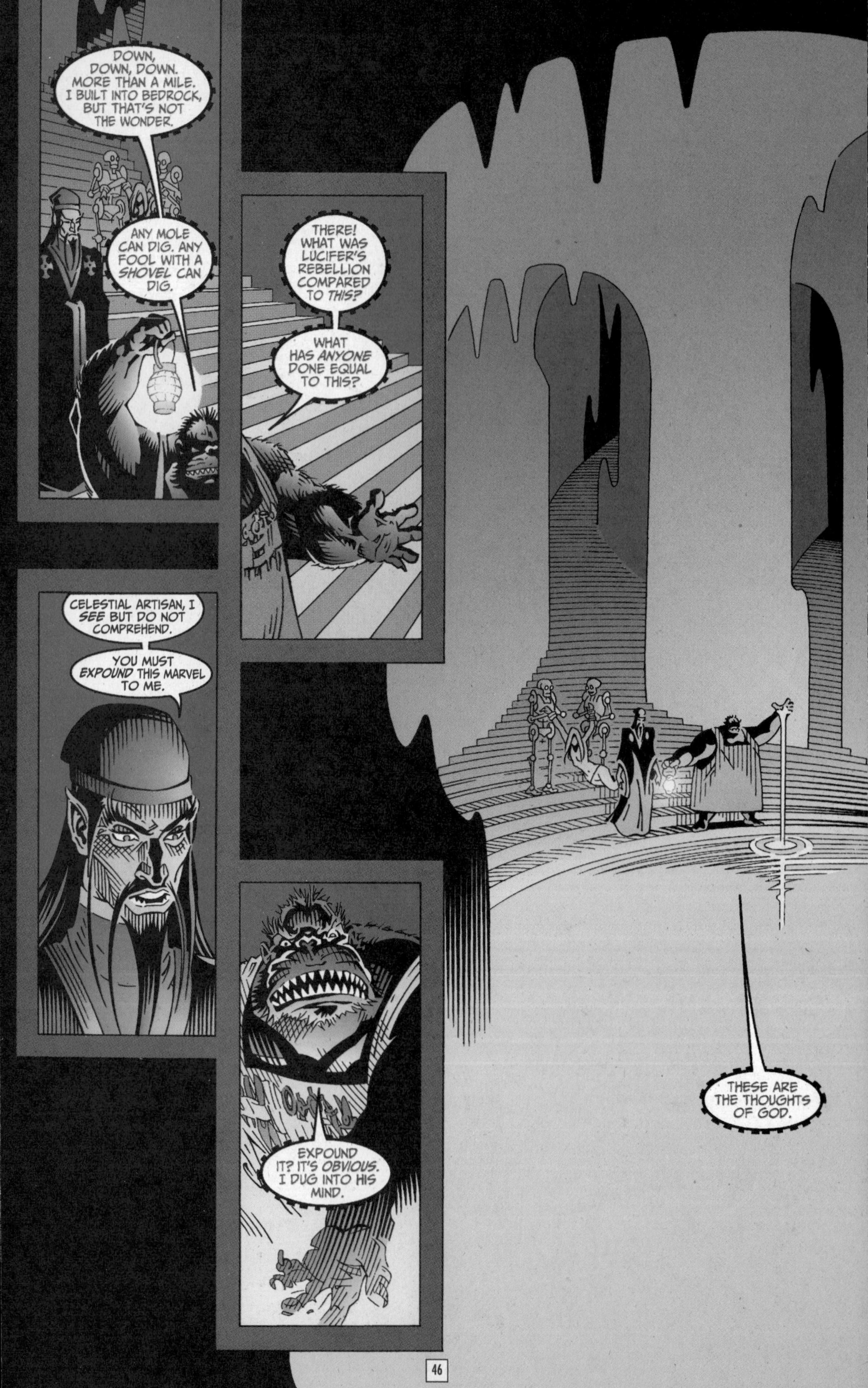
DOWN, DOWN, DOWN. MORE THAN A MILE. I BUILT INTO BEDROCK, BUT THAT'S NOT THE WONDER.
ANY MOLE CAN DIG. ANY FOOL WITH A SHOVEL CAN DIG.
THERE! WHAT WAS LUCIFER'S REBELLION COMPARED TO THIS?
WHAT HAS ANYONE DONE EQUAL TO THIS?
CELESTIAL ARTISAN, I SEE BUT DO NOT COMPREHEND.
YOU MUST EXPOUND THIS MARVEL TO ME.
EXPOUND IT? IT'S OBVIOUS. I DUG INTO HIS MIND.
THESE ARE THE THOUGHTS OF GOD.

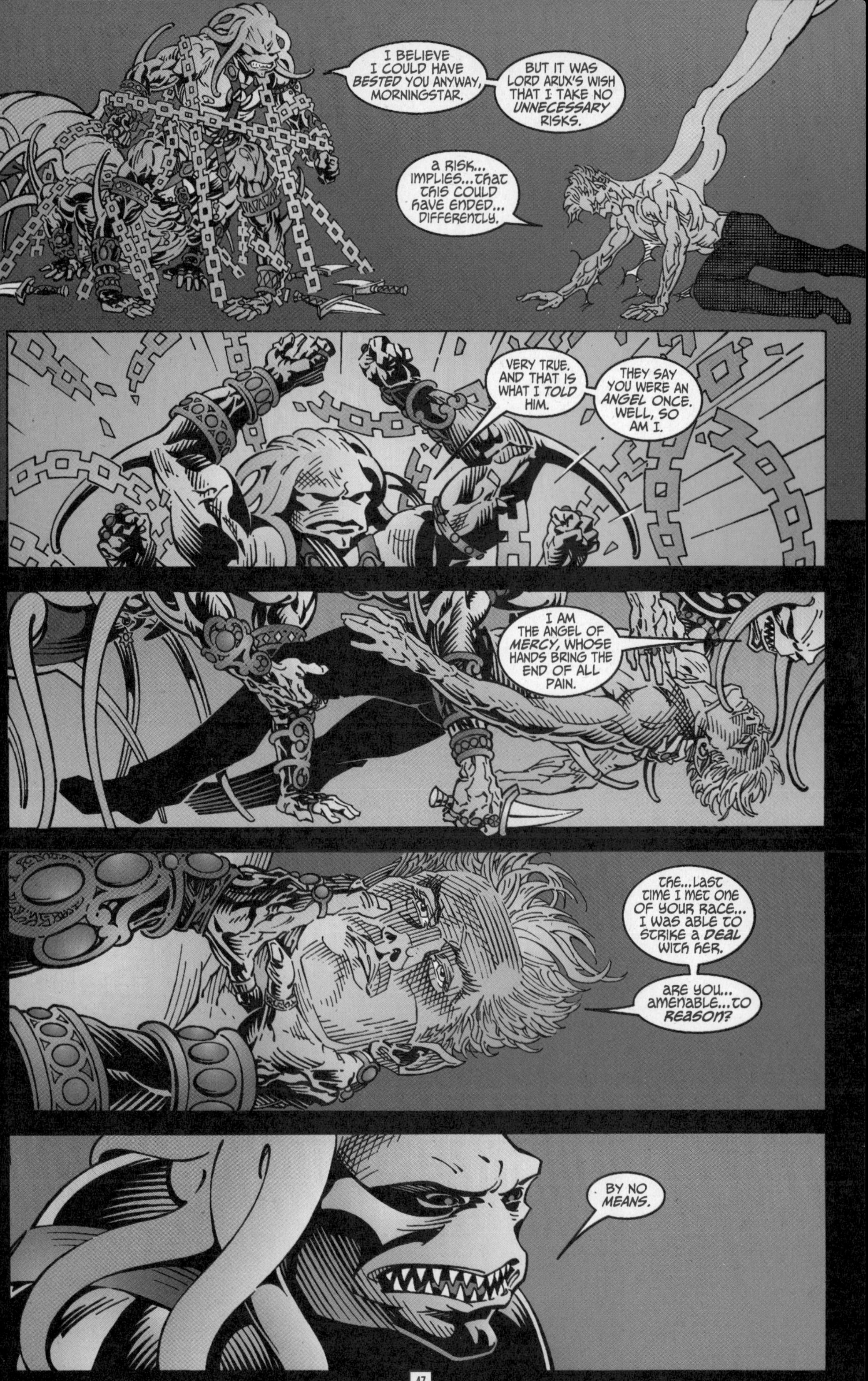
I BELIEVE I COULD HAVE BESTED YOU ANYWAY, MORNINGSTAR.
BUT IT WAS LORD ARUX'S WISH THAT I TAKE NO UNNECESSARY RISKS.
A RISK... IMPLIES...THAT THIS COULD HAVE ENDED... DIFFERENTLY.
VERY TRUE. AND THAT IS WHAT I TOLD HIM.
THEY SAY YOU WERE AN ANGEL ONCE. WELL, SO AM I.
I AM THE ANGEL OF MERCY, WHOSE HANDS BRING THE END OF ALL PAIN.
THE...LAST TIME I MET ONE OF YOUR RACE... I WAS ABLE TO STRIKE A DEAL WITH HER.
ARE YOU... AMENABLE...TO REASON?
BY NO MEANS.

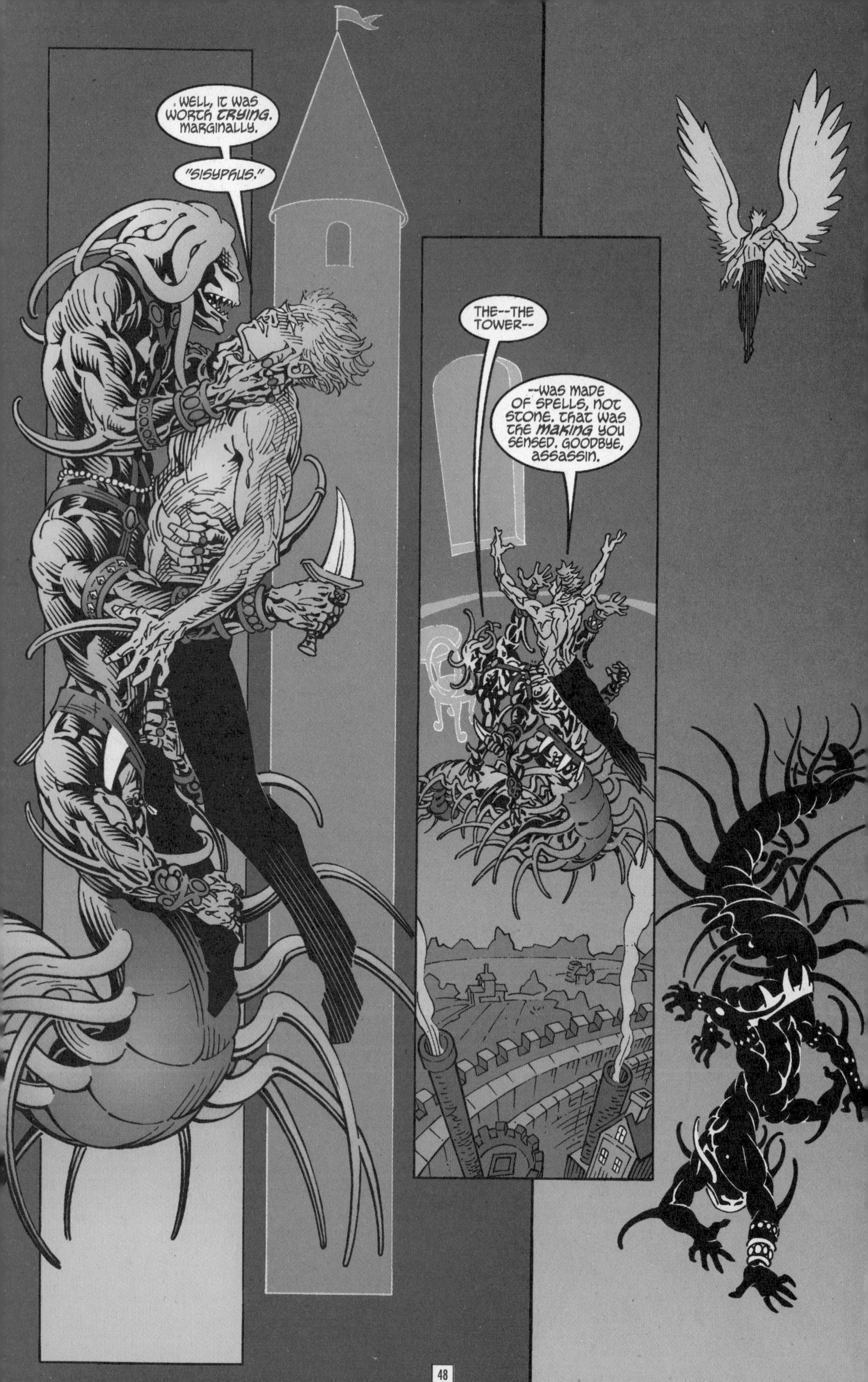
WELL, IT WAS WORTH TRYING. MARGINALLY.
"SISYPHUS."
THE--THE TOWER--
--WAS MADE OF SPELLS, NOT STONE. THAT WAS THE MAKING YOU SENSED. GOODBYE, assassin.

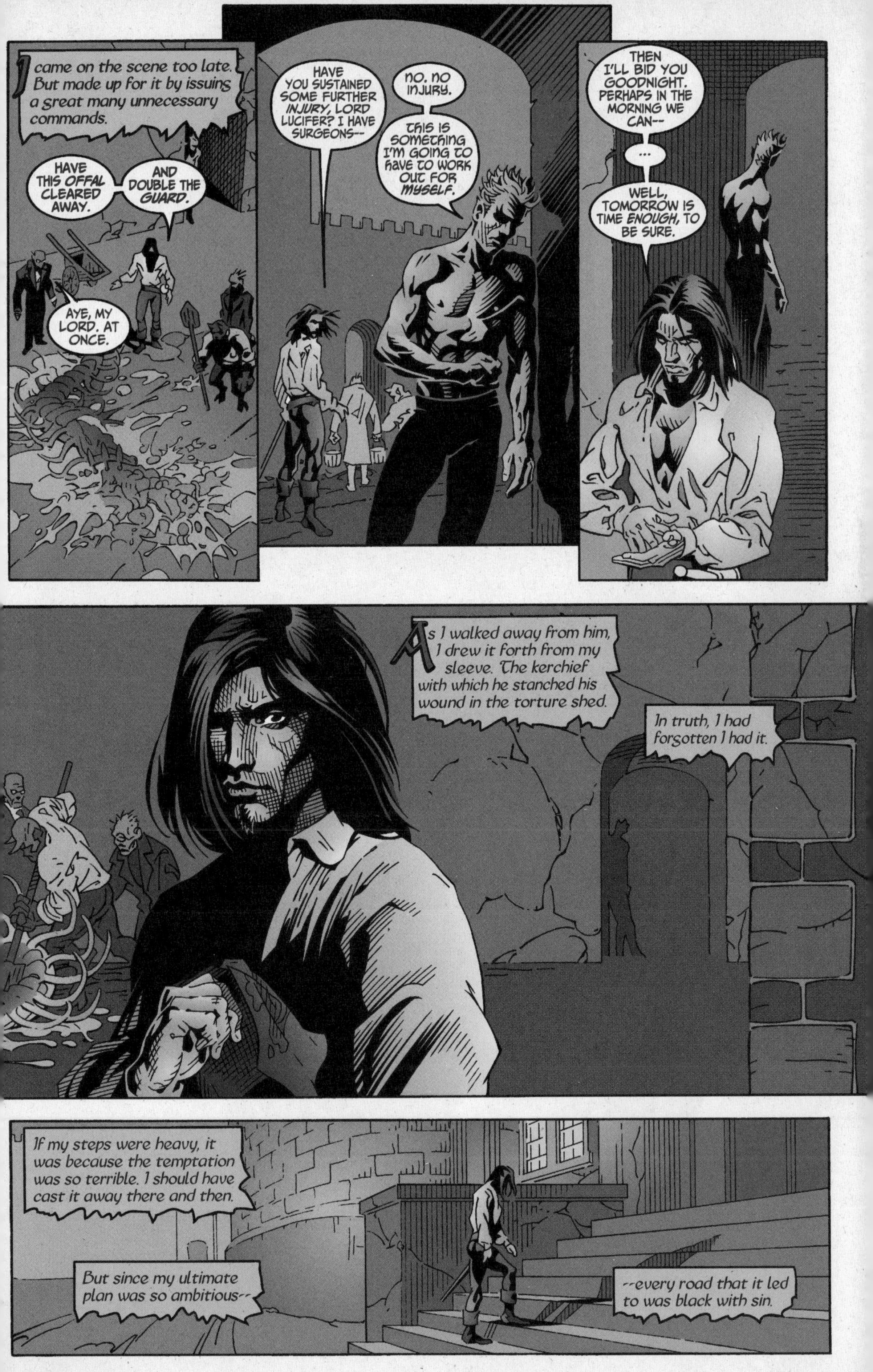
I came on the scene too late. But made up for it by issuing a great many unnecessary commands.
HAVE THIS OFFAL CLEARED AWAY.
AND DOUBLE THE GUARD.
AYE, MY LORD. AT ONCE.
HAVE YOU SUSTAINED SOME FURTHER INJURY, LORD LUCIFER? I HAVE SURGEONS--
NO. NO INJURY.
THIS IS SOMETHING I'M GOING TO HAVE TO WORK OUT FOR MYSELF.
THEN I'LL BID YOU GOODNIGHT. PERHAPS IN THE MORNING WE CAN--
...
WELL, TOMORROW IS TIME ENOUGH, TO BE SURE.
As I walked away from him, I drew it forth from my sleeve. The kerchief with which he stanched his wound in the torture shed.
In truth, I had forgotten I had it.
If my steps were heavy, it was because the temptation was so terrible. I should have cast it away there and then.
But since my ultimate plan was so ambitious--
--every road that it led to was black with sin.

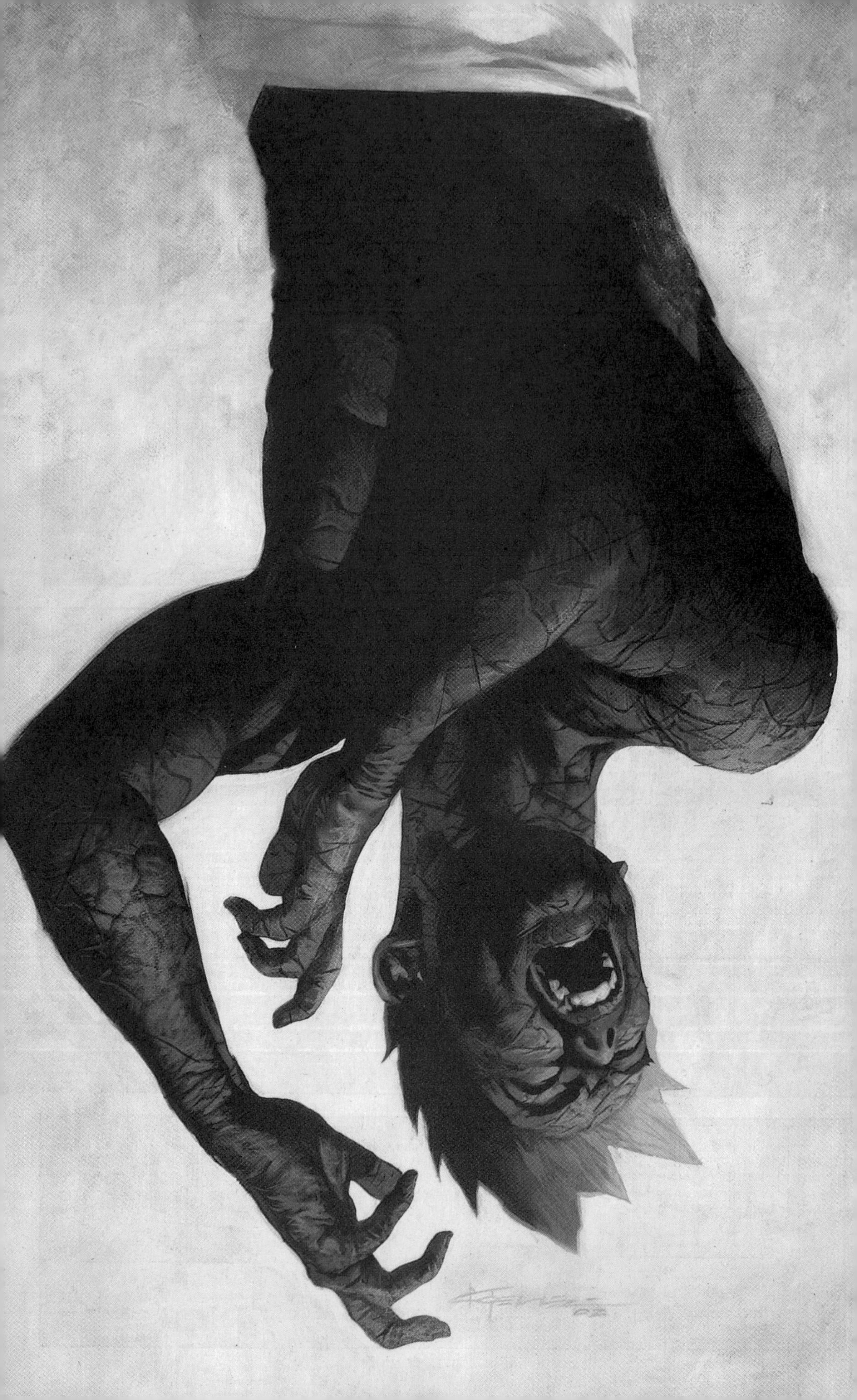

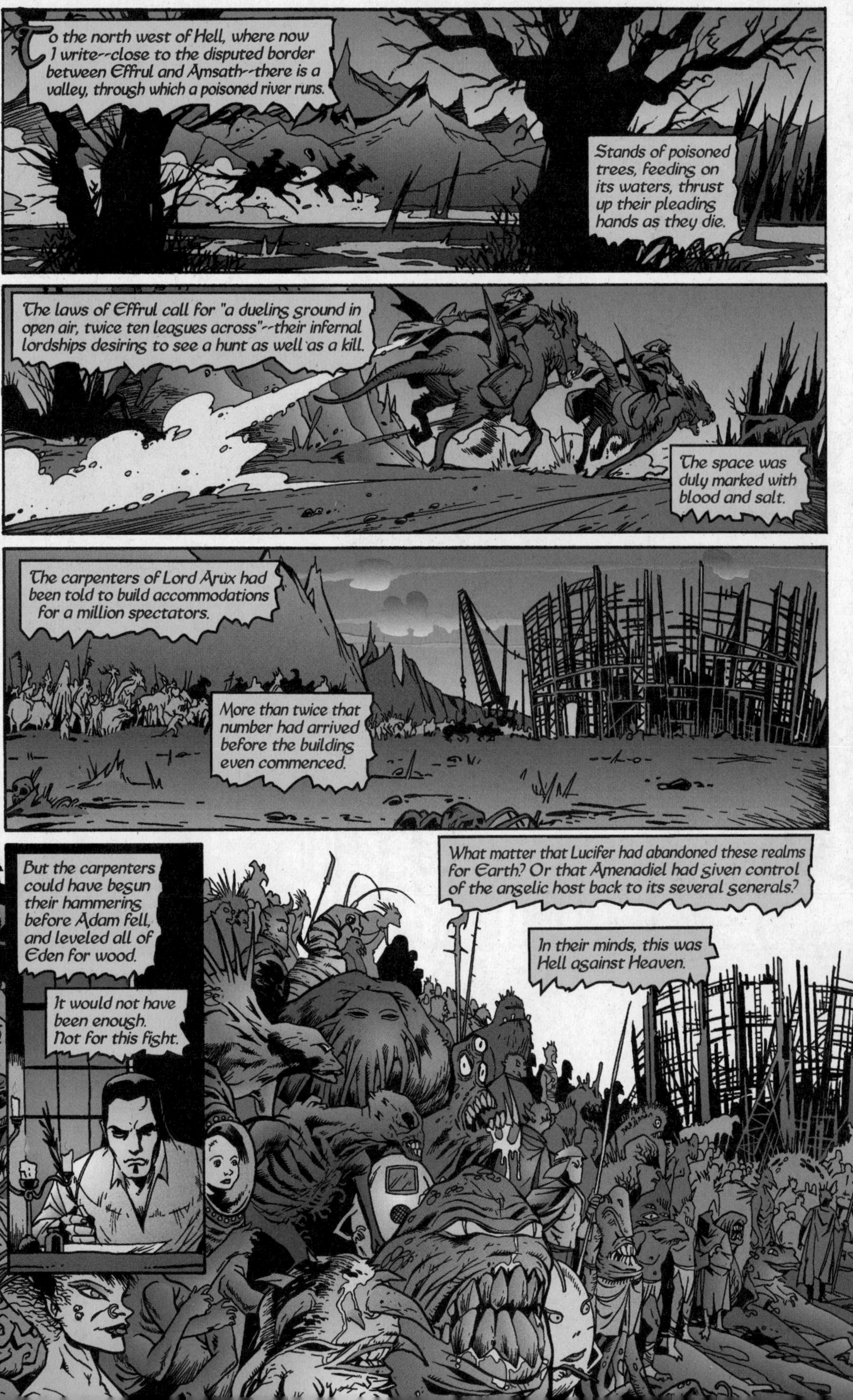
To the north west of Hell, where now I write--close to the disputed border between Effrul and Amsath--there is a valley, through which a poisoned river runs.
Stands of poisoned trees, feeding on its waters, thrust up their pleading hands as they die.
The laws of Effrul call for "a dueling ground in open air, twice ten leagues across"--their infernal lordships desiring to see a hunt as well as a kill.
The space was duly marked with blood and salt.
The carpenters of Lord Arux had been told to build accommodations for a million spectators.
More than twice that number had arrived before the building even commenced.
But the carpenters could have begun their hammering before Adam fell, and leveled all of Eden for wood.
It would not have been enough. Not for this fight.
What matter that Lucifer had abandoned these realms for Earth? Or that Amenadiel had given control of the angelic host back to its several generals?
In their minds, this was Hell against Heaven.

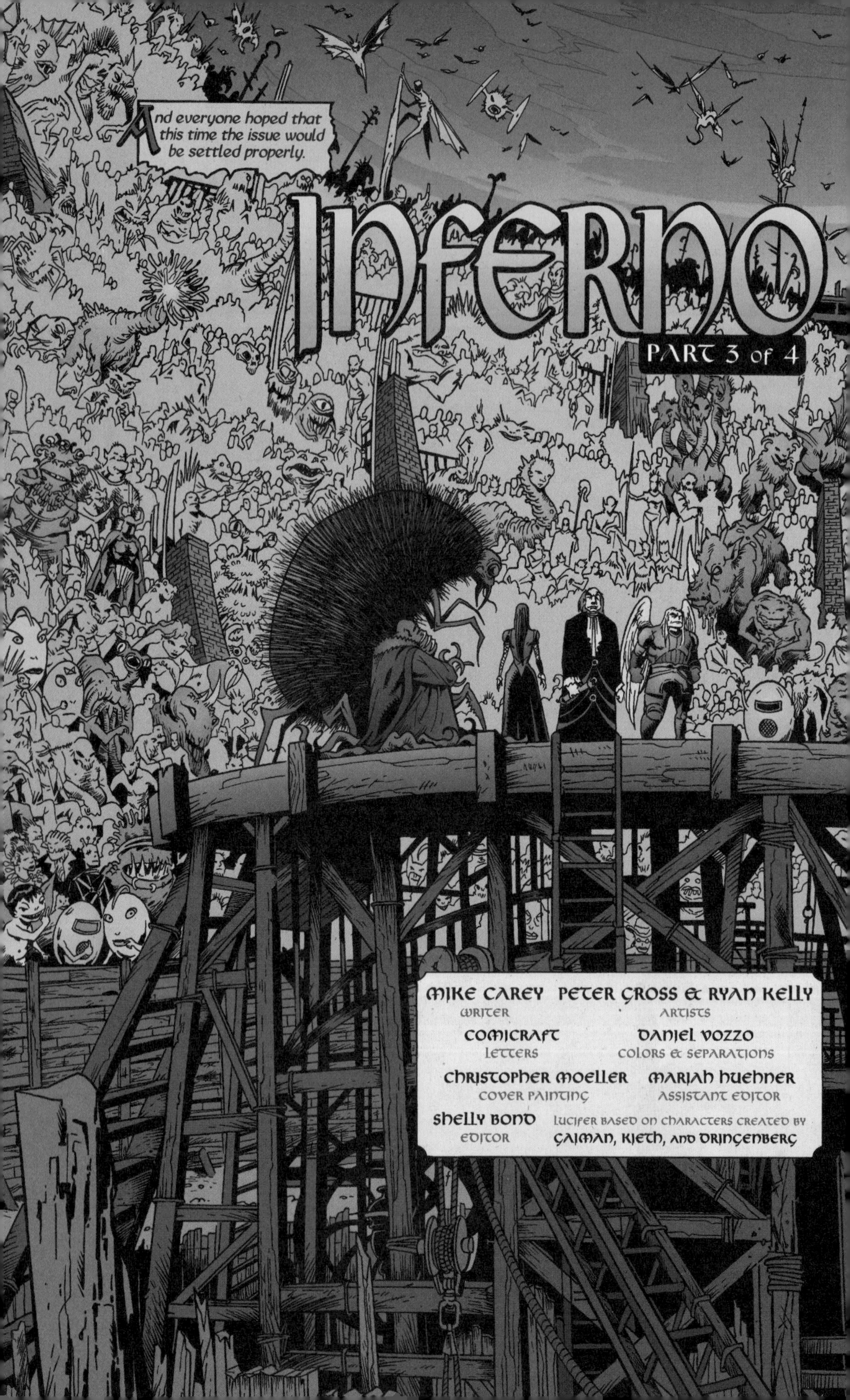
And everyone hoped that this time the issue would be settled properly.
INFERNO
PART 3 of 4
MIKE CAREY
WRITER
PETER GROSS & RYAN KELLY
ARTISTS
COMICRAFT
LETTERS
DANIEL VOZZO
COLORS & SEPARATIONS
CHRISTOPHER MOELLER
COVER PAINTING
MARIAH HUEHNER
ASSISTANT EDITOR
SHELLY BOND
EDITOR
LUCIFER BASED ON CHARACTERS CREATED BY
GAIMAN, KIETH, AND DRINGENBERG

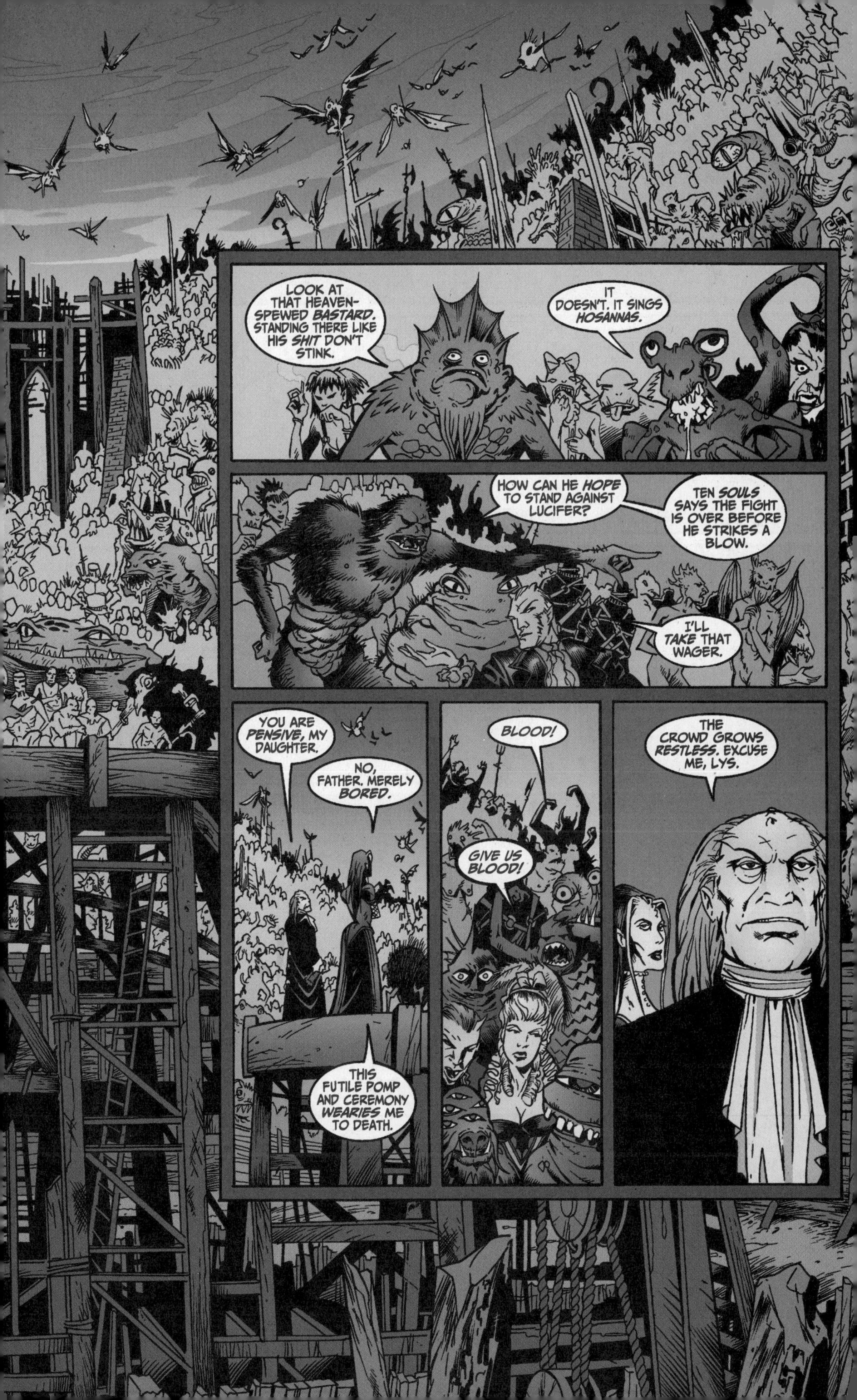
LOOK AT THAT HEAVEN-SPEWED BASTARD. STANDING THERE LIKE HIS SHIT DON'T STINK.
IT DOESN'T. IT SINGS HOSANNAS.
HOW CAN HE HOPE TO STAND AGAINST LUCIFER?
TEN SOULS SAYS THE FIGHT IS OVER BEFORE HE STRIKES A BLOW.
I'LL TAKE THAT WAGER.
YOU ARE PENSIVE, MY DAUGHTER.
NO, FATHER. MERELY BORED.
THIS FUTILE POMP AND CEREMONY WEARIES ME TO DEATH.
BLOOD!
GIVE US BLOOD!
THE CROWD GROWS RESTLESS. EXCUSE ME, LYS.

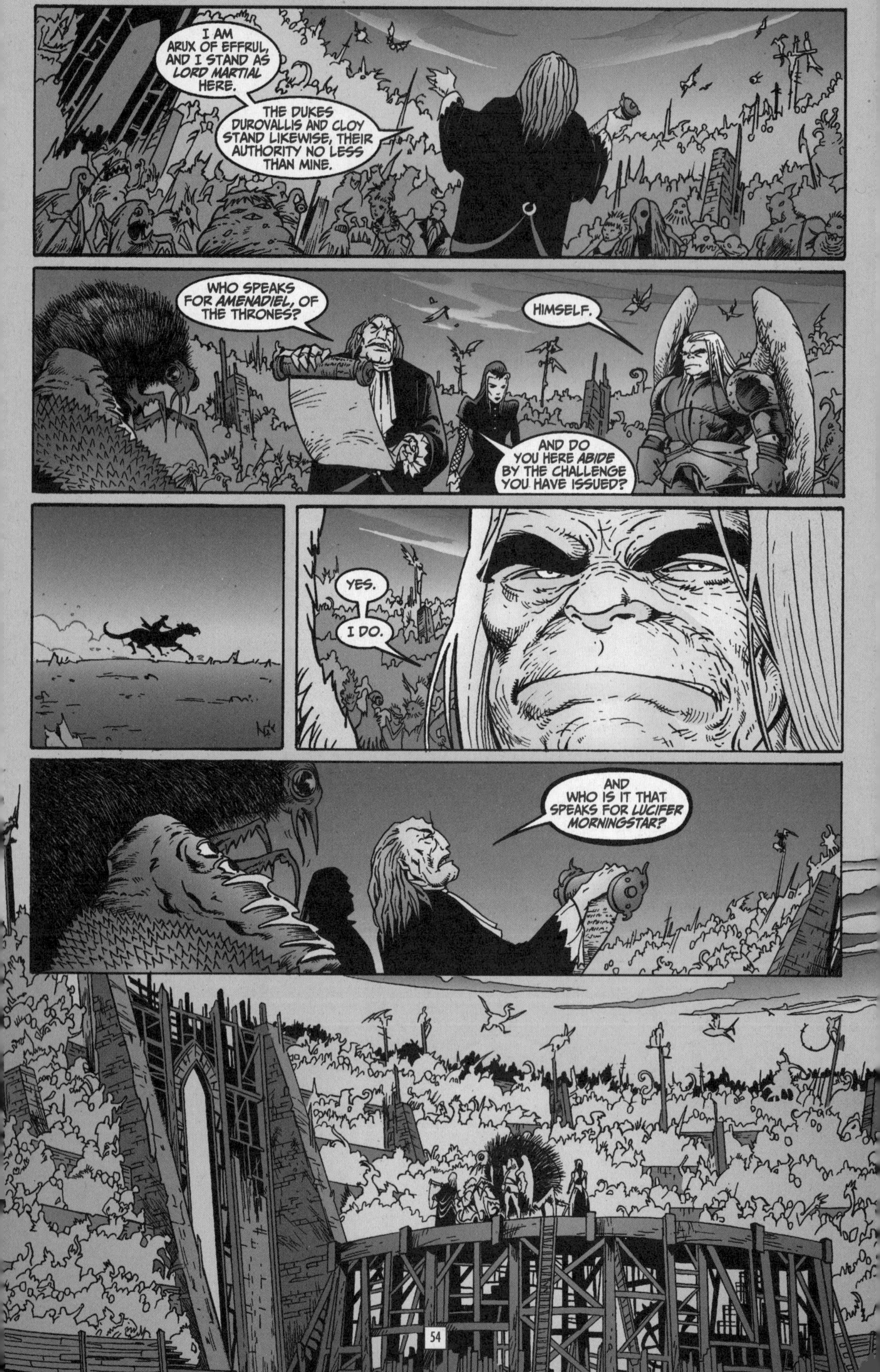
I AM ARUX OF EFFRUL, AND I STAND AS LORD MARTIAL HERE.
THE DUKES DUROVALLIS AND CLOY STAND LIKEWISE, THEIR AUTHORITY NO LESS THAN MINE.
WHO SPEAKS FOR AMENADIEL, OF THE THRONES?
HIMSELF.
AND DO YOU HERE ABIDE BY THE CHALLENGE YOU HAVE ISSUED?
YES.
I DO.
AND WHO IS IT THAT SPEAKS FOR LUCIFER MORNINGSTAR?

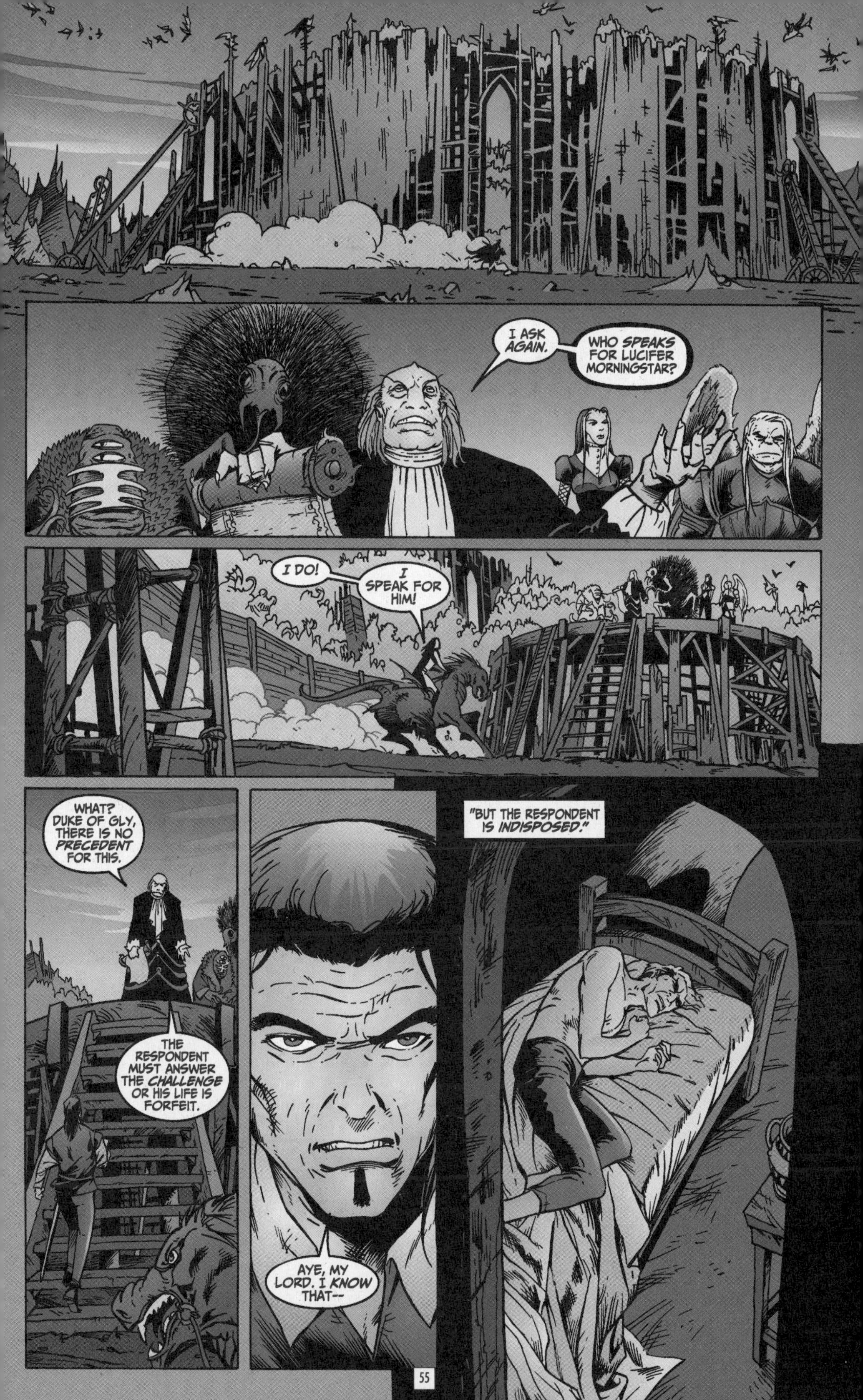
I ASK AGAIN.
WHO SPEAKS FOR LUCIFER MORNINGSTAR?
I DO!
I SPEAK FOR HIM!
WHAT? DUKE OF GLY, THERE IS NO PRECEDENT FOR THIS.
THE RESPONDENT MUST ANSWER THE CHALLENGE OR HIS LIFE IS FORFEIT.
AYE, MY LORD. I KNOW THAT--
"BUT THE RESPONDENT IS INDISPOSED."

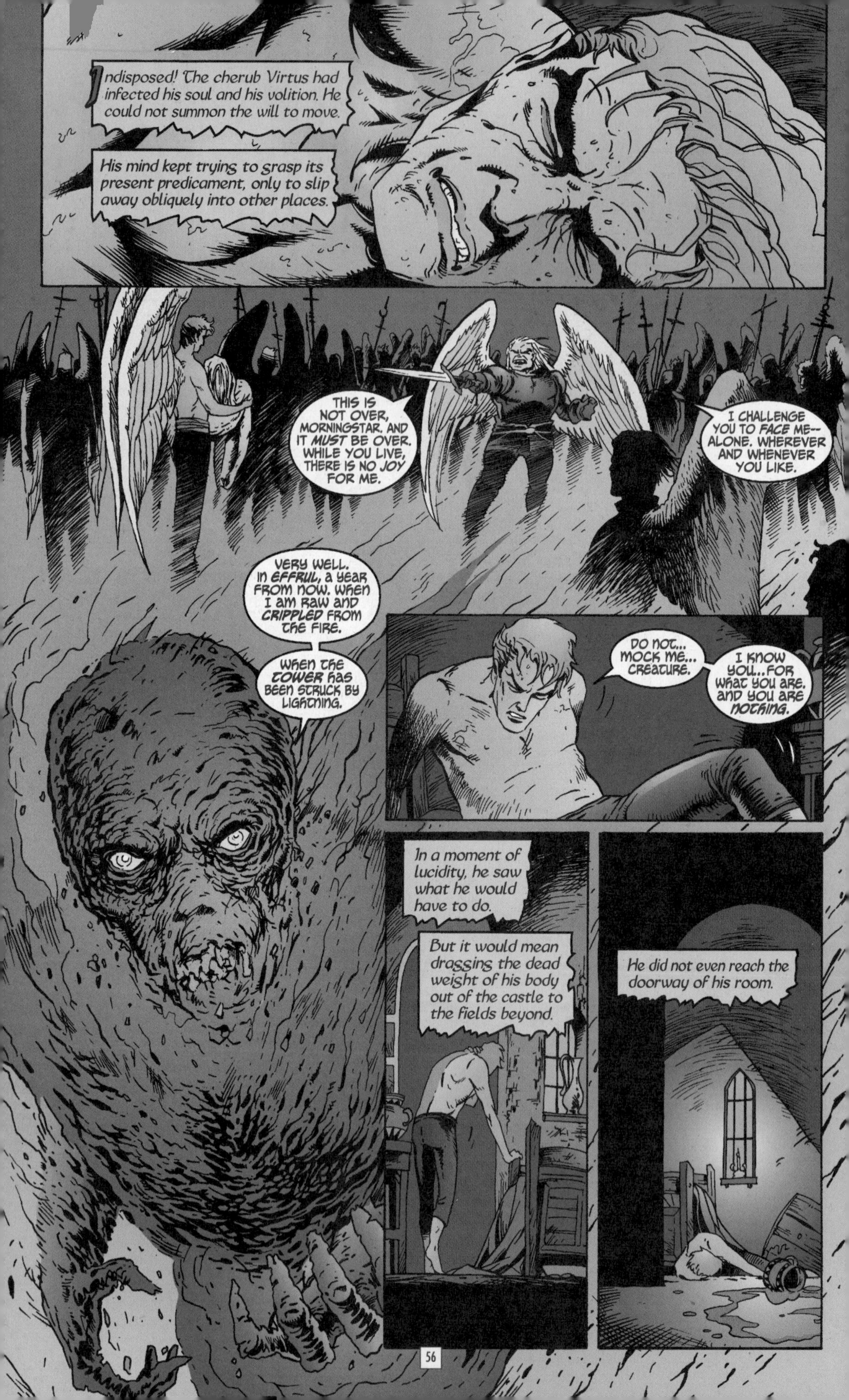
Indisposed! The cherub Virtus had infected his soul and his volition. He could not summon the will to move.
His mind kept trying to grasp its present predicament, only to slip away obliquely into other places.
THIS IS NOT OVER, MORNINGSTAR. AND IT MUST BE OVER. WHILE YOU LIVE, THERE IS NO JOY FOR ME.
I CHALLENGE YOU TO FACE ME-- ALONE. WHEREVER AND WHENEVER YOU LIKE.
VERY WELL. IN EFFRUL, A YEAR FROM NOW. WHEN I AM RAW AND CRIPPLED FROM THE FIRE.
WHEN THE TOWER HAS BEEN STRUCK BY LIGHTNING.
DO NOT... MOCK ME... CREATURE.
I KNOW YOU...FOR WHAT YOU ARE. AND YOU ARE NOTHING.
In a moment of lucidity, he saw what he would have to do.
But it would mean dragging the dead weight of his body out of the castle to the fields beyond.
He did not even reach the doorway of his room.

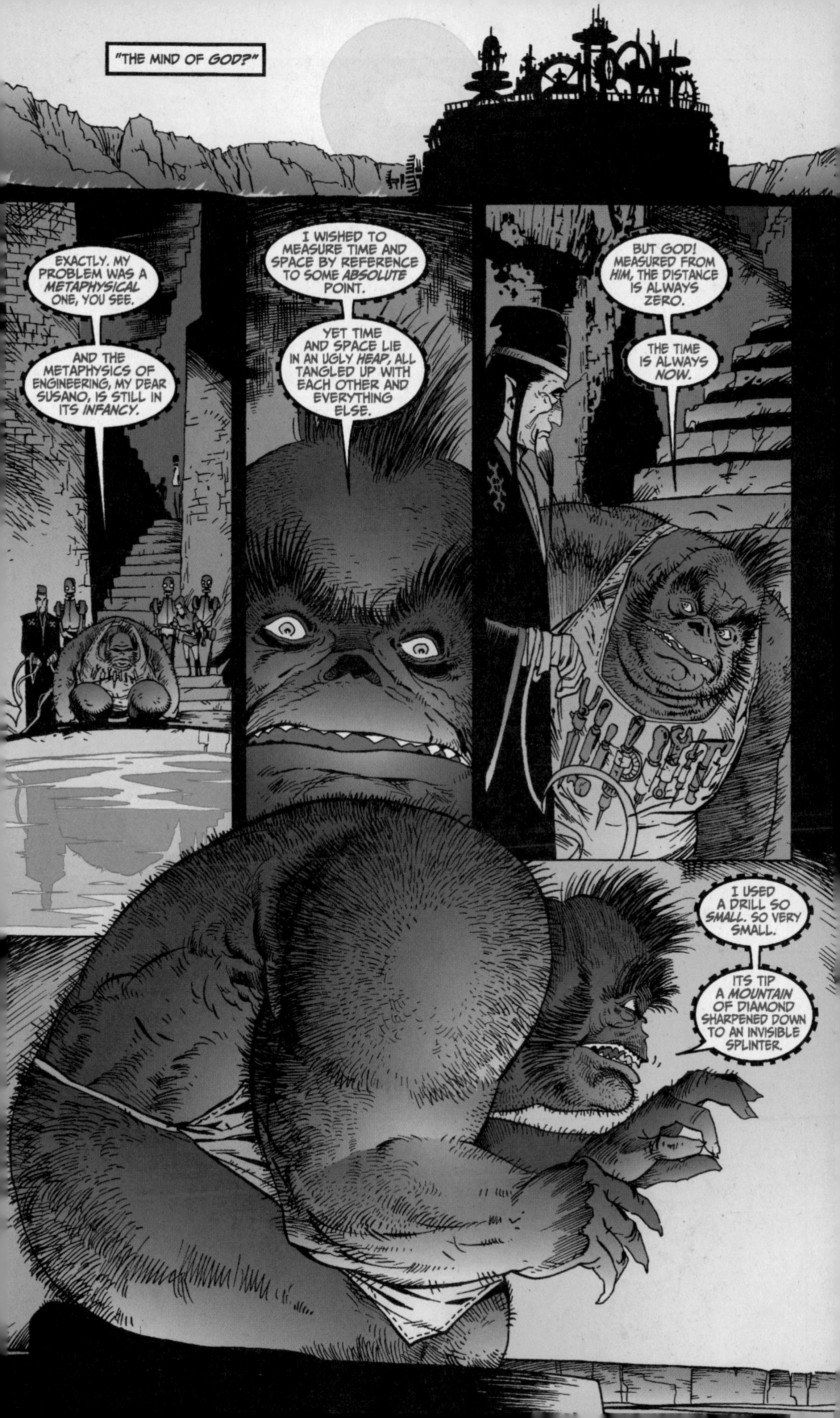
"THE MIND OF GOD?"
EXACTLY. MY PROBLEM WAS A METAPHYSICAL ONE, YOU SEE.
AND THE METAPHYSICS OF ENGINEERING, MY DEAR SUSANO, IS STILL IN ITS INFANCY.
I WISHED TO MEASURE TIME AND SPACE BY REFERENCE TO SOME ABSOLUTE POINT.
YET TIME AND SPACE LIE IN AN UGLY HEAP, ALL TANGLED UP WITH EACH OTHER AND EVERYTHING ELSE.
BUT GOD! MEASURED FROM HIM, THE DISTANCE IS ALWAYS ZERO.
THE TIME IS ALWAYS NOW.
I USED A DRILL SO SMALL. SO VERY SMALL.
ITS TIP A MOUNTAIN OF DIAMOND SHARPENED DOWN TO AN INVISIBLE SPLINTER.

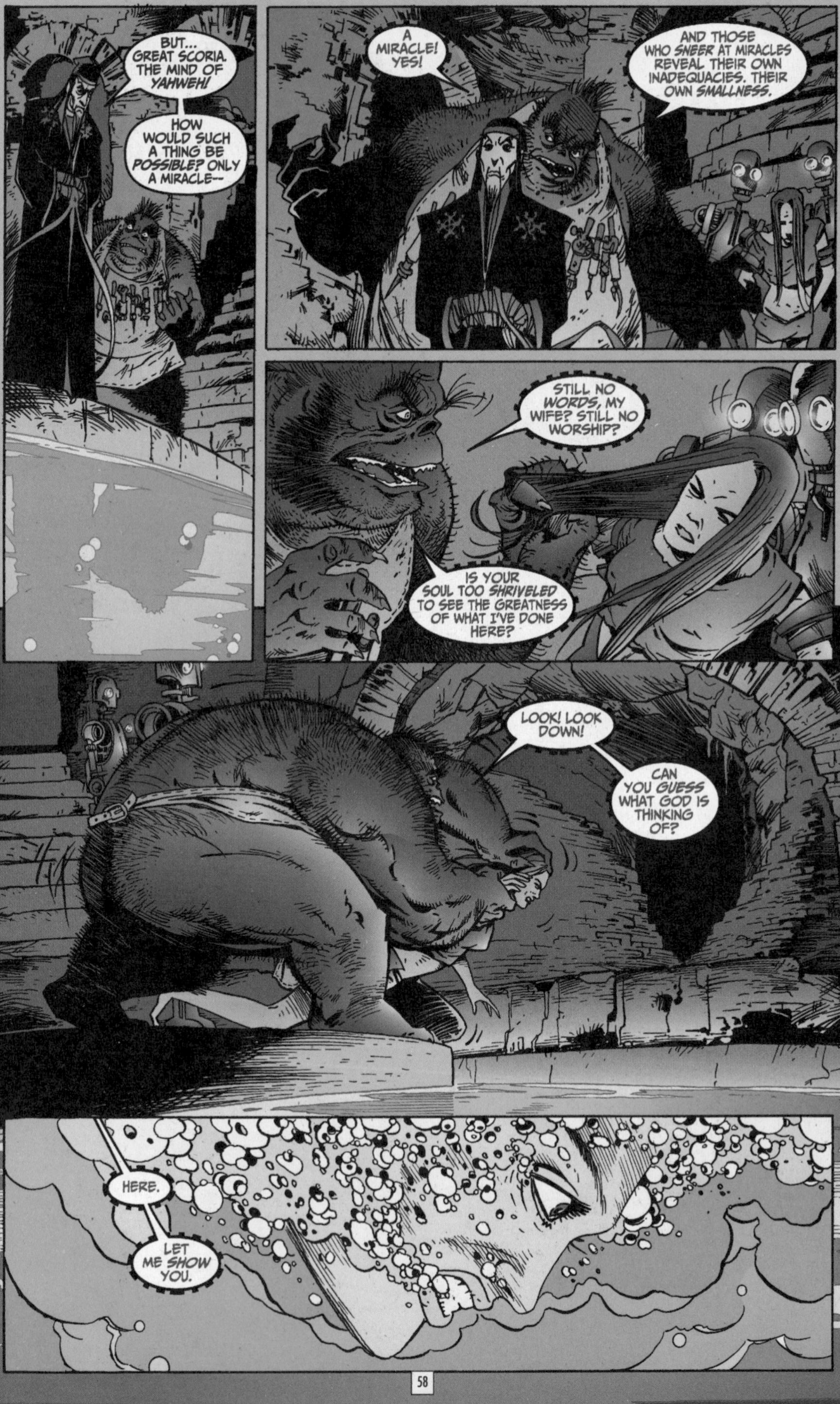

BUT... GREAT SCORIA. THE MIND OF YAHWEH!
HOW WOULD SUCH A THING BE POSSIBLE? ONLY A MIRACLE--
A MIRACLE! YES!
AND THOSE WHO SNEER AT MIRACLES REVEAL THEIR OWN INADEQUACIES. THEIR OWN SMALLNESS.
STILL NO WORDS, MY WIFE? STILL NO WORSHIP?
IS YOUR SOUL TOO SHRIVELED TO SEE THE GREATNESS OF WHAT I'VE DONE HERE?
LOOK! LOOK DOWN!
CAN YOU GUESS WHAT GOD IS THINKING OF?
HERE.
LET ME SHOW YOU.

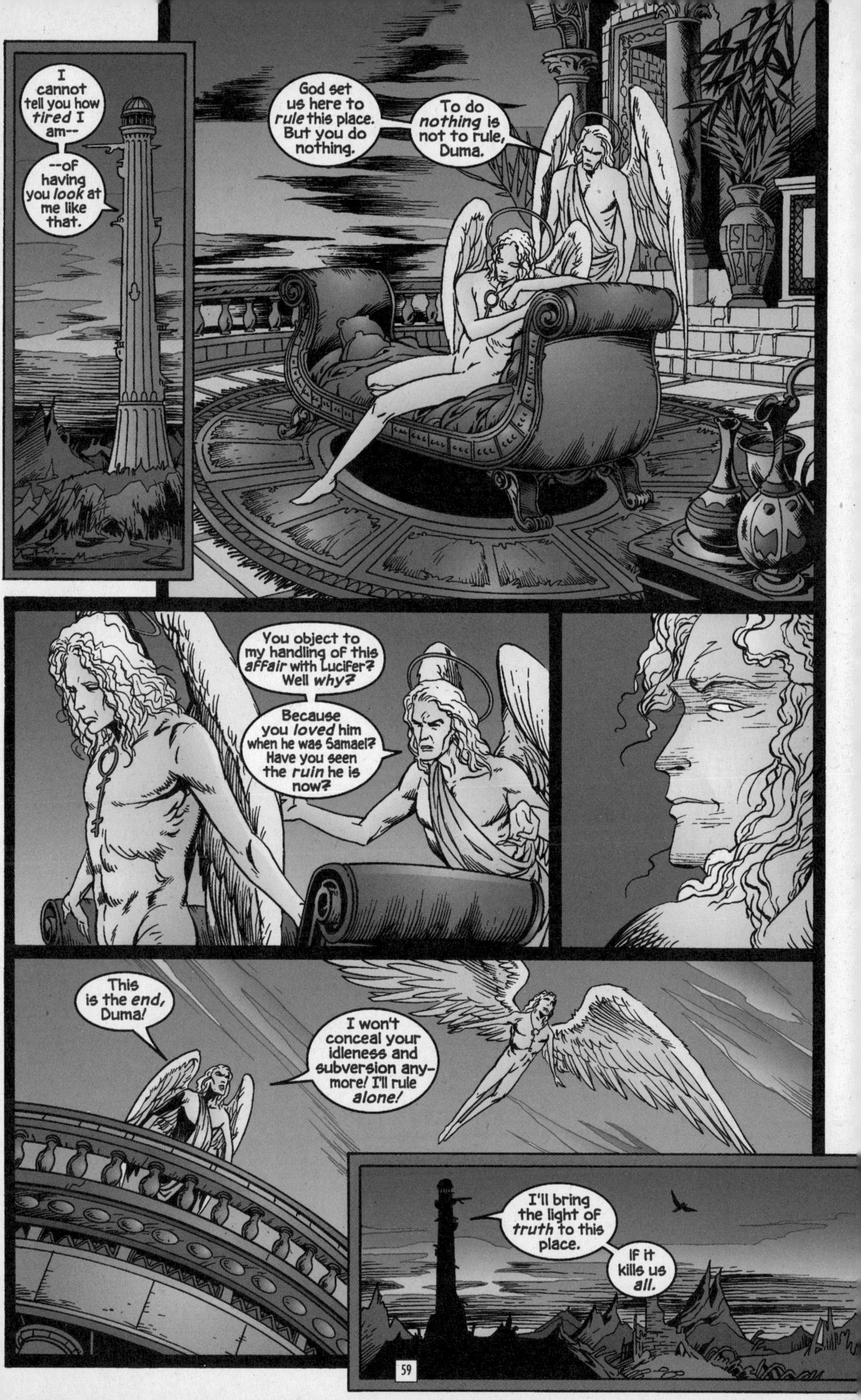
I cannot tell you how *tired* I am--
--of having you *look* at me like that.
God set us here to *rule* this place. But you do nothing.
To do *nothing* is not to rule, Duma.
You object to my handling of this *affair* with Lucifer? Well *why?*
Because you *loved* him when he was Samael? Have you seen the *ruin* he is now?
This is the *end*, Duma!
I won't conceal your idleness and subversion anymore! I'll rule *alone!*
I'll bring the light of *truth* to this place.
If it kills us *all.*

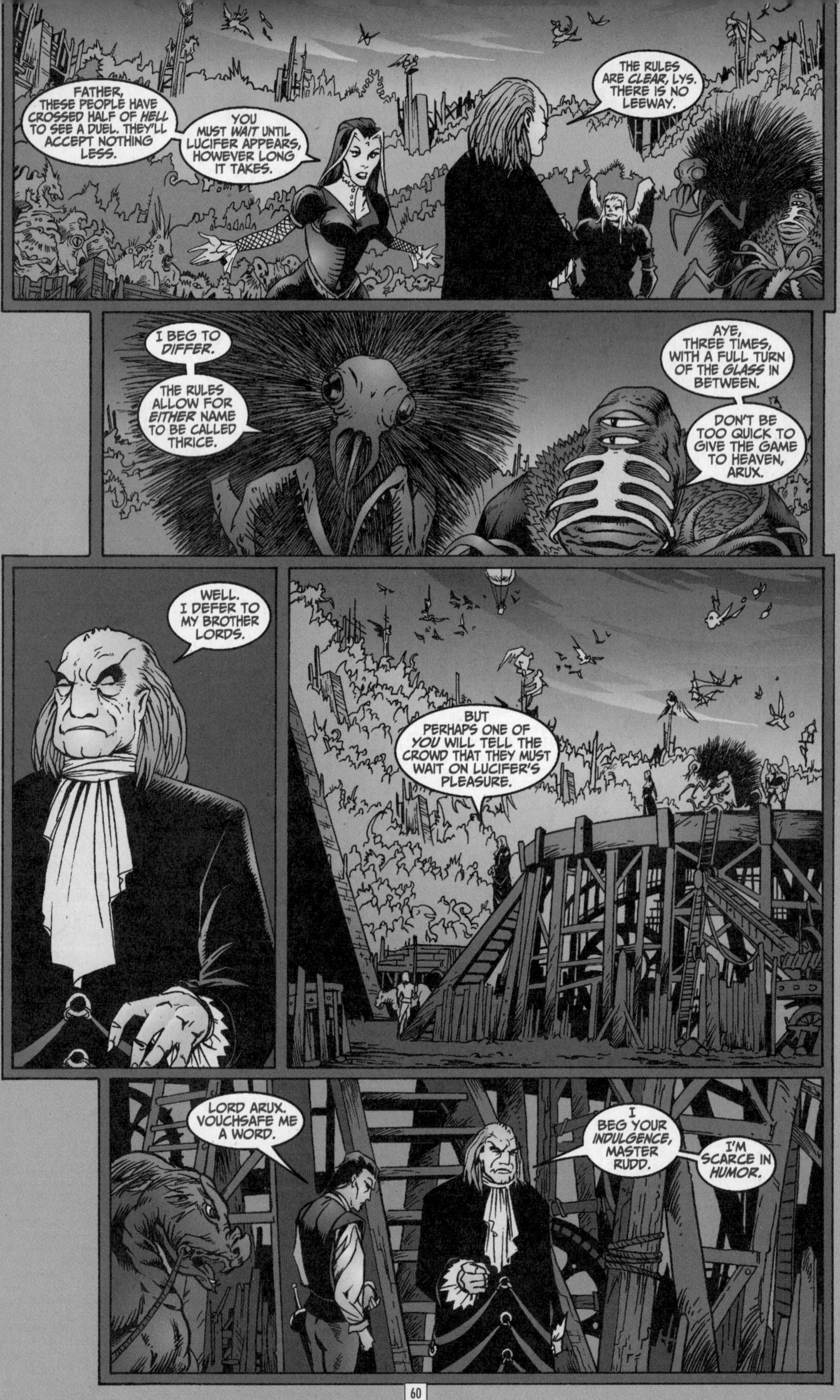
FATHER, THESE PEOPLE HAVE CROSSED HALF OF *HELL* TO SEE A DUEL. THEY'LL ACCEPT NOTHING LESS.
YOU MUST *WAIT* UNTIL LUCIFER APPEARS, HOWEVER LONG IT TAKES.
THE RULES ARE *CLEAR*, LYS. THERE IS NO LEEWAY.
I BEG TO *DIFFER*.
THE RULES ALLOW FOR *EITHER* NAME TO BE CALLED THRICE.
AYE, THREE TIMES, WITH A FULL TURN OF THE *GLASS* IN BETWEEN.
DON'T BE TOO QUICK TO GIVE THE GAME TO HEAVEN, ARUX.
WELL. I DEFER TO MY BROTHER LORDS.
BUT PERHAPS ONE OF *YOU* WILL TELL THE CROWD THAT THEY MUST WAIT ON LUCIFER'S PLEASURE.
LORD ARUX. VOUCHSAFE ME A WORD.
I BEG YOUR *INDULGENCE*, MASTER RUDD.
I'M SCARCE IN *HUMOR*.

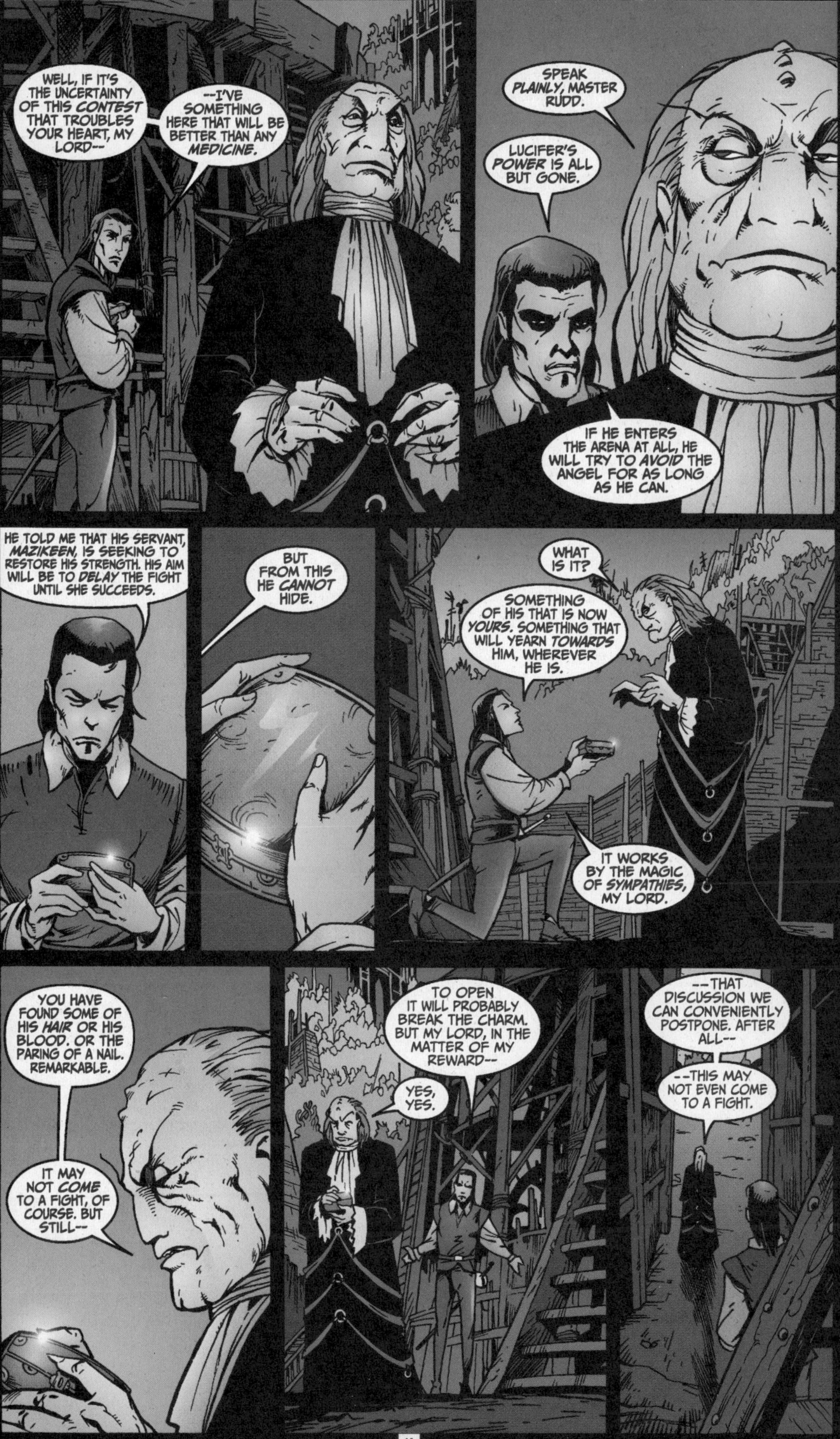
WELL, IF IT'S THE UNCERTAINTY OF THIS CONTEST THAT TROUBLES YOUR HEART, MY LORD--
--I'VE SOMETHING HERE THAT WILL BE BETTER THAN ANY MEDICINE.
SPEAK PLAINLY, MASTER RUDD.
LUCIFER'S POWER IS ALL BUT GONE.
IF HE ENTERS THE ARENA AT ALL, HE WILL TRY TO AVOID THE ANGEL FOR AS LONG AS HE CAN.
HE TOLD ME THAT HIS SERVANT, MAZIKEEN, IS SEEKING TO RESTORE HIS STRENGTH. HIS AIM WILL BE TO DELAY THE FIGHT UNTIL SHE SUCCEEDS.
BUT FROM THIS HE CANNOT HIDE.
WHAT IS IT?
SOMETHING OF HIS THAT IS NOW YOURS. SOMETHING THAT WILL YEARN TOWARDS HIM, WHEREVER HE IS.
IT WORKS BY THE MAGIC OF SYMPATHIES, MY LORD.
YOU HAVE FOUND SOME OF HIS HAIR OR HIS BLOOD. OR THE PARING OF A NAIL. REMARKABLE.
IT MAY NOT COME TO A FIGHT, OF COURSE. BUT STILL--
TO OPEN IT WILL PROBABLY BREAK THE CHARM. BUT MY LORD, IN THE MATTER OF MY REWARD--
YES, YES.
--THAT DISCUSSION WE CAN CONVENIENTLY POSTPONE. AFTER ALL--
--THIS MAY NOT EVEN COME TO A FIGHT.

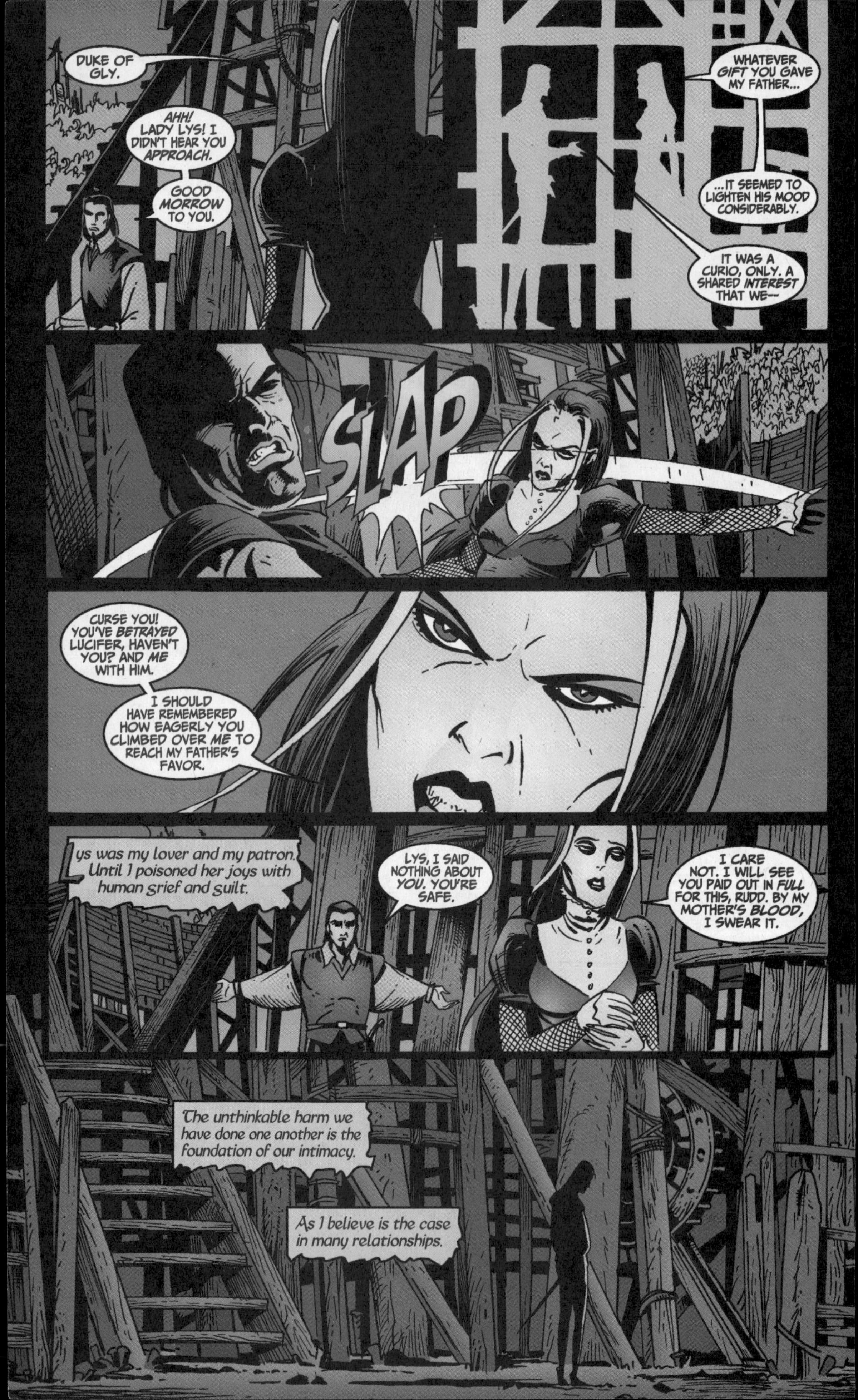
DUKE OF GLY.
AHH! LADY LYS! I DIDN'T HEAR YOU APPROACH.
GOOD MORROW TO YOU.
WHATEVER GIFT YOU GAVE MY FATHER...
...IT SEEMED TO LIGHTEN HIS MOOD CONSIDERABLY.
IT WAS A CURIO, ONLY. A SHARED INTEREST THAT WE--
SLAP
CURSE YOU! YOU'VE BETRAYED LUCIFER, HAVEN'T YOU? AND ME WITH HIM.
I SHOULD HAVE REMEMBERED HOW EAGERLY YOU CLIMBED OVER ME TO REACH MY FATHER'S FAVOR.
Lys was my lover and my patron. Until I poisoned her joys with human grief and guilt.
LYS, I SAID NOTHING ABOUT YOU. YOU'RE SAFE.
I CARE NOT. I WILL SEE YOU PAID OUT IN FULL FOR THIS, RUDD. BY MY MOTHER'S BLOOD, I SWEAR IT.
The unthinkable harm we have done one another is the foundation of our intimacy.
As I believe is the case in many relationships.

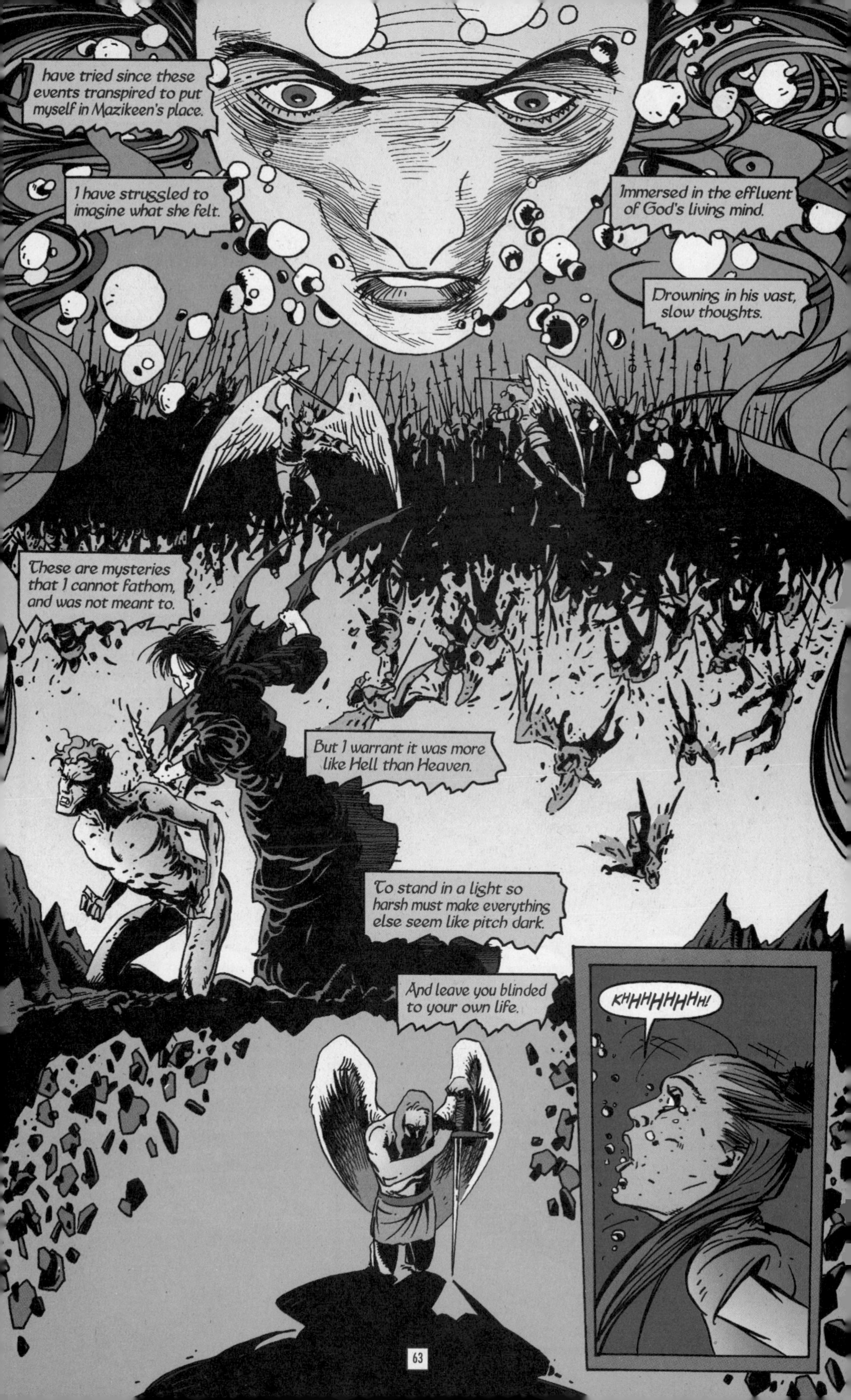

I have tried since these events transpired to put myself in Mazikeen's place.
I have struggled to imagine what she felt.
Immersed in the effluent of God's living mind.
Drowning in his vast, slow thoughts.
These are mysteries that I cannot fathom, and was not meant to.
But I warrant it was more like Hell than Heaven.
To stand in a light so harsh must make everything else seem like pitch dark.
And leave you blinded to your own life.
KHHHHHHHH!

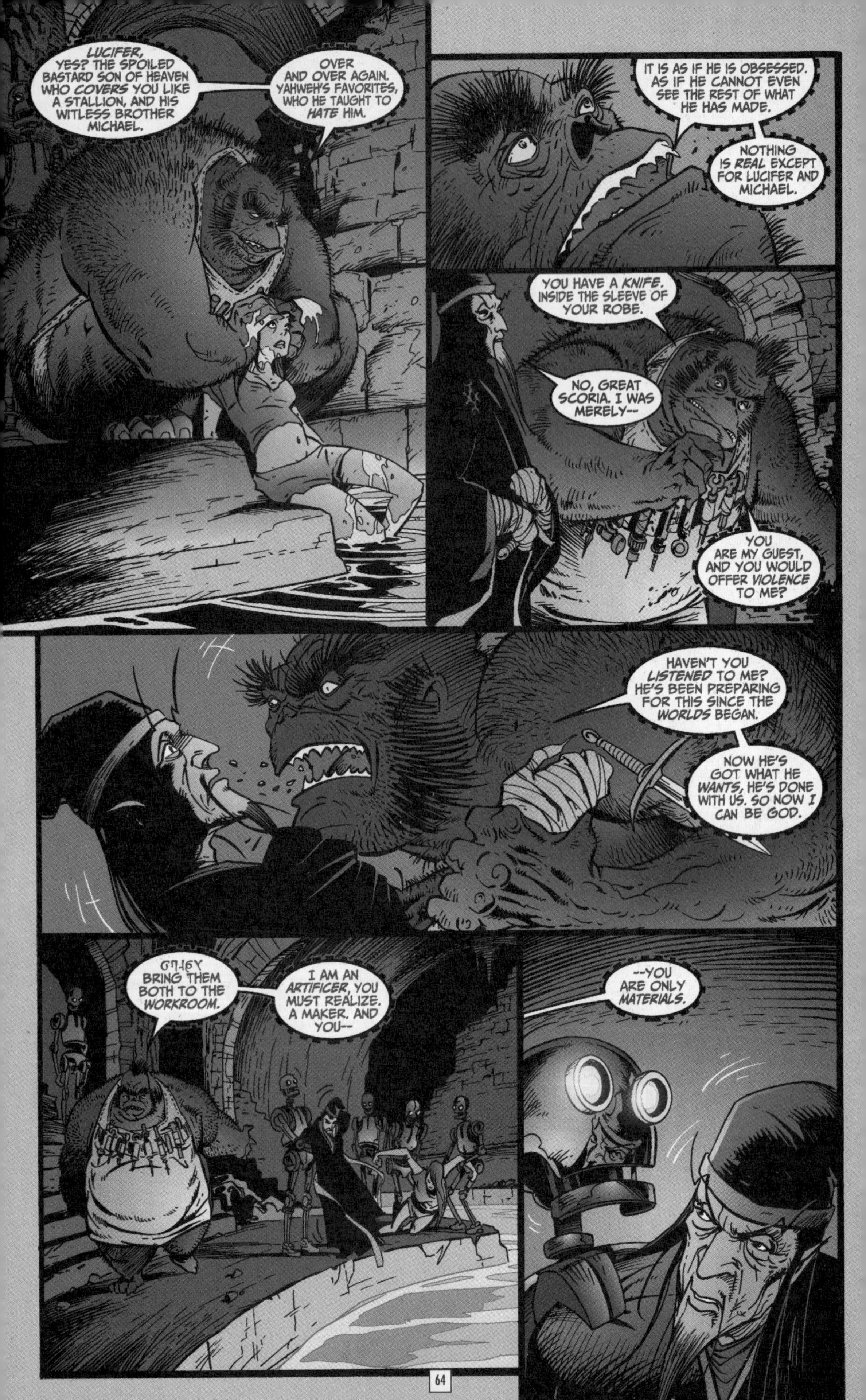
LUCIFER, YES? THE SPOILED BASTARD SON OF HEAVEN WHO COVERS YOU LIKE A STALLION, AND HIS WITLESS BROTHER MICHAEL.
OVER AND OVER AGAIN. YAHWEH'S FAVORITES, WHO HE TAUGHT TO HATE HIM.
IT IS AS IF HE IS OBSESSED. AS IF HE CANNOT EVEN SEE THE REST OF WHAT HE HAS MADE.
NOTHING IS REAL EXCEPT FOR LUCIFER AND MICHAEL.
YOU HAVE A KNIFE. INSIDE THE SLEEVE OF YOUR ROBE.
NO, GREAT SCORIA. I WAS MERELY--
YOU ARE MY GUEST, AND YOU WOULD OFFER VIOLENCE TO ME?
HAVEN'T YOU LISTENED TO ME? HE'S BEEN PREPARING FOR THIS SINCE THE WORLDS BEGAN.
NOW HE'S GOT WHAT HE WANTS, HE'S DONE WITH US. SO NOW I CAN BE GOD.
BRING THEM BOTH TO THE WORKROOM.
I AM AN ARTIFICER, YOU MUST REALIZE. A MAKER. AND YOU--
--YOU ARE ONLY MATERIALS.

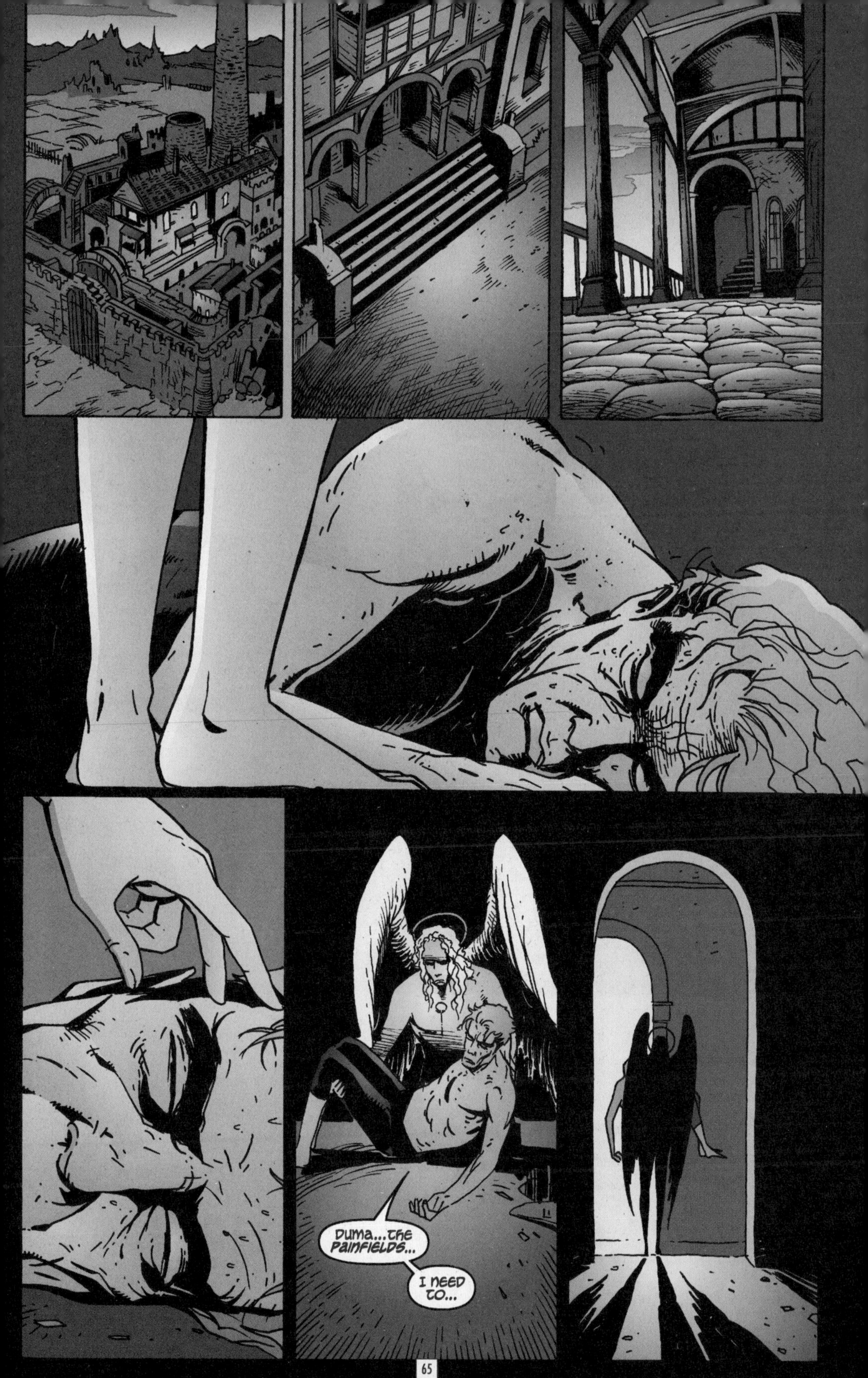
Duma...the painfields...
I need to...

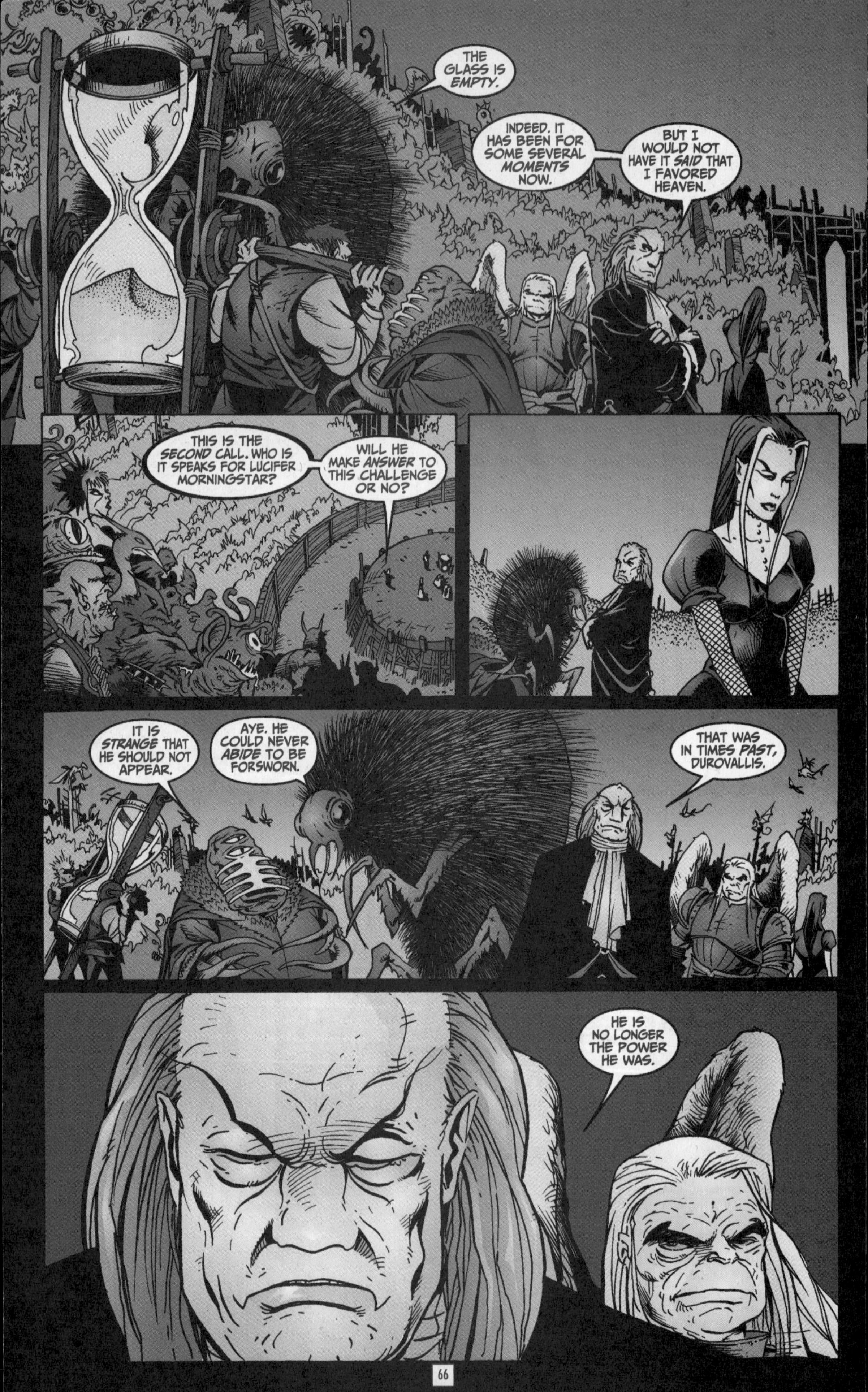
THE GLASS IS EMPTY.
INDEED. IT HAS BEEN FOR SOME SEVERAL MOMENTS NOW.
BUT I WOULD NOT HAVE IT SAID THAT I FAVORED HEAVEN.
THIS IS THE SECOND CALL. WHO IS IT SPEAKS FOR LUCIFER MORNINGSTAR?
WILL HE MAKE ANSWER TO THIS CHALLENGE OR NO?
IT IS STRANGE THAT HE SHOULD NOT APPEAR.
AYE. HE COULD NEVER ABIDE TO BE FORSWORN.
THAT WAS IN TIMES PAST, DUROVALLIS.
HE IS NO LONGER THE POWER HE WAS.

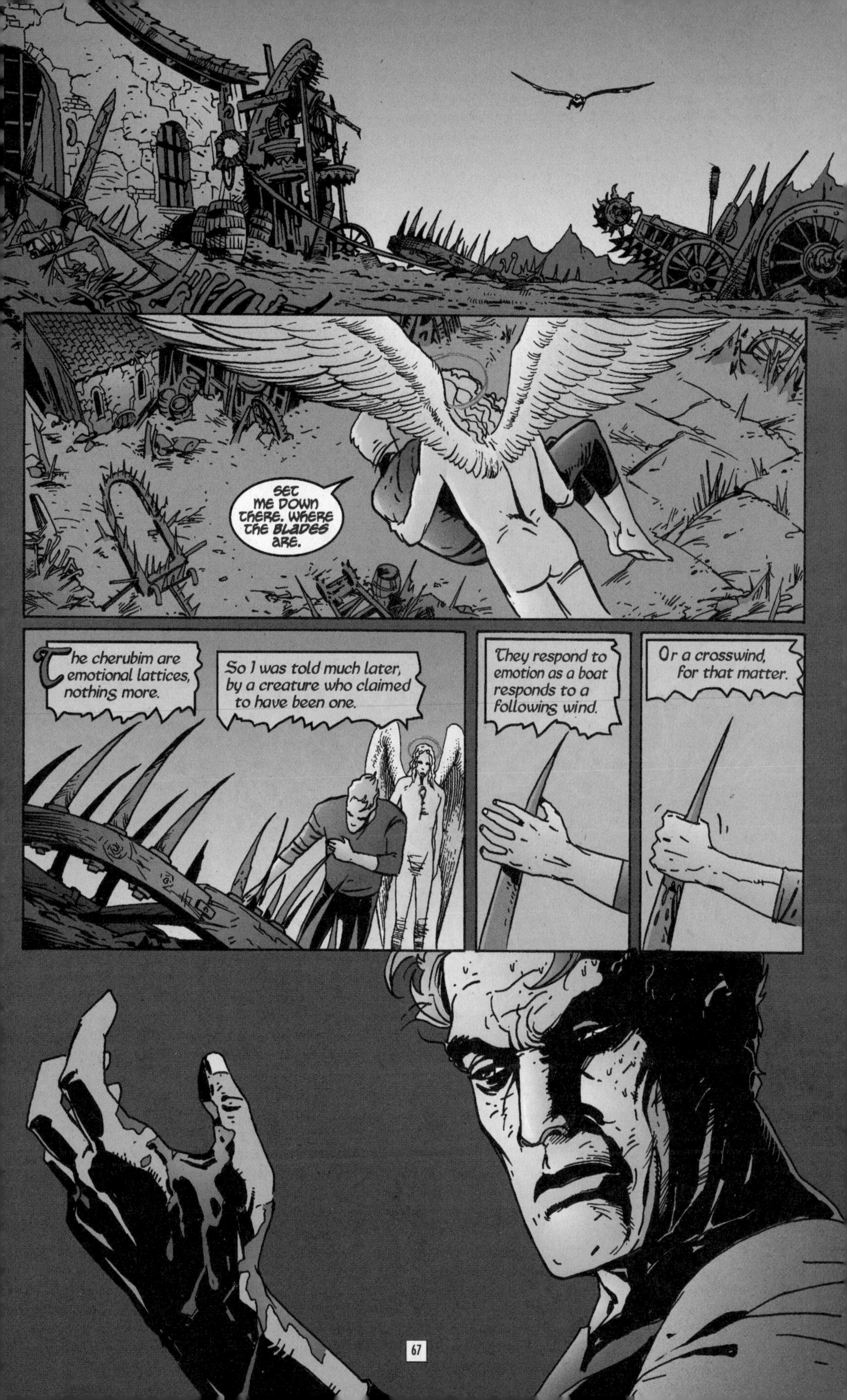

SET ME DOWN THERE. WHERE THE BLADES ARE.
The cherubim are emotional lattices, nothing more.
So I was told much later, by a creature who claimed to have been one.
They respond to emotion as a boat responds to a following wind.
Or a crosswind, for that matter.

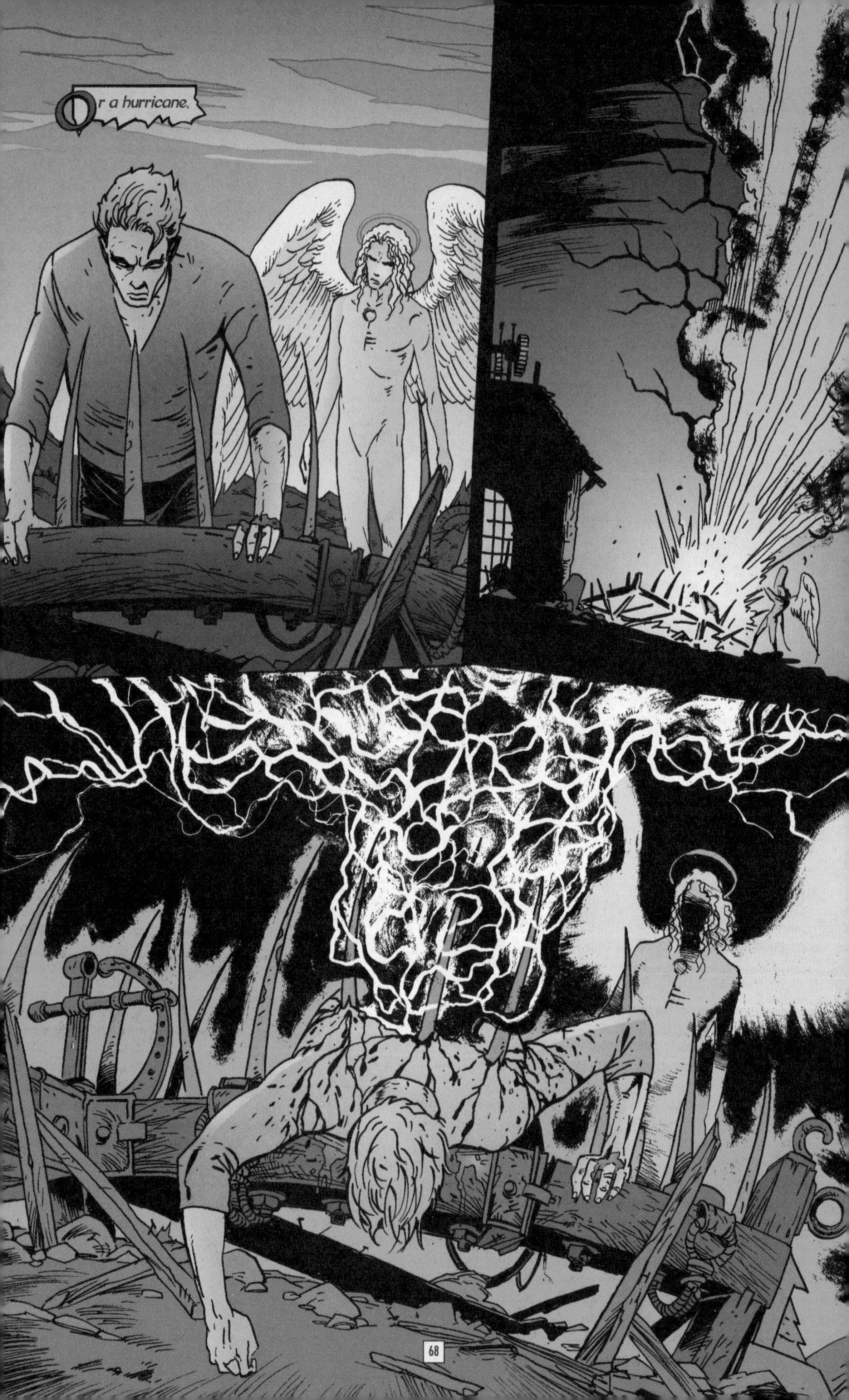
Or a hurricane.

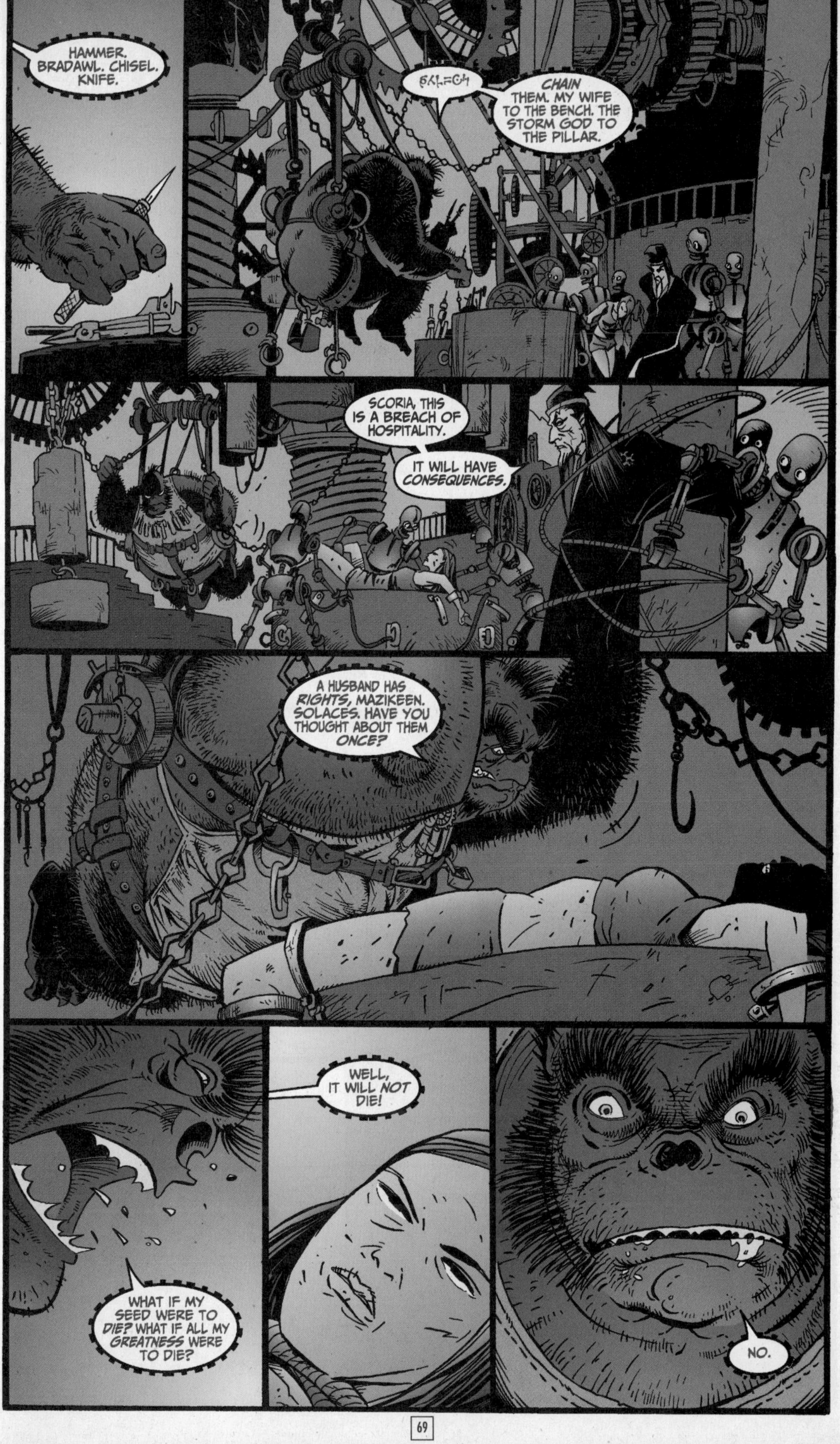
HAMMER. BRADAWL. CHISEL. KNIFE.
CHAIN THEM. MY WIFE TO THE BENCH. THE STORM GOD TO THE PILLAR.
SCORIA, THIS IS A BREACH OF HOSPITALITY.
IT WILL HAVE CONSEQUENCES.
A HUSBAND HAS RIGHTS, MAZIKEEN. SOLACES. HAVE YOU THOUGHT ABOUT THEM ONCE?
WHAT IF MY SEED WERE TO DIE? WHAT IF ALL MY GREATNESS WERE TO DIE?
WELL, IT WILL NOT DIE!
NO.

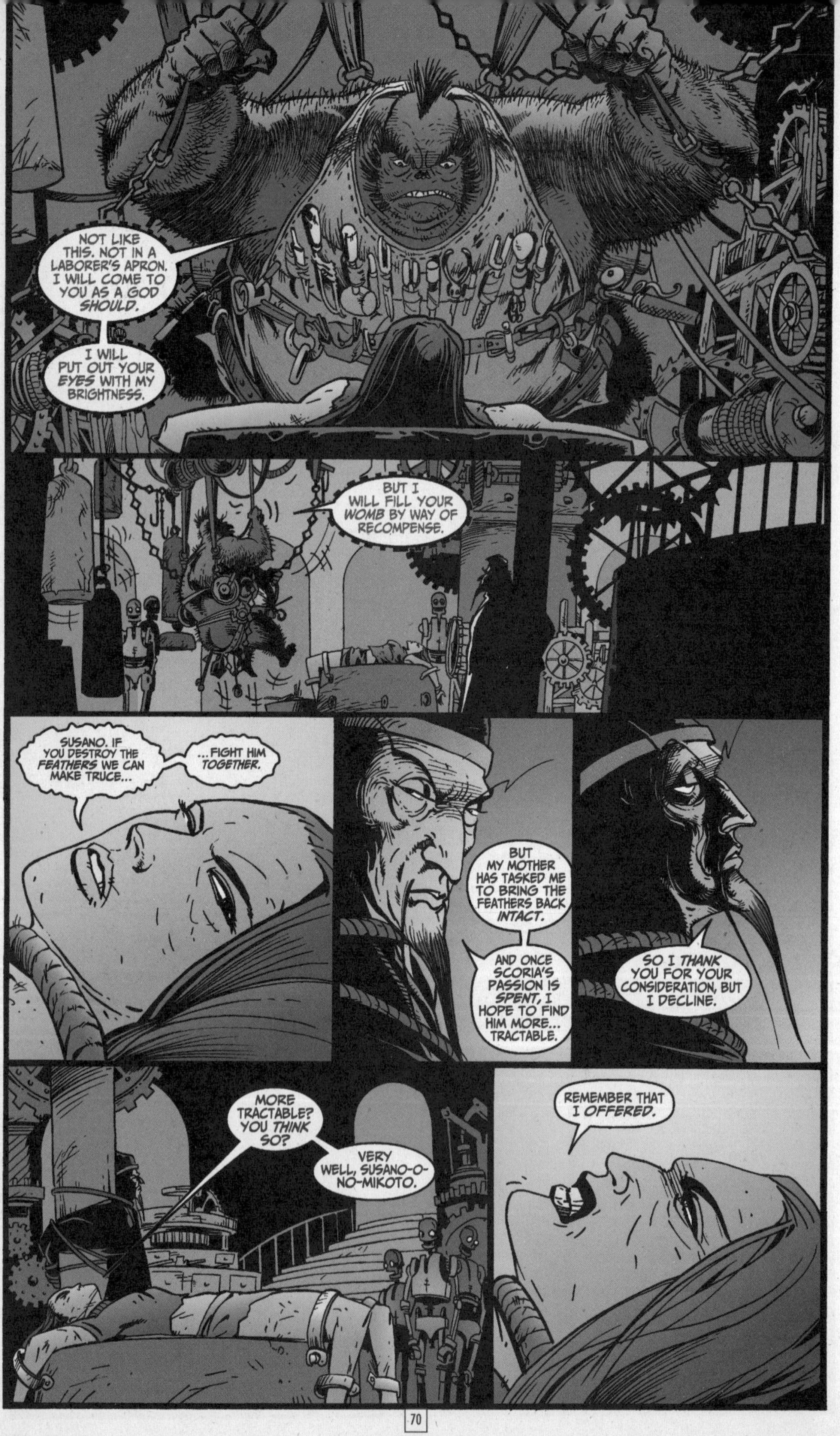
NOT LIKE THIS. NOT IN A LABORER'S APRON. I WILL COME TO YOU AS A GOD SHOULD.
I WILL PUT OUT YOUR EYES WITH MY BRIGHTNESS.
BUT I WILL FILL YOUR WOMB BY WAY OF RECOMPENSE.
SUSANO. IF YOU DESTROY THE FEATHERS WE CAN MAKE TRUCE...
...FIGHT HIM TOGETHER.
BUT MY MOTHER HAS TASKED ME TO BRING THE FEATHERS BACK INTACT.
AND ONCE SCORIA'S PASSION IS SPENT, I HOPE TO FIND HIM MORE... TRACTABLE.
SO I THANK YOU FOR YOUR CONSIDERATION, BUT I DECLINE.
MORE TRACTABLE? YOU THINK SO?
VERY WELL, SUSANO-O-NO-MIKOTO.
REMEMBER THAT I OFFERED.

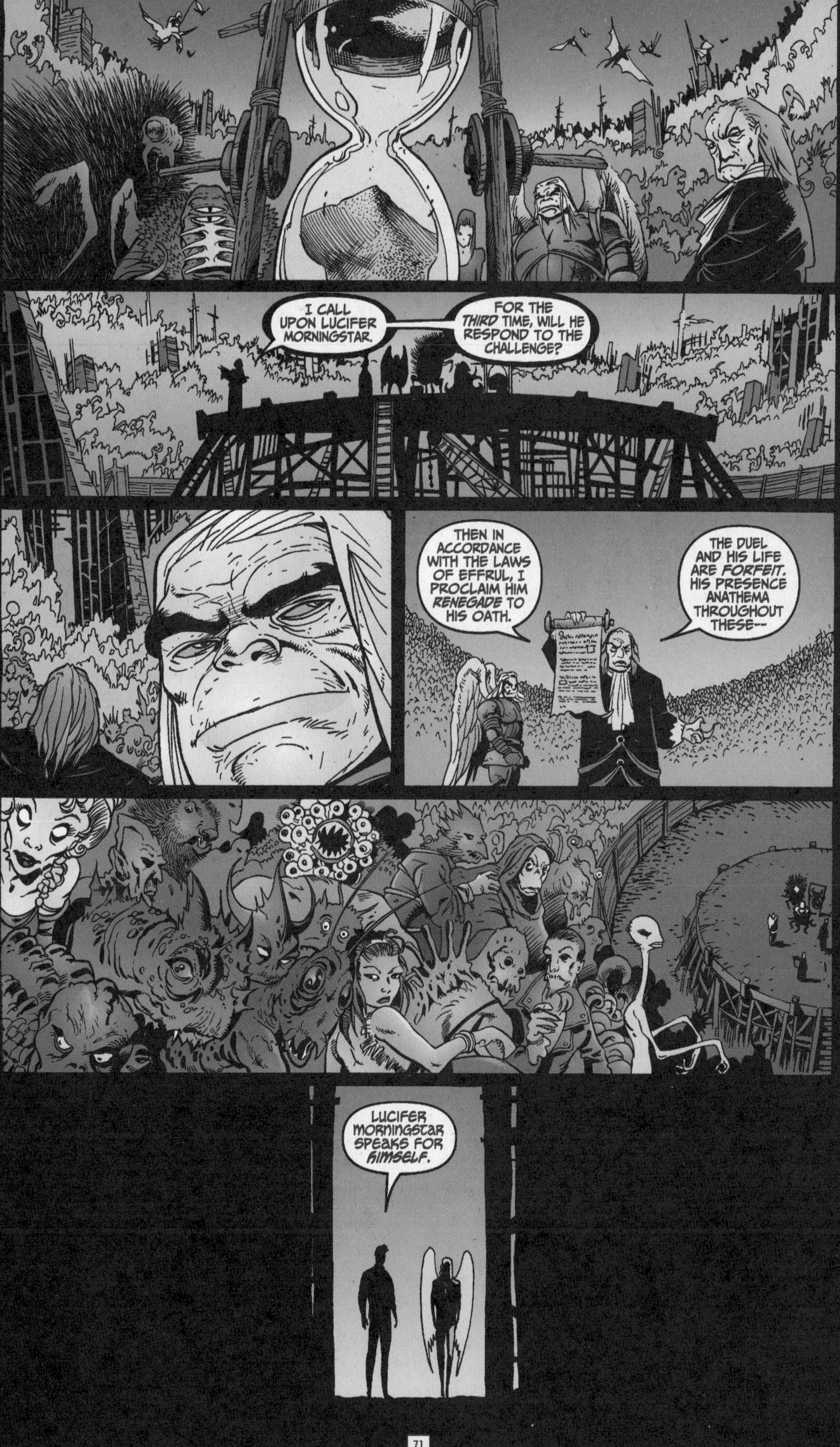
I CALL UPON LUCIFER MORNINGSTAR.
FOR THE *THIRD* TIME, WILL HE RESPOND TO THE CHALLENGE?
THEN IN ACCORDANCE WITH THE LAWS OF EFFRUL, I PROCLAIM HIM *RENEGADE* TO HIS OATH.
THE DUEL AND HIS LIFE ARE *FORFEIT*. HIS PRESENCE ANATHEMA THROUGHOUT THESE--
LUCIFER MORNINGSTAR SPEAKS FOR *HIMSELF*.

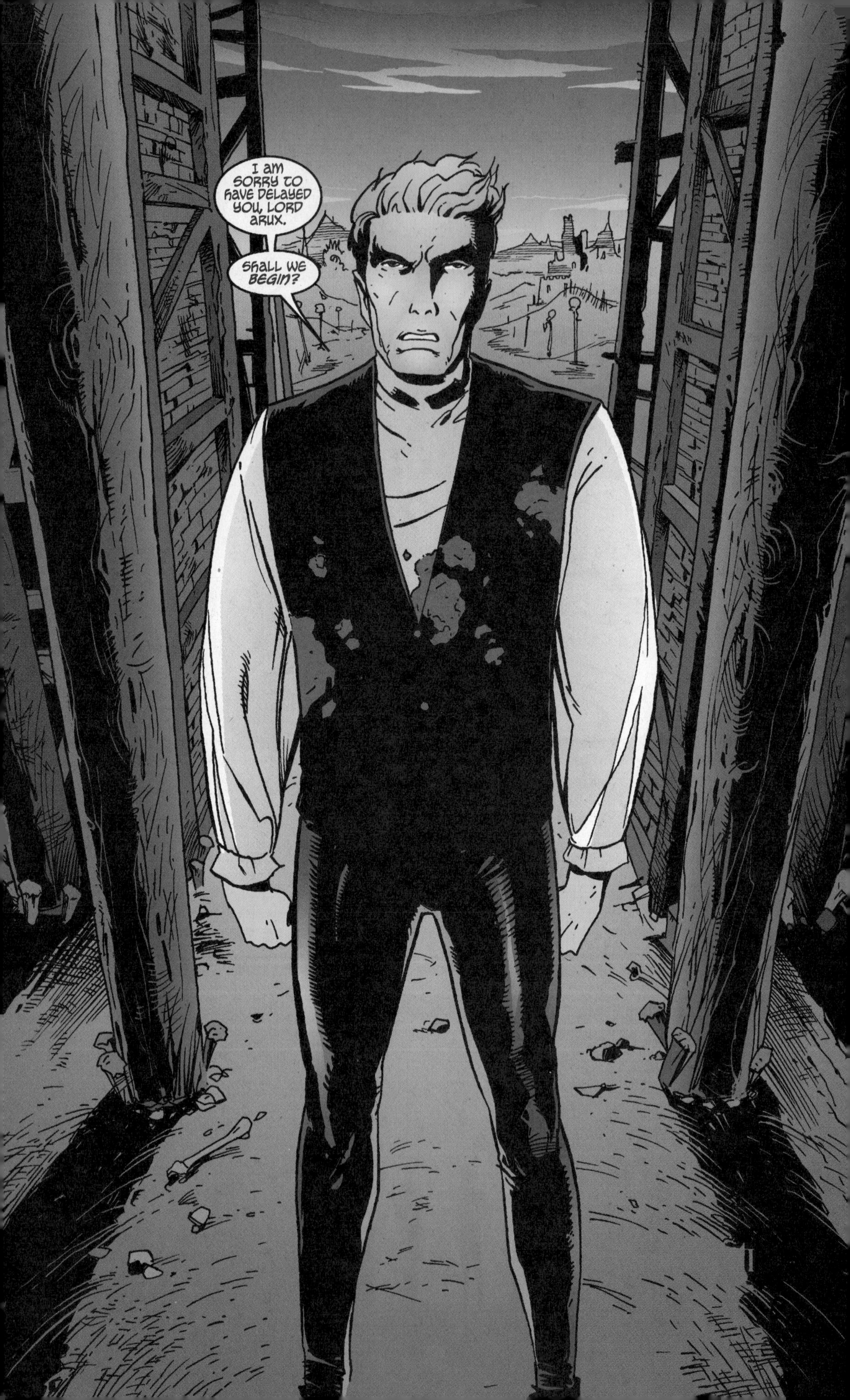
I AM SORRY TO HAVE DELAYED YOU, LORD ARUX.
SHALL WE *BEGIN?*

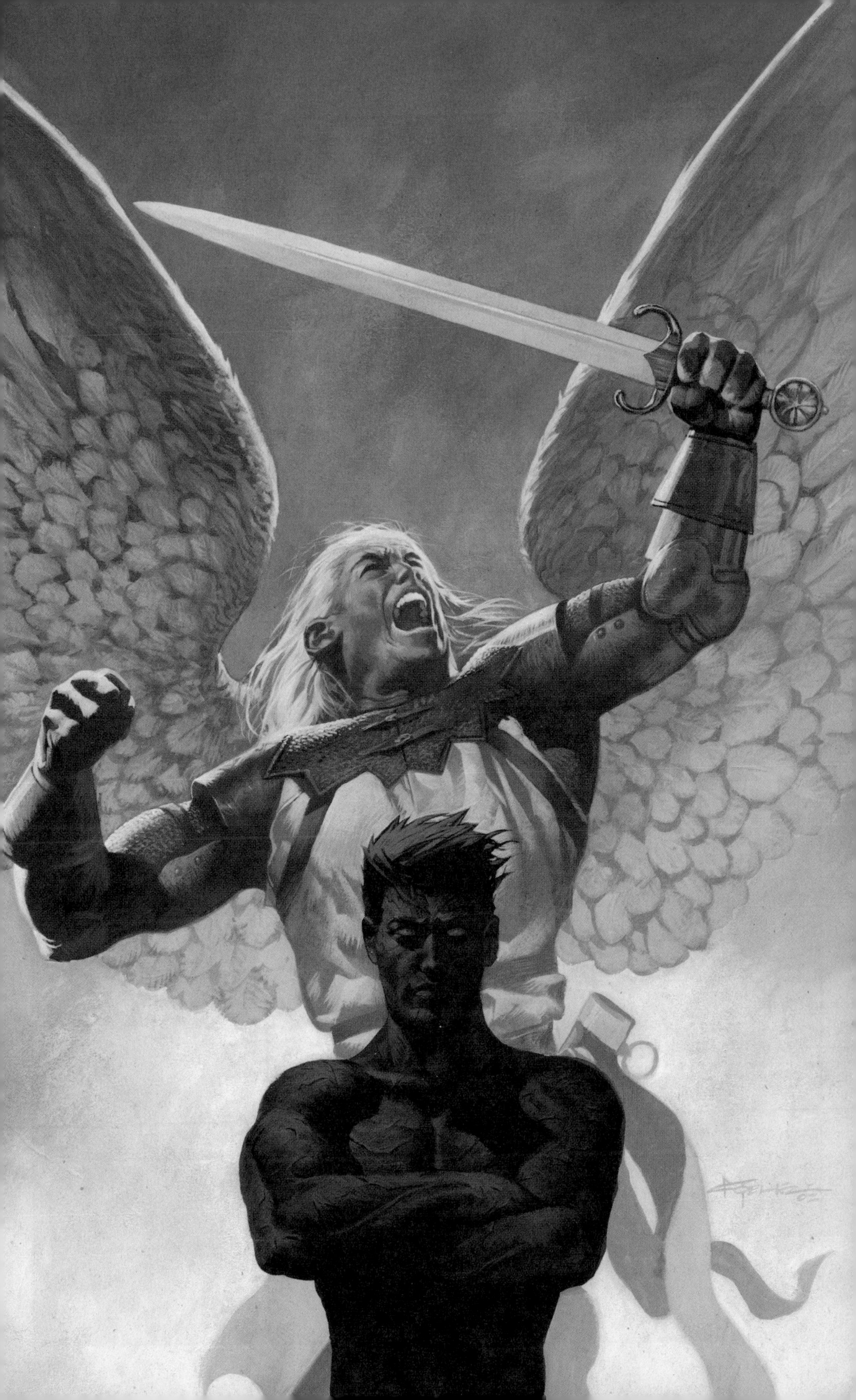

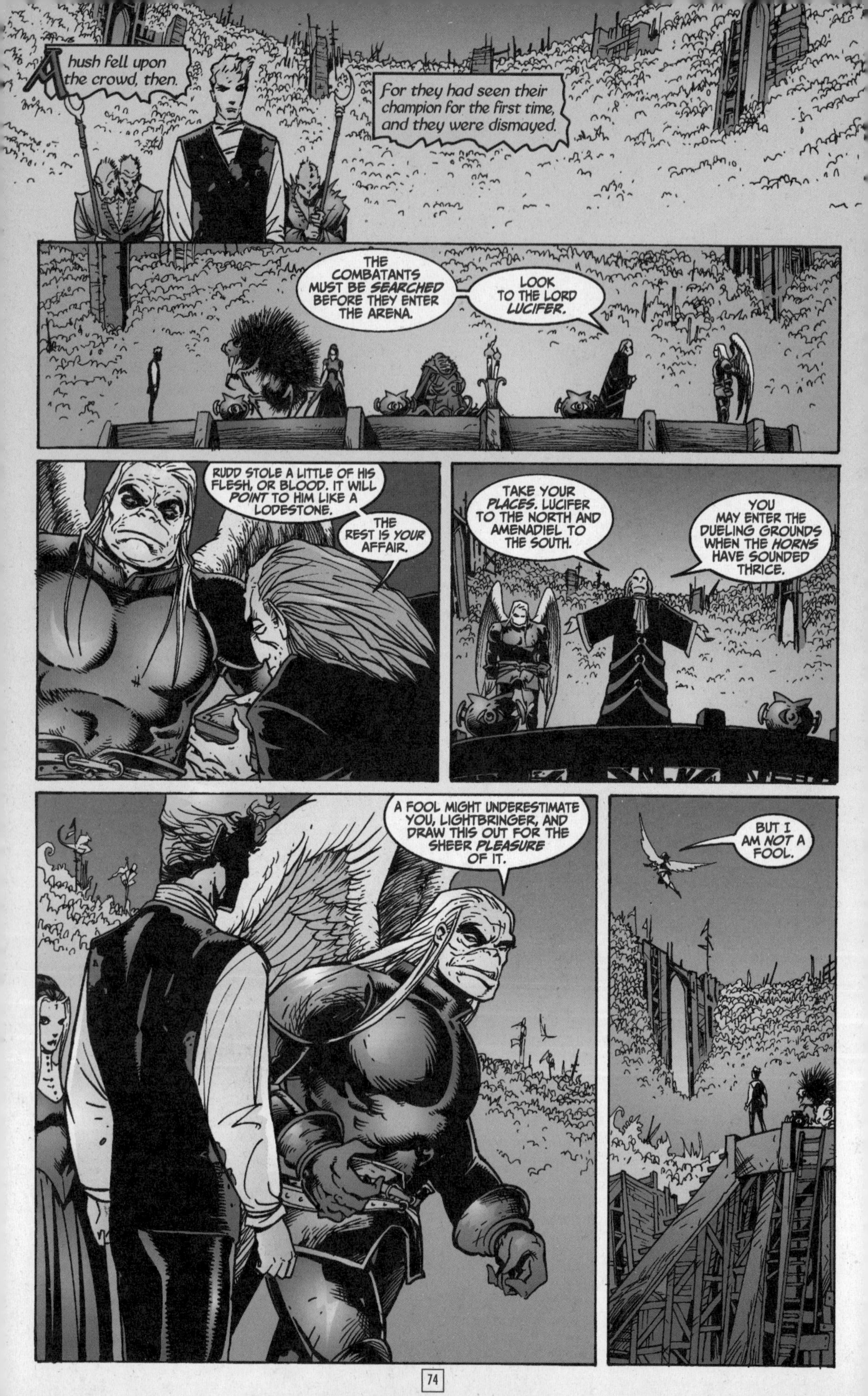
A hush fell upon the crowd, then.
For they had seen their champion for the first time, and they were dismayed.
THE COMBATANTS MUST BE SEARCHED BEFORE THEY ENTER THE ARENA.
LOOK TO THE LORD LUCIFER.
RUDD STOLE A LITTLE OF HIS FLESH, OR BLOOD. IT WILL POINT TO HIM LIKE A LODESTONE.
THE REST IS YOUR AFFAIR.
TAKE YOUR PLACES. LUCIFER TO THE NORTH AND AMENADIEL TO THE SOUTH.
YOU MAY ENTER THE DUELING GROUNDS WHEN THE HORNS HAVE SOUNDED THRICE.
A FOOL MIGHT UNDERESTIMATE YOU, LIGHTBRINGER, AND DRAW THIS OUT FOR THE SHEER PLEASURE OF IT.
BUT I AM NOT A FOOL.

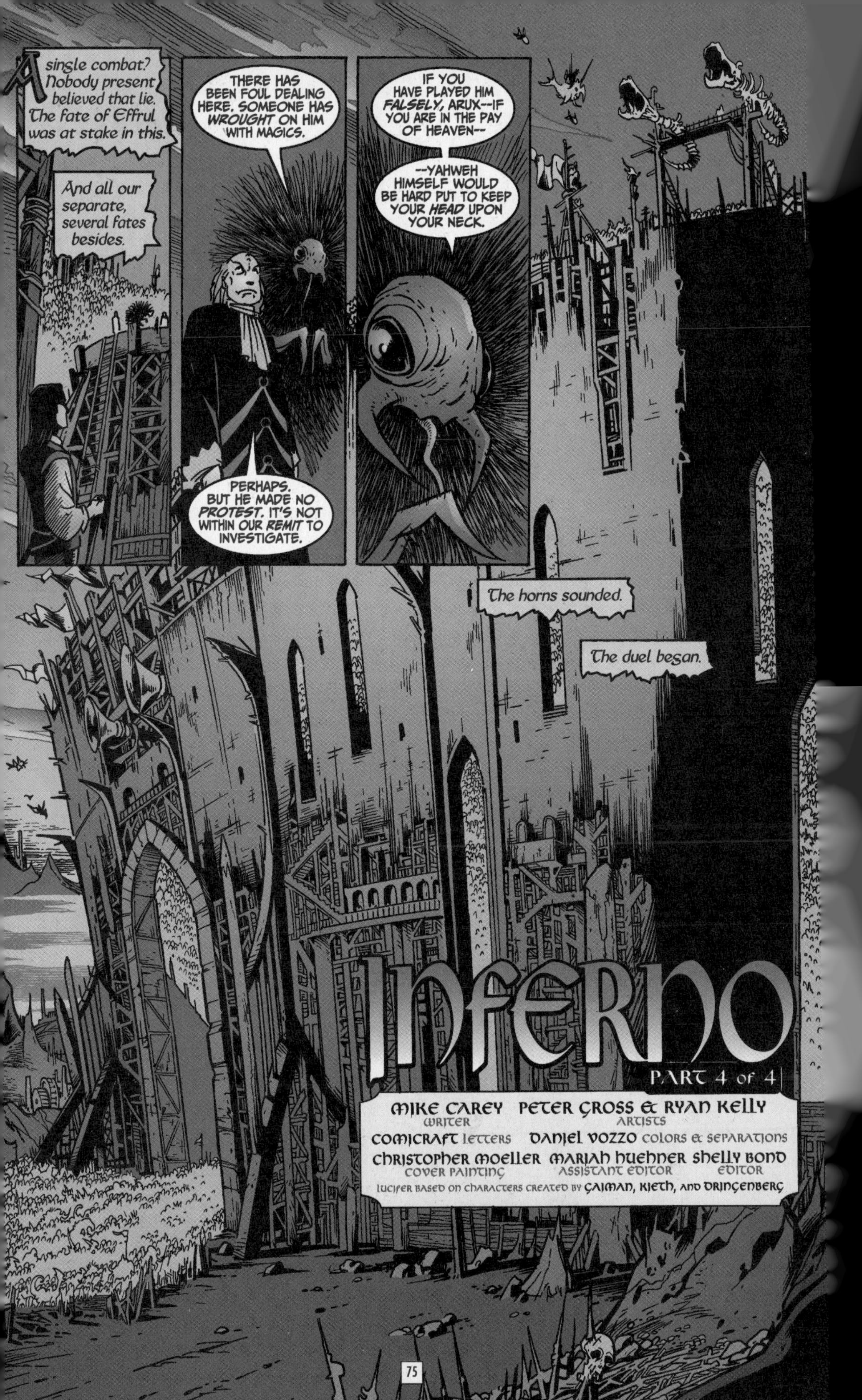

A single combat? Nobody present believed that lie. The fate of Effrul was at stake in this.
And all our separate, several fates besides.
THERE HAS BEEN FOUL DEALING HERE. SOMEONE HAS WROUGHT ON HIM WITH MAGICS.
PERHAPS. BUT HE MADE NO PROTEST. IT'S NOT WITHIN OUR REMIT TO INVESTIGATE.
IF YOU HAVE PLAYED HIM FALSELY, ARUX--IF YOU ARE IN THE PAY OF HEAVEN--
--YAHWEH HIMSELF WOULD BE HARD PUT TO KEEP YOUR HEAD UPON YOUR NECK.
The horns sounded.
The duel began.
INFERNO
PART 4 of 4
MIKE CAREY WRITER
PETER GROSS & RYAN KELLY ARTISTS
COMICRAFT LETTERS
DANIEL VOZZO COLORS & SEPARATIONS
CHRISTOPHER MOELLER COVER PAINTING
MARIAH HUEHNER ASSISTANT EDITOR
SHELLY BOND EDITOR
LUCIFER BASED ON CHARACTERS CREATED BY GAIMAN, KIETH, AND DRINGENBERG

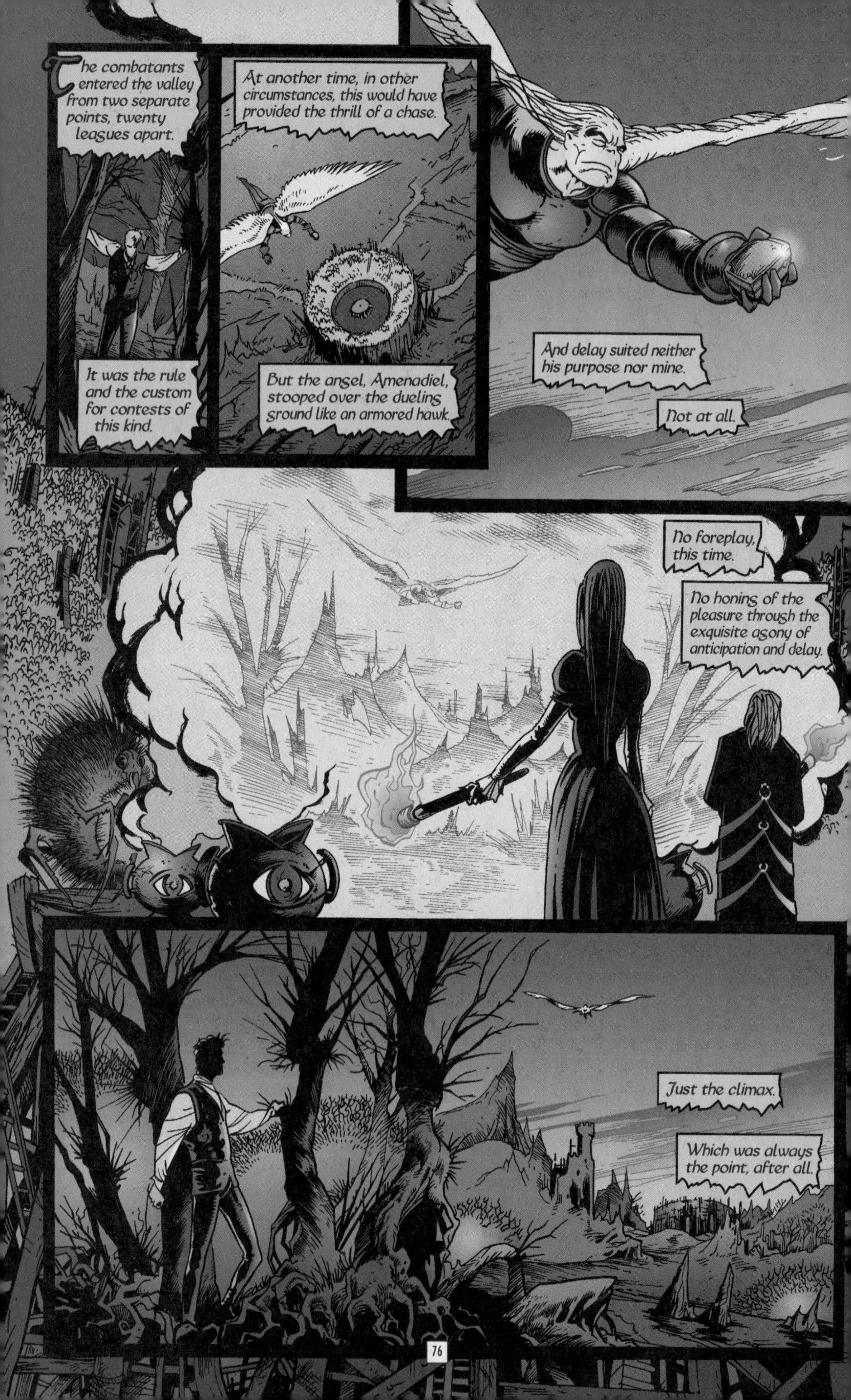
The combatants entered the valley from two separate points, twenty leagues apart.
It was the rule and the custom for contests of this kind.
At another time, in other circumstances, this would have provided the thrill of a chase.
But the angel, Amenadiel, stooped over the dueling ground like an armored hawk.
And delay suited neither his purpose nor mine.
Not at all.
No foreplay, this time.
No honing of the pleasure through the exquisite agony of anticipation and delay.
Just the climax.
Which was always the point, after all.

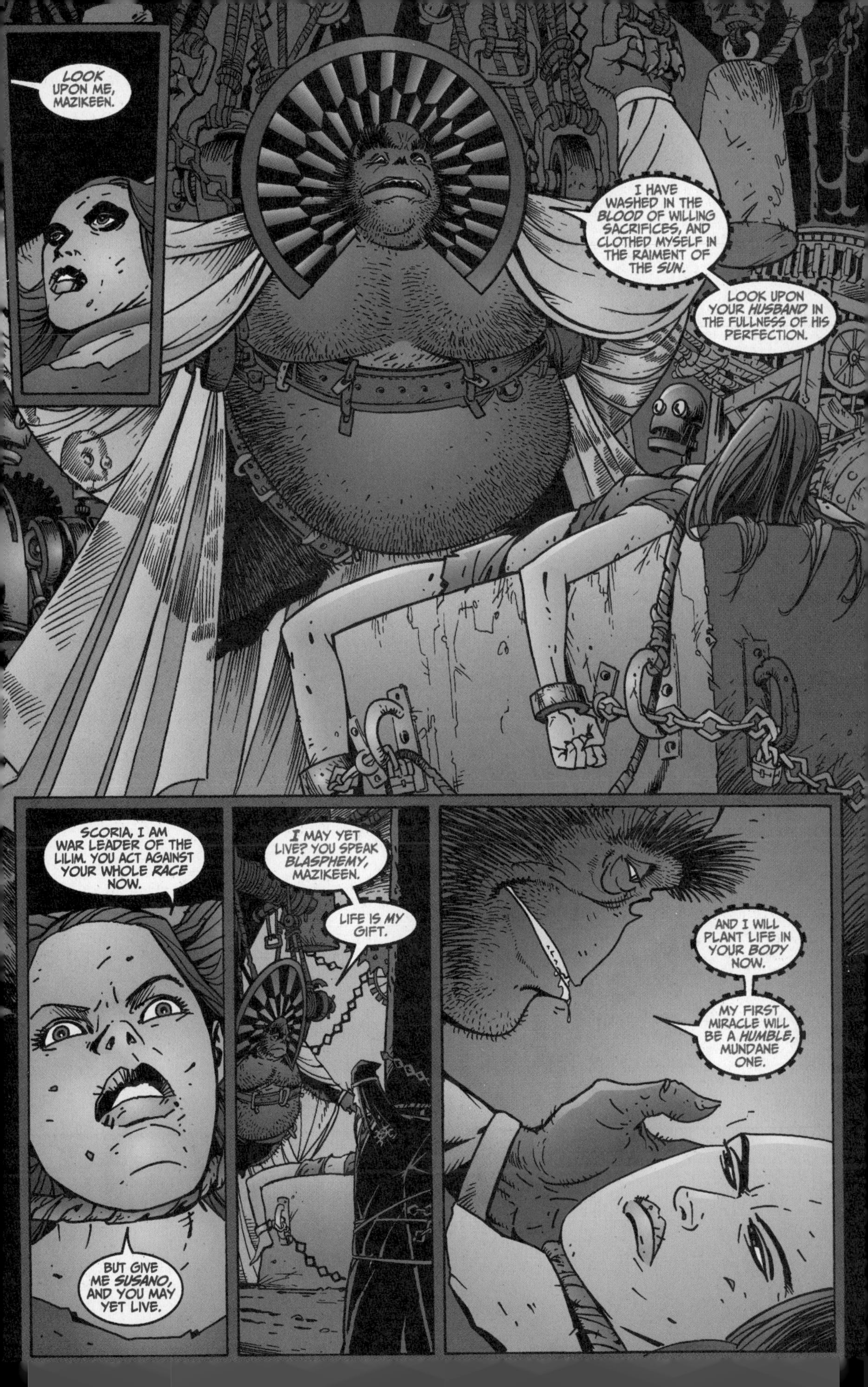
LOOK UPON ME, MAZIKEEN.
I HAVE WASHED IN THE BLOOD OF WILLING SACRIFICES, AND CLOTHED MYSELF IN THE RAIMENT OF THE SUN.
LOOK UPON YOUR HUSBAND IN THE FULLNESS OF HIS PERFECTION.
SCORIA, I AM WAR LEADER OF THE LILIM. YOU ACT AGAINST YOUR WHOLE RACE NOW.
BUT GIVE ME SUSANO, AND YOU MAY YET LIVE.
I MAY YET LIVE? YOU SPEAK BLASPHEMY, MAZIKEEN.
LIFE IS MY GIFT.
AND I WILL PLANT LIFE IN YOUR BODY NOW.
MY FIRST MIRACLE WILL BE A HUMBLE, MUNDANE ONE.

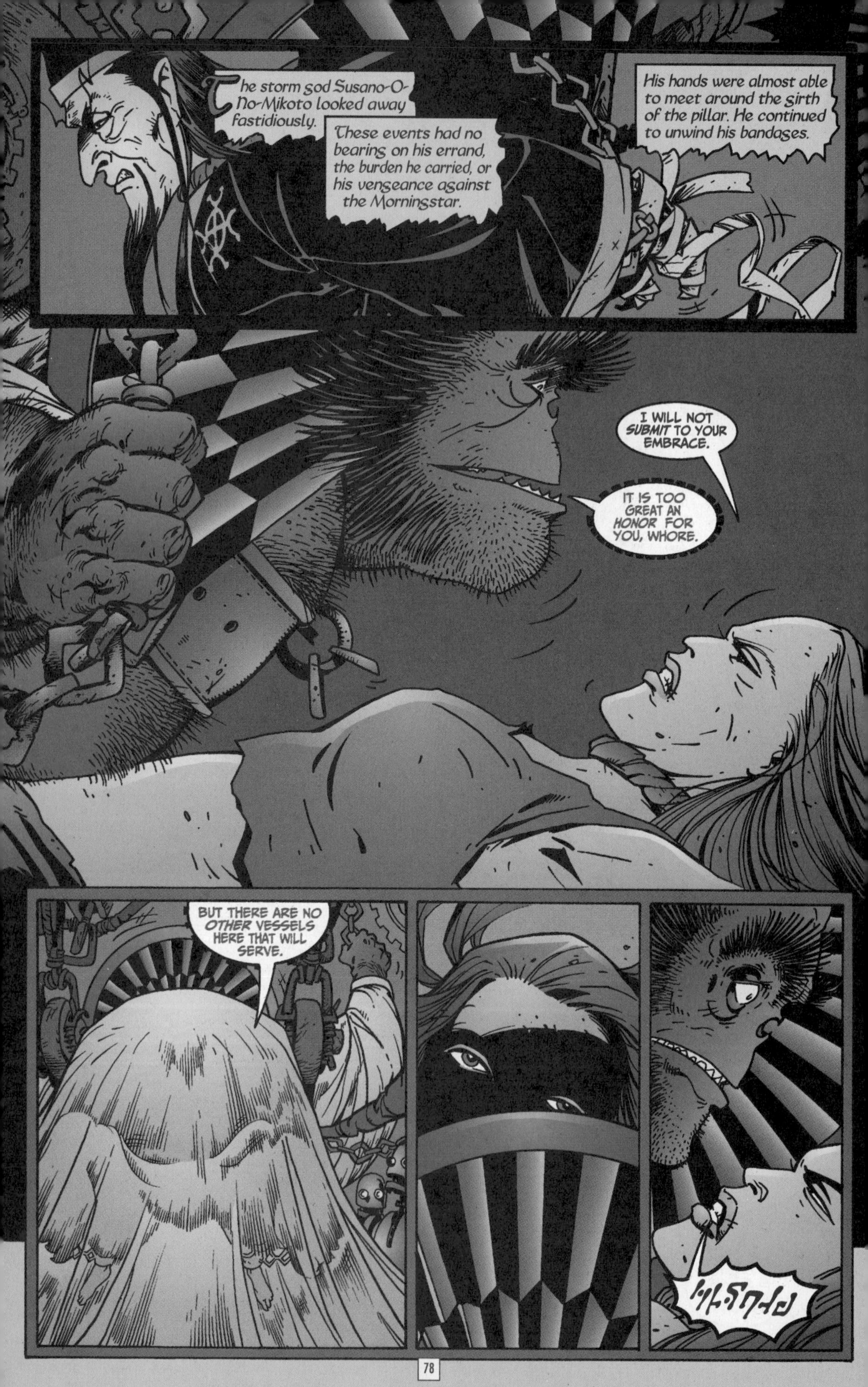
The storm god Susano-O-No-Mikoto looked away fastidiously.
These events had no bearing on his errand, the burden he carried, or his vengeance against the Morningstar.
His hands were almost able to meet around the girth of the pillar. He continued to unwind his bandages.
I WILL NOT SUBMIT TO YOUR EMBRACE.
IT IS TOO GREAT AN HONOR FOR YOU, WHORE.
BUT THERE ARE NO OTHER VESSELS HERE THAT WILL SERVE.
PFUSTT!

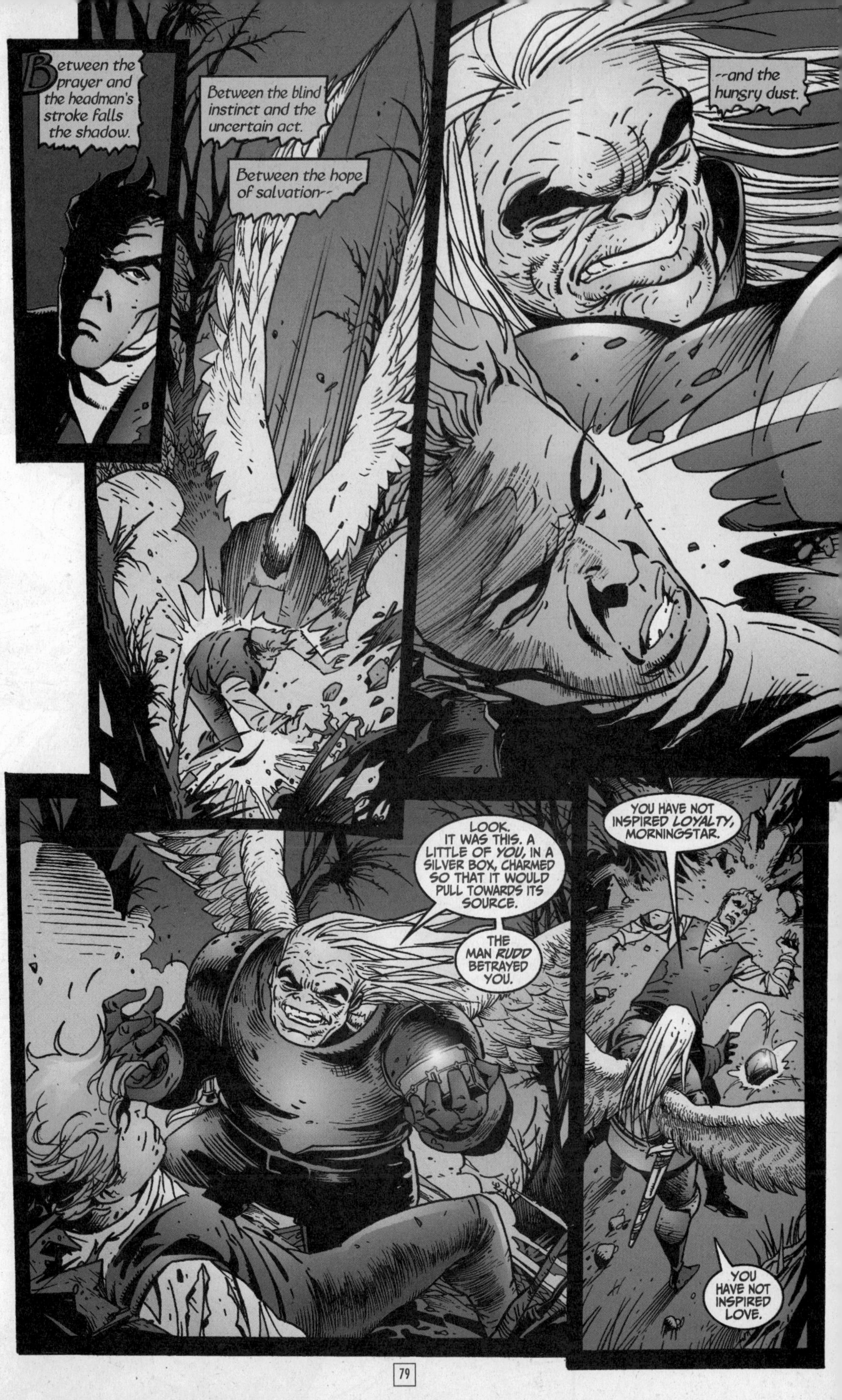
Between the prayer and the headman's stroke falls the shadow.
Between the blind instinct and the uncertain act.
Between the hope of salvation--
--and the hungry dust.
LOOK. IT WAS THIS. A LITTLE OF YOU, IN A SILVER BOX, CHARMED SO THAT IT WOULD PULL TOWARDS ITS SOURCE.
THE MAN RUDD BETRAYED YOU.
YOU HAVE NOT INSPIRED LOYALTY, MORNINGSTAR.
YOU HAVE NOT INSPIRED LOVE.

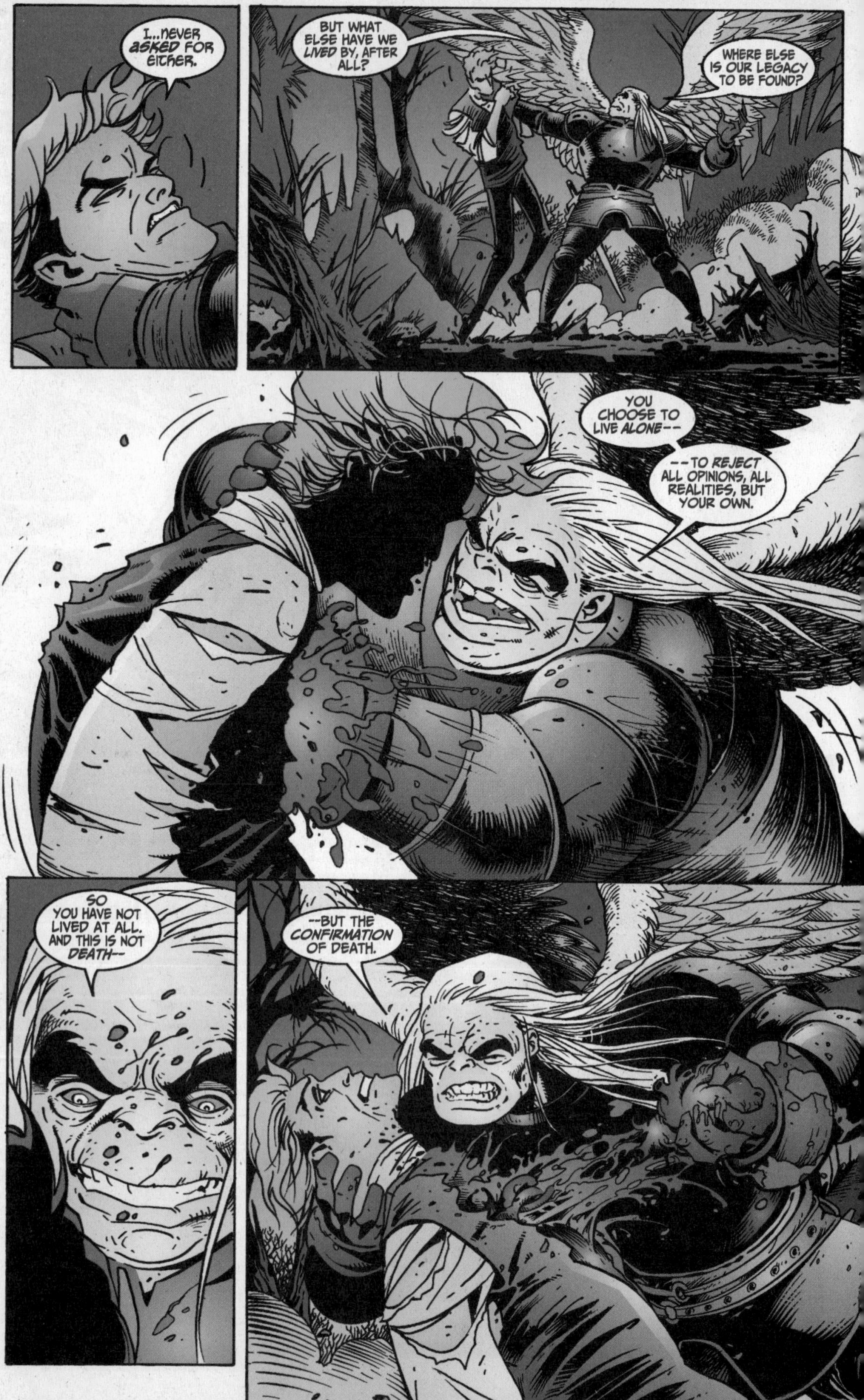
I...NEVER ASKED FOR EITHER.
BUT WHAT ELSE HAVE WE LIVED BY, AFTER ALL?
WHERE ELSE IS OUR LEGACY TO BE FOUND?
YOU CHOOSE TO LIVE ALONE--
--TO REJECT ALL OPINIONS, ALL REALITIES, BUT YOUR OWN.
SO YOU HAVE NOT LIVED AT ALL. AND THIS IS NOT DEATH--
--BUT THE CONFIRMATION OF DEATH.

HOLD FAST TO HIS *WINDPIPE.* DON'T LET HIM SPEAK.

BECAUSE I'M A *WOMAN,* MY FATHER WOULD NOT TEACH ME RUHOK.

BUT HE *SPOKE* IT OFTEN ENOUGH, SCORIA. AND I LISTENED.

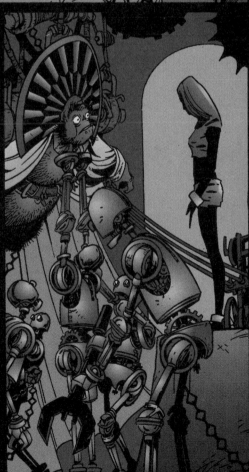

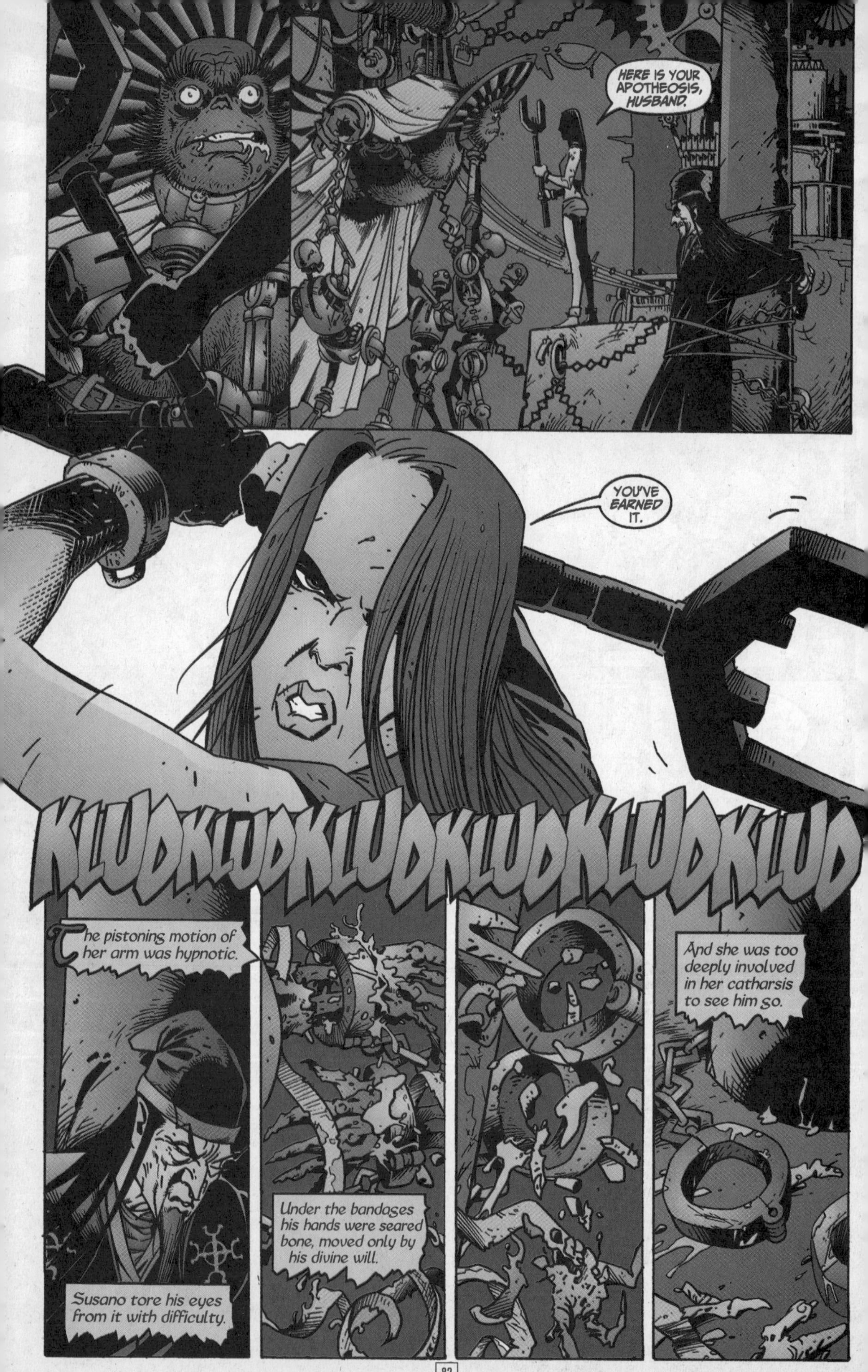
HERE IS YOUR APOTHEOSIS, HUSBAND.
YOU'VE EARNED IT.
KLUDKLUDKLUDKLUDKLUDKLUD
The pistoning motion of her arm was hypnotic.
Susano tore his eyes from it with difficulty.
Under the bandages his hands were seared bone, moved only by his divine will.
And she was too deeply involved in her catharsis to see him go.

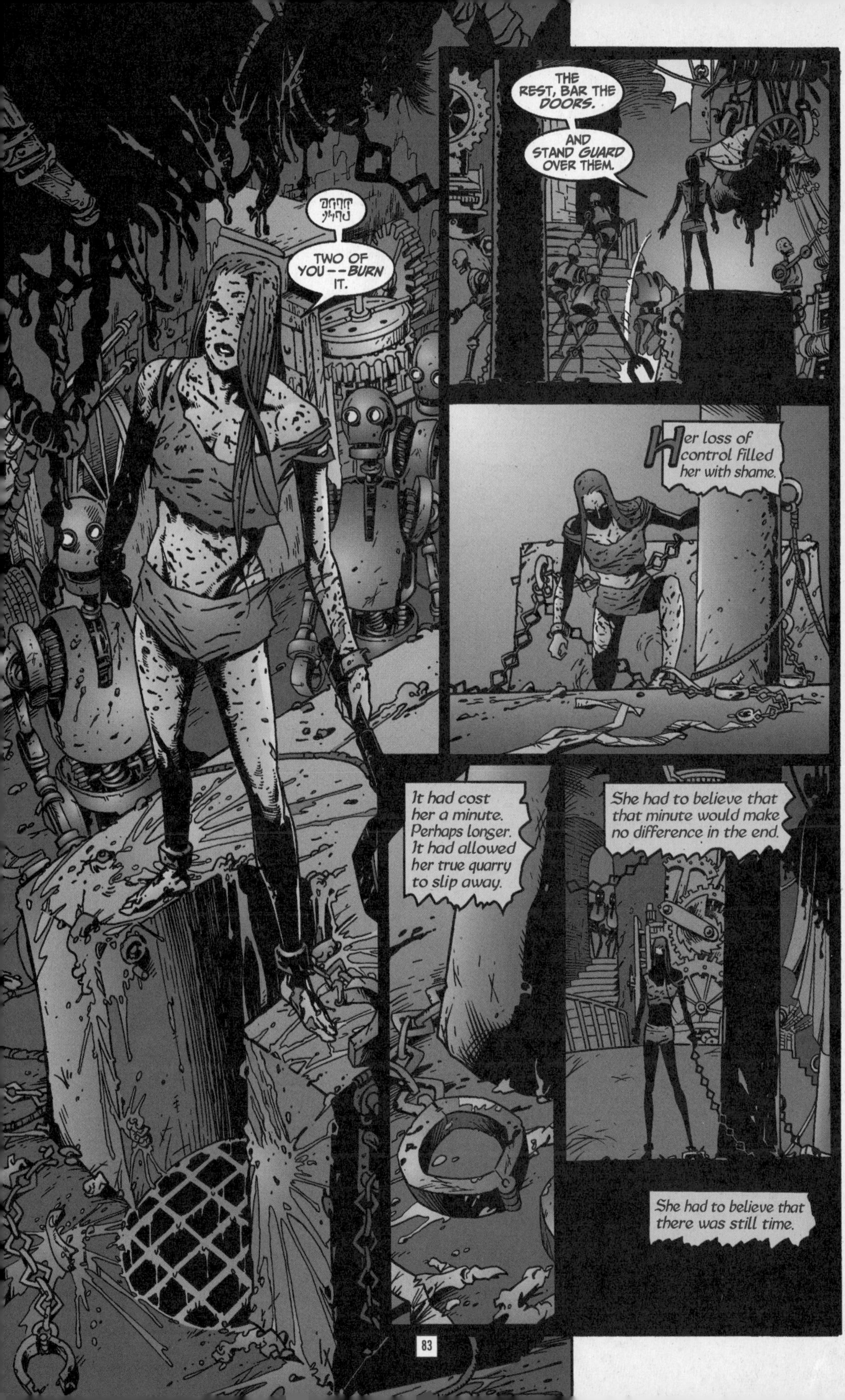

TWO OF YOU--BURN IT.
THE REST, BAR THE DOORS.
AND STAND GUARD OVER THEM.
Her loss of control filled her with shame.
It had cost her a minute. Perhaps longer. It had allowed her true quarry to slip away.
She had to believe that that minute would make no difference in the end.
She had to believe that there was still time.

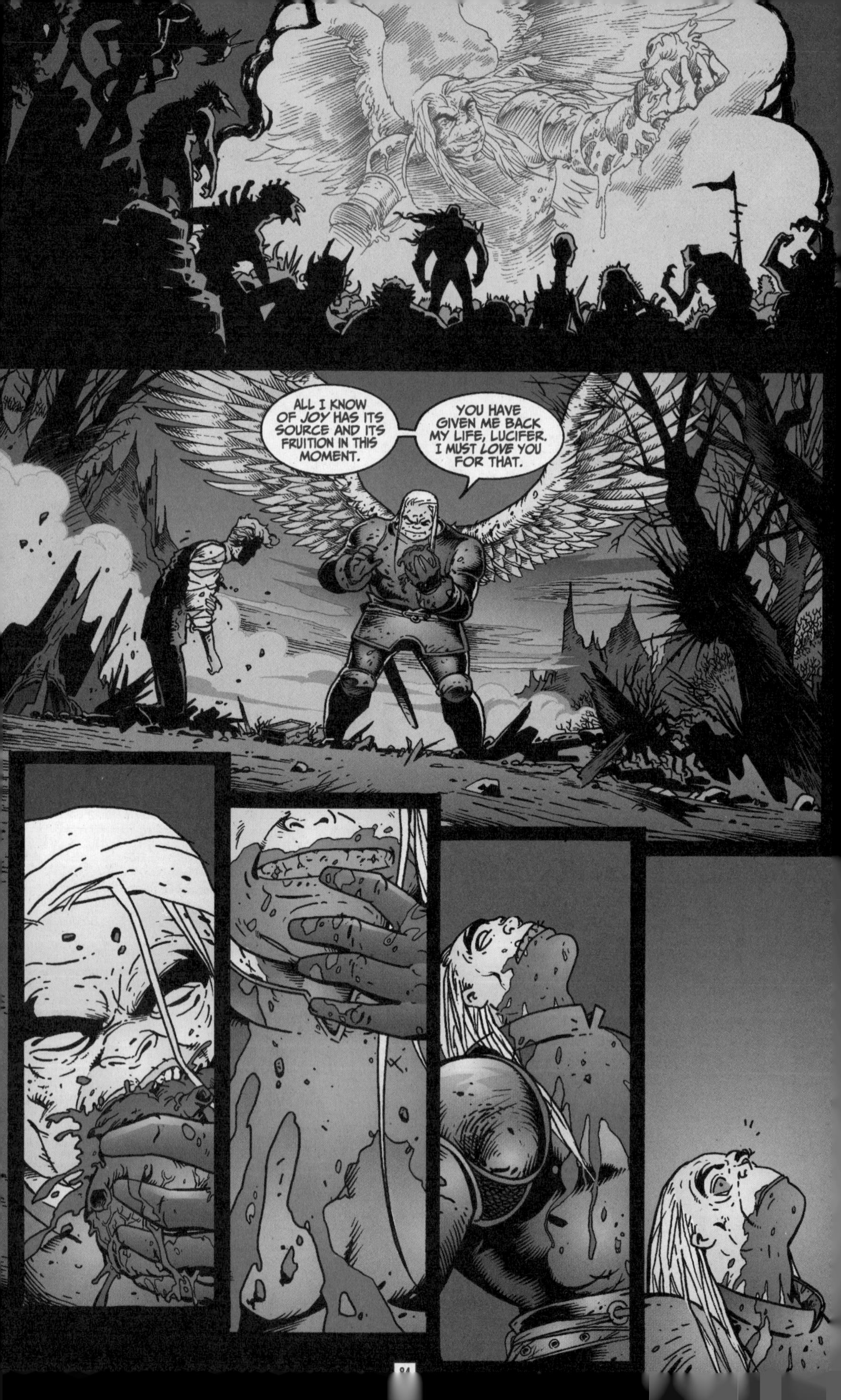
ALL I KNOW OF *JOY* HAS ITS SOURCE AND ITS FRUITION IN THIS MOMENT.
YOU HAVE GIVEN ME BACK MY LIFE, LUCIFER. I MUST *LOVE* YOU FOR THAT.

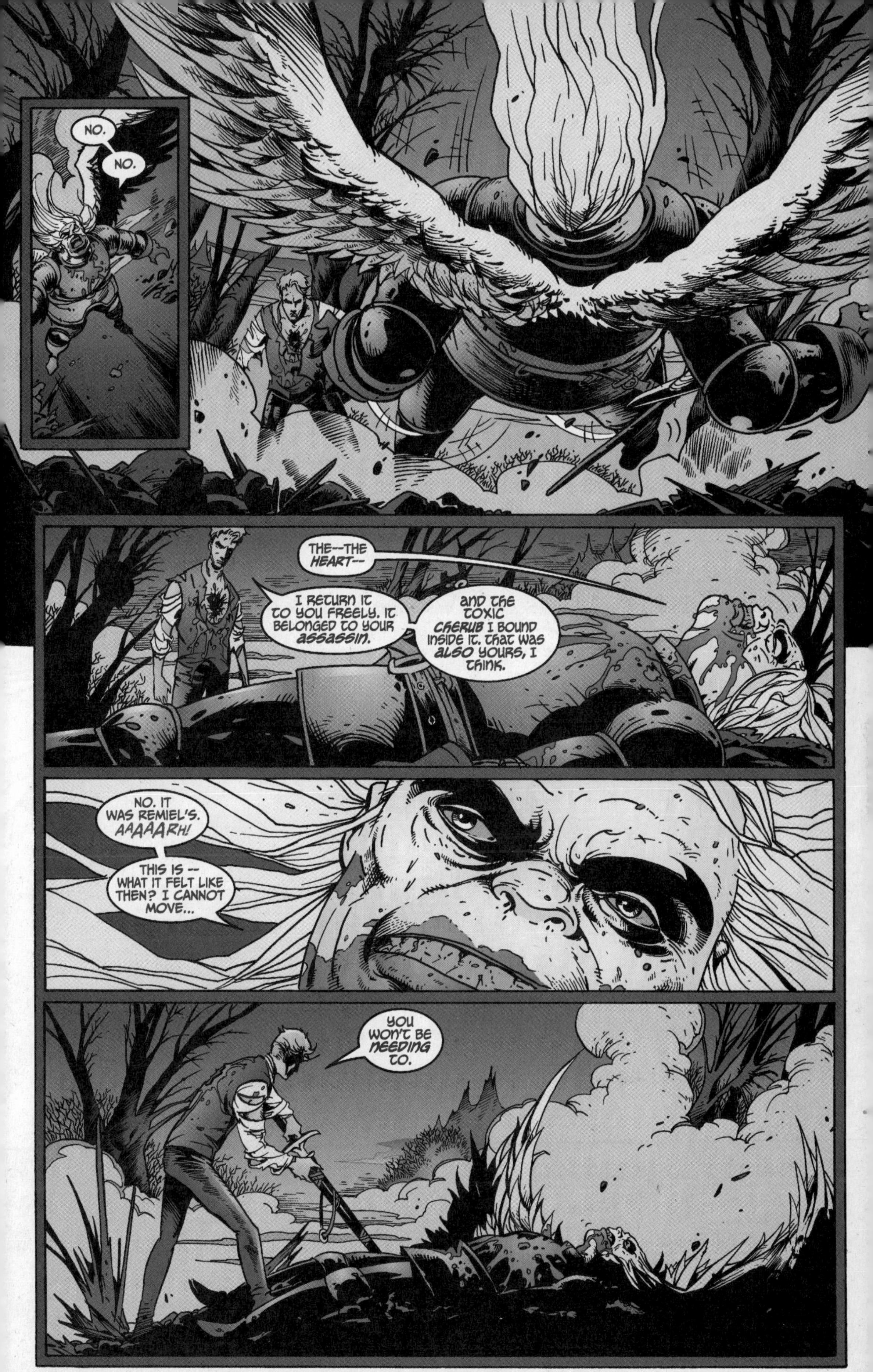
NO.
NO.
THE--THE HEART--
I RETURN IT TO YOU FREELY. IT BELONGED TO YOUR ASSASSIN.
AND THE TOXIC CHERUB I BOUND INSIDE IT. THAT WAS ALSO YOURS, I THINK.
NO. IT WAS REMIEL'S. AAAAARH!
THIS IS -- WHAT IT FELT LIKE THEN? I CANNOT MOVE...
YOU WON'T BE NEEDING TO.

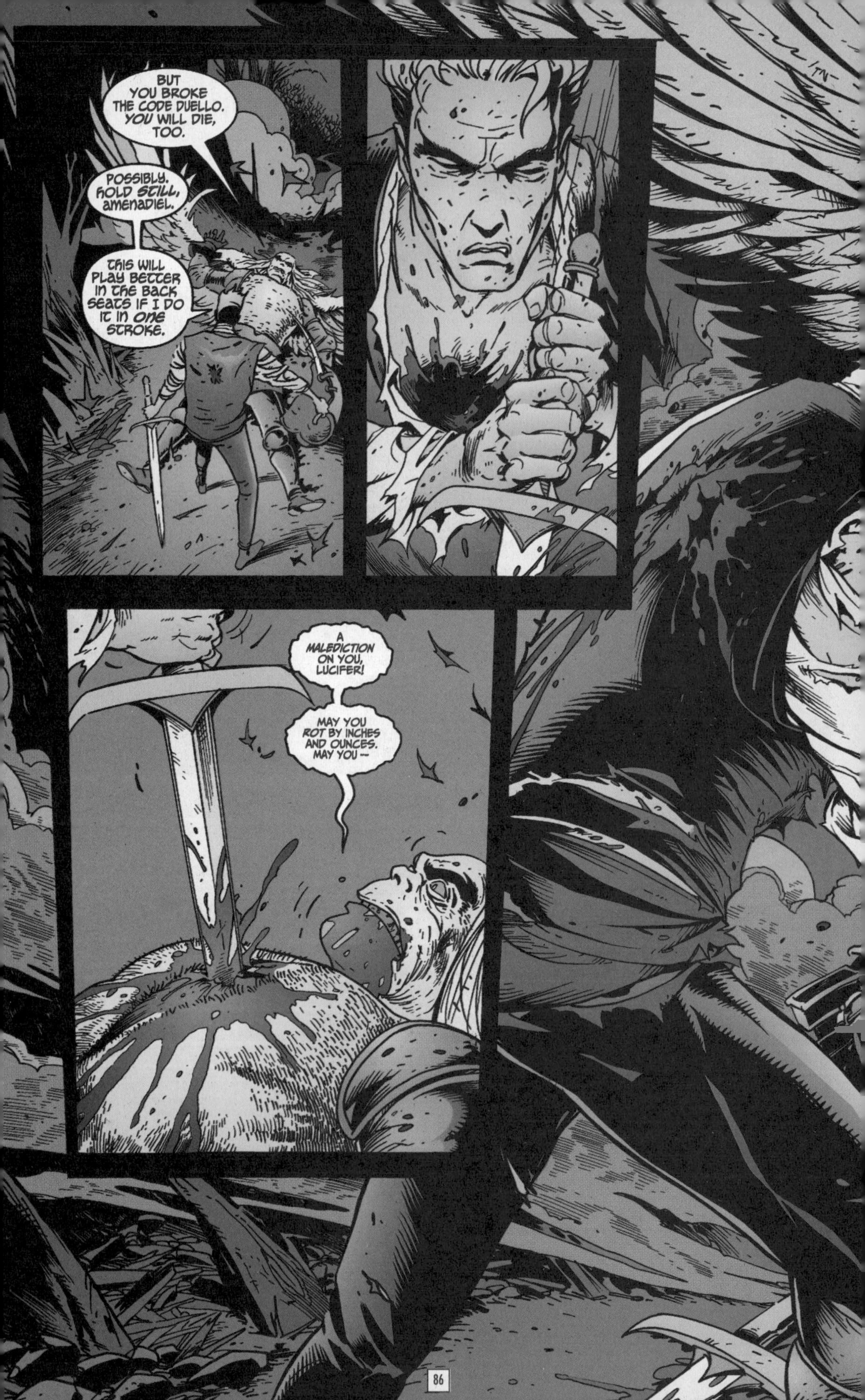

BUT YOU BROKE THE CODE DUELLO. YOU WILL DIE, TOO.
POSSIBLY. HOLD STILL, AMENADIEL.
THIS WILL PLAY BETTER IN THE BACK SEATS IF I DO IT IN ONE STROKE.
A MALEDICTION ON YOU, LUCIFER!
MAY YOU ROT BY INCHES AND OUNCES. MAY YOU --

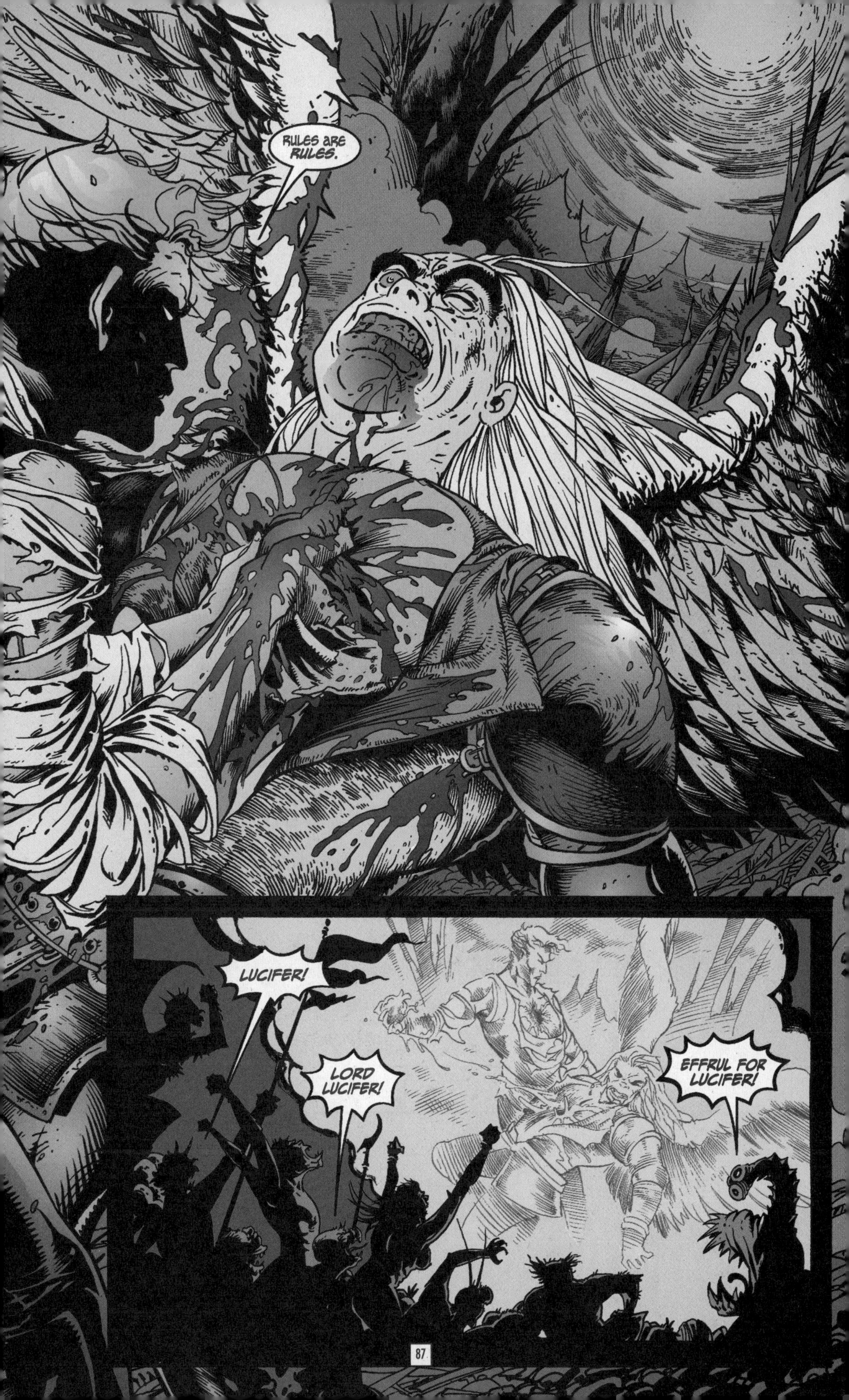
RULES ARE RULES.
LUCIFER!
LORD LUCIFER!
EFFRUL FOR LUCIFER!

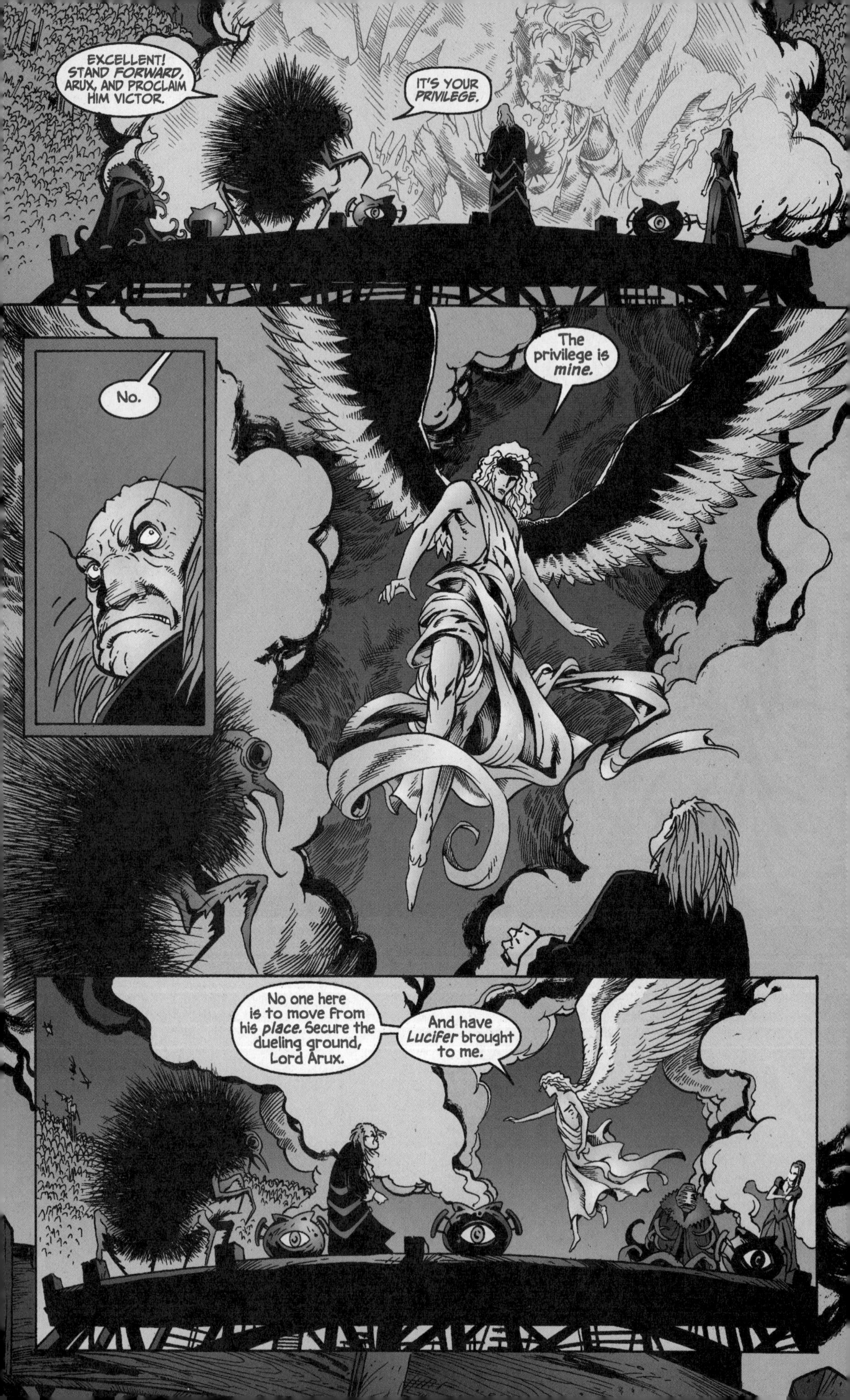
EXCELLENT! STAND FORWARD, ARUX, AND PROCLAIM HIM VICTOR.
IT'S YOUR PRIVILEGE.
No.
The privilege is mine.
No one here is to move from his place. Secure the dueling ground, Lord Arux.
And have Lucifer brought to me.

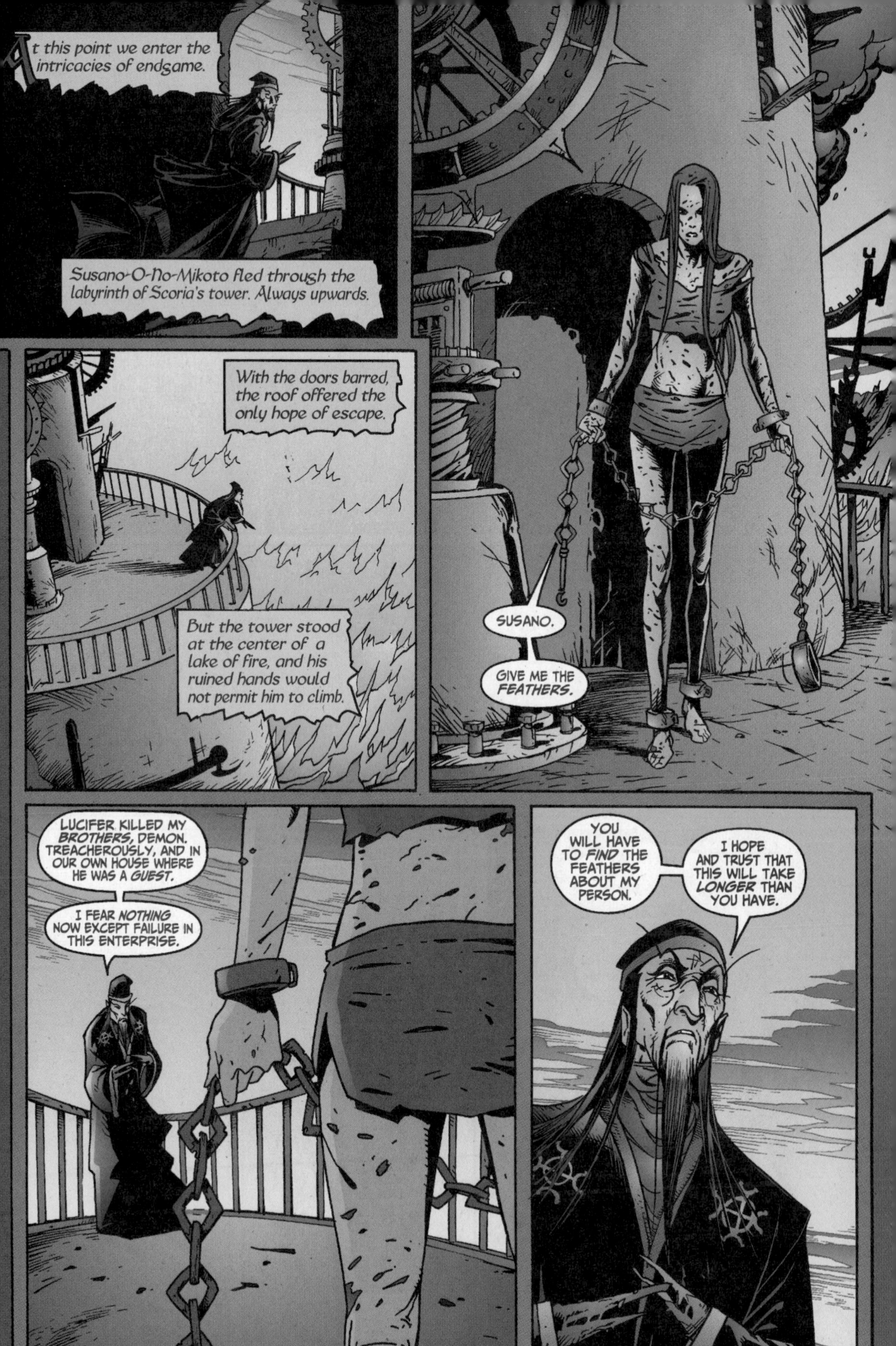
At this point we enter the intricacies of endgame.
Susano-O-No-Mikoto fled through the labyrinth of Scoria's tower. Always upwards.
With the doors barred, the roof offered the only hope of escape.
But the tower stood at the center of a lake of fire, and his ruined hands would not permit him to climb.
SUSANO.
GIVE ME THE FEATHERS.
LUCIFER KILLED MY BROTHERS, DEMON. TREACHEROUSLY, AND IN OUR OWN HOUSE WHERE HE WAS A GUEST.
I FEAR NOTHING NOW EXCEPT FAILURE IN THIS ENTERPRISE.
YOU WILL HAVE TO FIND THE FEATHERS ABOUT MY PERSON.
I HOPE AND TRUST THAT THIS WILL TAKE LONGER THAN YOU HAVE.

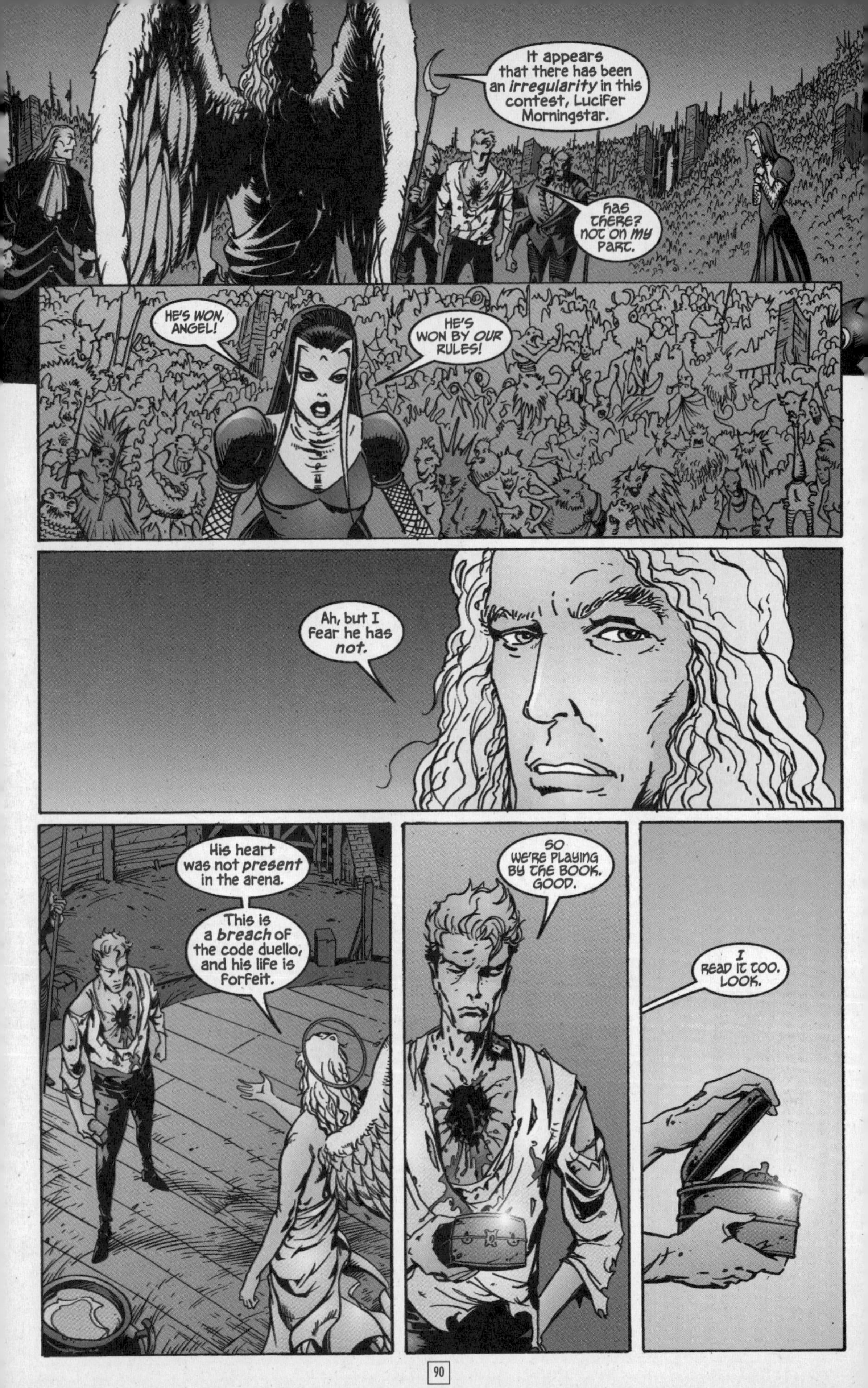
It appears that there has been an *irregularity* in this contest, Lucifer Morningstar.
HAS THERE? NOT ON *MY* PART.
HE'S *WON*, ANGEL!
HE'S WON BY *OUR* RULES!
Ah, but I fear he has *not*.
His heart was not *present* in the arena.
This is a *breach* of the code duello, and his life is forfeit.
SO WE'RE PLAYING BY THE BOOK. GOOD.
I READ IT TOO. LOOK.

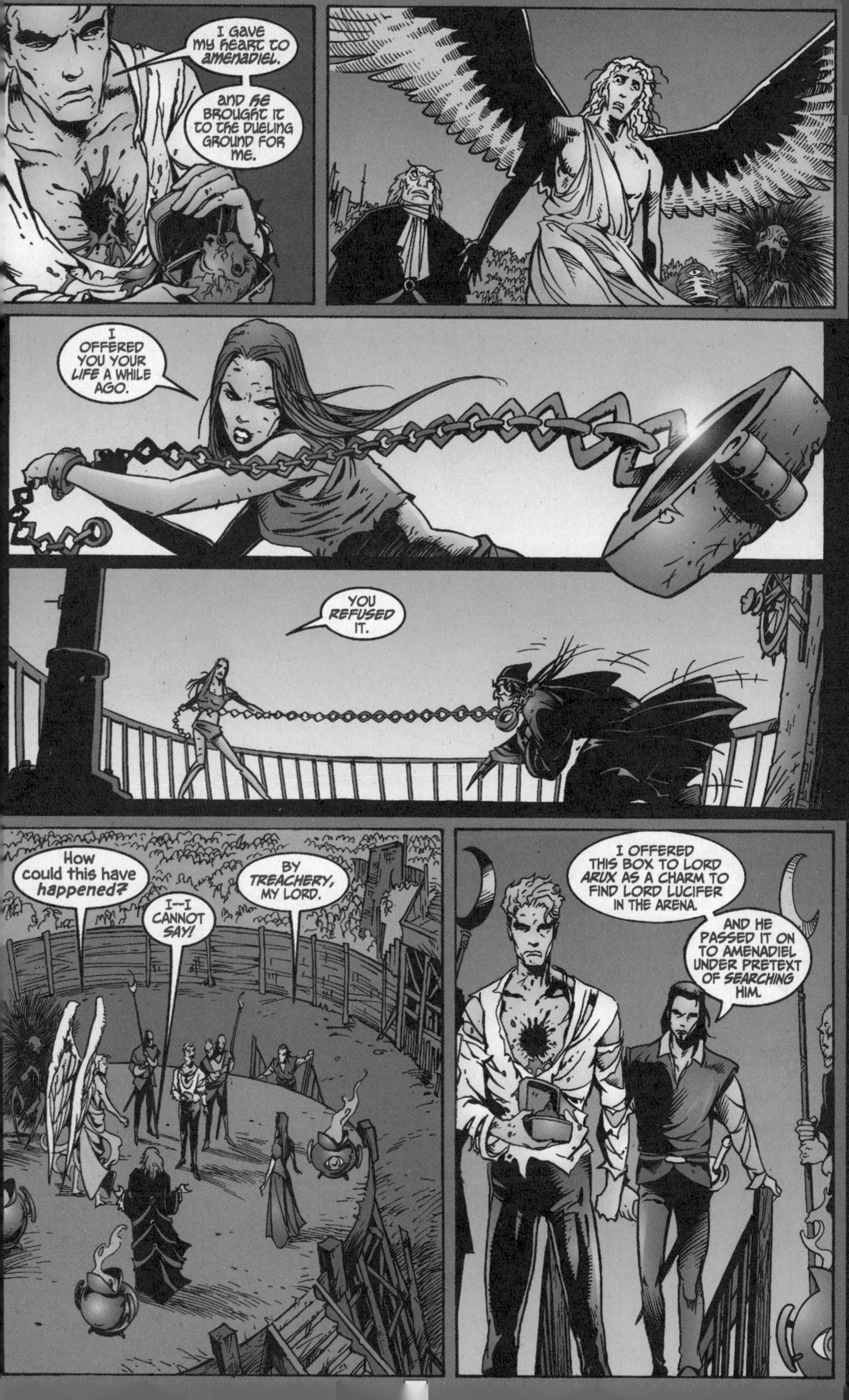
I GAVE MY HEART TO AMENADIEL.
AND HE BROUGHT IT TO THE DUELING GROUND FOR ME.
I OFFERED YOU YOUR LIFE A WHILE AGO.
YOU REFUSED IT.
How could this have happened?
I--I CANNOT SAY!
BY TREACHERY, MY LORD.
I OFFERED THIS BOX TO LORD ARUX AS A CHARM TO FIND LORD LUCIFER IN THE ARENA.
AND HE PASSED IT ON TO AMENADIEL UNDER PRETEXT OF SEARCHING HIM.

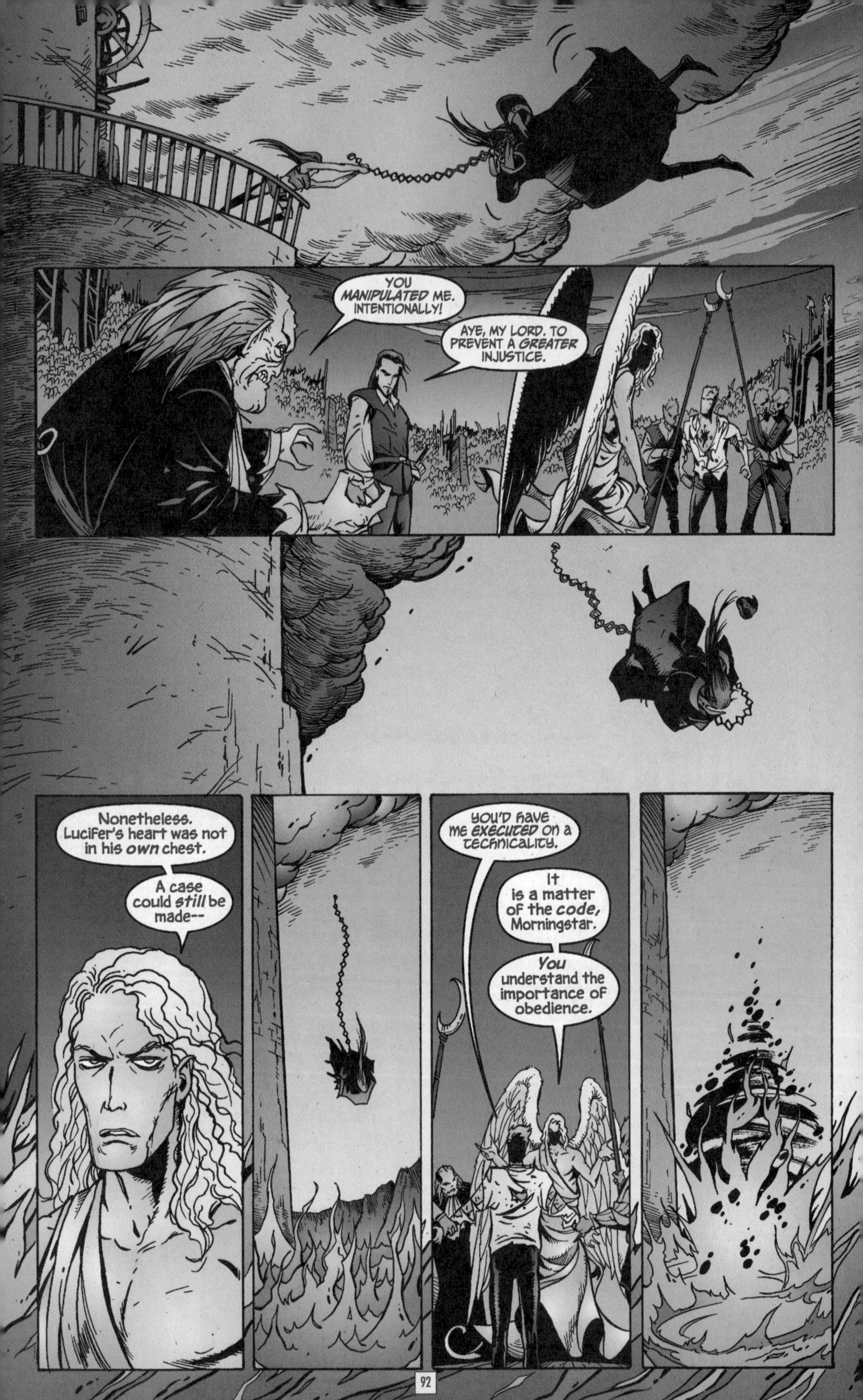
YOU *MANIPULATED* ME. INTENTIONALLY!
AYE, MY LORD. TO PREVENT A *GREATER* INJUSTICE.
Nonetheless. Lucifer's heart was not in his *own* chest.
A case could *still* be made--
YOU'D HAVE ME *EXECUTED* ON A TECHNICALITY.
It is a matter of the *code*, Morningstar.
You understand the importance of obedience.

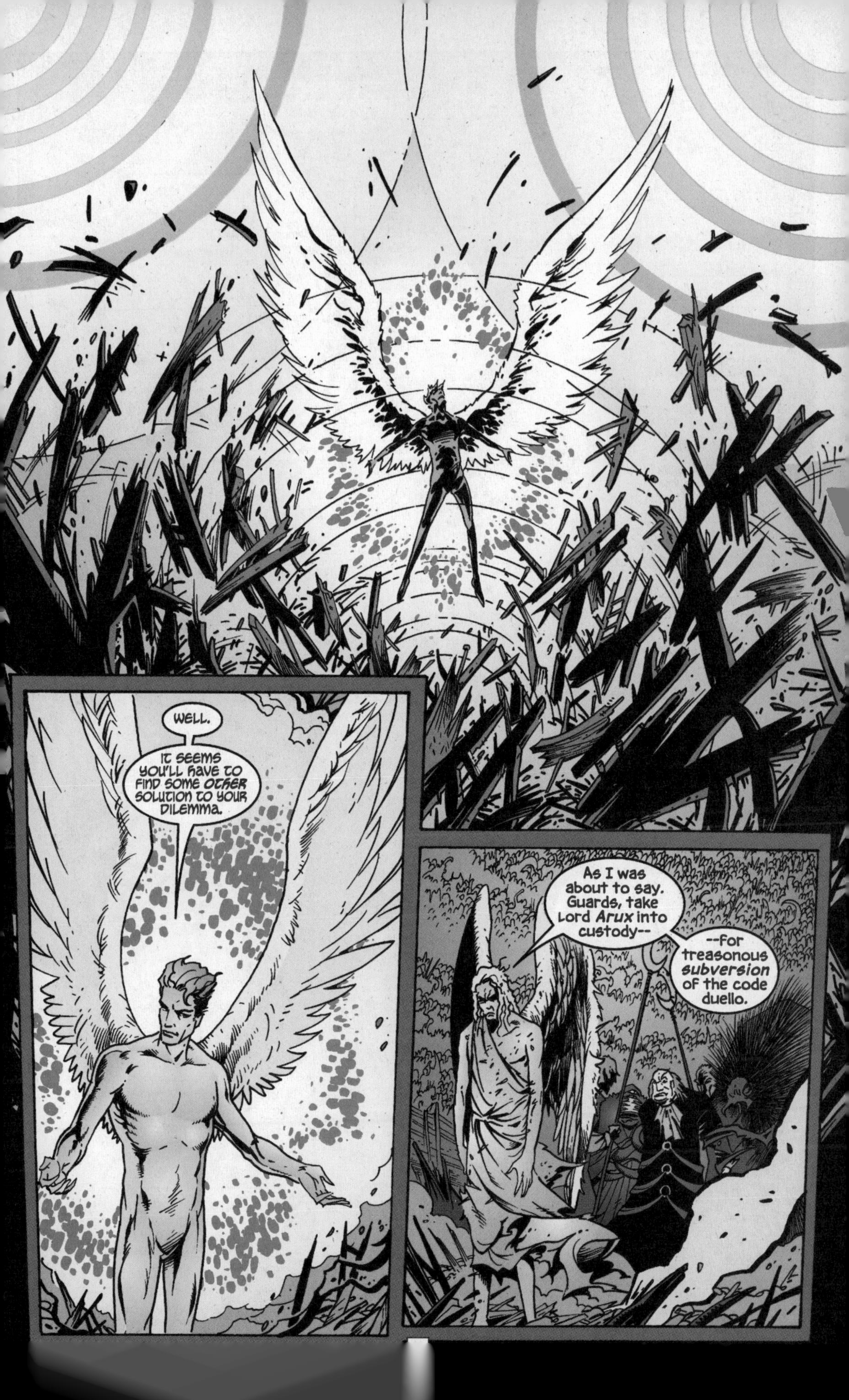

WELL.
IT SEEMS YOU'LL HAVE TO FIND SOME OTHER SOLUTION TO YOUR DILEMMA.
As I was about to say. Guards, take Lord Arux into custody--
--for treasonous subversion of the code duello.

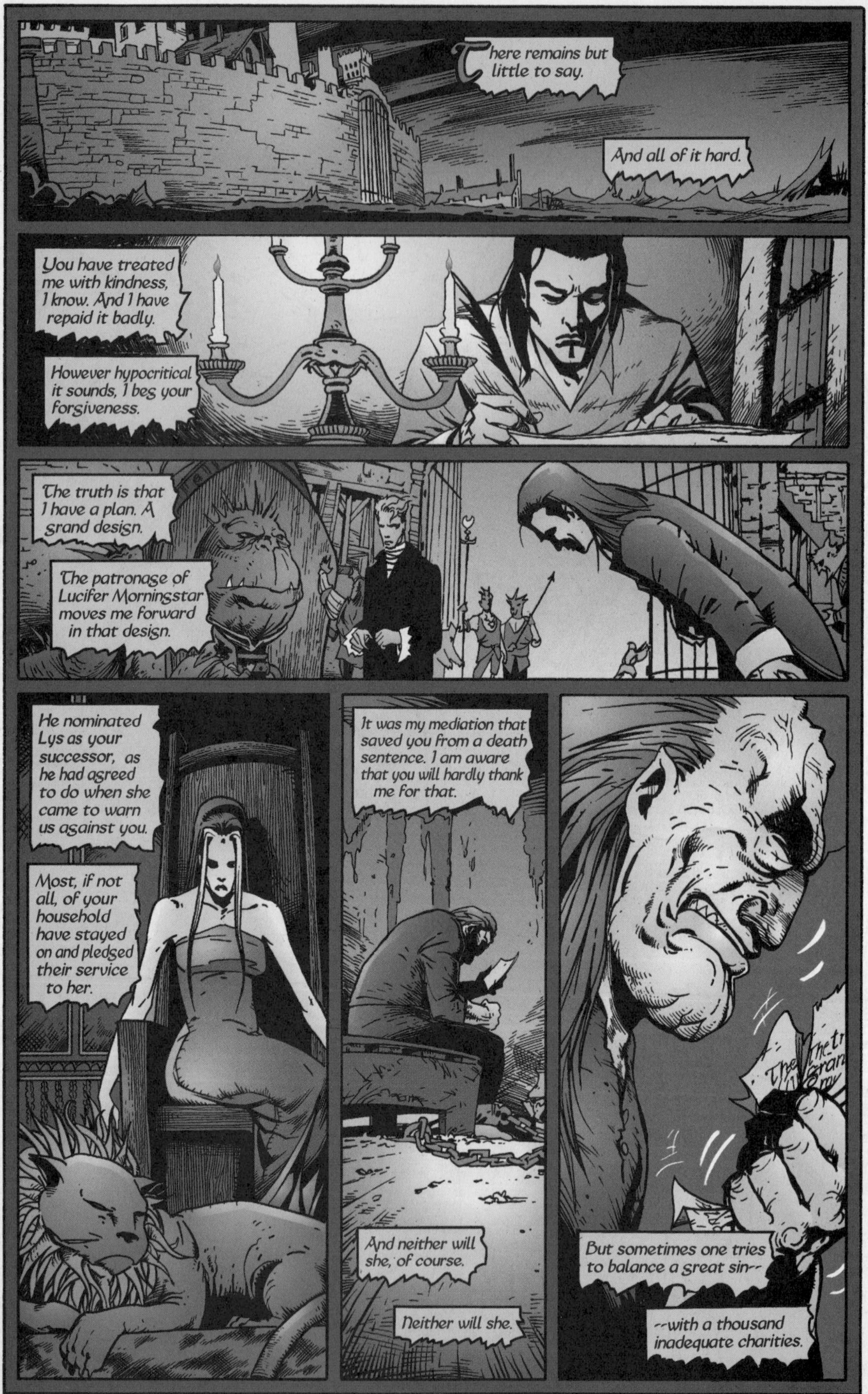
There remains but little to say.
And all of it hard.
You have treated me with kindness, I know. And I have repaid it badly.
However hypocritical it sounds, I beg your forgiveness.
The truth is that I have a plan. A grand design.
The patronage of Lucifer Morningstar moves me forward in that design.
He nominated Lys as your successor, as he had agreed to do when she came to warn us against you.
Most, if not all, of your household have stayed on and pledged their service to her.
It was my mediation that saved you from a death sentence. I am aware that you will hardly thank me for that.
And neither will she, of course.
Neither will she.
But sometimes one tries to balance a great sin--
--with a thousand inadequate charities.

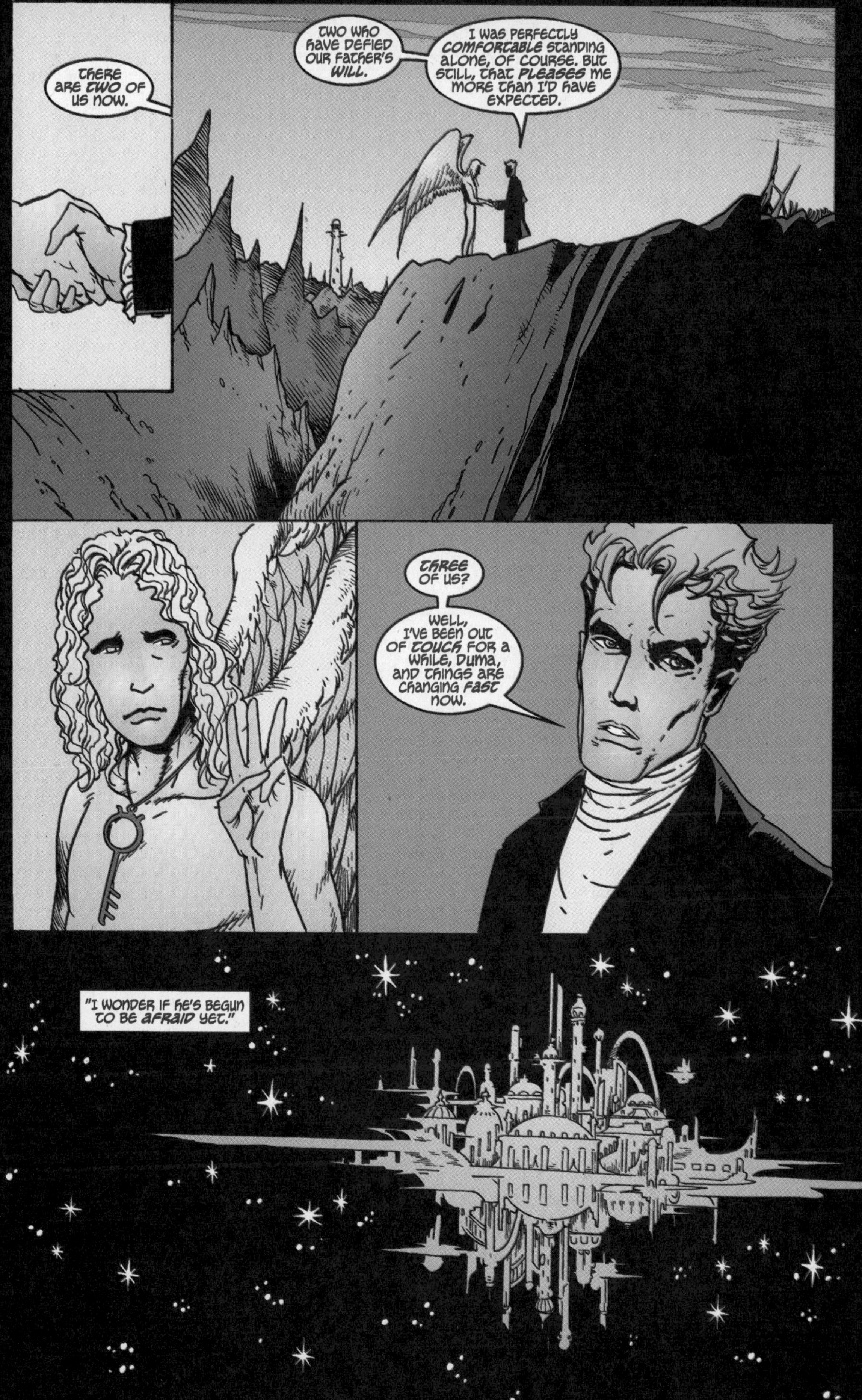

THERE ARE TWO OF US NOW.
TWO WHO HAVE DEFIED OUR FATHER'S WILL.
I WAS PERFECTLY COMFORTABLE STANDING ALONE, OF COURSE. BUT STILL, THAT PLEASES ME MORE THAN I'D HAVE EXPECTED.
THREE OF US?
WELL, I'VE BEEN OUT OF TOUCH FOR A WHILE, DUMA, AND THINGS ARE CHANGING FAST NOW.
"I WONDER IF HE'S BEGUN TO BE AFRAID YET."

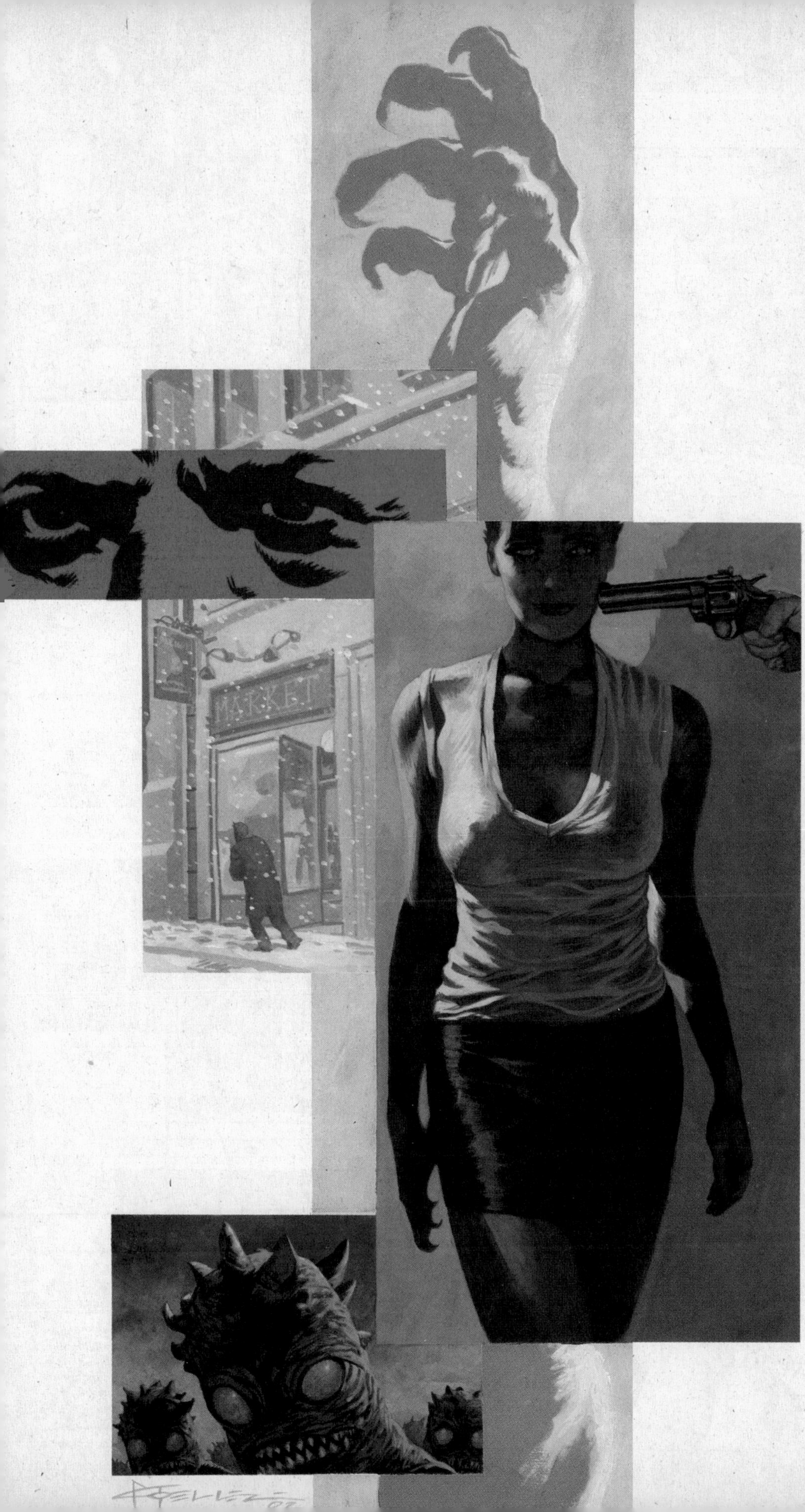
MARKET

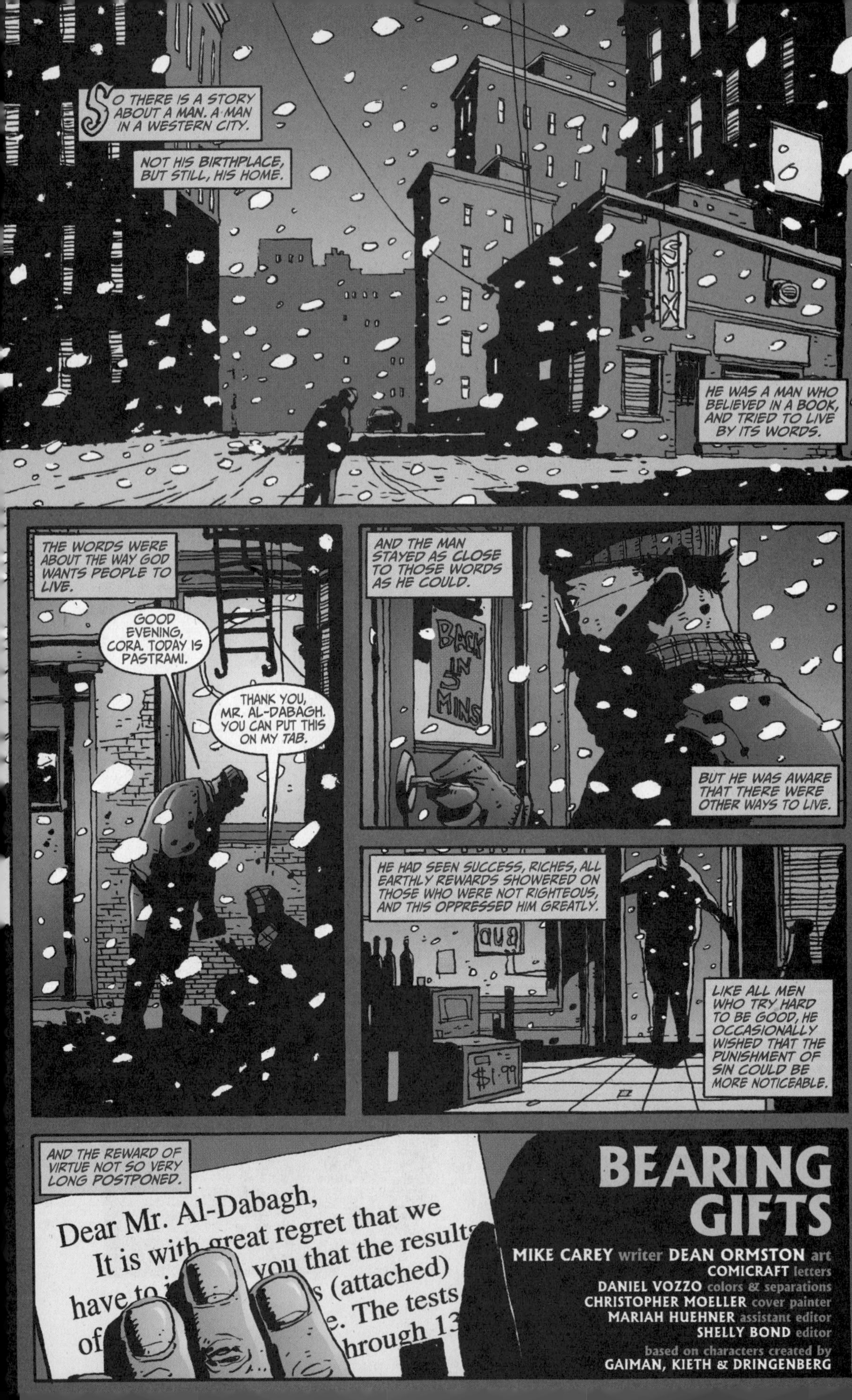

SO THERE IS A STORY ABOUT A MAN. A MAN IN A WESTERN CITY.
NOT HIS BIRTHPLACE, BUT STILL, HIS HOME.
SIX
HE WAS A MAN WHO BELIEVED IN A BOOK, AND TRIED TO LIVE BY ITS WORDS.
THE WORDS WERE ABOUT THE WAY GOD WANTS PEOPLE TO LIVE.
GOOD EVENING, CORA. TODAY IS PASTRAMI.
THANK YOU, MR. AL-DABAGH. YOU CAN PUT THIS ON MY TAB.
AND THE MAN STAYED AS CLOSE TO THOSE WORDS AS HE COULD.
BACK IN 5 MINS
BUT HE WAS AWARE THAT THERE WERE OTHER WAYS TO LIVE.
HE HAD SEEN SUCCESS, RICHES, ALL EARTHLY REWARDS SHOWERED ON THOSE WHO WERE NOT RIGHTEOUS, AND THIS OPPRESSED HIM GREATLY.
$1.99
LIKE ALL MEN WHO TRY HARD TO BE GOOD, HE OCCASIONALLY WISHED THAT THE PUNISHMENT OF SIN COULD BE MORE NOTICEABLE.
AND THE REWARD OF VIRTUE NOT SO VERY LONG POSTPONED.
Dear Mr. Al-Dabagh,
It is with great regret that we
have to i you that the results
s (attached)
e. The tests
of hrough 13

BEARING GIFTS

MIKE CAREY writer **DEAN ORMSTON** art
COMICRAFT letters
DANIEL VOZZO colors & separations
CHRISTOPHER MOELLER cover painter
MARIAH HUEHNER assistant editor
SHELLY BOND editor
based on characters created by
GAIMAN, KIETH & DRINGENBERG

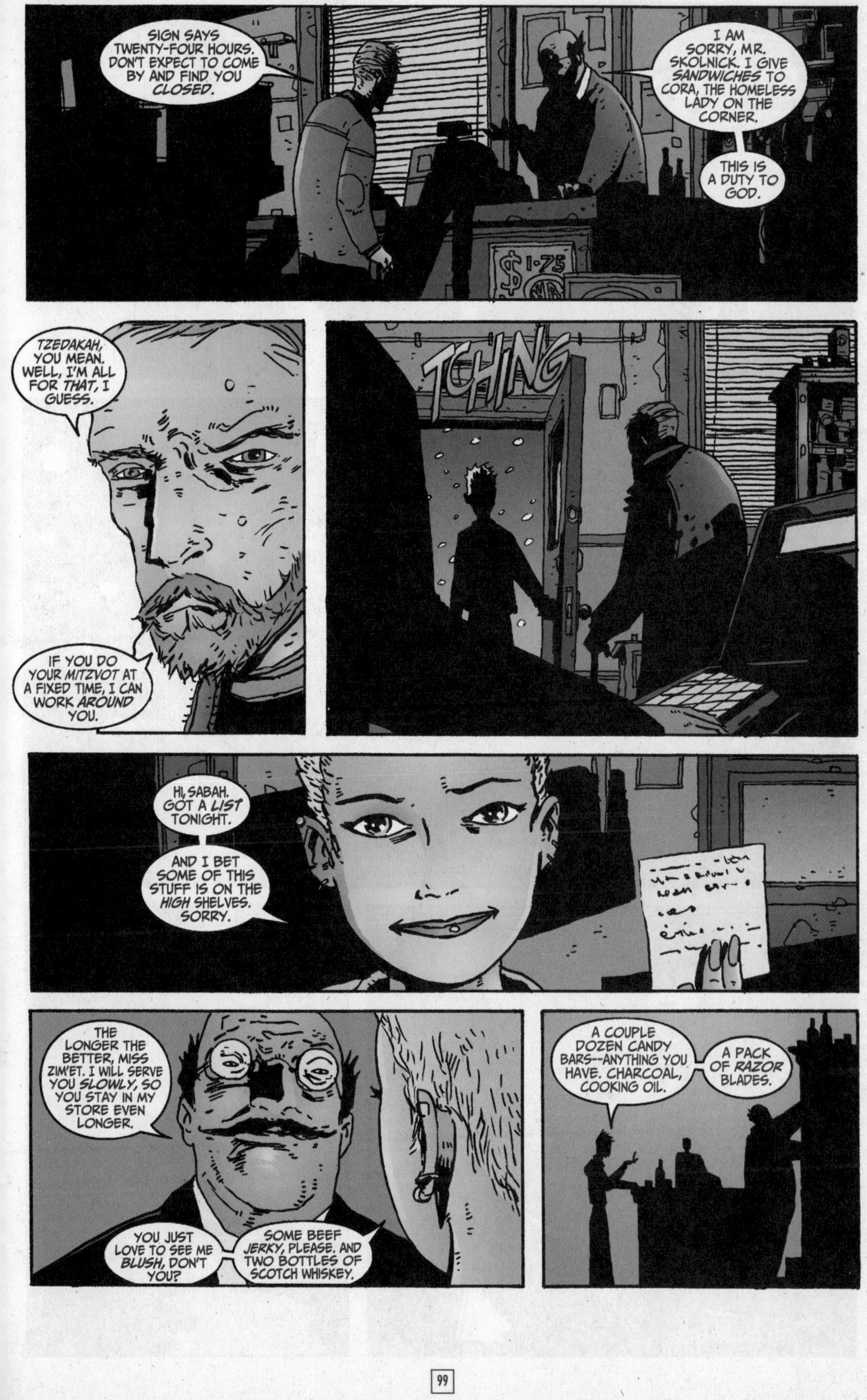
SIGN SAYS TWENTY-FOUR HOURS. DON'T EXPECT TO COME BY AND FIND YOU *CLOSED*.
I AM SORRY, MR. SKOLNICK. I GIVE *SANDWICHES* TO CORA, THE HOMELESS LADY ON THE CORNER.
THIS IS A DUTY TO GOD.
$1.75
TZEDAKAH, YOU MEAN. WELL, I'M ALL FOR *THAT*, I GUESS.
IF YOU DO YOUR *MITZVOT* AT A FIXED TIME, I CAN WORK *AROUND* YOU.
TCHING
HI, SABAH. GOT A *LIST* TONIGHT.
AND I BET SOME OF THIS STUFF IS ON THE *HIGH* SHELVES. SORRY.
THE LONGER THE BETTER, MISS ZIM'ET. I WILL SERVE YOU *SLOWLY*, SO YOU STAY IN MY STORE EVEN LONGER.
YOU JUST LOVE TO SEE ME *BLUSH*, DON'T YOU?
SOME BEEF *JERKY*, PLEASE. AND TWO BOTTLES OF SCOTCH WHISKEY.
A COUPLE DOZEN CANDY BARS--ANYTHING YOU HAVE. CHARCOAL, COOKING OIL.
A PACK OF *RAZOR* BLADES.

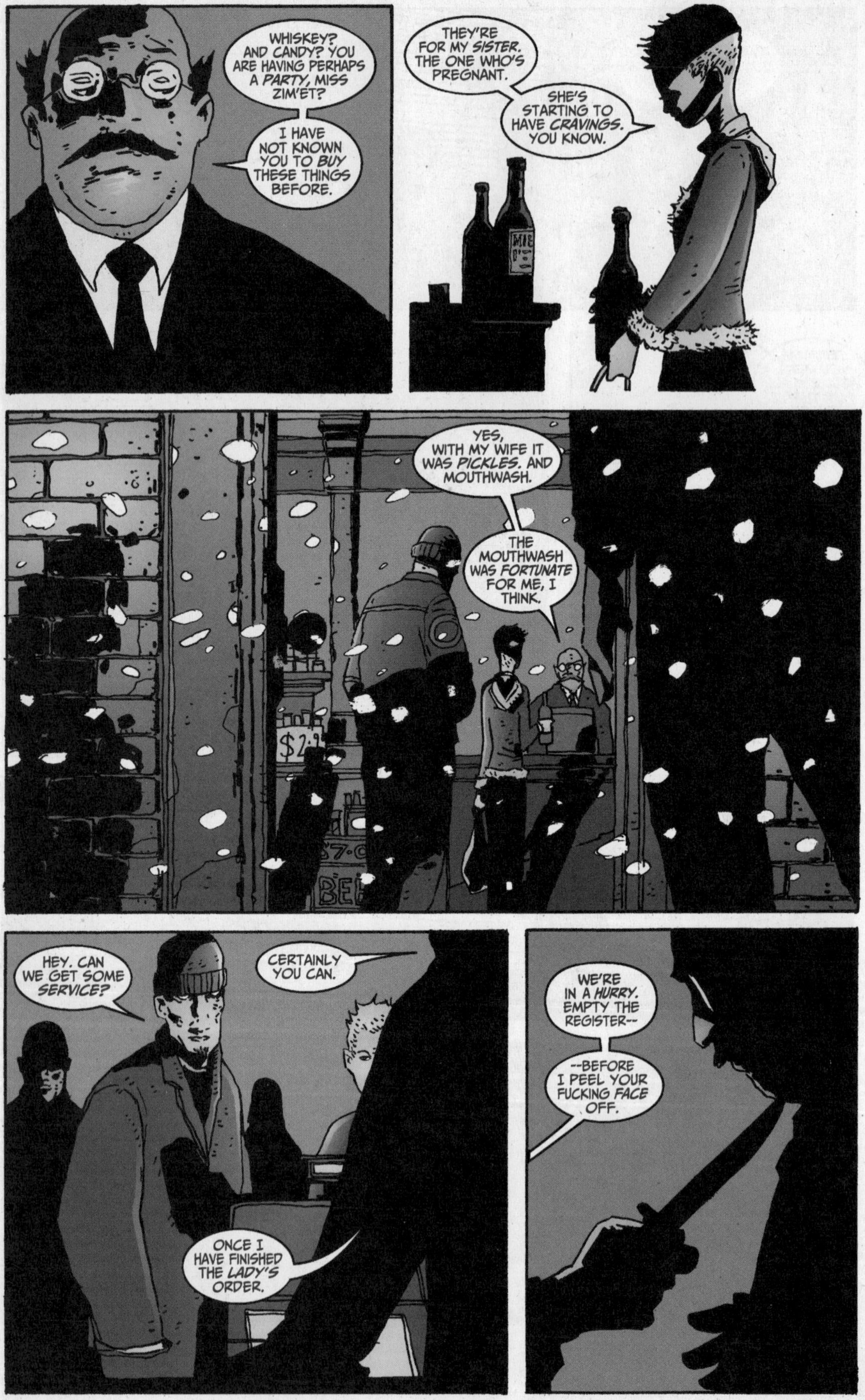
WHISKEY? AND CANDY? YOU ARE HAVING PERHAPS A PARTY, MISS ZIM'ET?
I HAVE NOT KNOWN YOU TO BUY THESE THINGS BEFORE.
THEY'RE FOR MY SISTER. THE ONE WHO'S PREGNANT.
SHE'S STARTING TO HAVE CRAVINGS. YOU KNOW.
YES, WITH MY WIFE IT WAS PICKLES. AND MOUTHWASH.
THE MOUTHWASH WAS FORTUNATE FOR ME, I THINK.
HEY. CAN WE GET SOME SERVICE?
CERTAINLY YOU CAN.
ONCE I HAVE FINISHED THE LADY'S ORDER.
WE'RE IN A HURRY. EMPTY THE REGISTER--
--BEFORE I PEEL YOUR FUCKING FACE OFF.

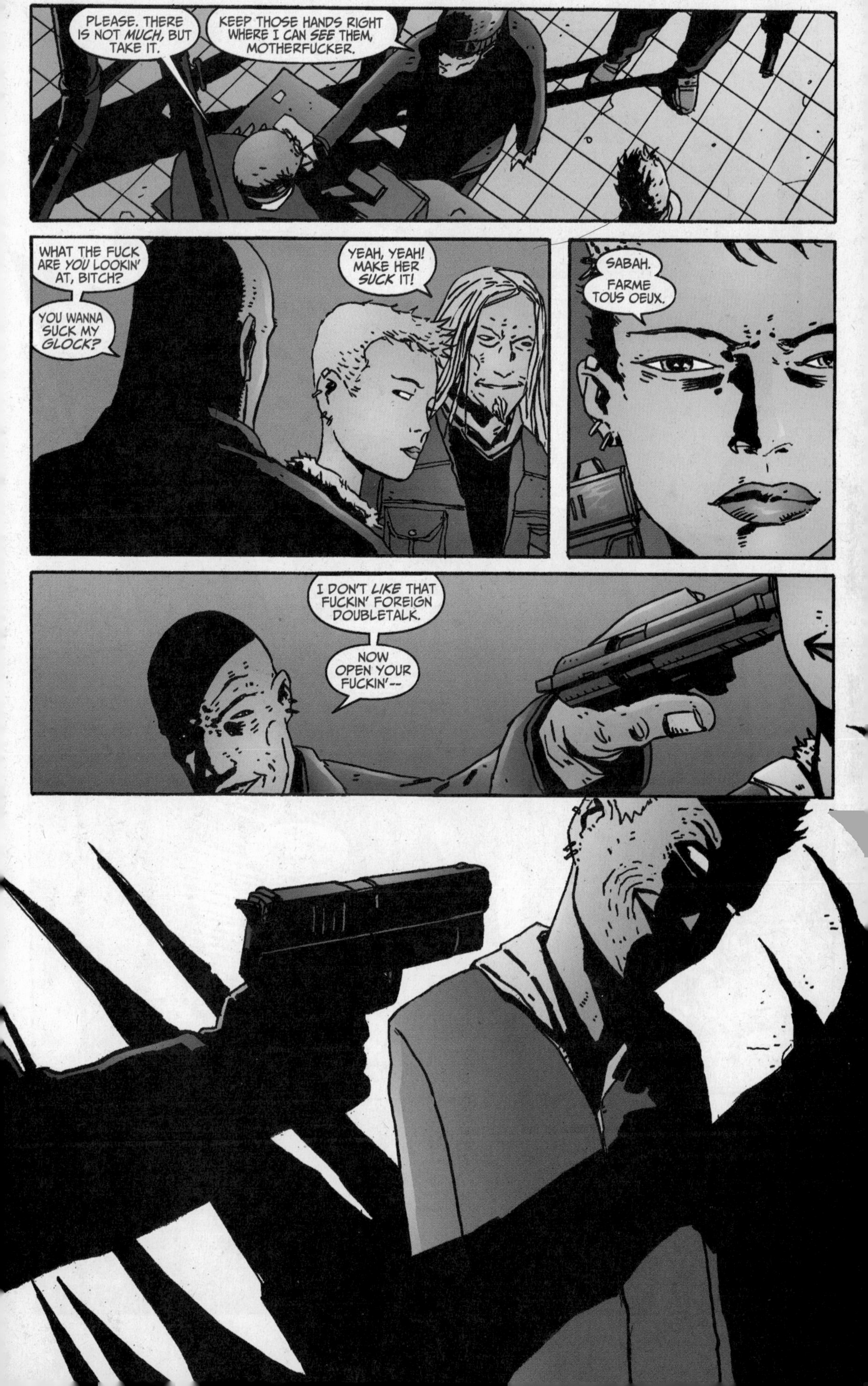
PLEASE. THERE IS NOT *MUCH*, BUT TAKE IT.
KEEP THOSE HANDS RIGHT WHERE I CAN *SEE* THEM, MOTHERFUCKER.
WHAT THE FUCK ARE *YOU* LOOKIN' AT, BITCH?
YOU WANNA SUCK MY *GLOCK?*
YEAH, YEAH! MAKE HER *SUCK* IT!
SABAH.
FARME TOUS OEUX.
I DON'T *LIKE* THAT FUCKIN' FOREIGN DOUBLETALK.
NOW OPEN YOUR FUCKIN'--

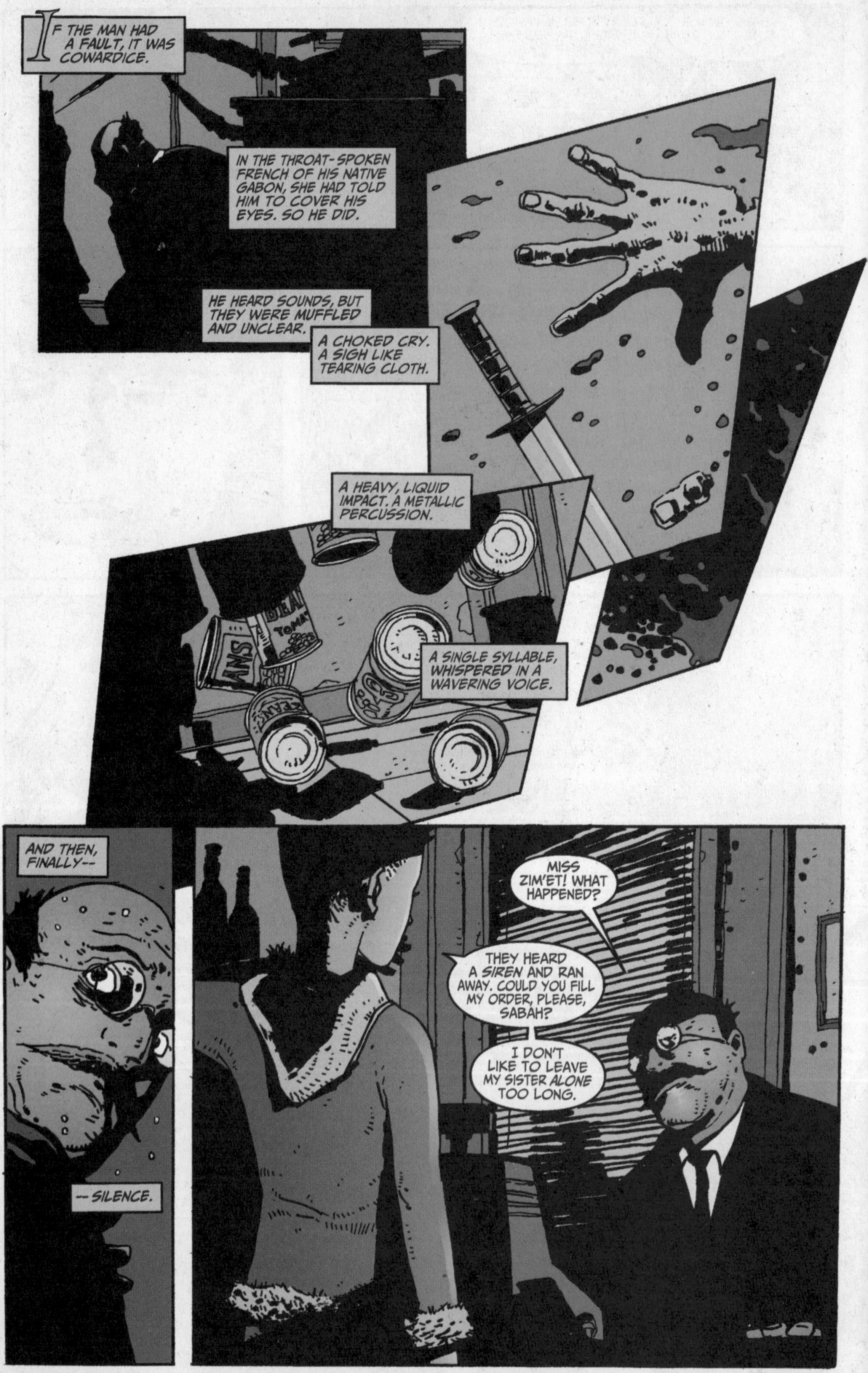
IF THE MAN HAD A FAULT, IT WAS COWARDICE.
IN THE THROAT-SPOKEN FRENCH OF HIS NATIVE GABON, SHE HAD TOLD HIM TO COVER HIS EYES. SO HE DID.
HE HEARD SOUNDS, BUT THEY WERE MUFFLED AND UNCLEAR.
A CHOKED CRY. A SIGH LIKE TEARING CLOTH.
A HEAVY, LIQUID IMPACT. A METALLIC PERCUSSION.
A SINGLE SYLLABLE, WHISPERED IN A WAVERING VOICE.
AND THEN, FINALLY--
-- SILENCE.
MISS ZIM'ET! WHAT HAPPENED?
THEY HEARD A SIREN AND RAN AWAY. COULD YOU FILL MY ORDER, PLEASE, SABAH?
I DON'T LIKE TO LEAVE MY SISTER ALONE TOO LONG.

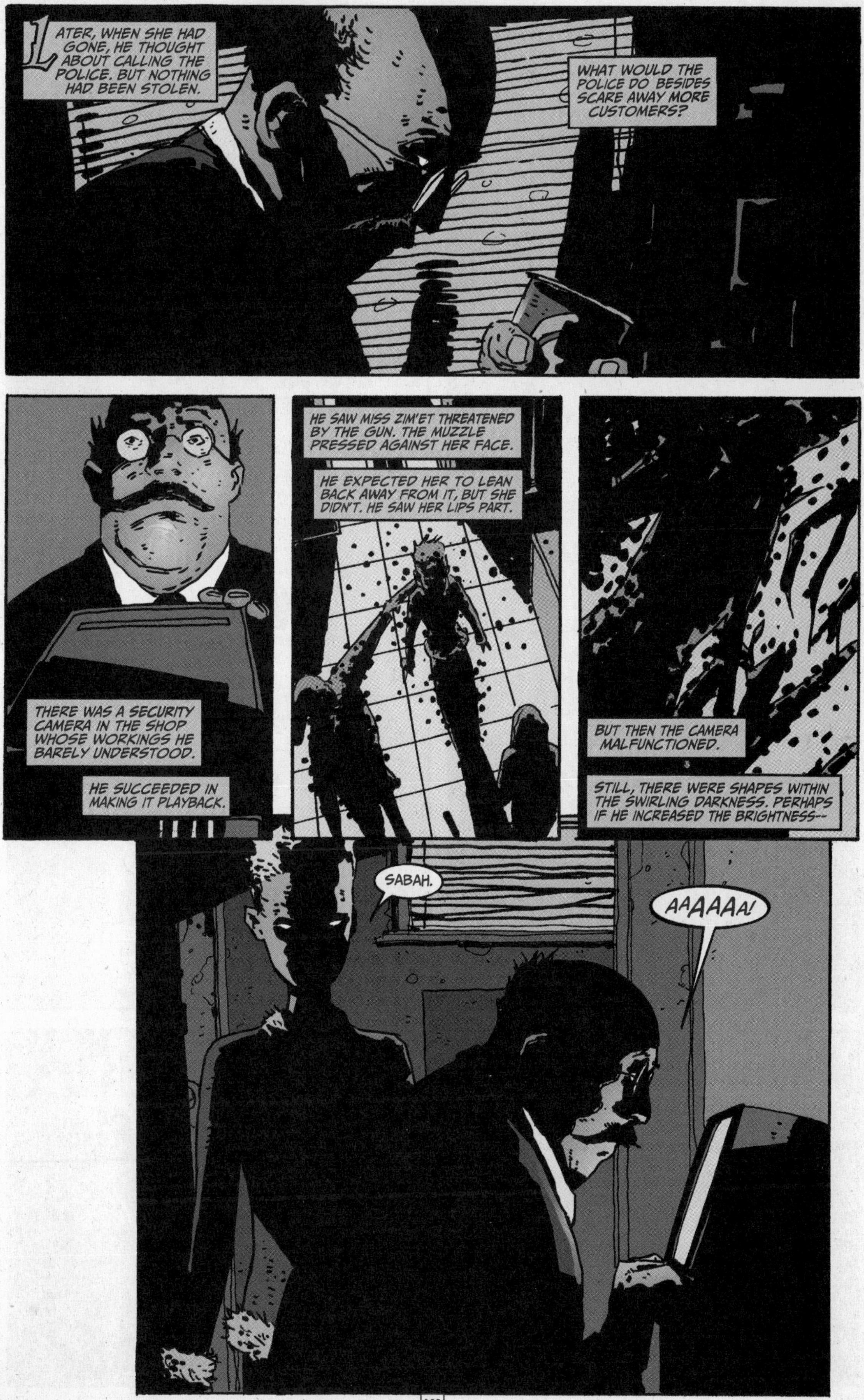
LATER, WHEN SHE HAD GONE, HE THOUGHT ABOUT CALLING THE POLICE. BUT NOTHING HAD BEEN STOLEN.
WHAT WOULD THE POLICE DO BESIDES SCARE AWAY MORE CUSTOMERS?
THERE WAS A SECURITY CAMERA IN THE SHOP WHOSE WORKINGS HE BARELY UNDERSTOOD.
HE SUCCEEDED IN MAKING IT PLAYBACK.
HE SAW MISS ZIM'ET THREATENED BY THE GUN. THE MUZZLE PRESSED AGAINST HER FACE.
HE EXPECTED HER TO LEAN BACK AWAY FROM IT, BUT SHE DIDN'T. HE SAW HER LIPS PART.
BUT THEN THE CAMERA MALFUNCTIONED.
STILL, THERE WERE SHAPES WITHIN THE SWIRLING DARKNESS. PERHAPS IF HE INCREASED THE BRIGHTNESS--
SABAH.
AAAAAA!

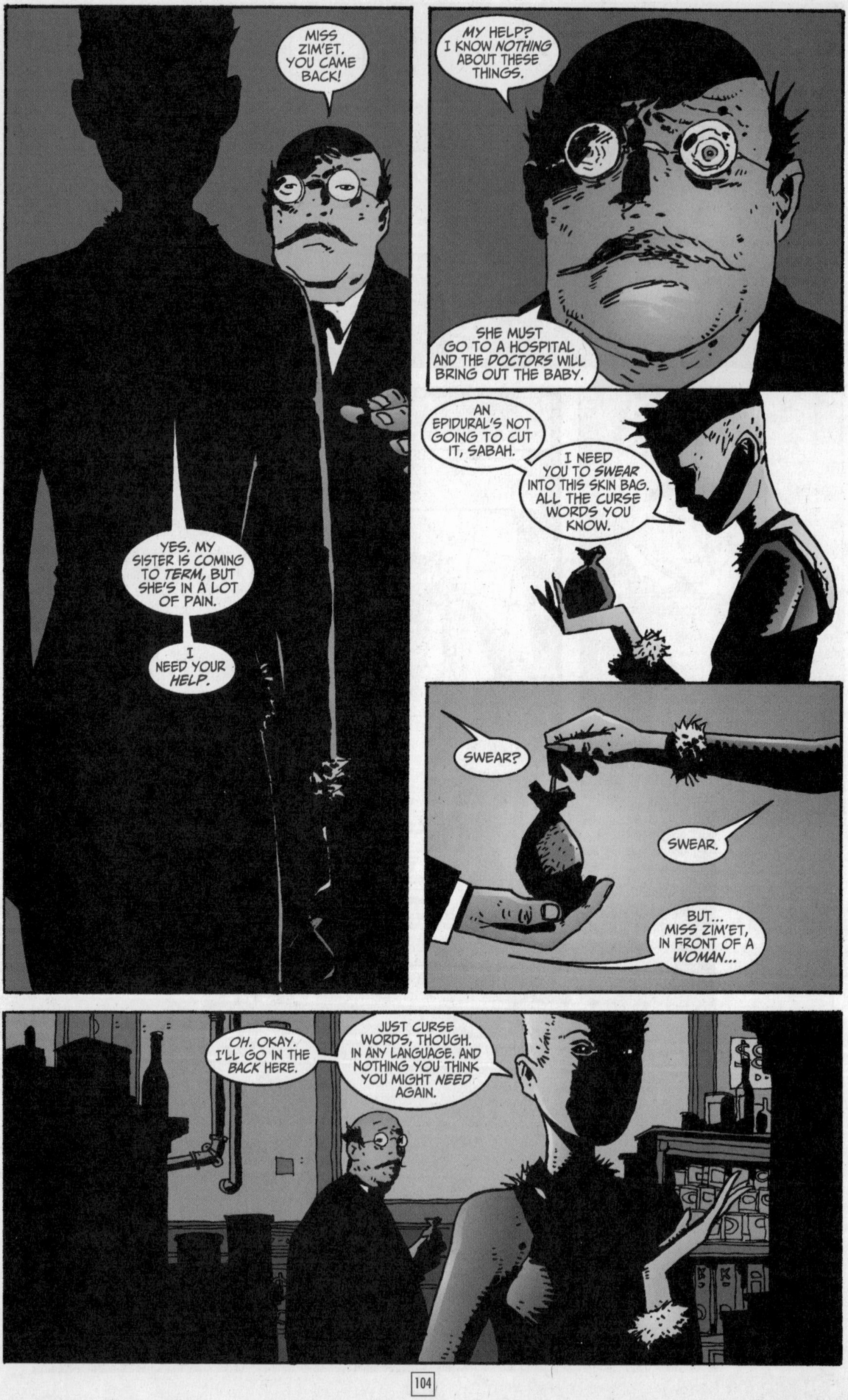
MISS ZIM'ET. YOU CAME BACK!
YES. MY SISTER IS COMING TO TERM, BUT SHE'S IN A LOT OF PAIN.
I NEED YOUR HELP.
MY HELP? I KNOW NOTHING ABOUT THESE THINGS.
SHE MUST GO TO A HOSPITAL AND THE DOCTORS WILL BRING OUT THE BABY.
AN EPIDURAL'S NOT GOING TO CUT IT, SABAH.
I NEED YOU TO SWEAR INTO THIS SKIN BAG. ALL THE CURSE WORDS YOU KNOW.
SWEAR?
SWEAR.
BUT... MISS ZIM'ET, IN FRONT OF A WOMAN...
OH. OKAY. I'LL GO IN THE BACK HERE.
JUST CURSE WORDS, THOUGH. IN ANY LANGUAGE. AND NOTHING YOU THINK YOU MIGHT NEED AGAIN.

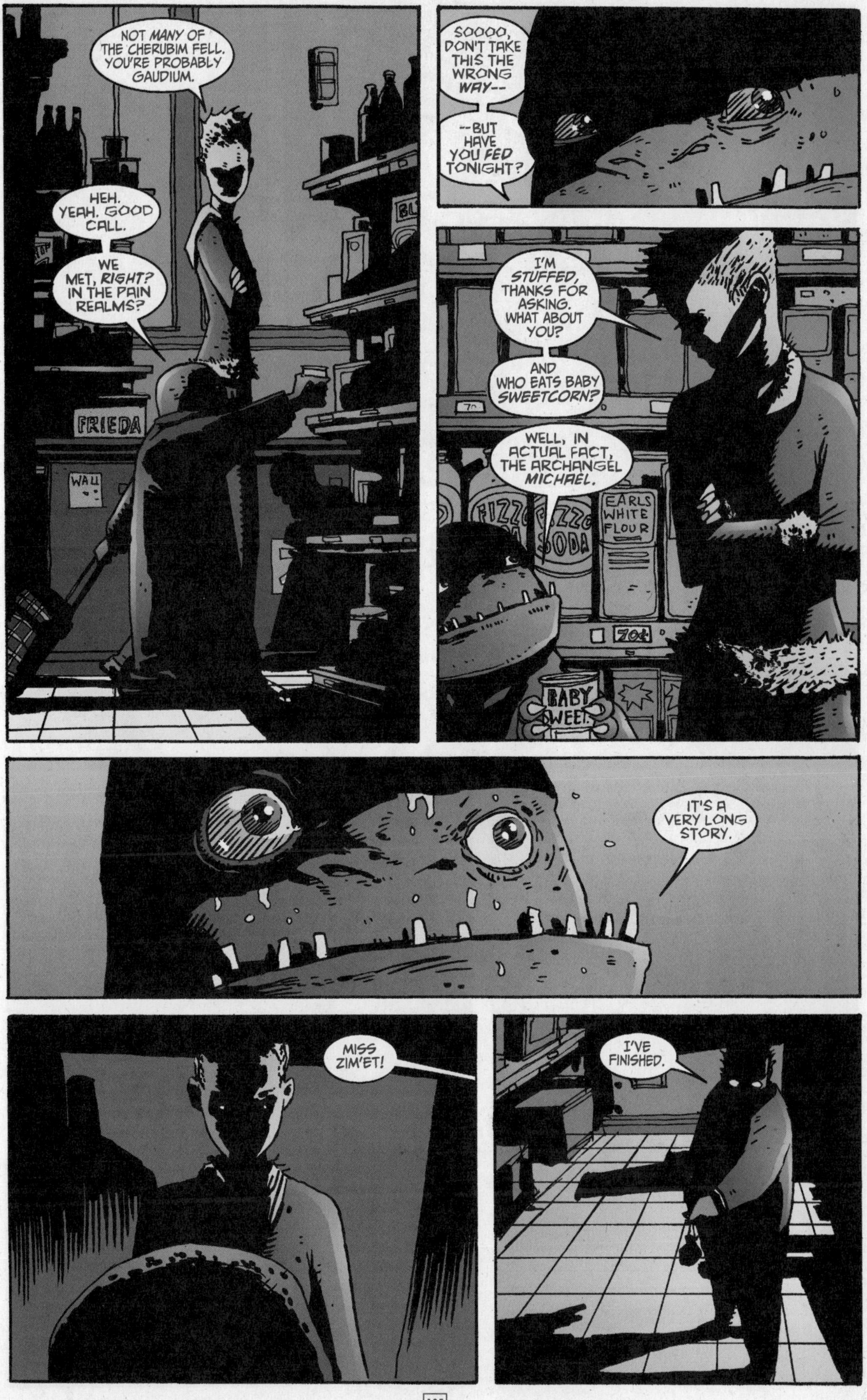
NOT MANY OF THE CHERUBIM FELL. YOU'RE PROBABLY GAUDIUM.
HEH. YEAH. GOOD CALL.
WE MET, RIGHT? IN THE PAIN REALMS?
FRIEDA
SOOOO, DON'T TAKE THIS THE WRONG WAY--
--BUT HAVE YOU FED TONIGHT?
I'M STUFFED, THANKS FOR ASKING. WHAT ABOUT YOU?
AND WHO EATS BABY SWEETCORN?
WELL, IN ACTUAL FACT, THE ARCHANGEL MICHAEL.
EARLS WHITE FLOUR
SODA
BABY SWEET
IT'S A VERY LONG STORY.
MISS ZIM'ET!
I'VE FINISHED.

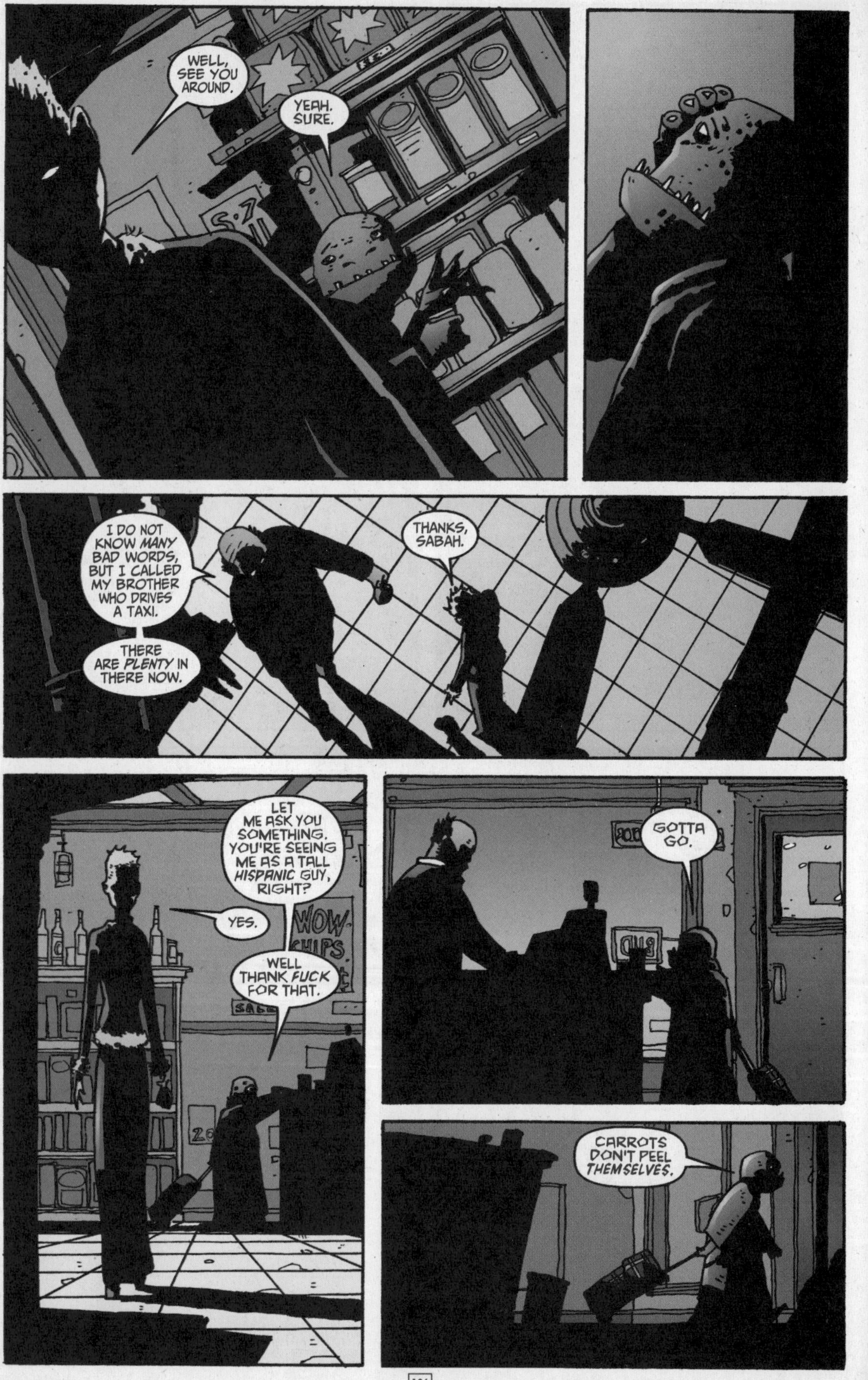
WELL, SEE YOU AROUND.
YEAH. SURE.
I DO NOT KNOW MANY BAD WORDS, BUT I CALLED MY BROTHER WHO DRIVES A TAXI.
THERE ARE PLENTY IN THERE NOW.
THANKS, SABAH.
LET ME ASK YOU SOMETHING. YOU'RE SEEING ME AS A TALL HISPANIC GUY, RIGHT?
YES.
WELL THANK FUCK FOR THAT.
GOTTA GO.
CARROTS DON'T PEEL THEMSELVES.

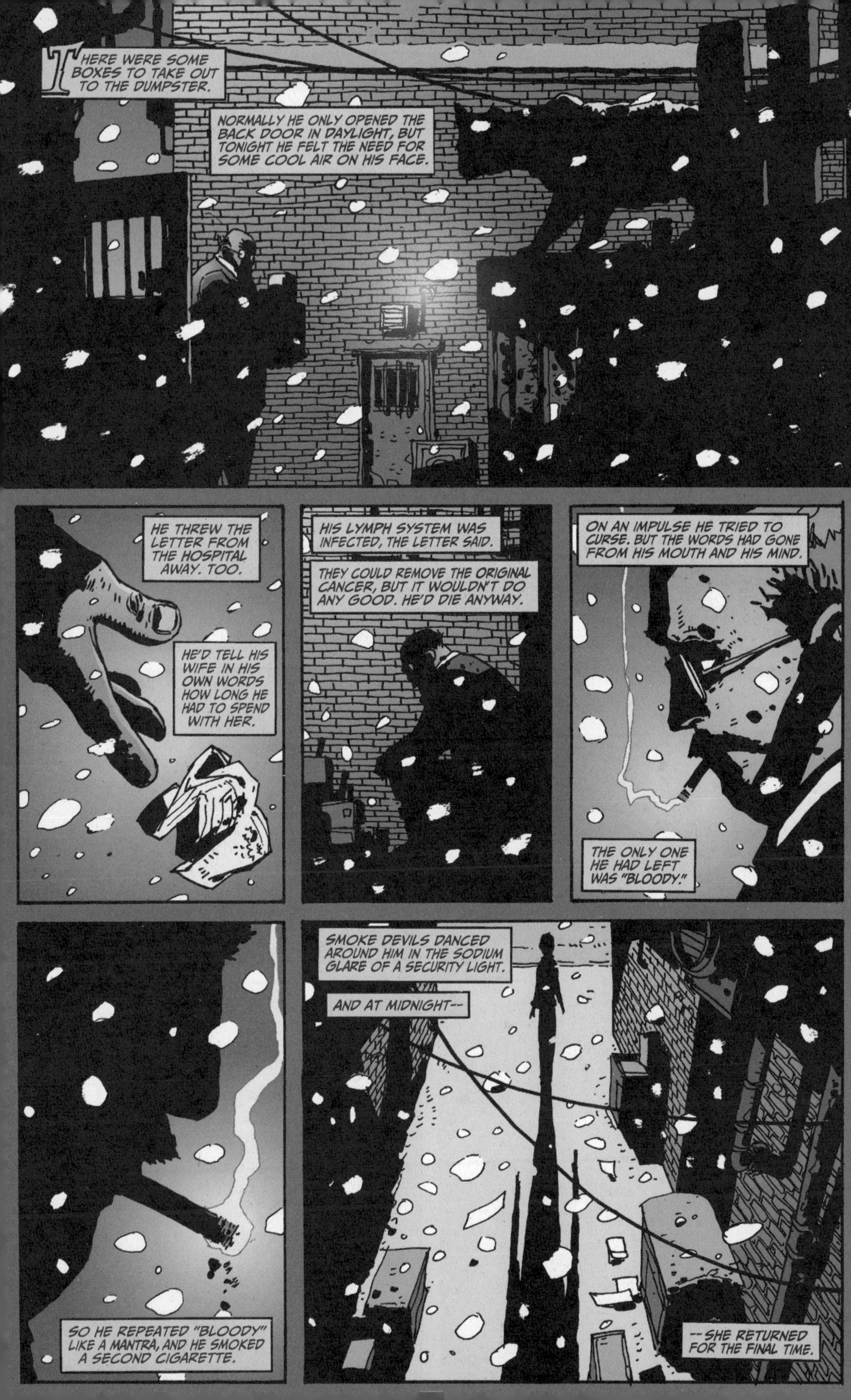
THERE WERE SOME BOXES TO TAKE OUT TO THE DUMPSTER.
NORMALLY HE ONLY OPENED THE BACK DOOR IN DAYLIGHT, BUT TONIGHT HE FELT THE NEED FOR SOME COOL AIR ON HIS FACE.
HE THREW THE LETTER FROM THE HOSPITAL AWAY, TOO.
HE'D TELL HIS WIFE IN HIS OWN WORDS HOW LONG HE HAD TO SPEND WITH HER.
HIS LYMPH SYSTEM WAS INFECTED, THE LETTER SAID.
THEY COULD REMOVE THE ORIGINAL CANCER, BUT IT WOULDN'T DO ANY GOOD. HE'D DIE ANYWAY.
ON AN IMPULSE HE TRIED TO CURSE. BUT THE WORDS HAD GONE FROM HIS MOUTH AND HIS MIND.
THE ONLY ONE HE HAD LEFT WAS "BLOODY."
SO HE REPEATED "BLOODY" LIKE A MANTRA, AND HE SMOKED A SECOND CIGARETTE.
SMOKE DEVILS DANCED AROUND HIM IN THE SODIUM GLARE OF A SECURITY LIGHT.
AND AT MIDNIGHT--
--SHE RETURNED FOR THE FINAL TIME.

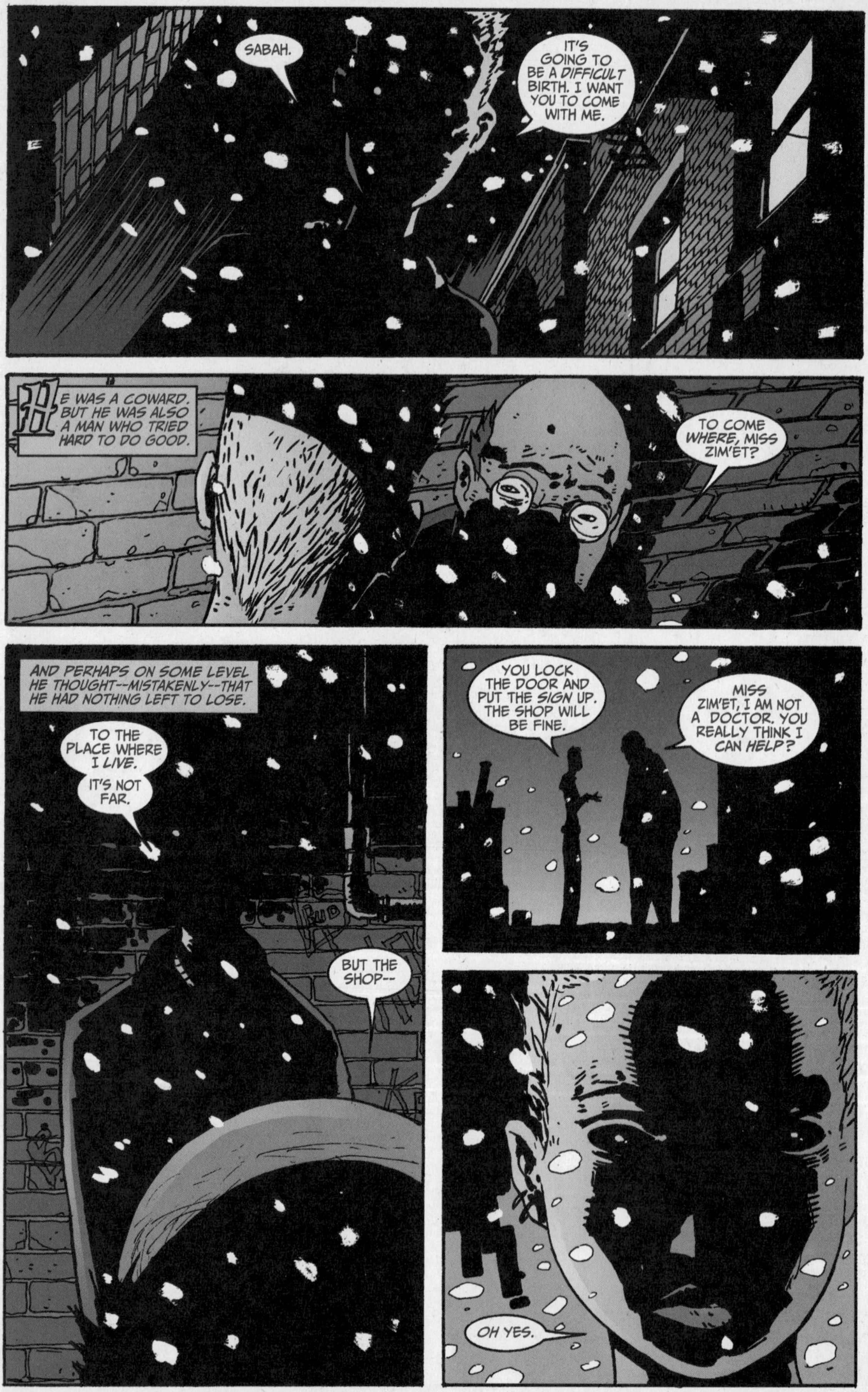
SABAH.
IT'S GOING TO BE A *DIFFICULT* BIRTH. I WANT YOU TO COME WITH ME.
HE WAS A COWARD. BUT HE WAS ALSO A MAN WHO TRIED HARD TO DO GOOD.
TO COME *WHERE*, MISS ZIM'ET?
AND PERHAPS ON SOME LEVEL HE THOUGHT--MISTAKENLY--THAT HE HAD NOTHING LEFT TO LOSE.
TO THE PLACE WHERE I *LIVE*.
IT'S NOT FAR.
BUT THE SHOP--
YOU LOCK THE DOOR AND PUT THE *SIGN* UP. THE SHOP WILL BE FINE.
MISS ZIM'ET, I AM NOT A DOCTOR. YOU REALLY THINK I CAN *HELP*?
OH YES.

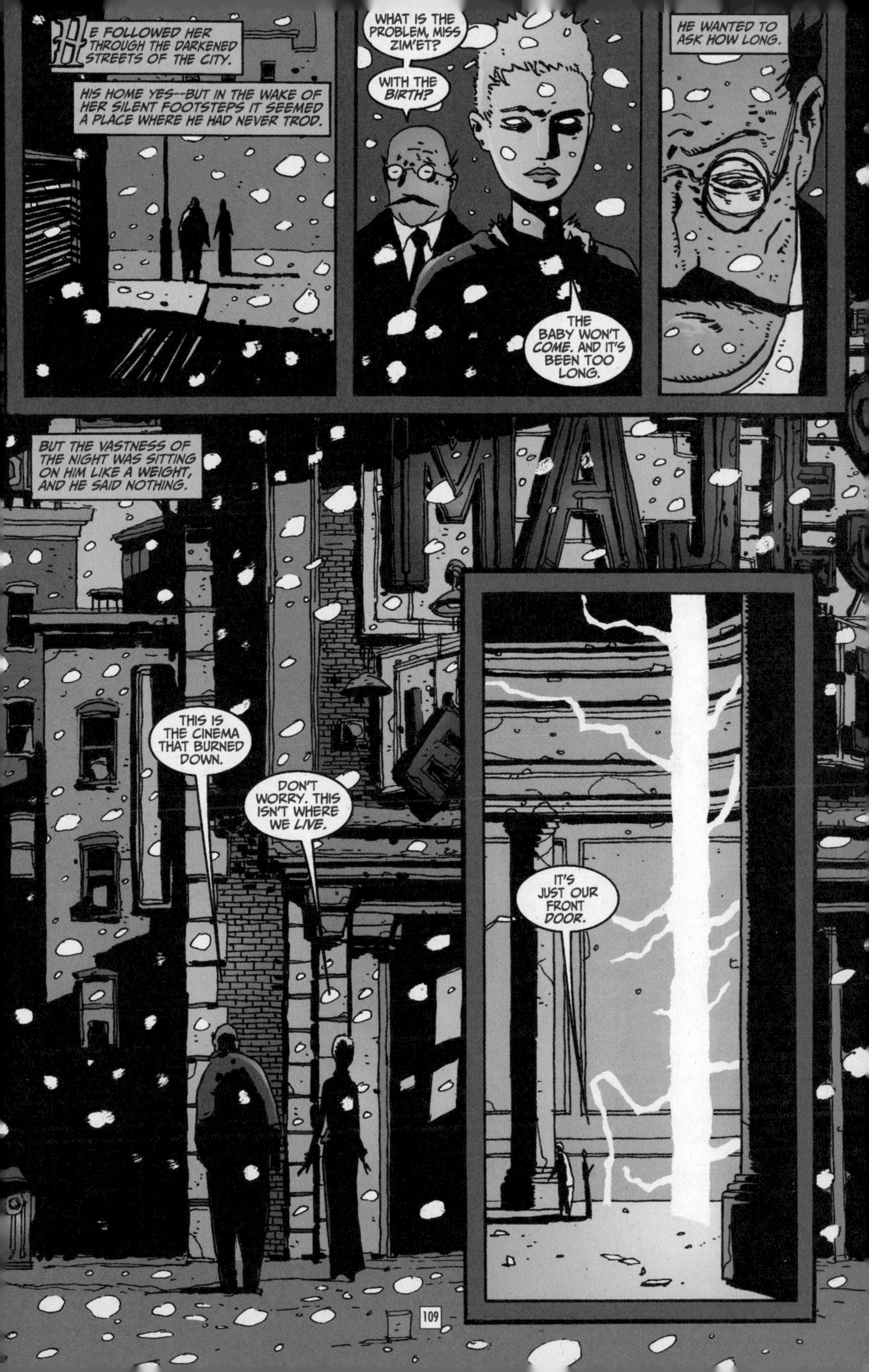
He followed her through the darkened streets of the city.
His home yes--but in the wake of her silent footsteps it seemed a place where he had never trod.
What is the problem, Miss Zim'et?
With the birth?
The baby won't come. And it's been too long.
He wanted to ask how long.
But the vastness of the night was sitting on him like a weight, and he said nothing.
This is the cinema that burned down.
Don't worry. This isn't where we live.
It's just our front door.

MISS ZIM'ET--

THIS...THIS *PLACE* WE ARE GOING TO--

YOU'RE WITH *ME*, SABAH. BELIEVE ME, NOTHING'S GOING TO TOUCH YOU.

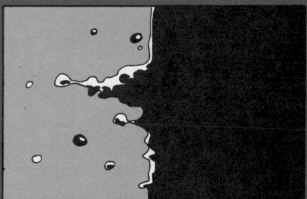

BUT IT'S PROBABLY BEST IF YOU DON'T LET GO OF MY *HAND*.

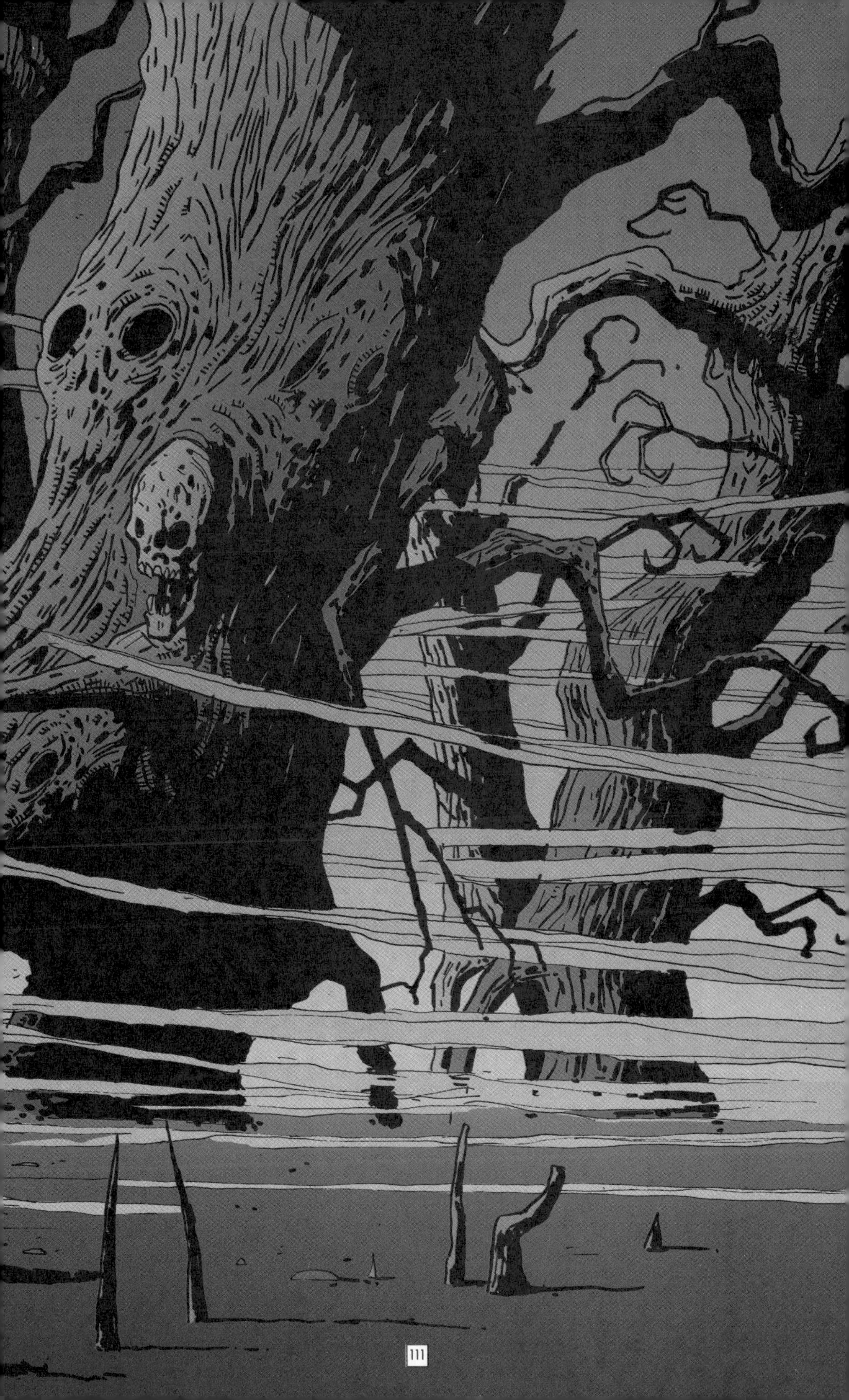

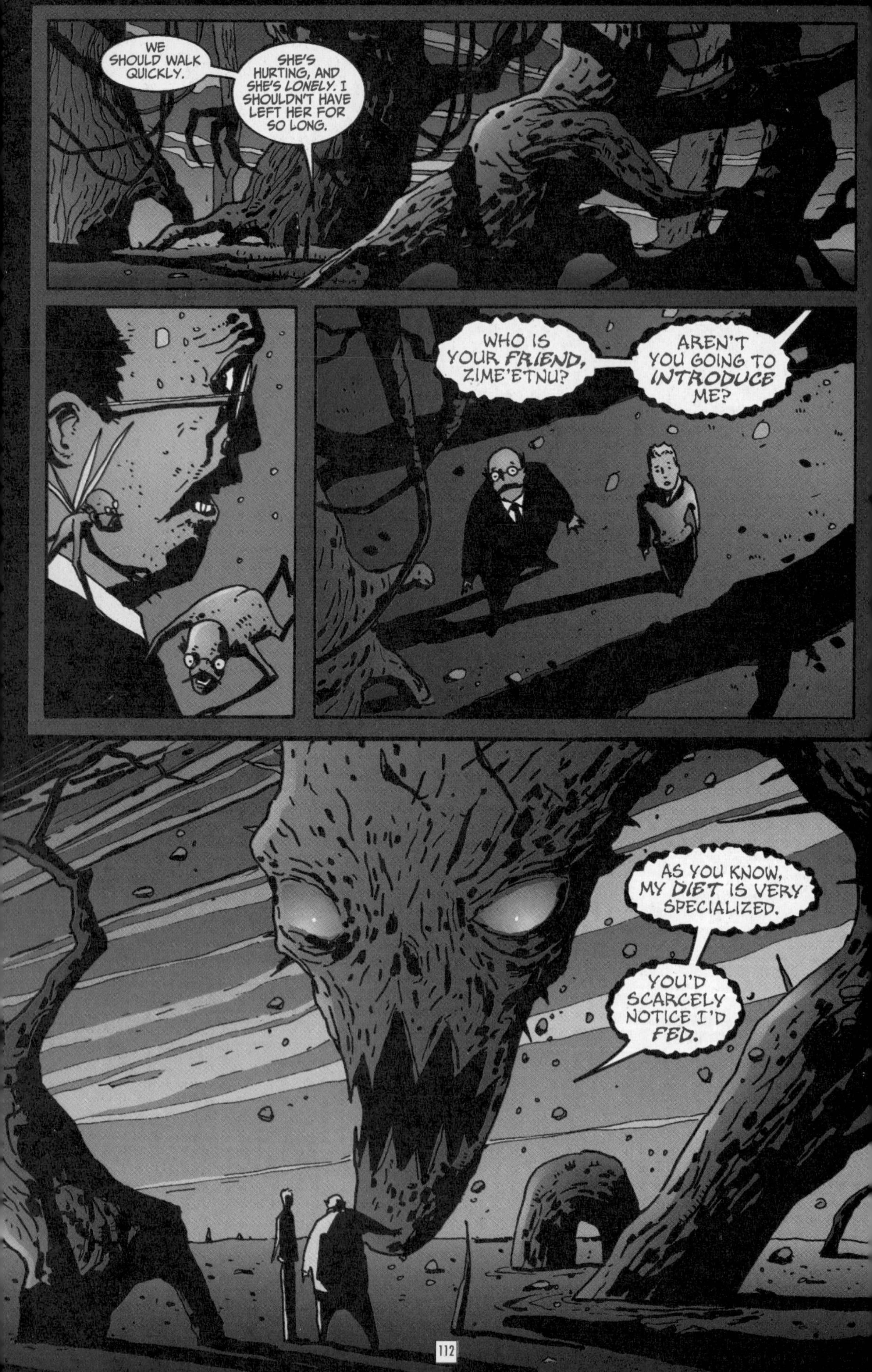
WE SHOULD WALK QUICKLY.
SHE'S HURTING, AND SHE'S LONELY. I SHOULDN'T HAVE LEFT HER FOR SO LONG.
WHO IS YOUR FRIEND, ZIME'ETNU?
AREN'T YOU GOING TO INTRODUCE ME?
AS YOU KNOW, MY DIET IS VERY SPECIALIZED.
YOU'D SCARCELY NOTICE I'D FED.

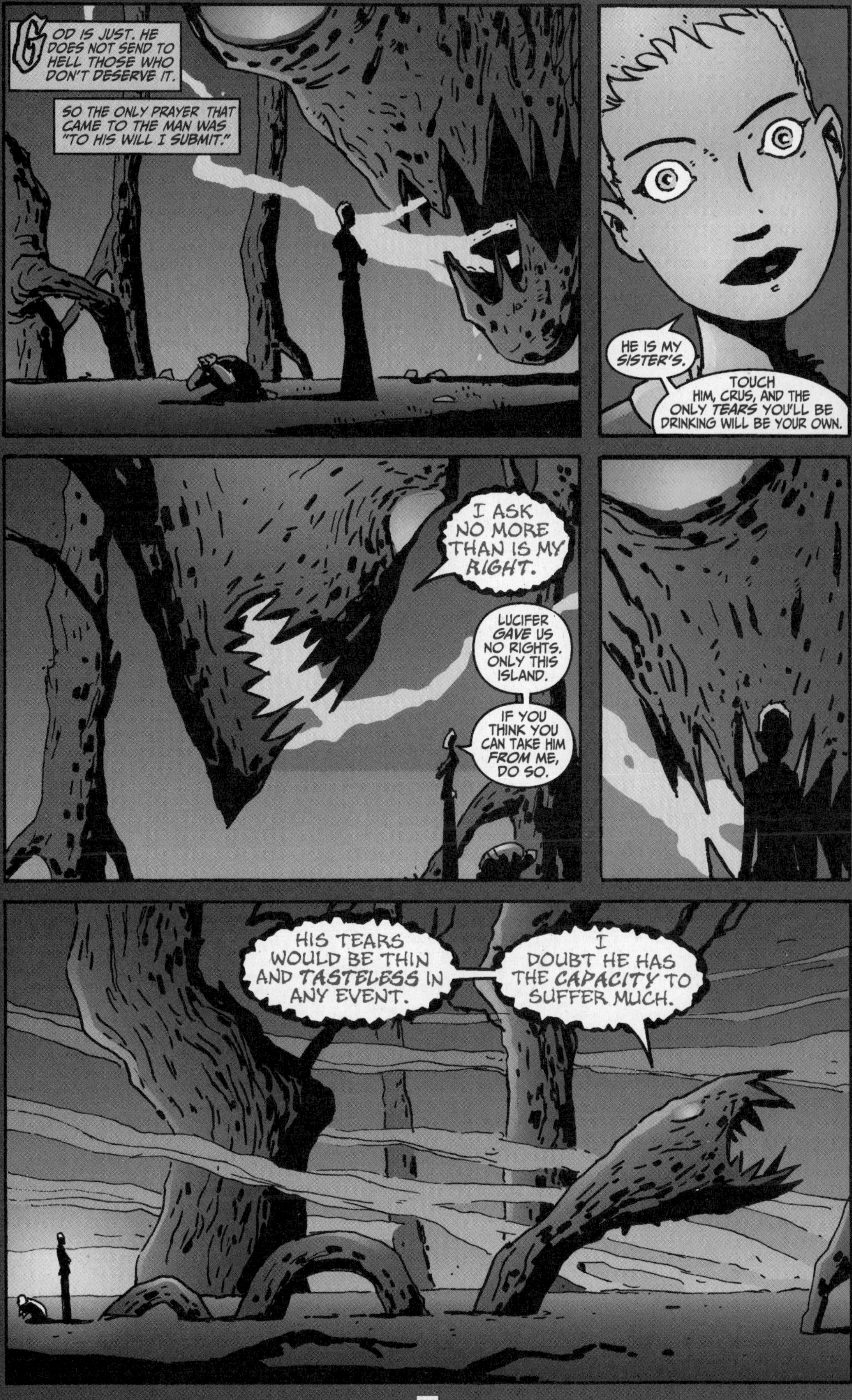
GOD IS JUST. HE DOES NOT SEND TO HELL THOSE WHO DON'T DESERVE IT.
SO THE ONLY PRAYER THAT CAME TO THE MAN WAS "TO HIS WILL I SUBMIT."
HE IS MY SISTER'S.
TOUCH HIM, CRUS, AND THE ONLY TEARS YOU'LL BE DRINKING WILL BE YOUR OWN.
I ASK NO MORE THAN IS MY RIGHT.
LUCIFER GAVE US NO RIGHTS. ONLY THIS ISLAND.
IF YOU THINK YOU CAN TAKE HIM FROM ME, DO SO.
HIS TEARS WOULD BE THIN AND TASTELESS IN ANY EVENT.
I DOUBT HE HAS THE CAPACITY TO SUFFER MUCH.

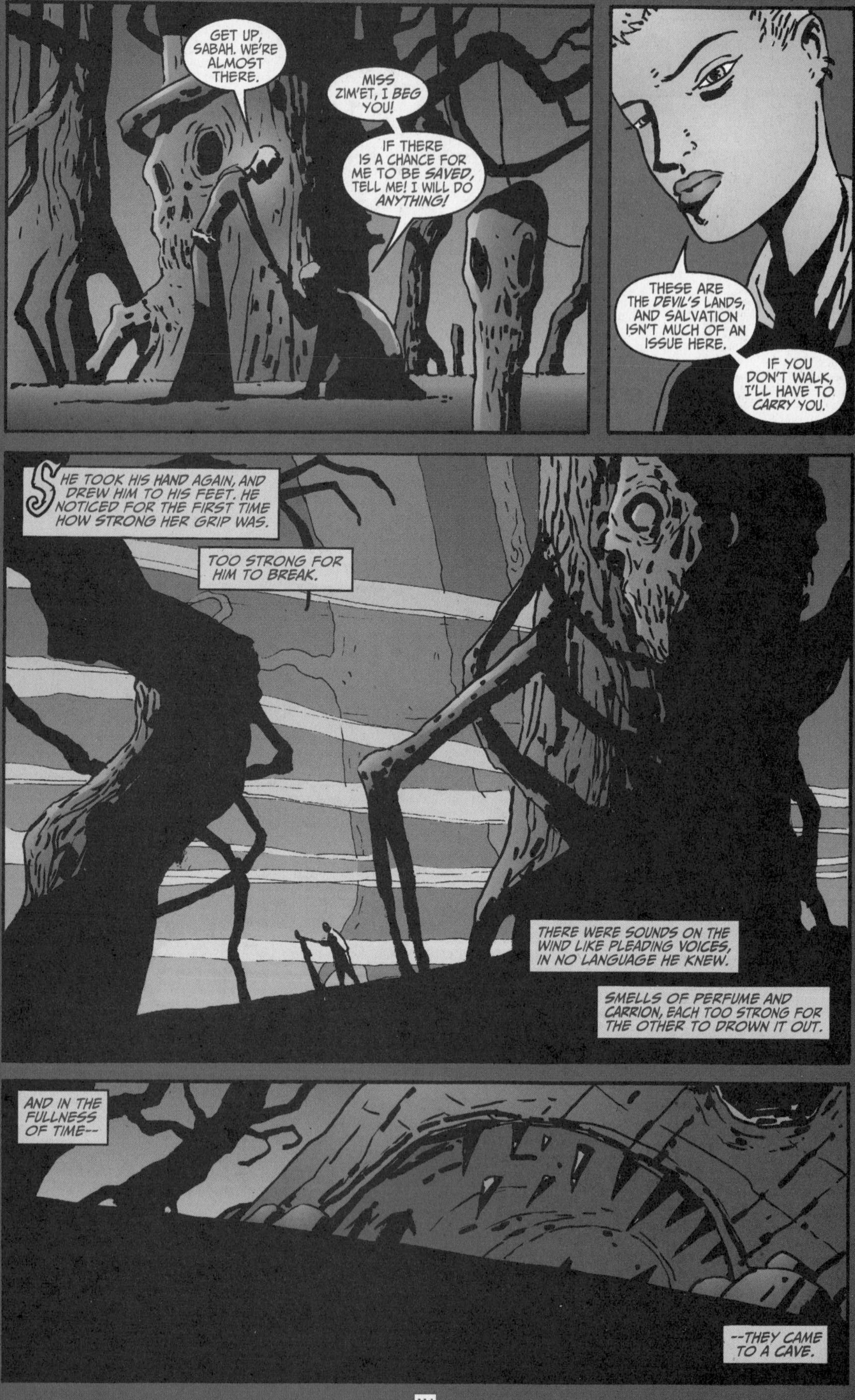

GET UP, SABAH. WE'RE ALMOST THERE.
MISS ZIM'ET, I *BEG* YOU!
IF THERE IS A CHANCE FOR ME TO BE *SAVED*, TELL ME! I WILL DO *ANYTHING!*
THESE ARE THE *DEVIL'S* LANDS, AND SALVATION ISN'T MUCH OF AN ISSUE HERE.
IF YOU DON'T WALK, I'LL HAVE TO *CARRY* YOU.
SHE TOOK HIS HAND AGAIN, AND DREW HIM TO HIS FEET. HE NOTICED FOR THE FIRST TIME HOW STRONG HER GRIP WAS.
TOO STRONG FOR HIM TO BREAK.
THERE WERE SOUNDS ON THE WIND LIKE PLEADING VOICES, IN NO LANGUAGE HE KNEW.
SMELLS OF PERFUME AND CARRION, EACH TOO STRONG FOR THE OTHER TO DROWN IT OUT.
AND IN THE FULLNESS OF TIME--
--THEY CAME TO A CAVE.

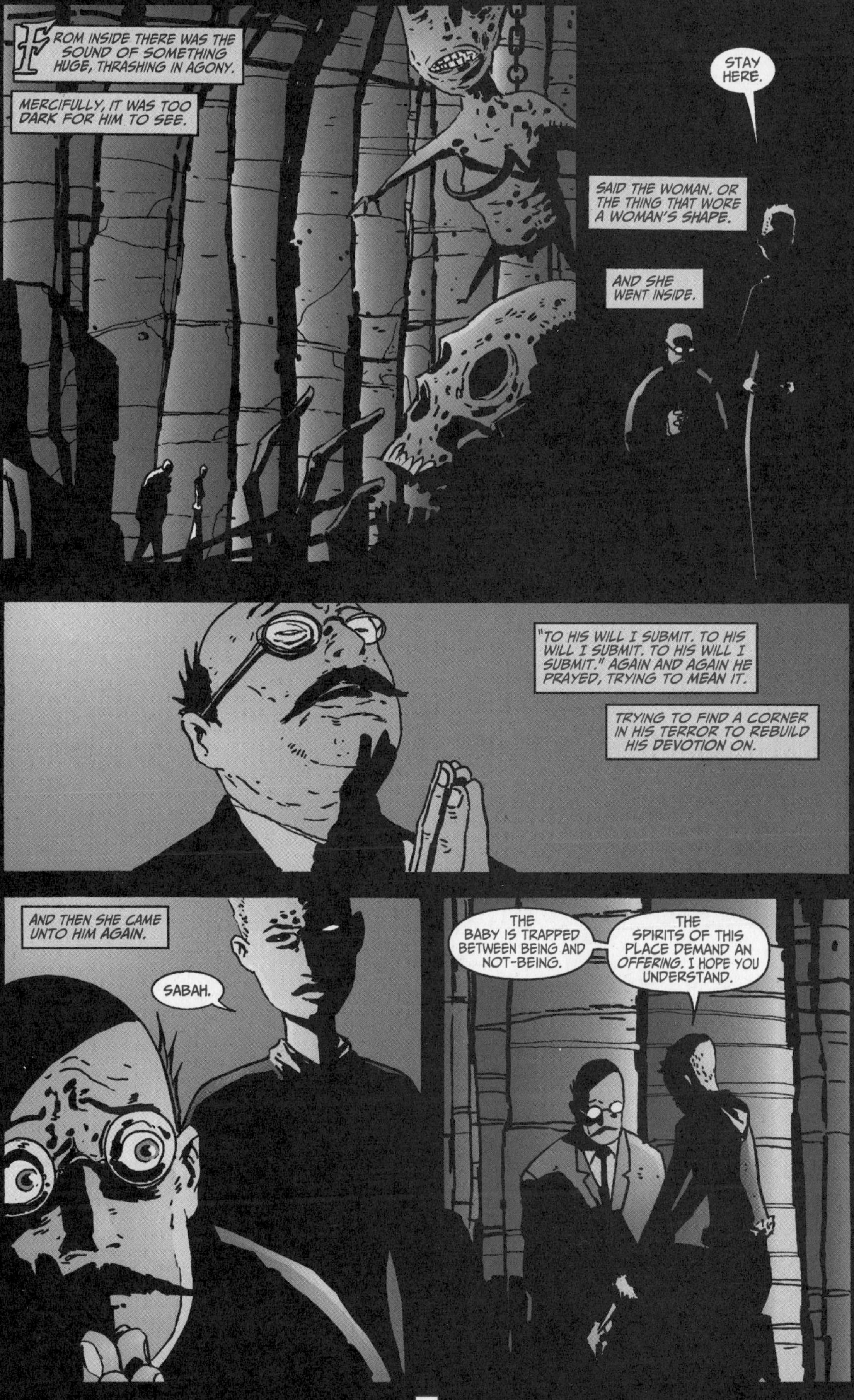
FROM INSIDE THERE WAS THE SOUND OF SOMETHING HUGE, THRASHING IN AGONY.
MERCIFULLY, IT WAS TOO DARK FOR HIM TO SEE.
STAY HERE.
SAID THE WOMAN. OR THE THING THAT WORE A WOMAN'S SHAPE.
AND SHE WENT INSIDE.
"TO HIS WILL I SUBMIT. TO HIS WILL I SUBMIT. TO HIS WILL I SUBMIT." AGAIN AND AGAIN HE PRAYED, TRYING TO MEAN IT.
TRYING TO FIND A CORNER IN HIS TERROR TO REBUILD HIS DEVOTION ON.
AND THEN SHE CAME UNTO HIM AGAIN.
SABAH.
THE BABY IS TRAPPED BETWEEN BEING AND NOT-BEING.
THE SPIRITS OF THIS PLACE DEMAND AN OFFERING. I HOPE YOU UNDERSTAND.

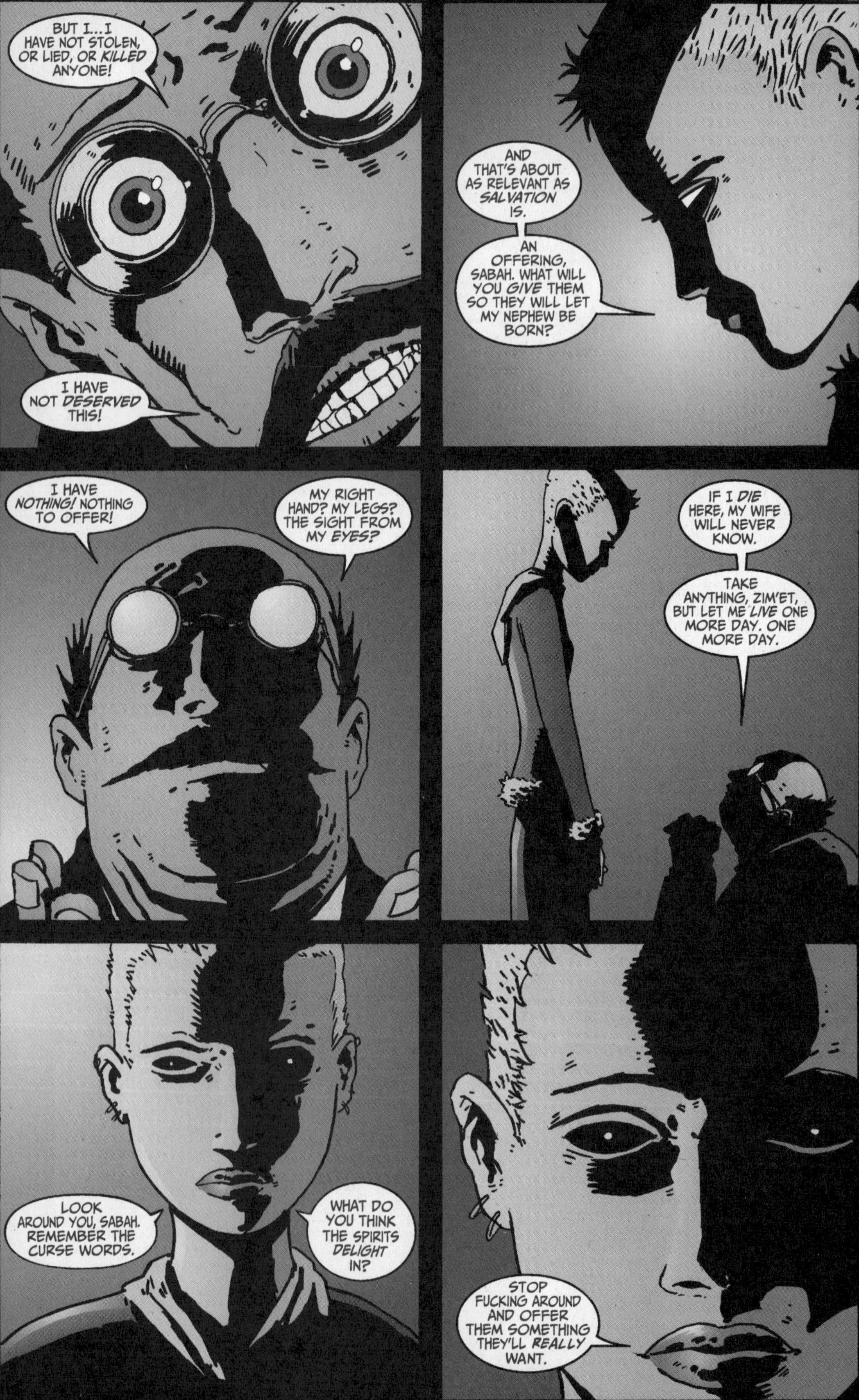

BUT I...I HAVE NOT STOLEN, OR LIED, OR *KILLED* ANYONE!
I HAVE NOT *DESERVED* THIS!
AND THAT'S ABOUT AS RELEVANT AS *SALVATION* IS.
AN OFFERING, SABAH. WHAT WILL YOU *GIVE* THEM SO THEY WILL LET MY NEPHEW BE BORN?
I HAVE *NOTHING!* NOTHING TO OFFER!
MY RIGHT HAND? MY LEGS? THE SIGHT FROM MY *EYES?*
IF I *DIE* HERE, MY WIFE WILL NEVER KNOW.
TAKE ANYTHING, ZIM'ET, BUT LET ME *LIVE* ONE MORE DAY. ONE MORE DAY.
LOOK AROUND YOU, SABAH. REMEMBER THE CURSE WORDS.
WHAT DO YOU THINK THE SPIRITS *DELIGHT* IN?
STOP FUCKING AROUND AND OFFER THEM SOMETHING THEY'LL *REALLY* WANT.

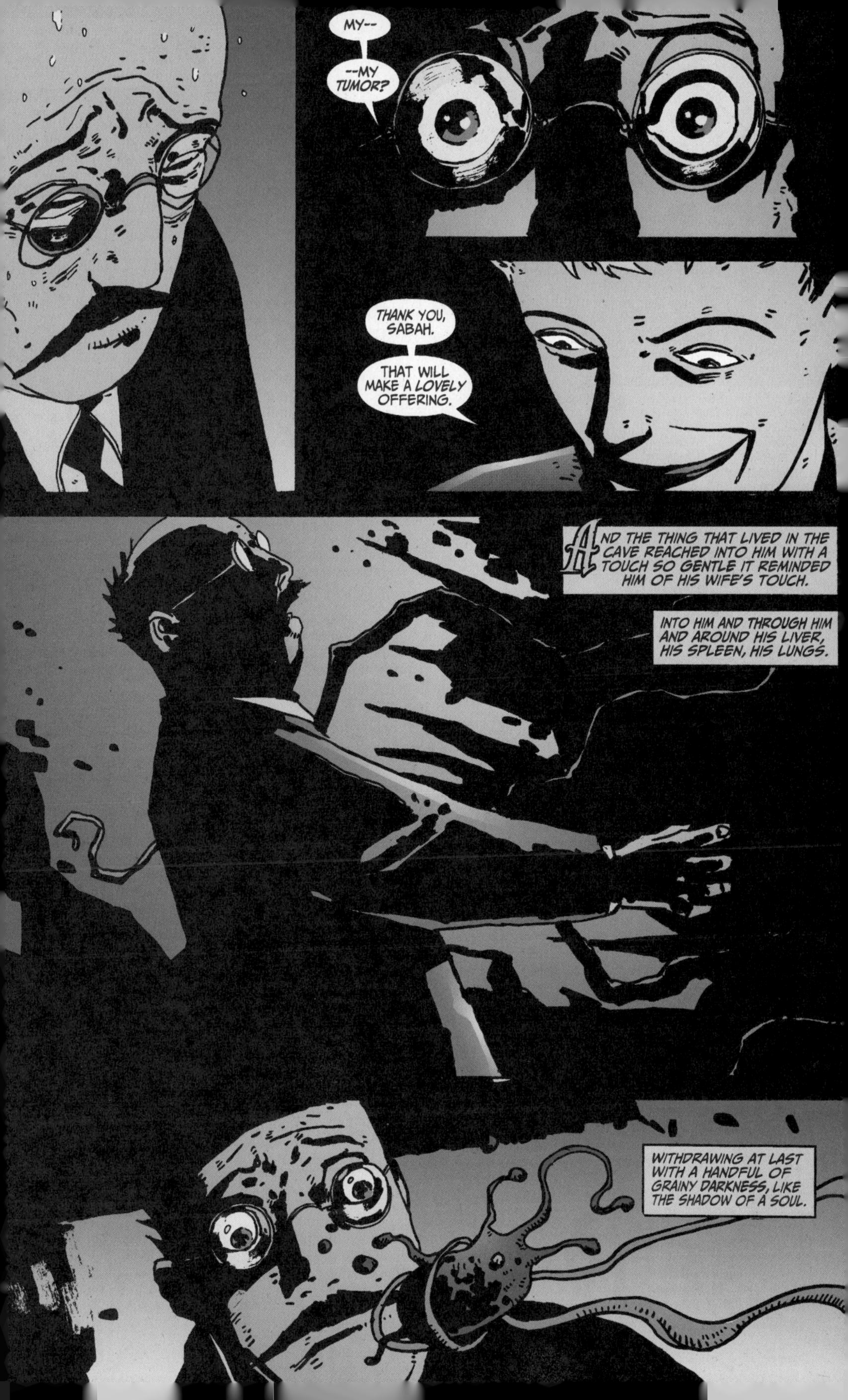

MY--
--MY TUMOR?
THANK YOU, SABAH.
THAT WILL MAKE A LOVELY OFFERING.
AND THE THING THAT LIVED IN THE CAVE REACHED INTO HIM WITH A TOUCH SO GENTLE IT REMINDED HIM OF HIS WIFE'S TOUCH.
INTO HIM AND THROUGH HIM AND AROUND HIS LIVER, HIS SPLEEN, HIS LUNGS.
WITHDRAWING AT LAST WITH A HANDFUL OF GRAINY DARKNESS, LIKE THE SHADOW OF A SOUL.

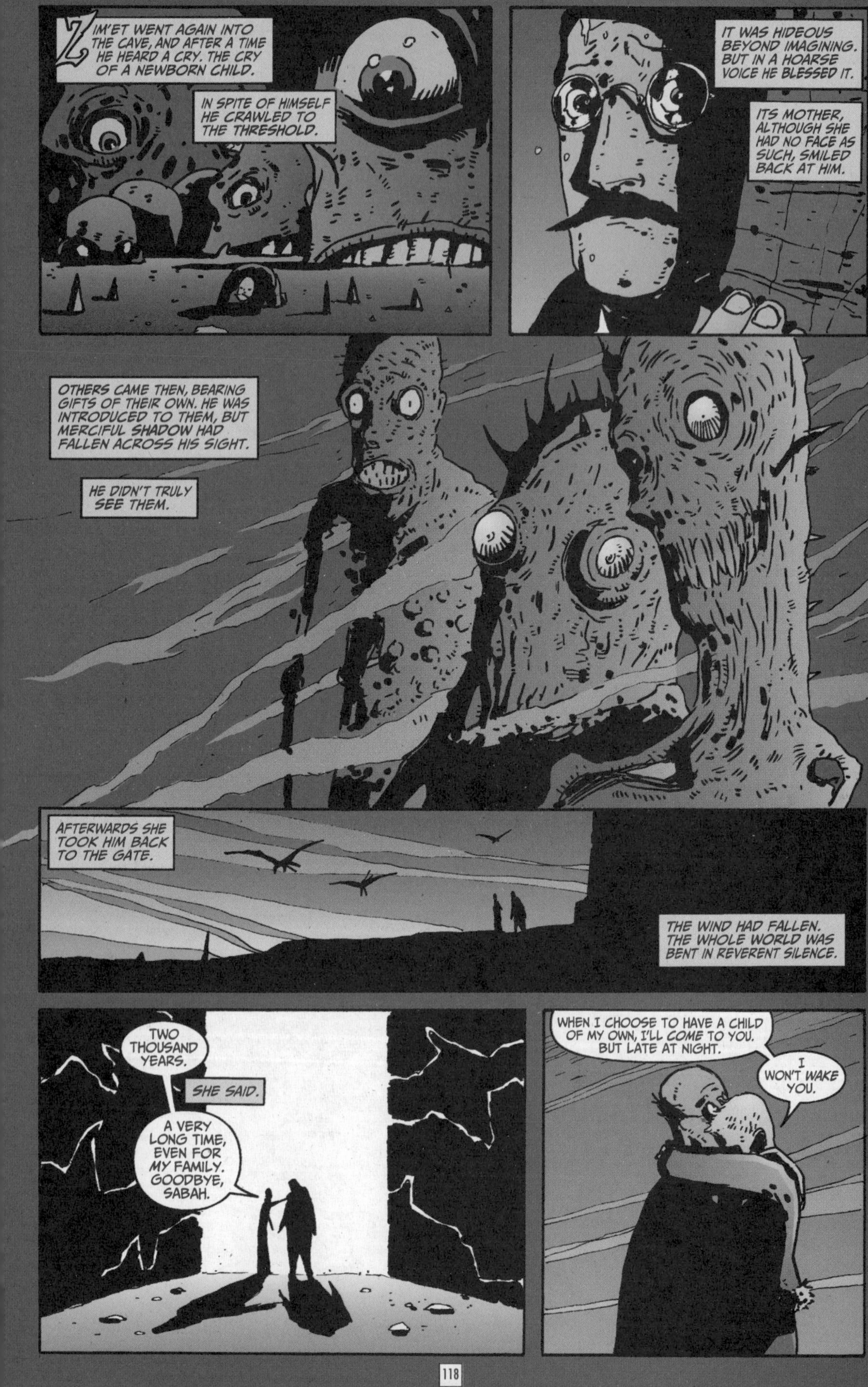
Zim'et went again into the cave, and after a time he heard a cry. The cry of a newborn child.
In spite of himself he crawled to the threshold.
It was hideous beyond imagining. But in a hoarse voice he blessed it.
Its mother, although she had no face as such, smiled back at him.
Others came then, bearing gifts of their own. He was introduced to them, but merciful shadow had fallen across his sight.
He didn't truly see them.
Afterwards she took him back to the gate.
The wind had fallen. The whole world was bent in reverent silence.
Two thousand years.
She said.
A very long time, even for my family. Goodbye, Sabah.
When I choose to have a child of my own, I'll come to you. But late at night.
I won't wake you.

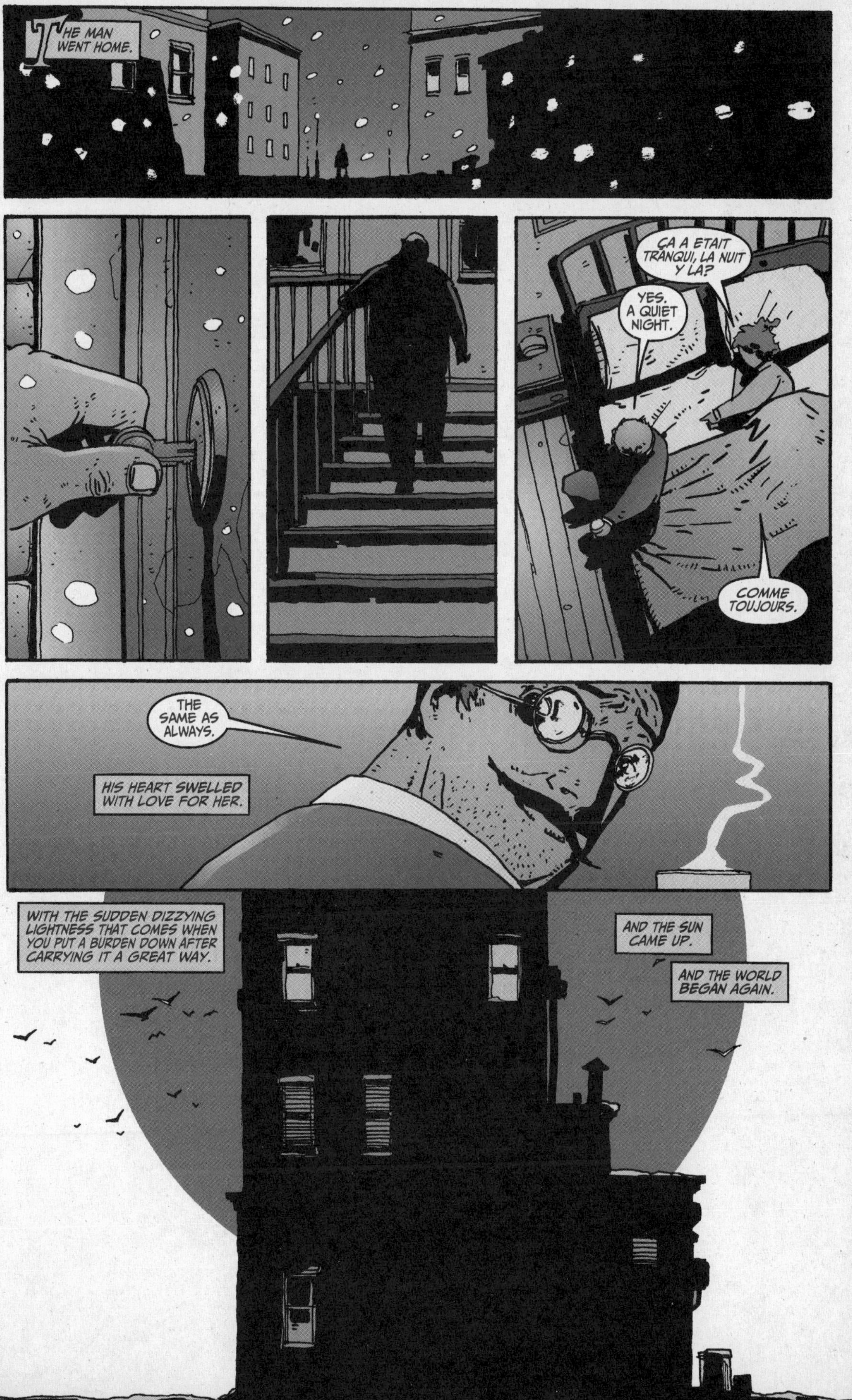
THE MAN WENT HOME.
ÇA A ETAIT TRANQUI, LA NUIT Y LA?
YES. A QUIET NIGHT.
COMME TOUJOURS.
THE SAME AS ALWAYS.
HIS HEART SWELLED WITH LOVE FOR HER.
WITH THE SUDDEN DIZZYING LIGHTNESS THAT COMES WHEN YOU PUT A BURDEN DOWN AFTER CARRYING IT A GREAT WAY.
AND THE SUN CAME UP.
AND THE WORLD BEGAN AGAIN.

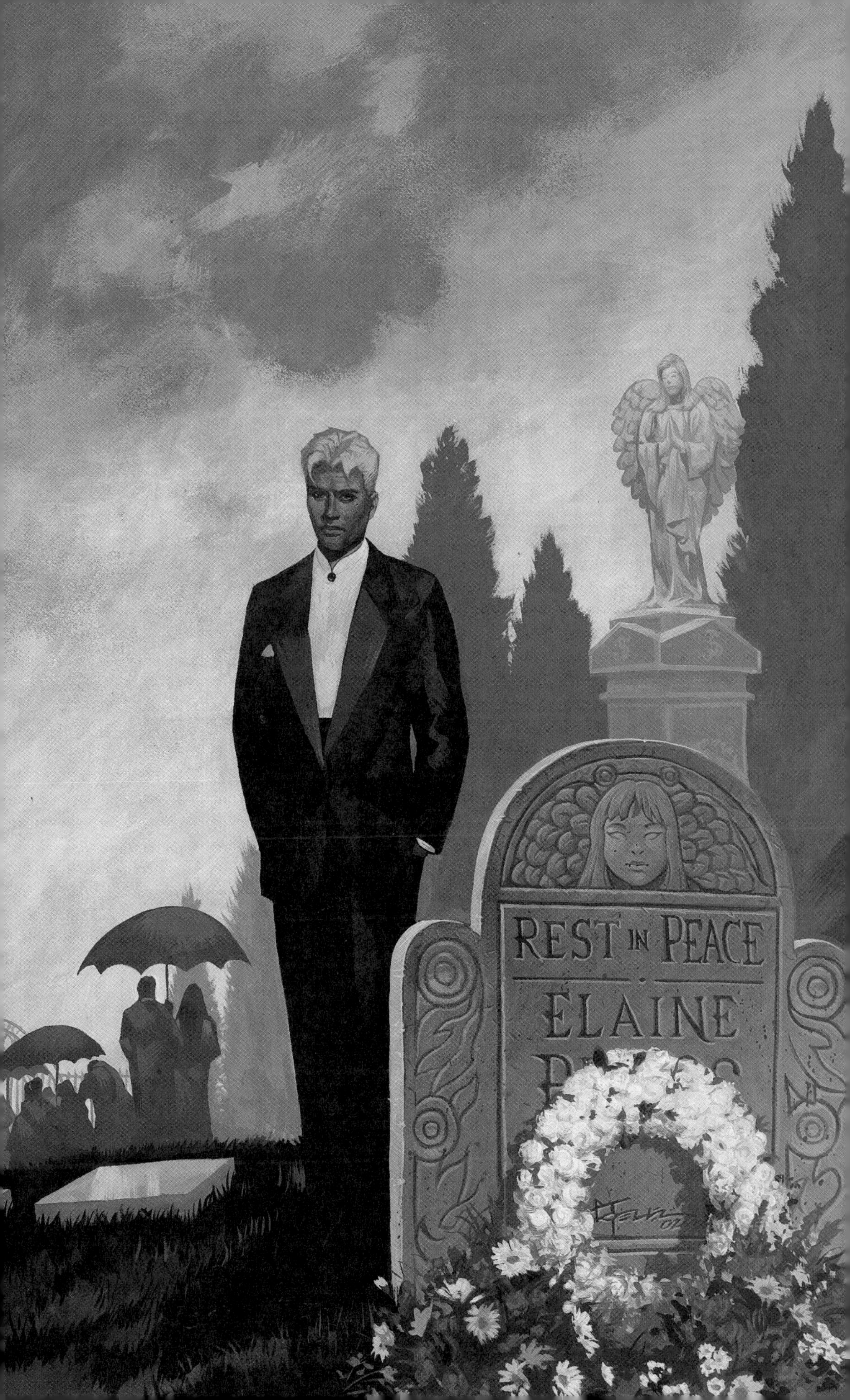
REST IN PEACE
ELAINE

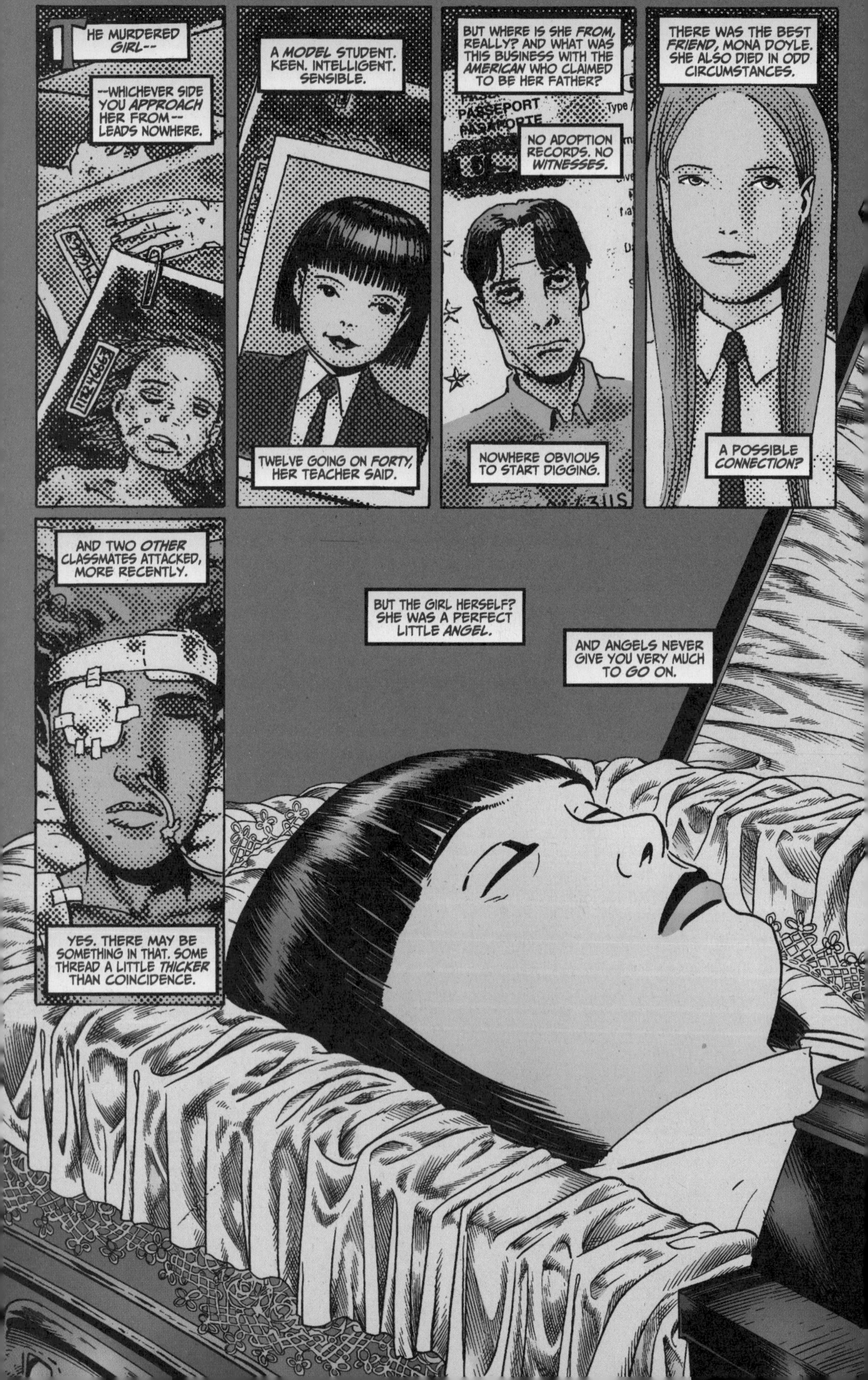
THE MURDERED GIRL--
--WHICHEVER SIDE YOU APPROACH HER FROM--LEADS NOWHERE.
A MODEL STUDENT. KEEN. INTELLIGENT. SENSIBLE.
TWELVE GOING ON FORTY, HER TEACHER SAID.
BUT WHERE IS SHE FROM, REALLY? AND WHAT WAS THIS BUSINESS WITH THE AMERICAN WHO CLAIMED TO BE HER FATHER?
PASSPORT
NO ADOPTION RECORDS. NO WITNESSES.
NOWHERE OBVIOUS TO START DIGGING.
THERE WAS THE BEST FRIEND, MONA DOYLE. SHE ALSO DIED IN ODD CIRCUMSTANCES.
A POSSIBLE CONNECTION?
AND TWO OTHER CLASSMATES ATTACKED, MORE RECENTLY.
YES. THERE MAY BE SOMETHING IN THAT. SOME THREAD A LITTLE THICKER THAN COINCIDENCE.
BUT THE GIRL HERSELF? SHE WAS A PERFECT LITTLE ANGEL.
AND ANGELS NEVER GIVE YOU VERY MUCH TO GO ON.

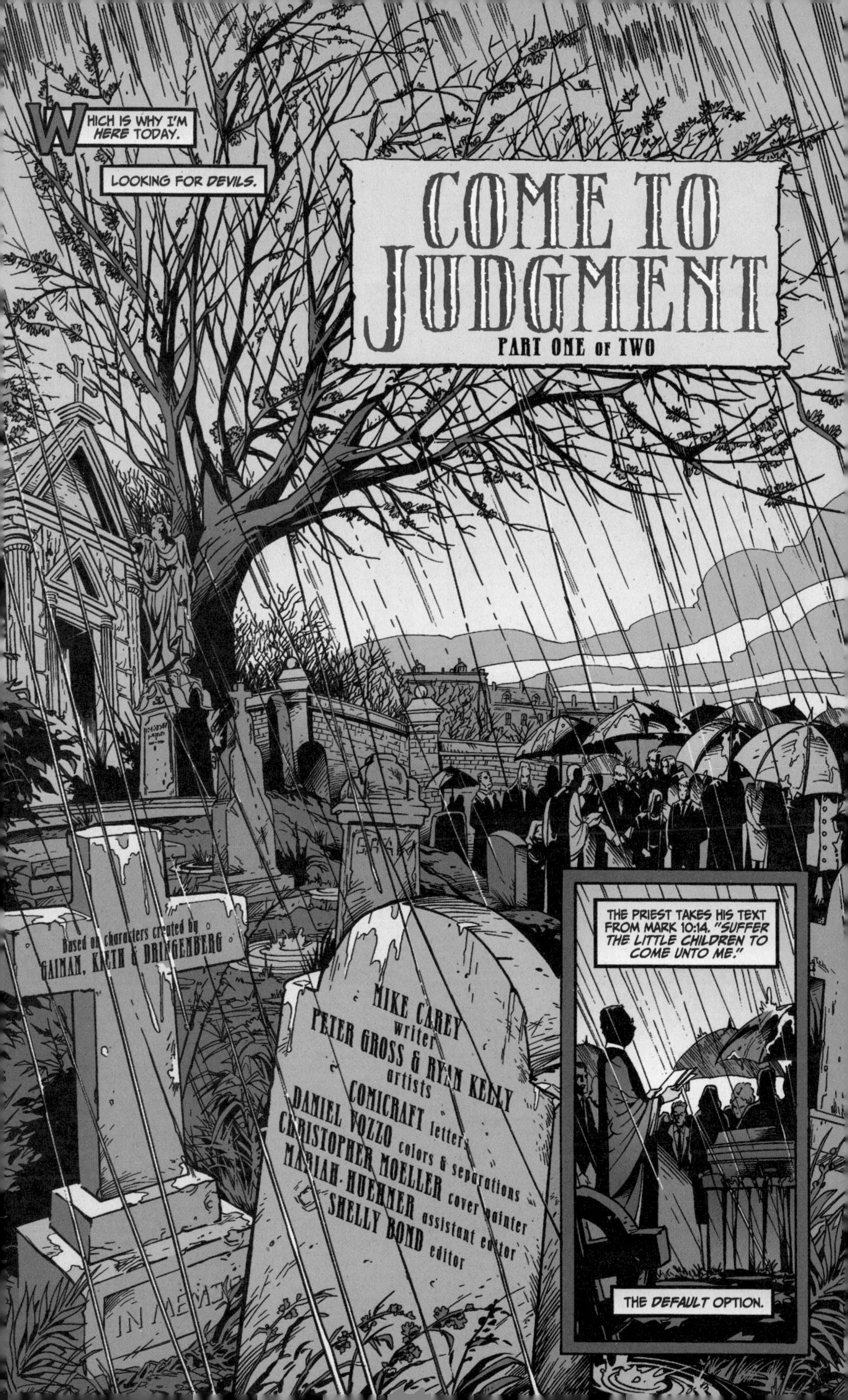
WHICH IS WHY I'M HERE TODAY.
LOOKING FOR DEVILS.
COME TO JUDGMENT
PART ONE OF TWO
Based on characters created by
GAIMAN, KIETH & DRINGENBERG
MIKE CAREY writer
PETER GROSS & RYAN KELLY artists
COMICRAFT letters
DANIEL VOZZO colors & separations
CHRISTOPHER MOELLER cover painter
MARIAH HUEHNER assistant editor
SHELLY BOND editor
IN MEM
THE PRIEST TAKES HIS TEXT FROM MARK 10:14. "SUFFER THE LITTLE CHILDREN TO COME UNTO ME."
THE DEFAULT OPTION.

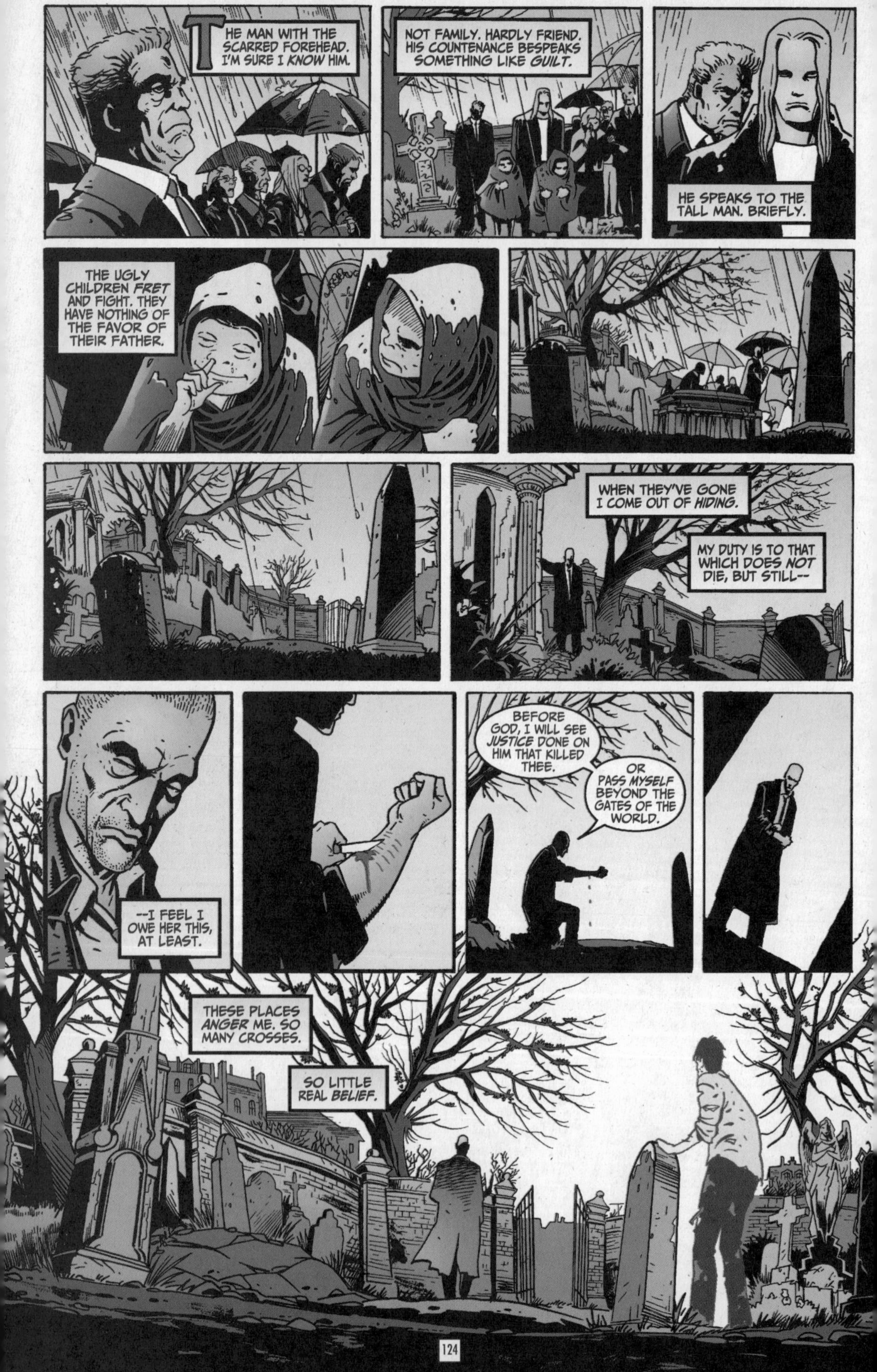
THE MAN WITH THE SCARRED FOREHEAD. I'M SURE I KNOW HIM.
NOT FAMILY. HARDLY FRIEND. HIS COUNTENANCE BESPEAKS SOMETHING LIKE GUILT.
HE SPEAKS TO THE TALL MAN. BRIEFLY.
THE UGLY CHILDREN FRET AND FIGHT. THEY HAVE NOTHING OF THE FAVOR OF THEIR FATHER.
WHEN THEY'VE GONE I COME OUT OF HIDING.
MY DUTY IS TO THAT WHICH DOES NOT DIE, BUT STILL--
--I FEEL I OWE HER THIS, AT LEAST.
BEFORE GOD, I WILL SEE JUSTICE DONE ON HIM THAT KILLED THEE.
OR PASS MYSELF BEYOND THE GATES OF THE WORLD.
THESE PLACES ANGER ME. SO MANY CROSSES.
SO LITTLE REAL BELIEF.

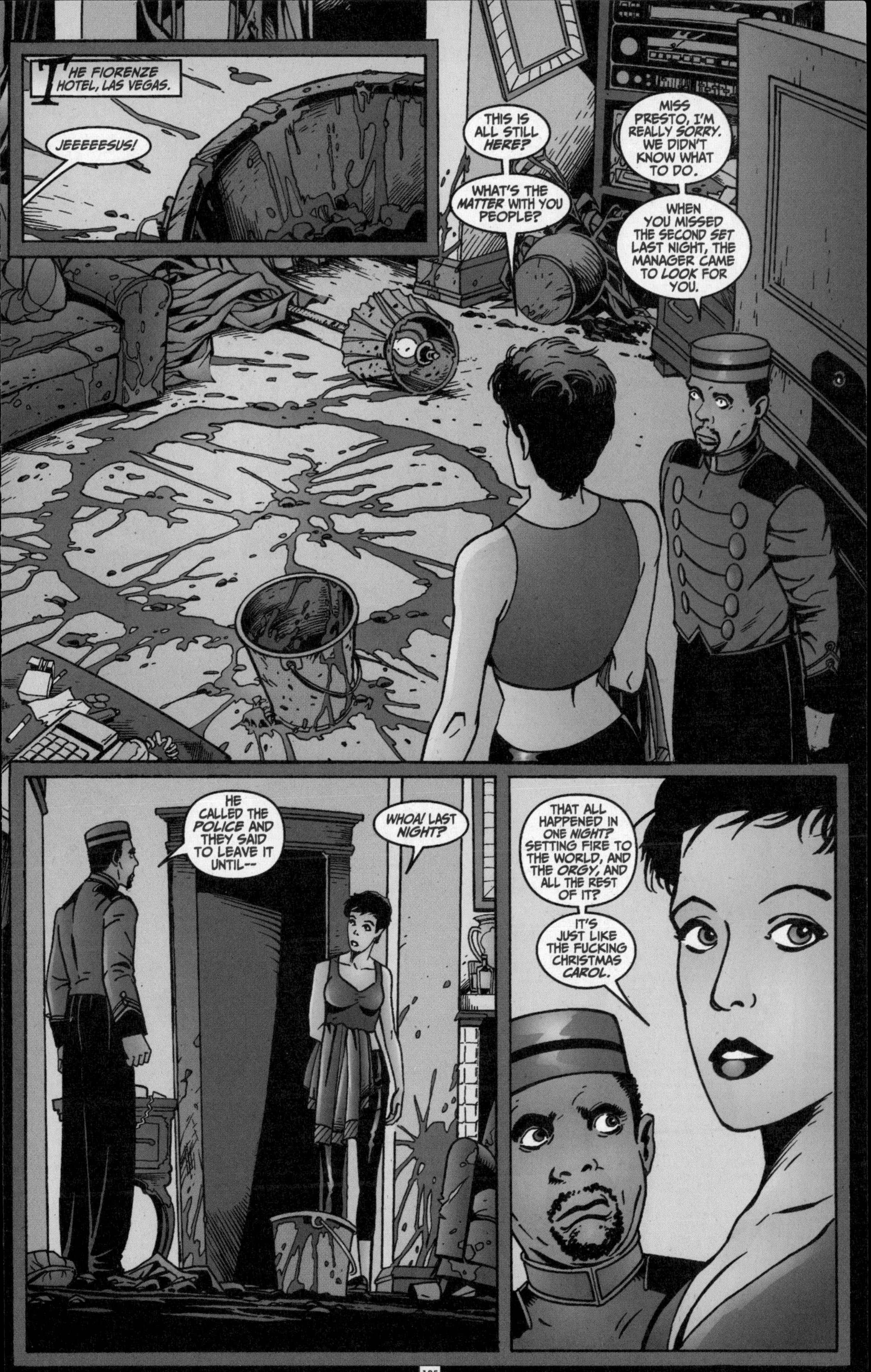
THE FIORENZE HOTEL, LAS VEGAS.
JEEEEESUS!
THIS IS ALL STILL HERE?
WHAT'S THE MATTER WITH YOU PEOPLE?
MISS PRESTO, I'M REALLY SORRY. WE DIDN'T KNOW WHAT TO DO.
WHEN YOU MISSED THE SECOND SET LAST NIGHT, THE MANAGER CAME TO LOOK FOR YOU.
HE CALLED THE POLICE AND THEY SAID TO LEAVE IT UNTIL--
WHOA! LAST NIGHT?
THAT ALL HAPPENED IN ONE NIGHT? SETTING FIRE TO THE WORLD, AND THE ORGY, AND ALL THE REST OF IT?
IT'S JUST LIKE THE FUCKING CHRISTMAS CAROL.

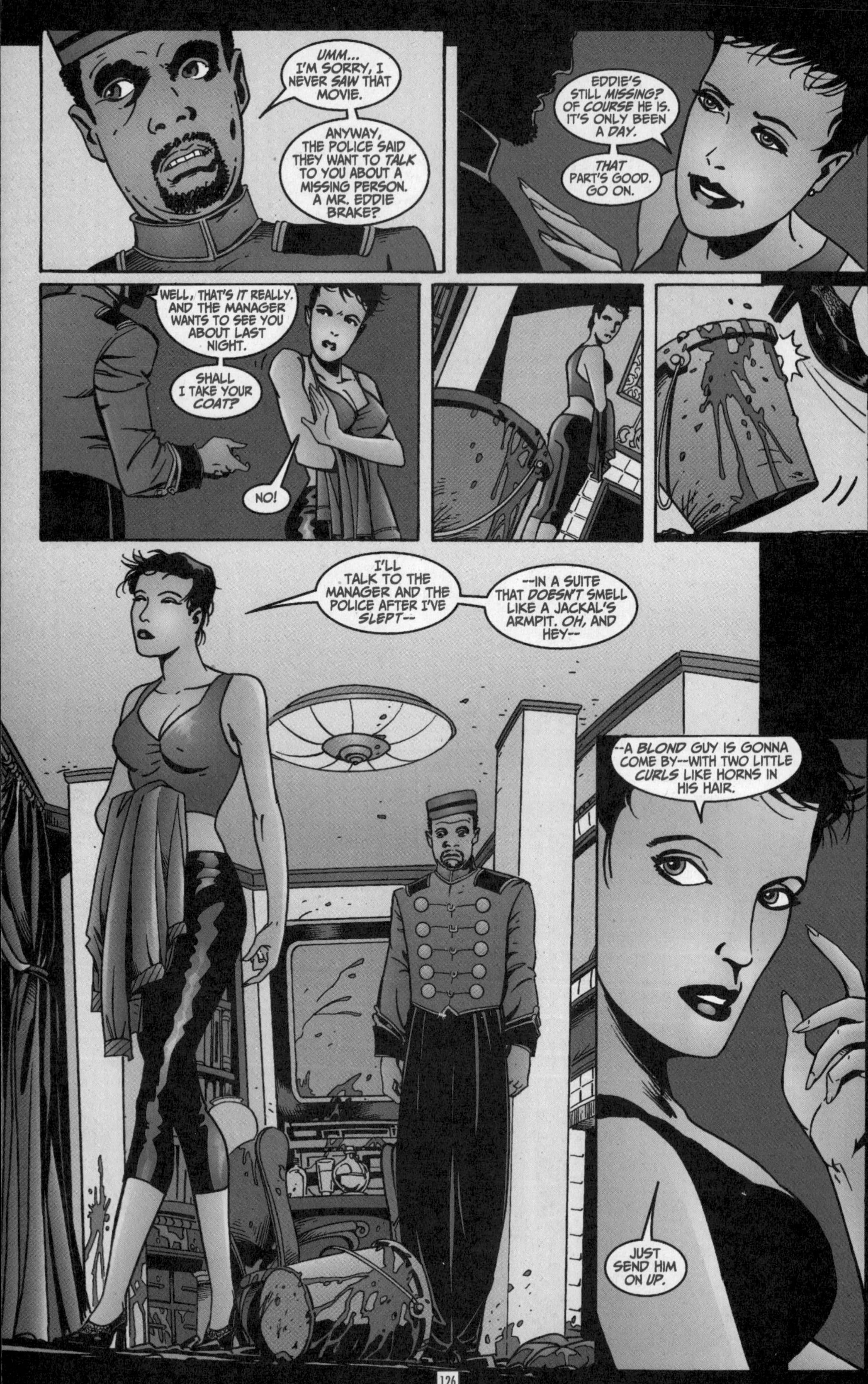
UMM... I'M SORRY, I NEVER SAW THAT MOVIE.
ANYWAY, THE POLICE SAID THEY WANT TO TALK TO YOU ABOUT A MISSING PERSON. A MR. EDDIE BRAKE?
EDDIE'S STILL MISSING? OF COURSE HE IS. IT'S ONLY BEEN A DAY.
THAT PART'S GOOD. GO ON.
WELL, THAT'S IT REALLY. AND THE MANAGER WANTS TO SEE YOU ABOUT LAST NIGHT.
SHALL I TAKE YOUR COAT?
NO!
I'LL TALK TO THE MANAGER AND THE POLICE AFTER I'VE SLEPT--
--IN A SUITE THAT DOESN'T SMELL LIKE A JACKAL'S ARMPIT. OH, AND HEY--
--A BLOND GUY IS GONNA COME BY--WITH TWO LITTLE CURLS LIKE HORNS IN HIS HAIR.
JUST SEND HIM ON UP.

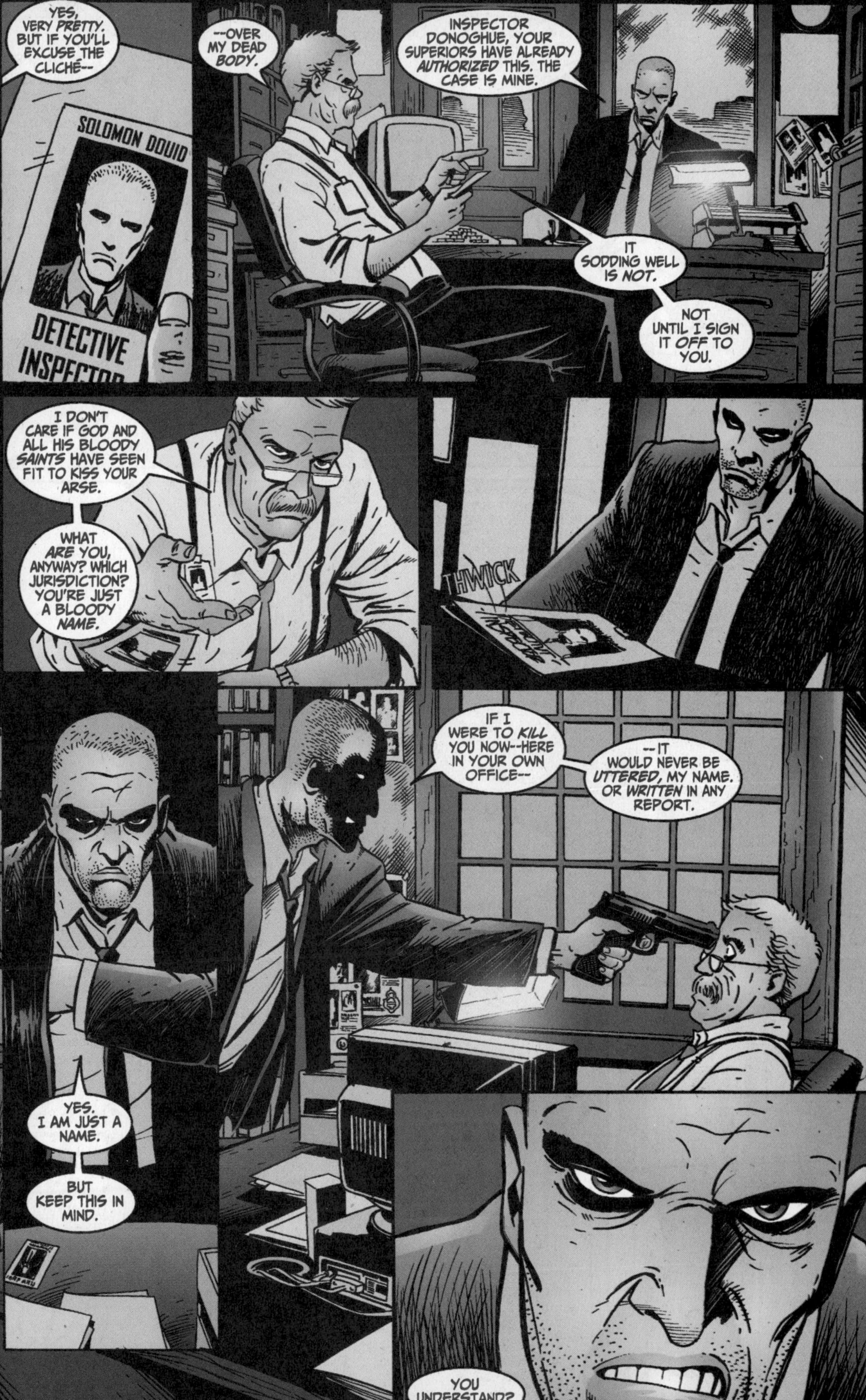
YES, VERY PRETTY. BUT IF YOU'LL EXCUSE THE CLICHÉ--
SOLOMON DOUID
DETECTIVE INSPECTOR
--OVER MY DEAD BODY.
INSPECTOR DONOGHUE, YOUR SUPERIORS HAVE ALREADY AUTHORIZED THIS. THE CASE IS MINE.
IT SODDING WELL IS NOT.
NOT UNTIL I SIGN IT OFF TO YOU.
I DON'T CARE IF GOD AND ALL HIS BLOODY SAINTS HAVE SEEN FIT TO KISS YOUR ARSE.
WHAT ARE YOU, ANYWAY? WHICH JURISDICTION? YOU'RE JUST A BLOODY NAME.
THWICK
IF I WERE TO KILL YOU NOW--HERE IN YOUR OWN OFFICE--
--IT WOULD NEVER BE UTTERED, MY NAME. OR WRITTEN IN ANY REPORT.
YES. I AM JUST A NAME.
BUT KEEP THIS IN MIND.
YOU UNDERSTAND?

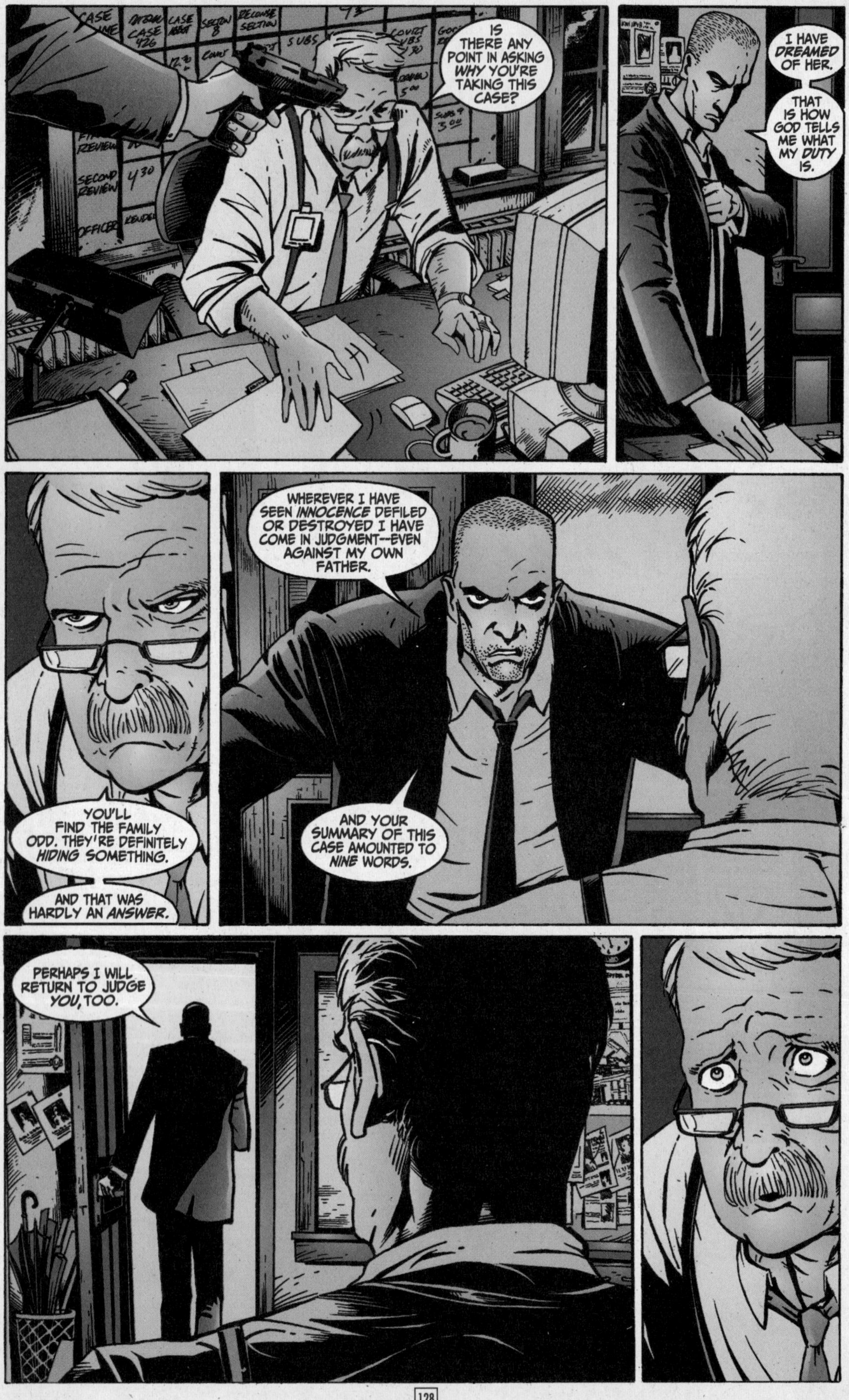
IS THERE ANY POINT IN ASKING WHY YOU'RE TAKING THIS CASE?
I HAVE DREAMED OF HER.
THAT IS HOW GOD TELLS ME WHAT MY DUTY IS.
YOU'LL FIND THE FAMILY ODD. THEY'RE DEFINITELY HIDING SOMETHING.
AND THAT WAS HARDLY AN ANSWER.
WHEREVER I HAVE SEEN INNOCENCE DEFILED OR DESTROYED I HAVE COME IN JUDGMENT--EVEN AGAINST MY OWN FATHER.
AND YOUR SUMMARY OF THIS CASE AMOUNTED TO NINE WORDS.
PERHAPS I WILL RETURN TO JUDGE YOU, TOO.

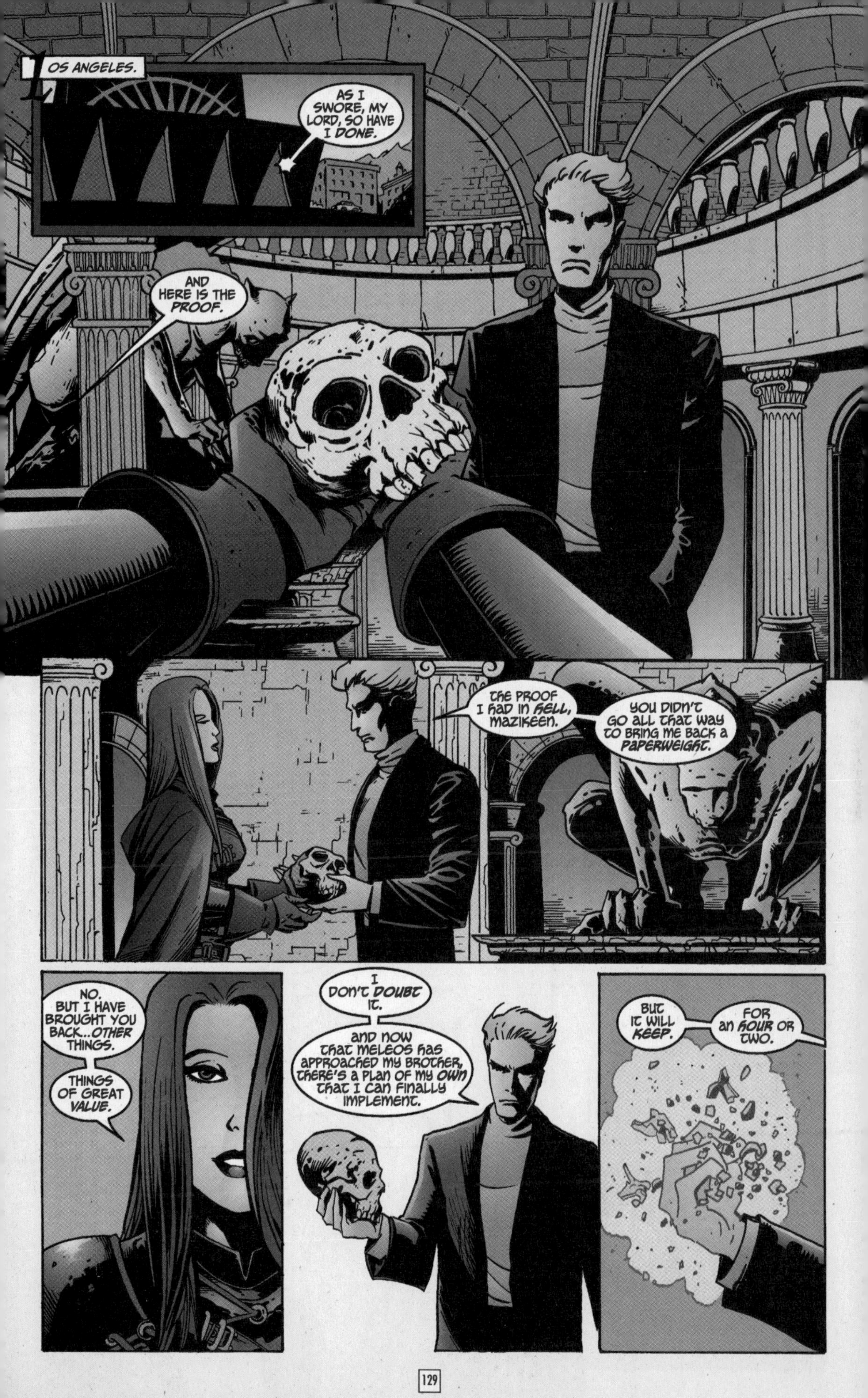
LOS ANGELES.
AS I SWORE, MY LORD, SO HAVE I DONE.
AND HERE IS THE PROOF.
THE PROOF I HAD IN HELL, MAZIKEEN.
YOU DIDN'T GO ALL THAT WAY TO BRING ME BACK A PAPERWEIGHT.
NO. BUT I HAVE BROUGHT YOU BACK...OTHER THINGS.
THINGS OF GREAT VALUE.
I DON'T DOUBT IT.
AND NOW THAT MELEOS HAS APPROACHED MY BROTHER, THERE'S A PLAN OF MY OWN THAT I CAN FINALLY IMPLEMENT.
BUT IT WILL KEEP.
FOR AN HOUR OR TWO.

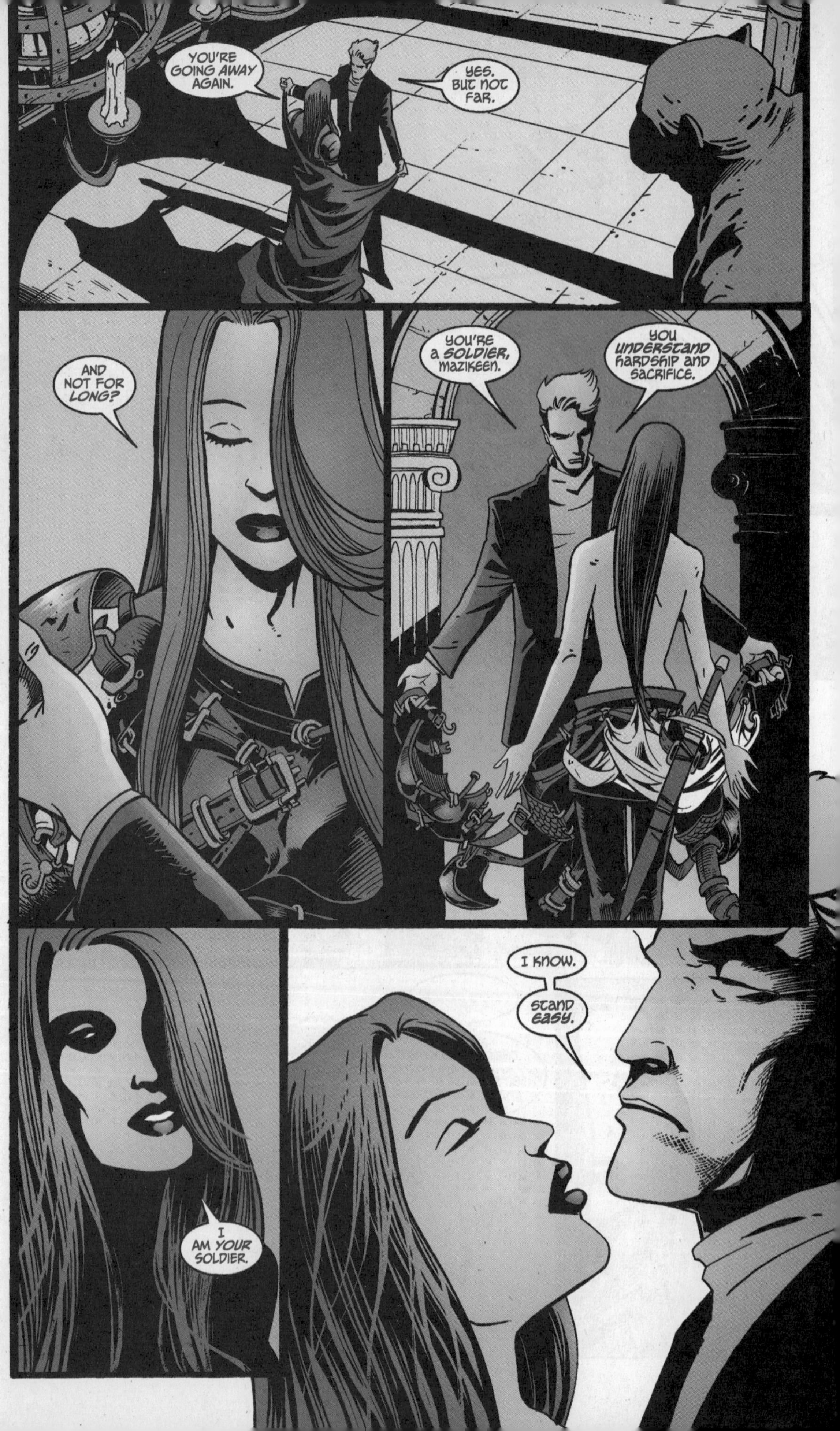
YOU'RE GOING AWAY AGAIN.
YES. BUT NOT FAR.
AND NOT FOR LONG?
YOU'RE A SOLDIER, MAZIKEEN.
YOU UNDERSTAND HARDSHIP AND SACRIFICE.
I AM YOUR SOLDIER.
I KNOW.
STAND EASY.

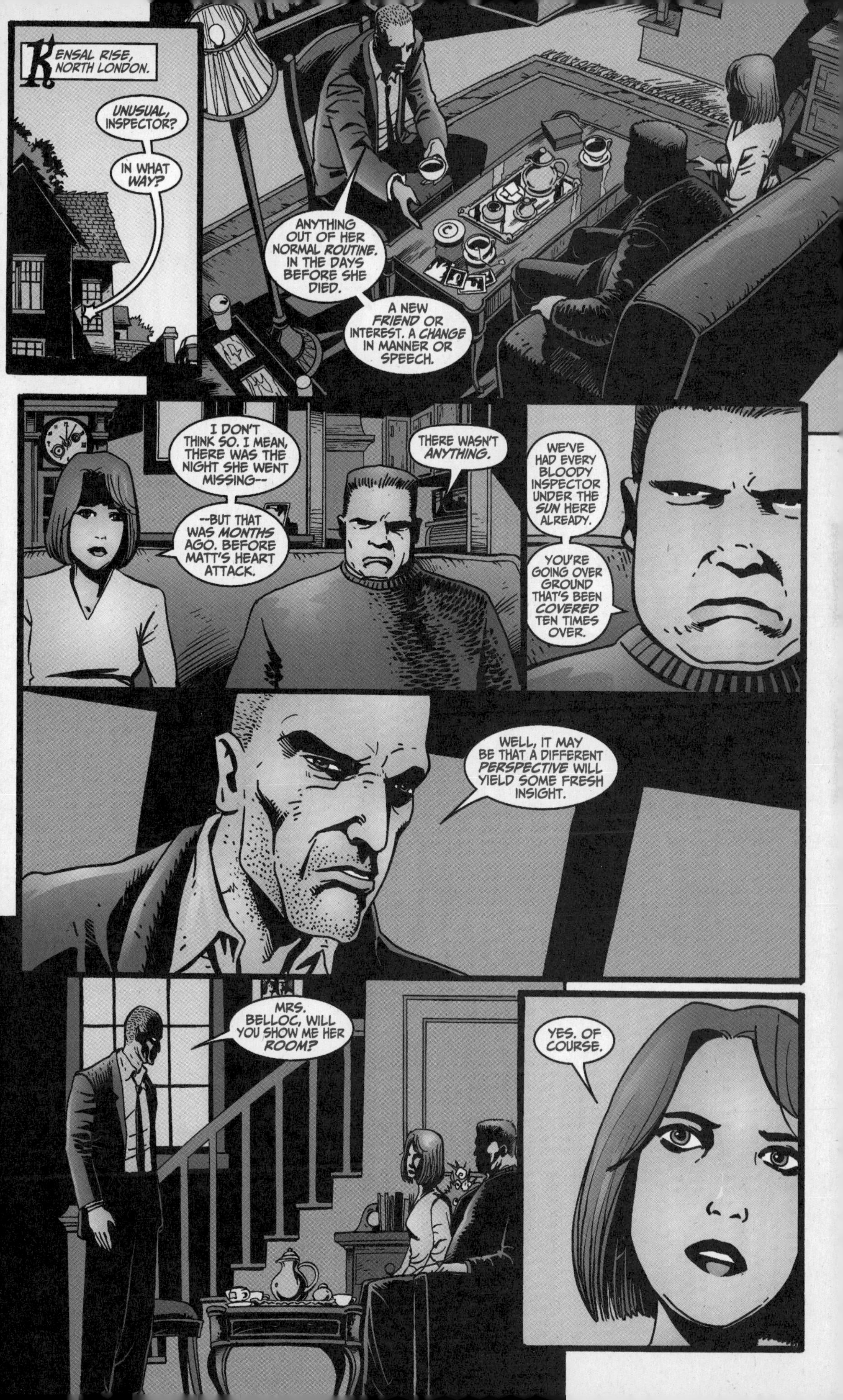
KENSAL RISE, NORTH LONDON.
UNUSUAL, INSPECTOR?
IN WHAT WAY?
ANYTHING OUT OF HER NORMAL ROUTINE. IN THE DAYS BEFORE SHE DIED.
A NEW FRIEND OR INTEREST. A CHANGE IN MANNER OR SPEECH.
I DON'T THINK SO. I MEAN, THERE WAS THE NIGHT SHE WENT MISSING--
--BUT THAT WAS MONTHS AGO. BEFORE MATT'S HEART ATTACK.
THERE WASN'T ANYTHING.
WE'VE HAD EVERY BLOODY INSPECTOR UNDER THE SUN HERE ALREADY.
YOU'RE GOING OVER GROUND THAT'S BEEN COVERED TEN TIMES OVER.
WELL, IT MAY BE THAT A DIFFERENT PERSPECTIVE WILL YIELD SOME FRESH INSIGHT.
MRS. BELLOC, WILL YOU SHOW ME HER ROOM?
YES. OF COURSE.

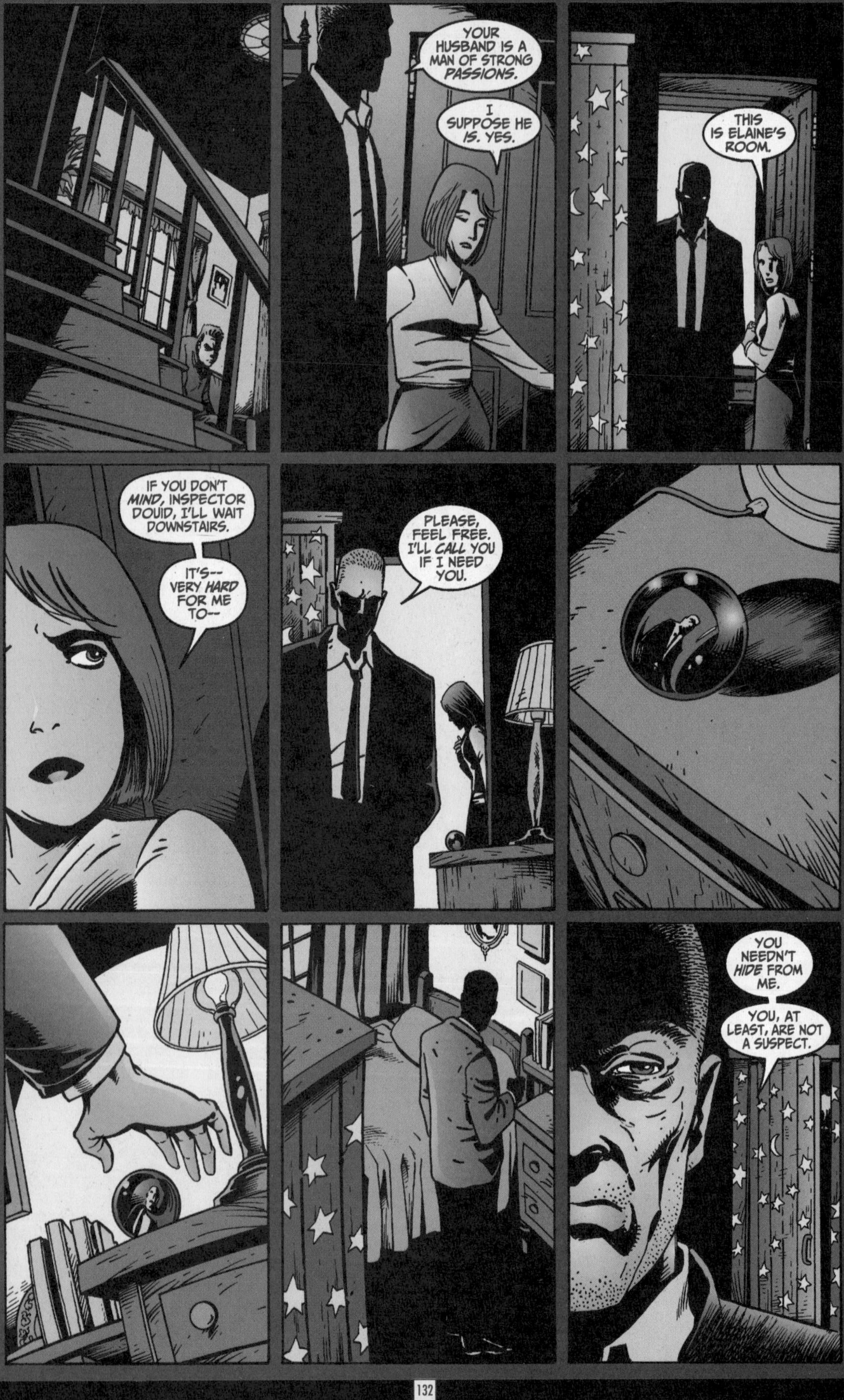
YOUR HUSBAND IS A MAN OF STRONG PASSIONS.
I SUPPOSE HE IS. YES.
THIS IS ELAINE'S ROOM.
IF YOU DON'T MIND, INSPECTOR DOUID, I'LL WAIT DOWNSTAIRS.
IT'S-- VERY HARD FOR ME TO--
PLEASE, FEEL FREE. I'LL CALL YOU IF I NEED YOU.
YOU NEEDN'T HIDE FROM ME.
YOU, AT LEAST, ARE NOT A SUSPECT.

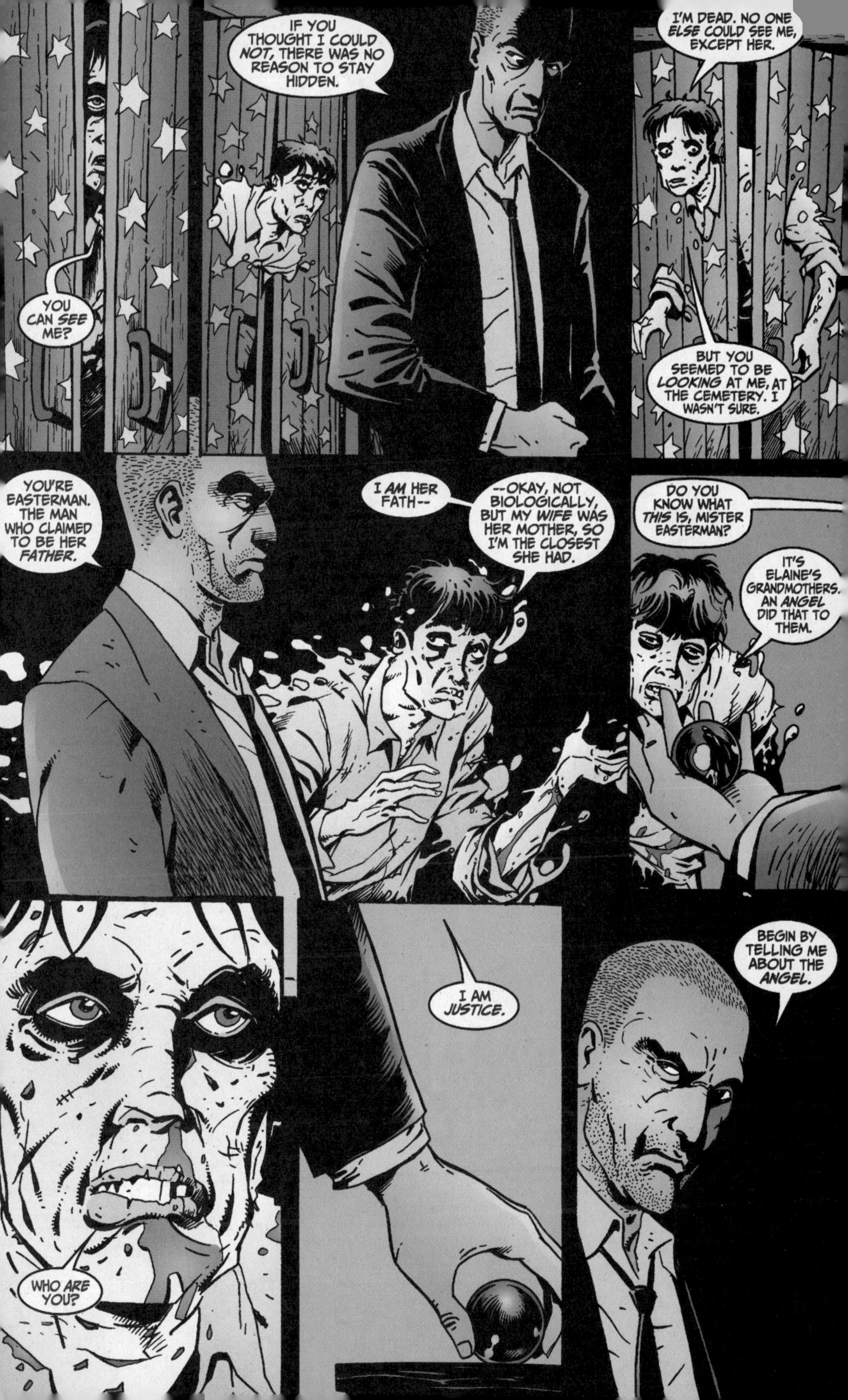

YOU CAN SEE ME?
IF YOU THOUGHT I COULD NOT, THERE WAS NO REASON TO STAY HIDDEN.
I'M DEAD. NO ONE ELSE COULD SEE ME, EXCEPT HER.
BUT YOU SEEMED TO BE LOOKING AT ME, AT THE CEMETERY. I WASN'T SURE.
YOU'RE EASTERMAN. THE MAN WHO CLAIMED TO BE HER FATHER.
I AM HER FATH--
--OKAY, NOT BIOLOGICALLY, BUT MY WIFE WAS HER MOTHER, SO I'M THE CLOSEST SHE HAD.
DO YOU KNOW WHAT THIS IS, MISTER EASTERMAN?
IT'S ELAINE'S GRANDMOTHERS. AN ANGEL DID THAT TO THEM.
WHO ARE YOU?
I AM JUSTICE.
BEGIN BY TELLING ME ABOUT THE ANGEL.

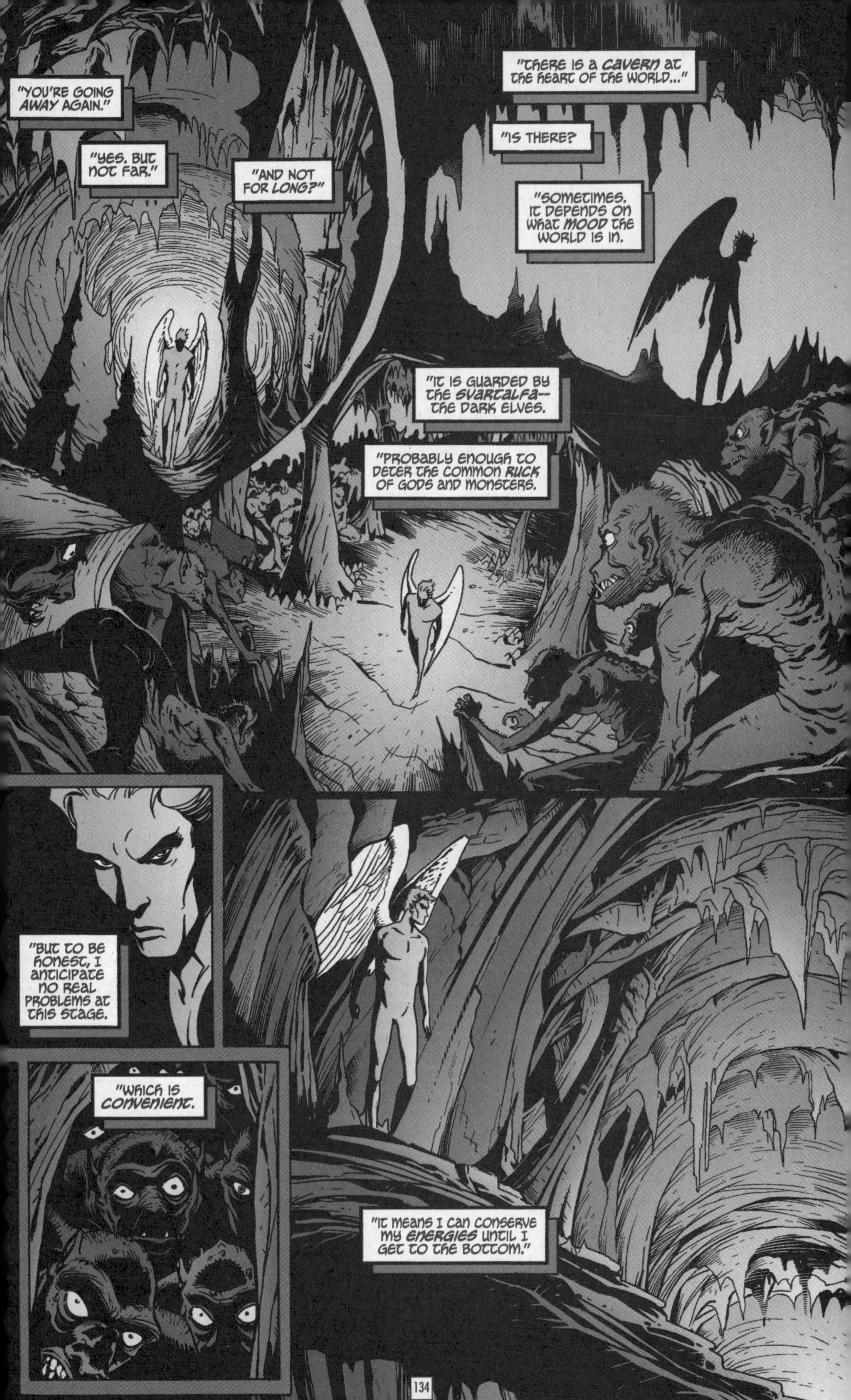
"YOU'RE GOING AWAY AGAIN."
"YES. BUT NOT FAR."
"AND NOT FOR LONG?"
"THERE IS A CAVERN AT THE HEART OF THE WORLD..."
"IS THERE?
"SOMETIMES. IT DEPENDS ON WHAT MOOD THE WORLD IS IN.
"IT IS GUARDED BY THE SVARTALFA-- THE DARK ELVES.
"PROBABLY ENOUGH TO DETER THE COMMON RUCK OF GODS AND MONSTERS.
"BUT TO BE HONEST, I ANTICIPATE NO REAL PROBLEMS AT THIS STAGE.
"WHICH IS CONVENIENT.
"IT MEANS I CAN CONSERVE MY ENERGIES UNTIL I GET TO THE BOTTOM."

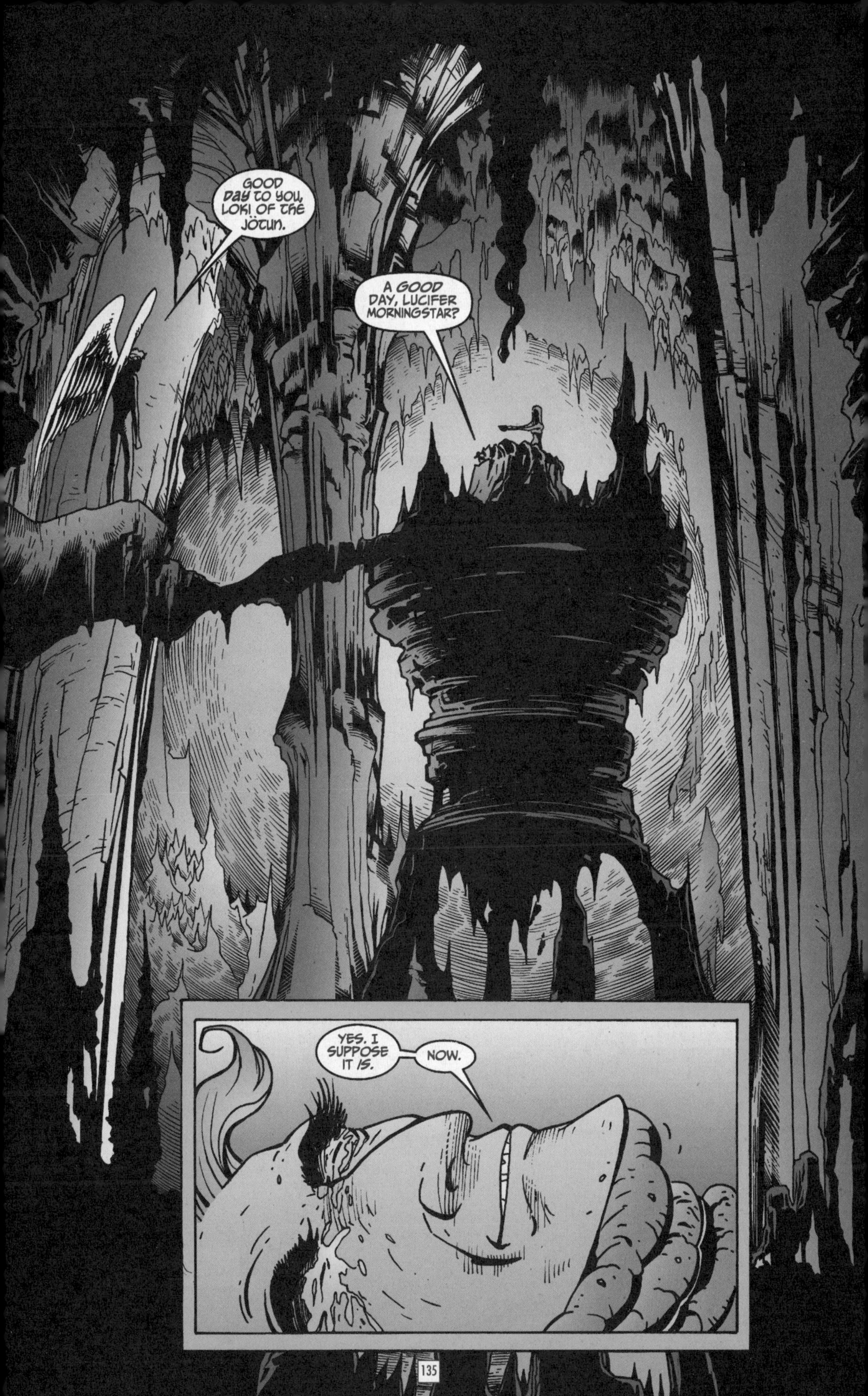
GOOD DAY TO YOU, LOKI OF THE JÖTUN.
A GOOD DAY, LUCIFER MORNINGSTAR?
YES. I SUPPOSE IT IS.
NOW.

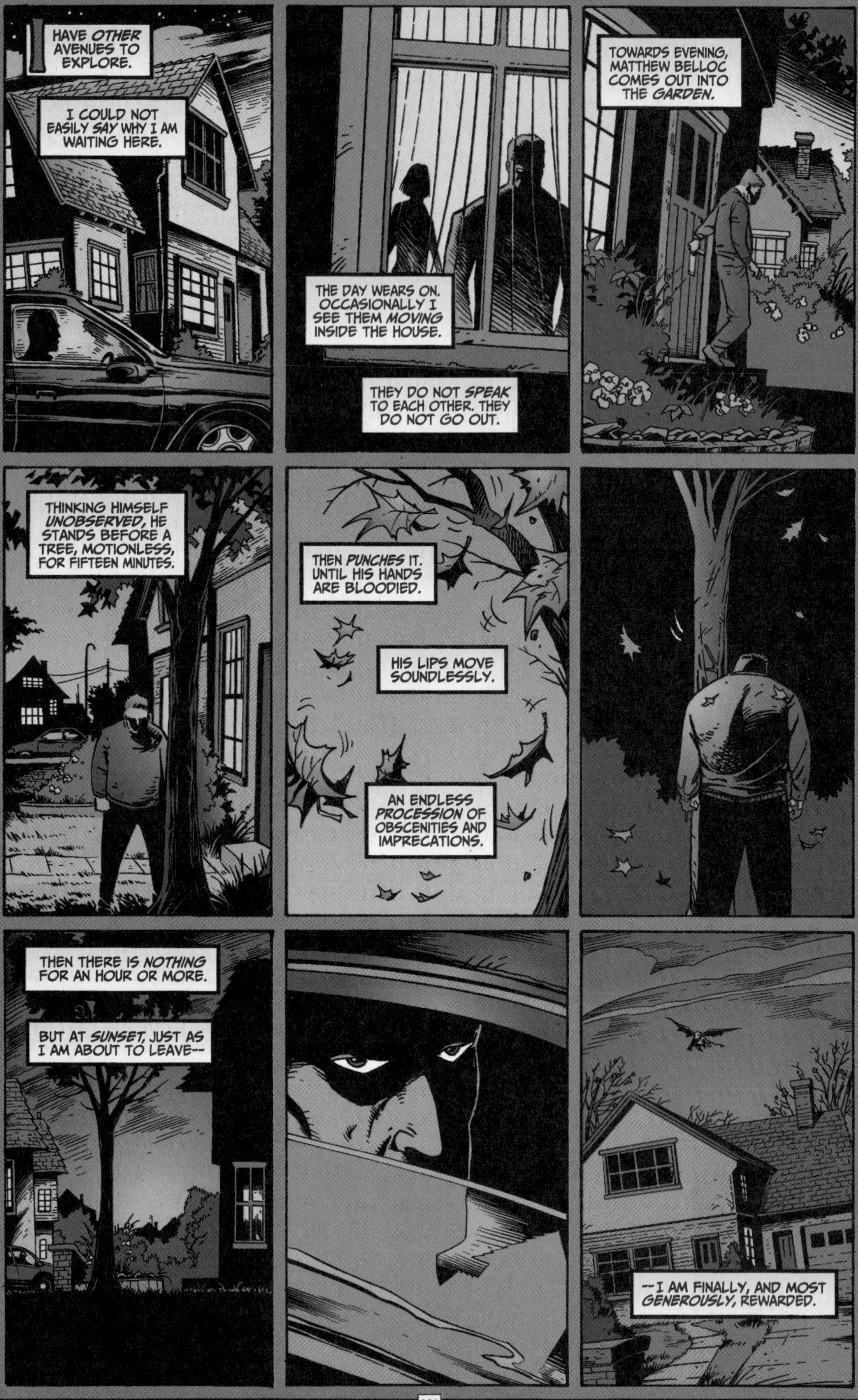
HAVE OTHER AVENUES TO EXPLORE.
I COULD NOT EASILY SAY WHY I AM WAITING HERE.
THE DAY WEARS ON. OCCASIONALLY I SEE THEM MOVING INSIDE THE HOUSE.
THEY DO NOT SPEAK TO EACH OTHER. THEY DO NOT GO OUT.
TOWARDS EVENING, MATTHEW BELLOC COMES OUT INTO THE GARDEN.
THINKING HIMSELF UNOBSERVED, HE STANDS BEFORE A TREE, MOTIONLESS, FOR FIFTEEN MINUTES.
THEN PUNCHES IT. UNTIL HIS HANDS ARE BLOODIED.
HIS LIPS MOVE SOUNDLESSLY.
AN ENDLESS PROCESSION OF OBSCENITIES AND IMPRECATIONS.
THEN THERE IS NOTHING FOR AN HOUR OR MORE.
BUT AT SUNSET, JUST AS I AM ABOUT TO LEAVE--
--I AM FINALLY, AND MOST GENEROUSLY, REWARDED.

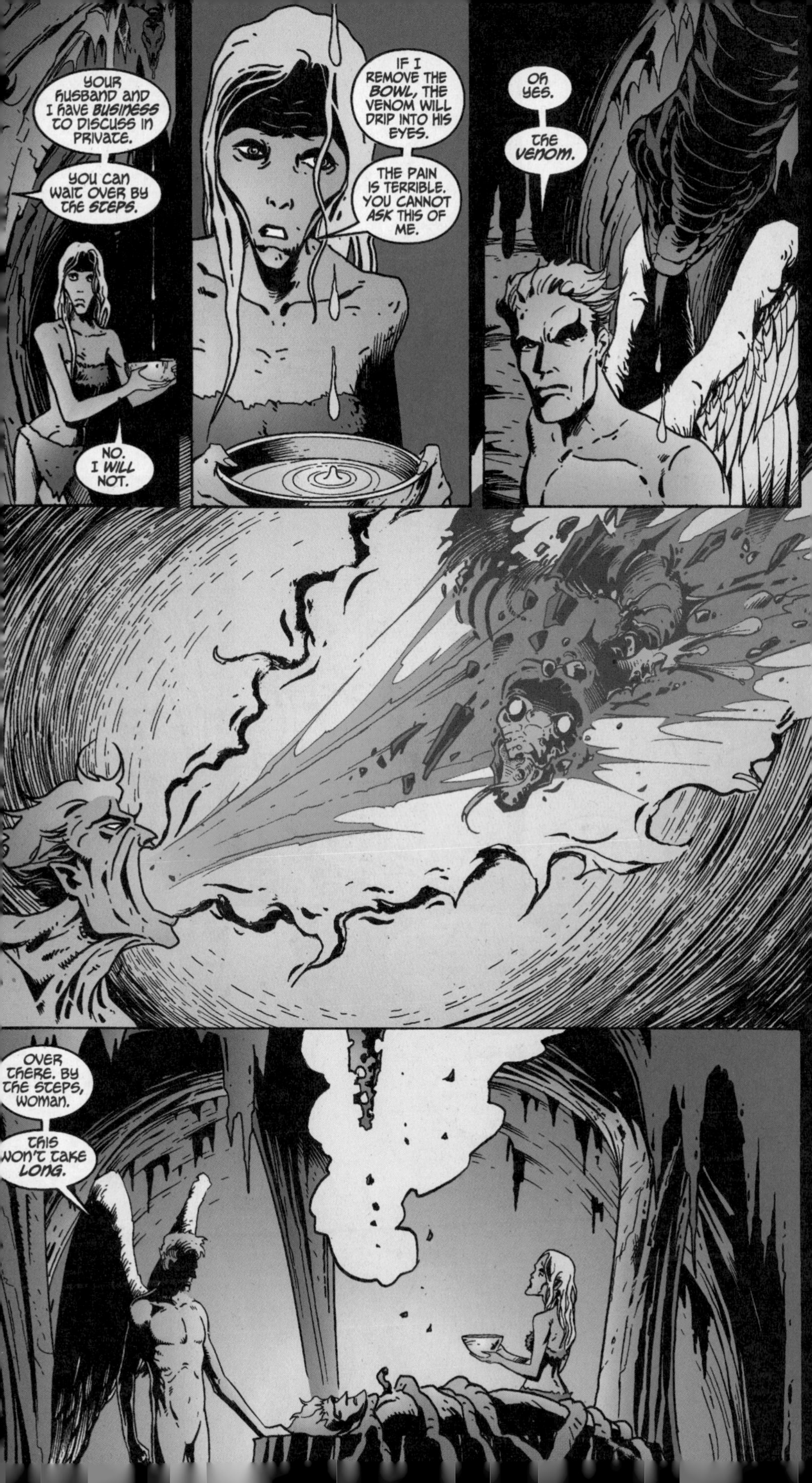
YOUR HUSBAND AND I HAVE BUSINESS TO DISCUSS IN PRIVATE.
YOU CAN WAIT OVER BY THE STEPS.
NO. I WILL NOT.
IF I REMOVE THE BOWL, THE VENOM WILL DRIP INTO HIS EYES.
THE PAIN IS TERRIBLE. YOU CANNOT ASK THIS OF ME.
OH YES.
THE VENOM.
OVER THERE. BY THE STEPS, WOMAN.
THIS WON'T TAKE LONG.

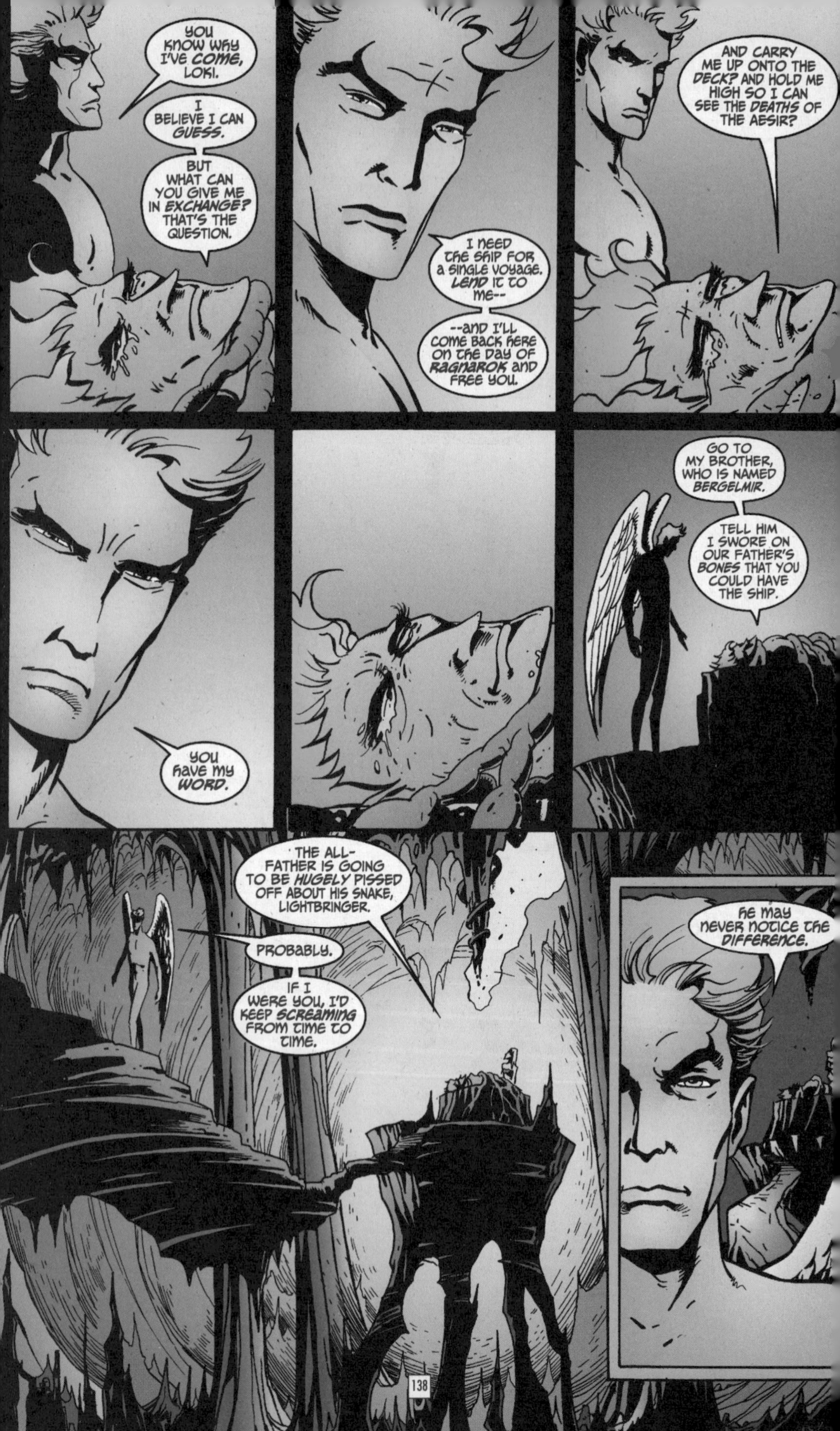
YOU KNOW WHY I'VE COME, LOKI.
I BELIEVE I CAN GUESS.
BUT WHAT CAN YOU GIVE ME IN EXCHANGE? THAT'S THE QUESTION.
I NEED THE SHIP FOR A SINGLE VOYAGE. LEND IT TO ME--
--AND I'LL COME BACK HERE ON THE DAY OF RAGNAROK AND FREE YOU.
AND CARRY ME UP ONTO THE DECK? AND HOLD ME HIGH SO I CAN SEE THE DEATHS OF THE AESIR?
YOU HAVE MY WORD.
GO TO MY BROTHER, WHO IS NAMED BERGELMIR.
TELL HIM I SWORE ON OUR FATHER'S BONES THAT YOU COULD HAVE THE SHIP.
THE ALL-FATHER IS GOING TO BE HUGELY PISSED OFF ABOUT HIS SNAKE, LIGHTBRINGER.
PROBABLY.
IF I WERE YOU, I'D KEEP SCREAMING FROM TIME TO TIME.
HE MAY NEVER NOTICE THE DIFFERENCE.

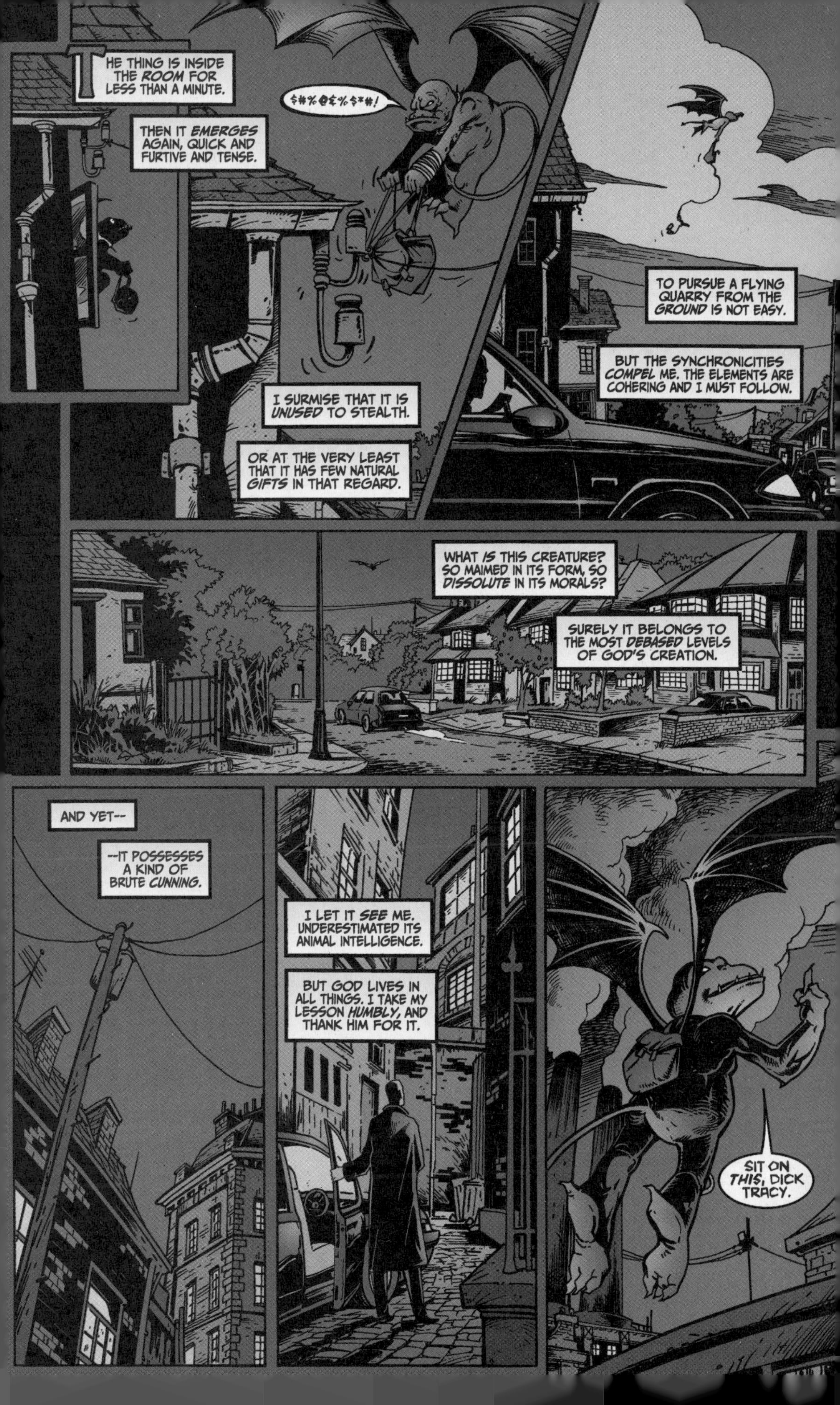
THE THING IS INSIDE THE ROOM FOR LESS THAN A MINUTE.
THEN IT EMERGES AGAIN, QUICK AND FURTIVE AND TENSE.
$#%@£%$*#!
I SURMISE THAT IT IS UNUSED TO STEALTH.
OR AT THE VERY LEAST THAT IT HAS FEW NATURAL GIFTS IN THAT REGARD.
TO PURSUE A FLYING QUARRY FROM THE GROUND IS NOT EASY.
BUT THE SYNCHRONICITIES COMPEL ME. THE ELEMENTS ARE COHERING AND I MUST FOLLOW.
WHAT IS THIS CREATURE? SO MAIMED IN ITS FORM, SO DISSOLUTE IN ITS MORALS?
SURELY IT BELONGS TO THE MOST DEBASED LEVELS OF GOD'S CREATION.
AND YET--
--IT POSSESSES A KIND OF BRUTE CUNNING.
I LET IT SEE ME. UNDERESTIMATED ITS ANIMAL INTELLIGENCE.
BUT GOD LIVES IN ALL THINGS. I TAKE MY LESSON HUMBLY, AND THANK HIM FOR IT.
SIT ON THIS, DICK TRACY.

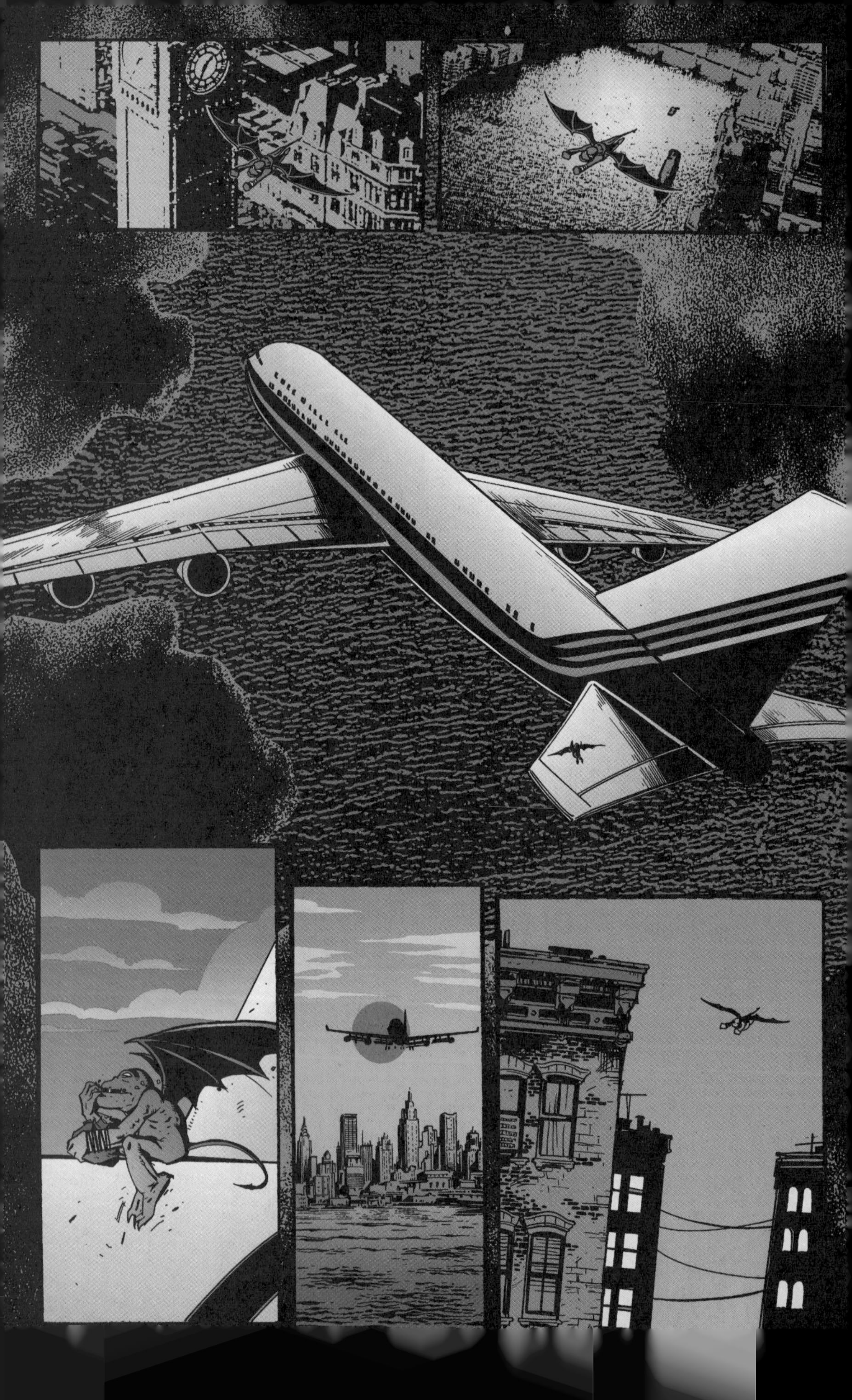

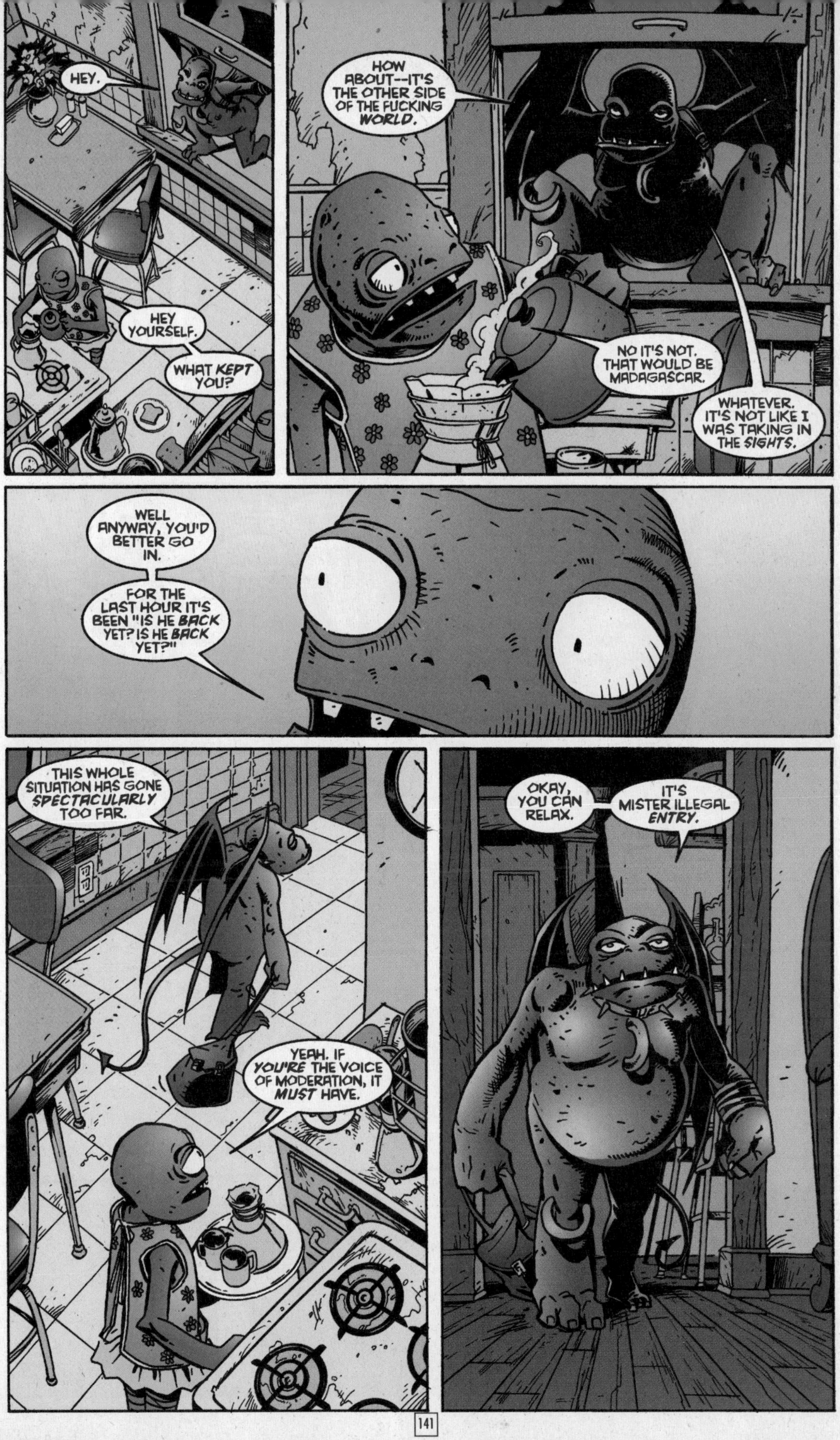
HEY.
HEY YOURSELF.
WHAT KEPT YOU?
HOW ABOUT--IT'S THE OTHER SIDE OF THE FUCKING WORLD.
NO IT'S NOT. THAT WOULD BE MADAGASCAR.
WHATEVER. IT'S NOT LIKE I WAS TAKING IN THE SIGHTS.
WELL ANYWAY, YOU'D BETTER GO IN.
FOR THE LAST HOUR IT'S BEEN "IS HE BACK YET? IS HE BACK YET?"
THIS WHOLE SITUATION HAS GONE SPECTACULARLY TOO FAR.
YEAH. IF YOU'RE THE VOICE OF MODERATION, IT MUST HAVE.
OKAY, YOU CAN RELAX.
IT'S MISTER ILLEGAL ENTRY.

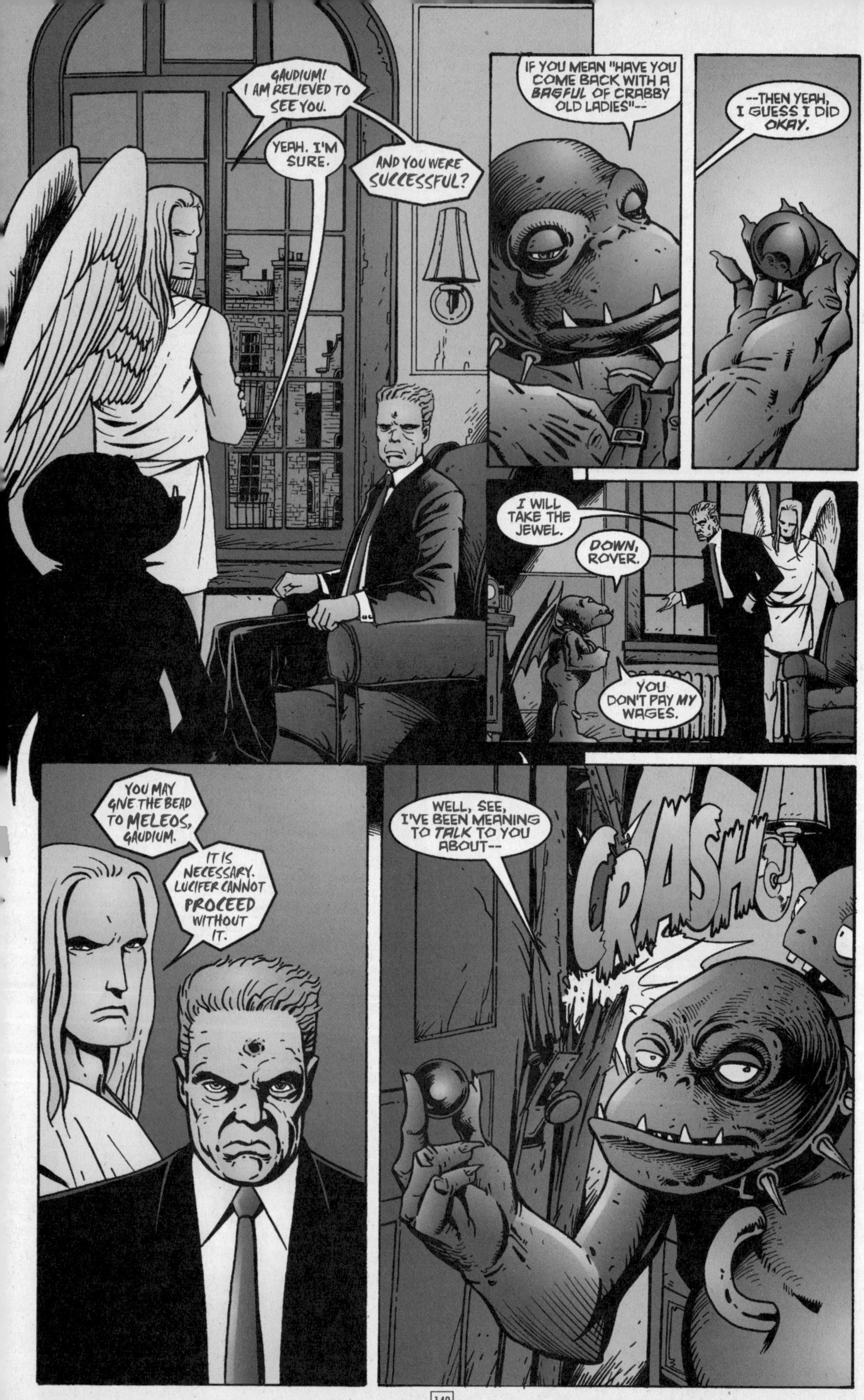
GAUDIUM! I AM RELIEVED TO SEE YOU.
YEAH. I'M SURE.
AND YOU WERE SUCCESSFUL?
IF YOU MEAN "HAVE YOU COME BACK WITH A BAGFUL OF CRABBY OLD LADIES"--
--THEN YEAH, I GUESS I DID OKAY.
I WILL TAKE THE JEWEL.
DOWN, ROVER.
YOU DON'T PAY MY WAGES.
YOU MAY GIVE THE BEAD TO MELEOS, GAUDIUM.
IT IS NECESSARY. LUCIFER CANNOT PROCEED WITHOUT IT.
WELL, SEE, I'VE BEEN MEANING TO TALK TO YOU ABOUT--
CRASH

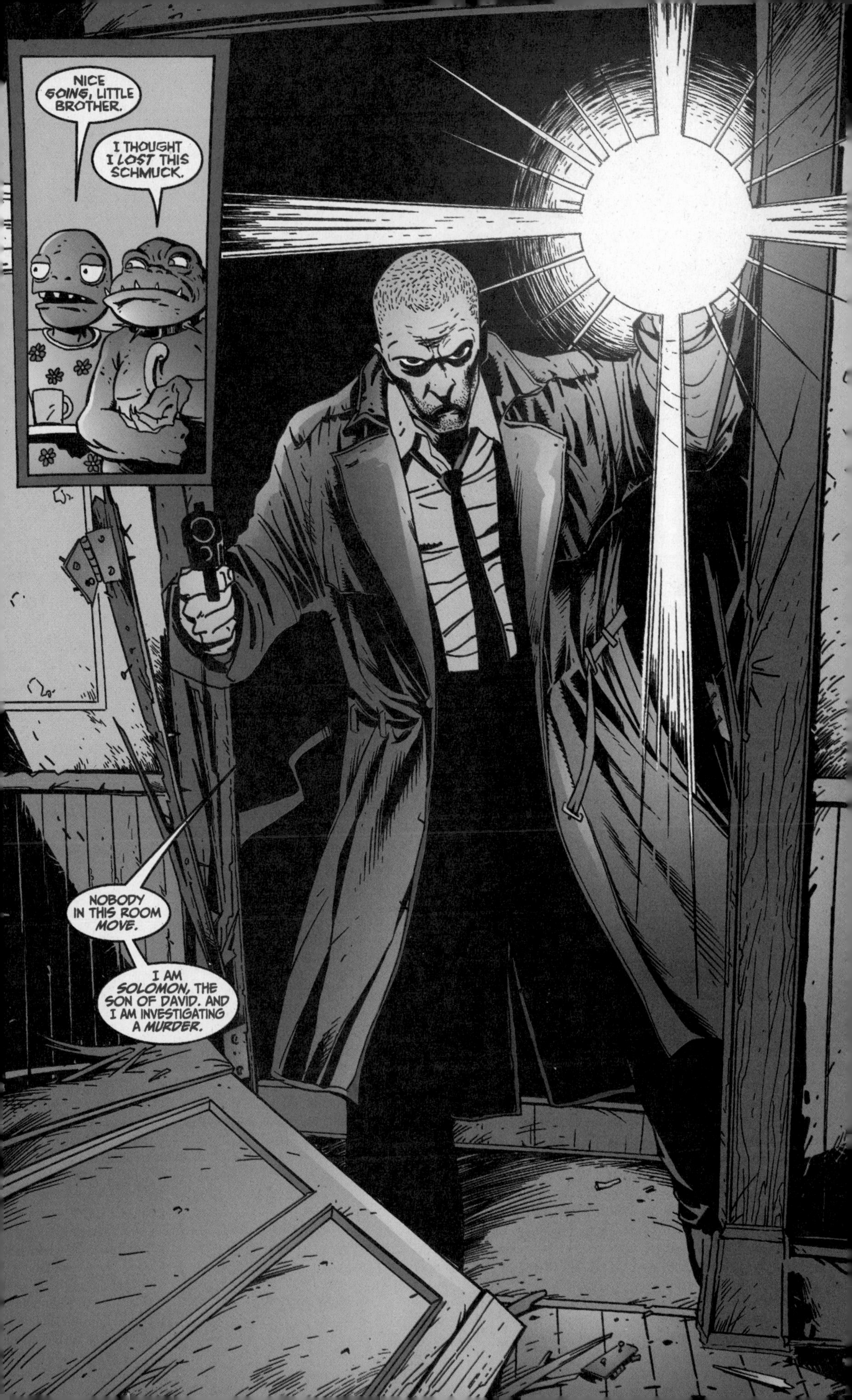
NICE GOING, LITTLE BROTHER.
I THOUGHT I LOST THIS SCHMUCK.
NOBODY IN THIS ROOM MOVE.
I AM SOLOMON, THE SON OF DAVID. AND I AM INVESTIGATING A MURDER.

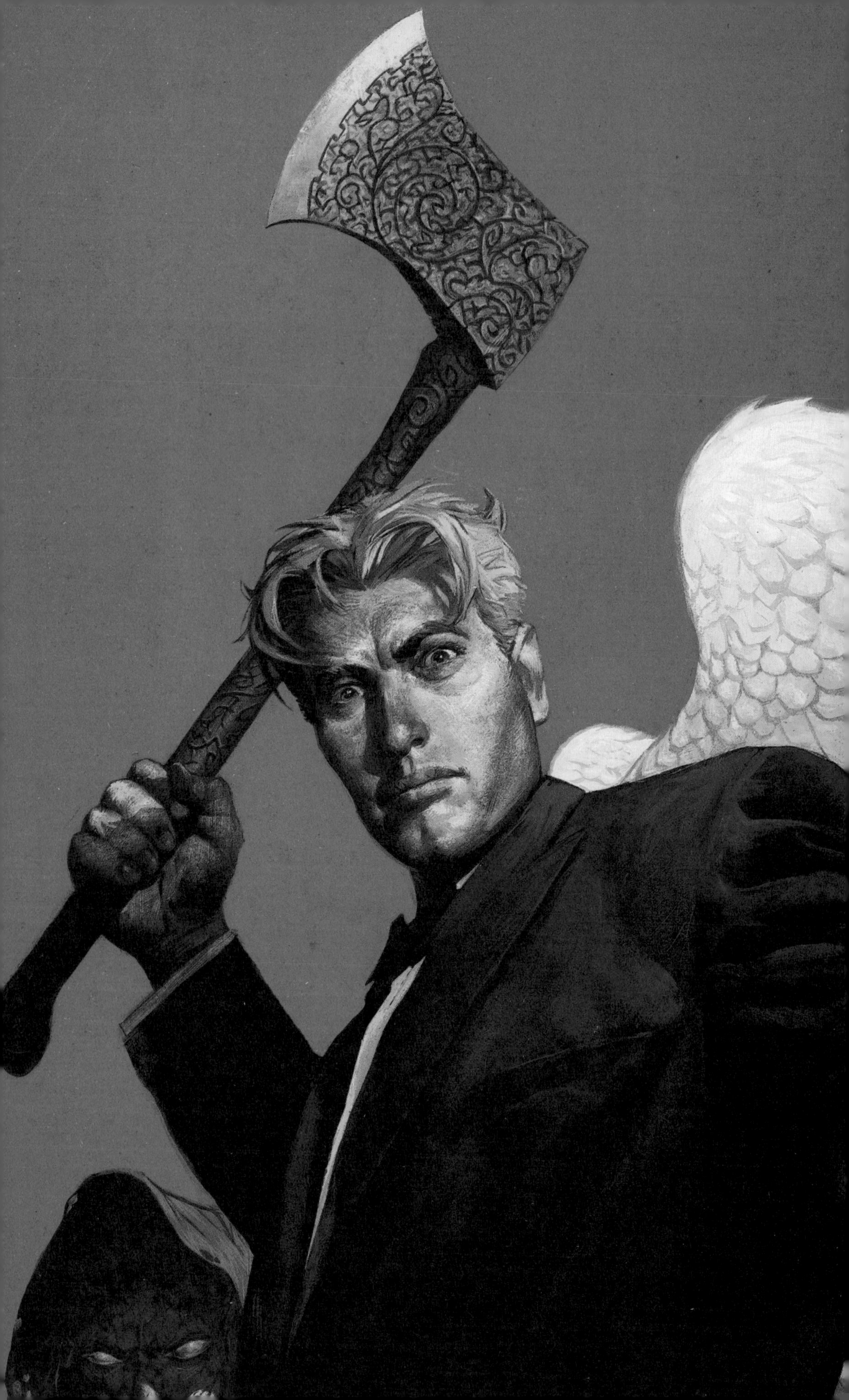

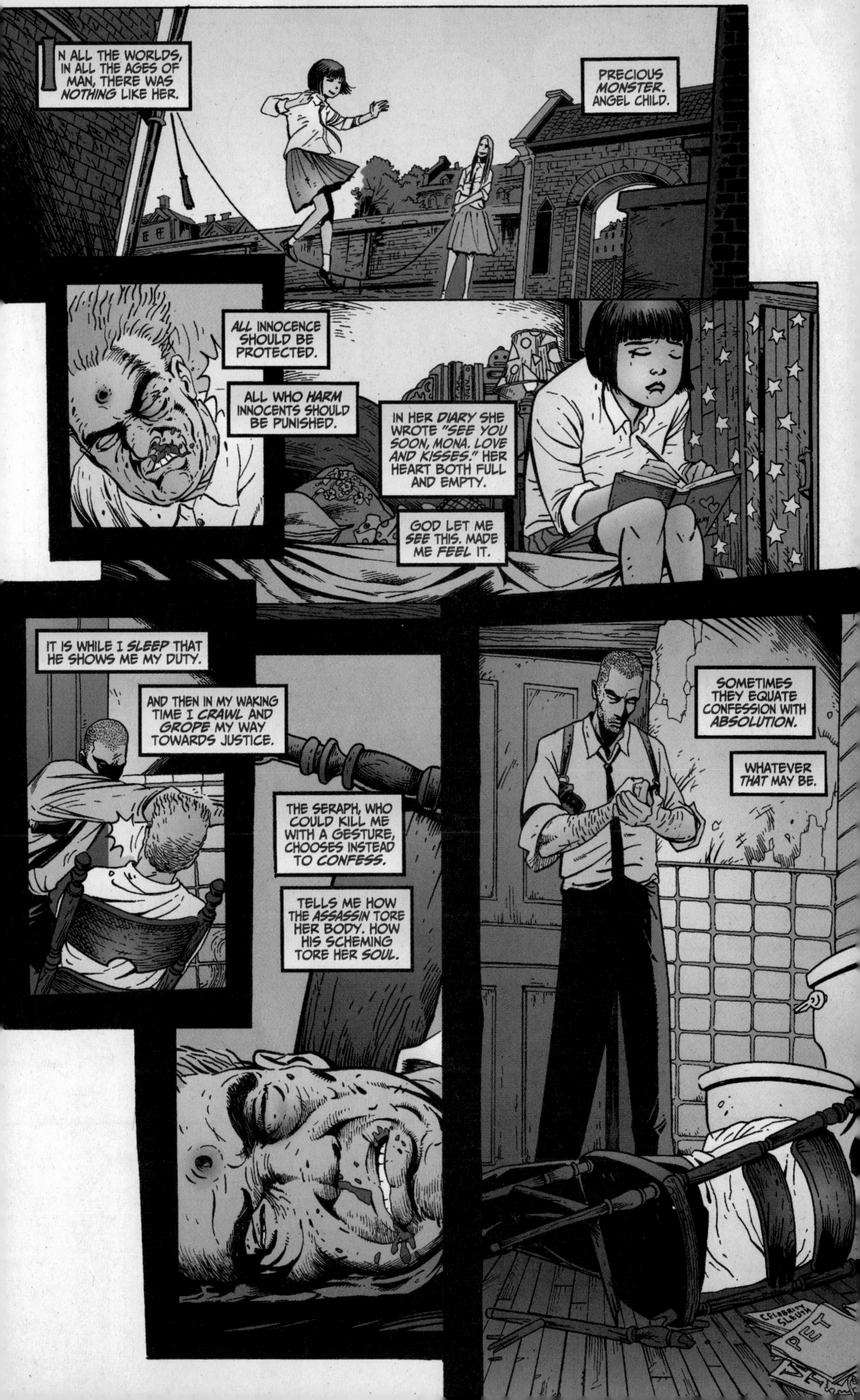
IN ALL THE WORLDS, IN ALL THE AGES OF MAN, THERE WAS NOTHING LIKE HER.
PRECIOUS MONSTER. ANGEL CHILD.
ALL INNOCENCE SHOULD BE PROTECTED.
ALL WHO HARM INNOCENTS SHOULD BE PUNISHED.
IN HER DIARY SHE WROTE "SEE YOU SOON, MONA. LOVE AND KISSES." HER HEART BOTH FULL AND EMPTY.
GOD LET ME SEE THIS. MADE ME FEEL IT.
IT IS WHILE I SLEEP THAT HE SHOWS ME MY DUTY.
AND THEN IN MY WAKING TIME I CRAWL AND GROPE MY WAY TOWARDS JUSTICE.
THE SERAPH, WHO COULD KILL ME WITH A GESTURE, CHOOSES INSTEAD TO CONFESS.
TELLS ME HOW THE ASSASSIN TORE HER BODY. HOW HIS SCHEMING TORE HER SOUL.
SOMETIMES THEY EQUATE CONFESSION WITH ABSOLUTION.
WHATEVER THAT MAY BE.
CELEBRITY SLEUTH
PET

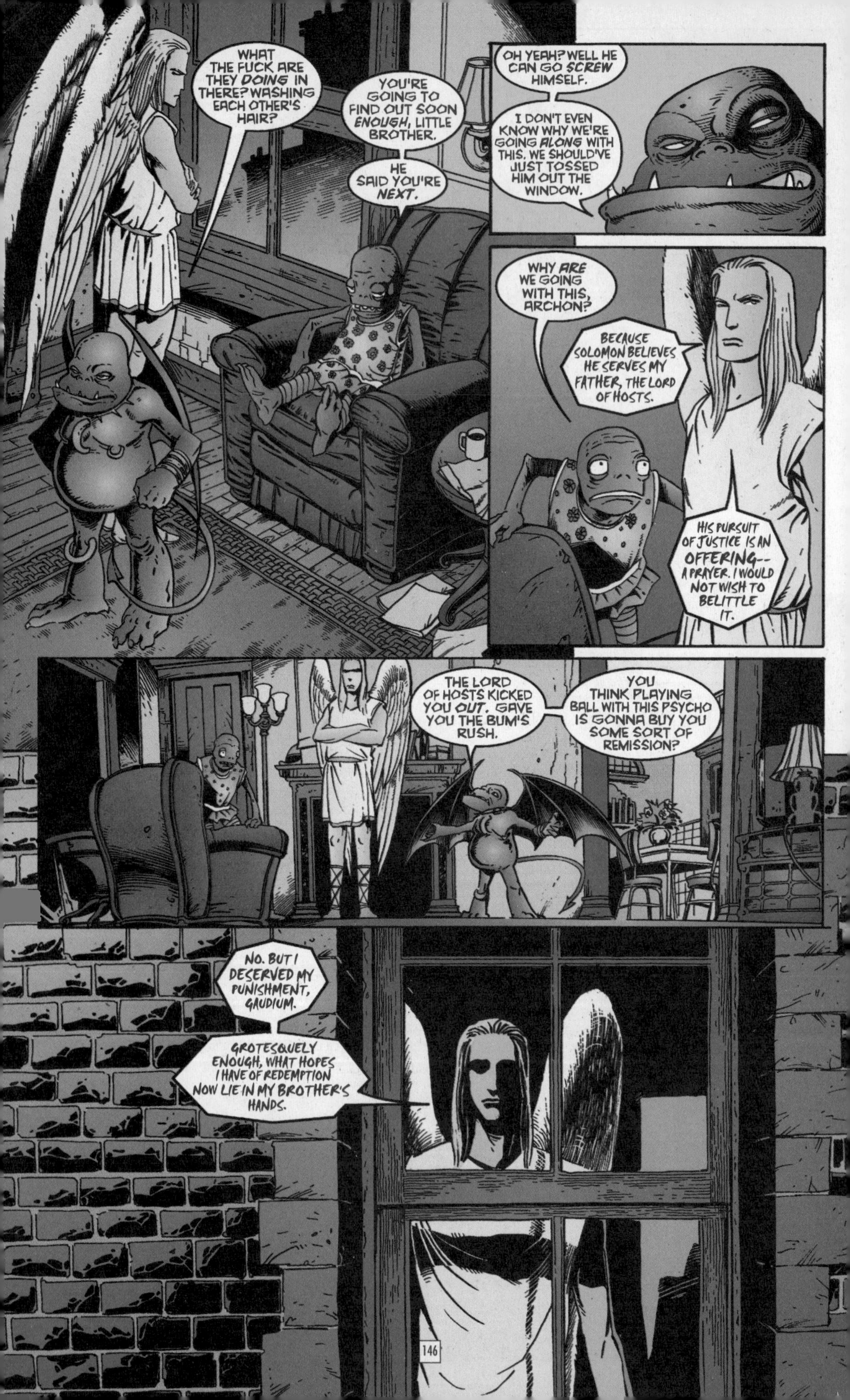
WHAT THE FUCK ARE THEY DOING IN THERE? WASHING EACH OTHER'S HAIR?
YOU'RE GOING TO FIND OUT SOON ENOUGH, LITTLE BROTHER.
HE SAID YOU'RE NEXT.
OH YEAH? WELL HE CAN GO SCREW HIMSELF.
I DON'T EVEN KNOW WHY WE'RE GOING ALONG WITH THIS. WE SHOULD'VE JUST TOSSED HIM OUT THE WINDOW.
WHY ARE WE GOING WITH THIS, ARCHON?
BECAUSE SOLOMON BELIEVES HE SERVES MY FATHER, THE LORD OF HOSTS.
HIS PURSUIT OF JUSTICE IS AN OFFERING-- A PRAYER. I WOULD NOT WISH TO BELITTLE IT.
THE LORD OF HOSTS KICKED YOU OUT. GAVE YOU THE BUM'S RUSH.
YOU THINK PLAYING BALL WITH THIS PSYCHO IS GONNA BUY YOU SOME SORT OF REMISSION?
NO. BUT I DESERVED MY PUNISHMENT, GAUDIUM.
GROTESQUELY ENOUGH, WHAT HOPES I HAVE OF REDEMPTION NOW LIE IN MY BROTHER'S HANDS.

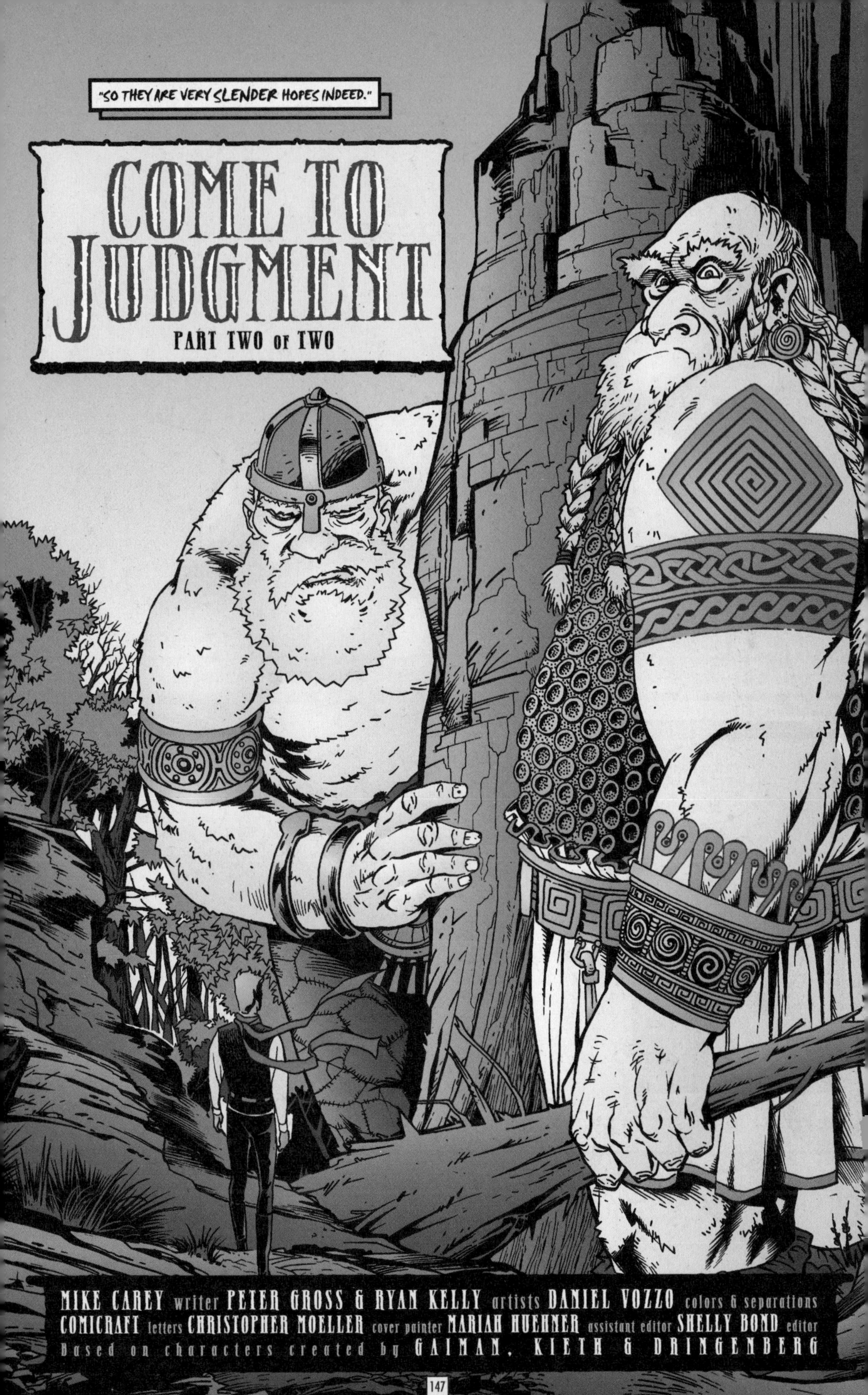
"SO THEY ARE VERY SLENDER HOPES INDEED."
COME TO JUDGMENT
PART TWO OF TWO
MIKE CAREY writer PETER GROSS & RYAN KELLY artists DANIEL VOZZO colors & separations
COMICRAFT letters CHRISTOPHER MOELLER cover painter MARIAH HUEHNER assistant editor SHELLY BOND editor
Based on characters created by GAIMAN, KIETH & DRINGENBERG

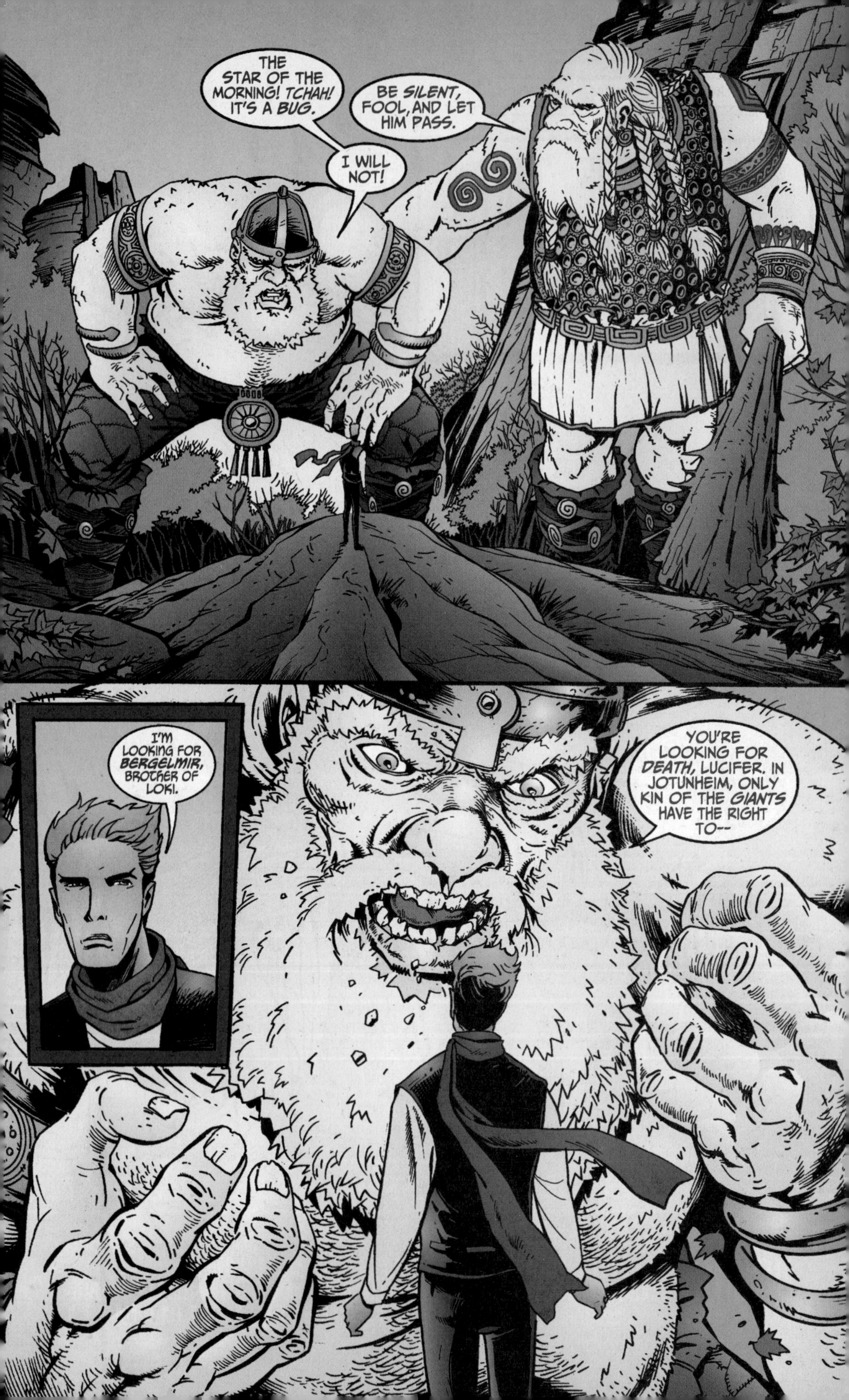
THE STAR OF THE MORNING! *TCHAH!* IT'S A *BUG.*
BE *SILENT,* FOOL, AND LET HIM PASS.
I WILL NOT!
I'M LOOKING FOR ***BERGELMIR,*** BROTHER OF LOKI.
YOU'RE LOOKING FOR *DEATH,* LUCIFER. IN JOTUNHEIM, ONLY KIN OF THE *GIANTS* HAVE THE RIGHT TO--

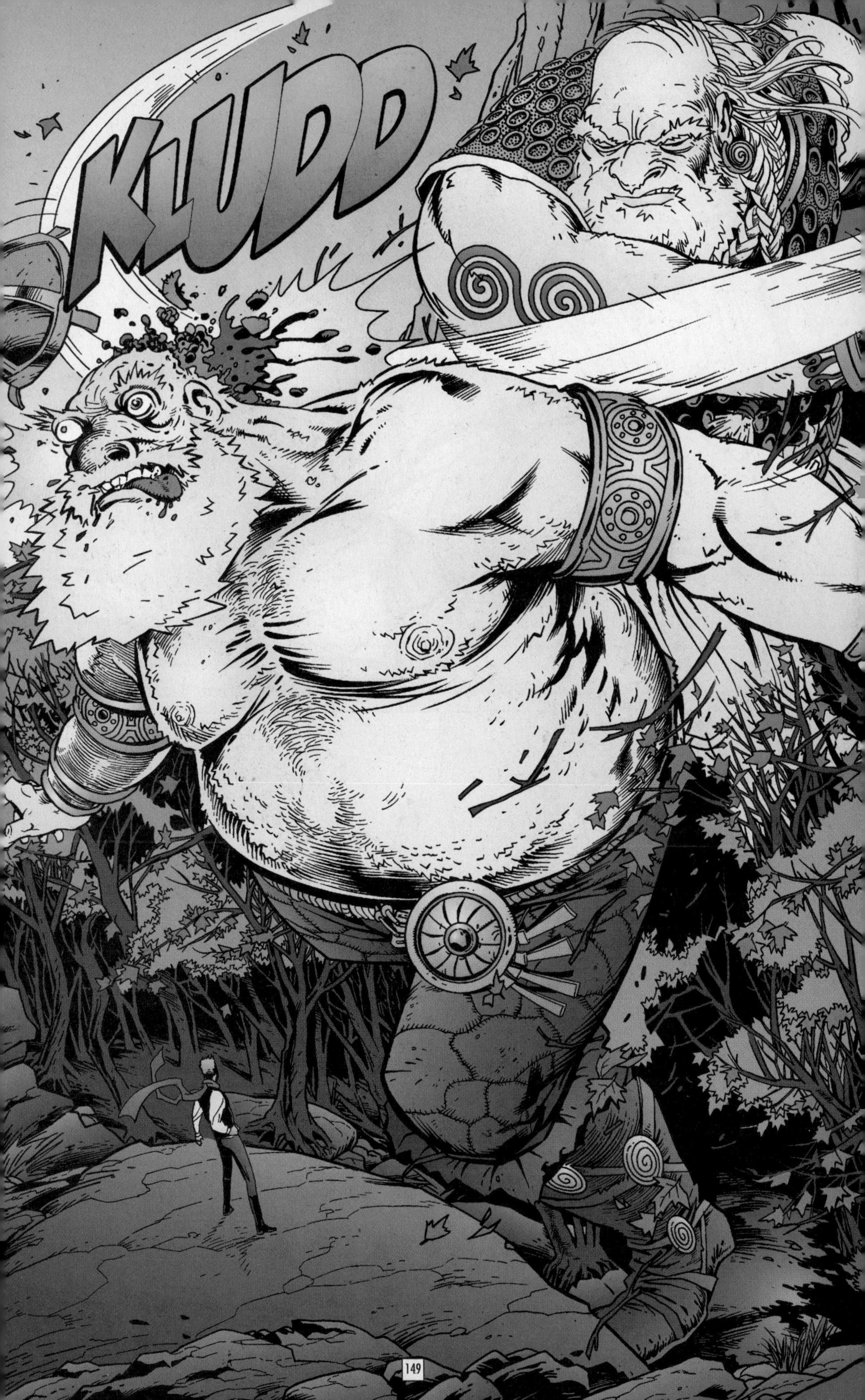
KLUDD

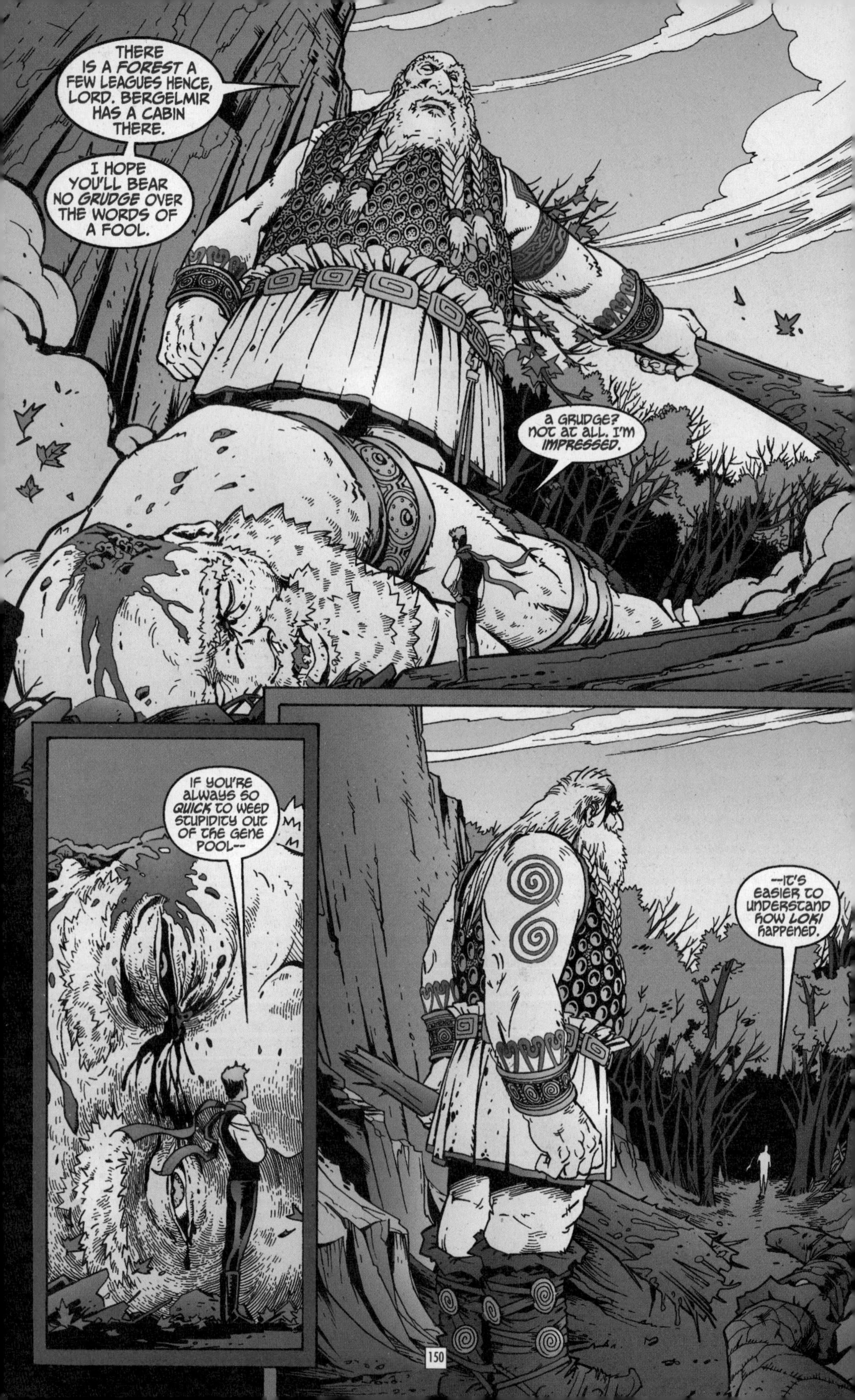
THERE IS A FOREST A FEW LEAGUES HENCE, LORD. BERGELMIR HAS A CABIN THERE.
I HOPE YOU'LL BEAR NO GRUDGE OVER THE WORDS OF A FOOL.
A GRUDGE? NOT AT ALL. I'M IMPRESSED.
IF YOU'RE ALWAYS SO QUICK TO WEED STUPIDITY OUT OF THE GENE POOL--
--IT'S EASIER TO UNDERSTAND HOW LOKI HAPPENED.

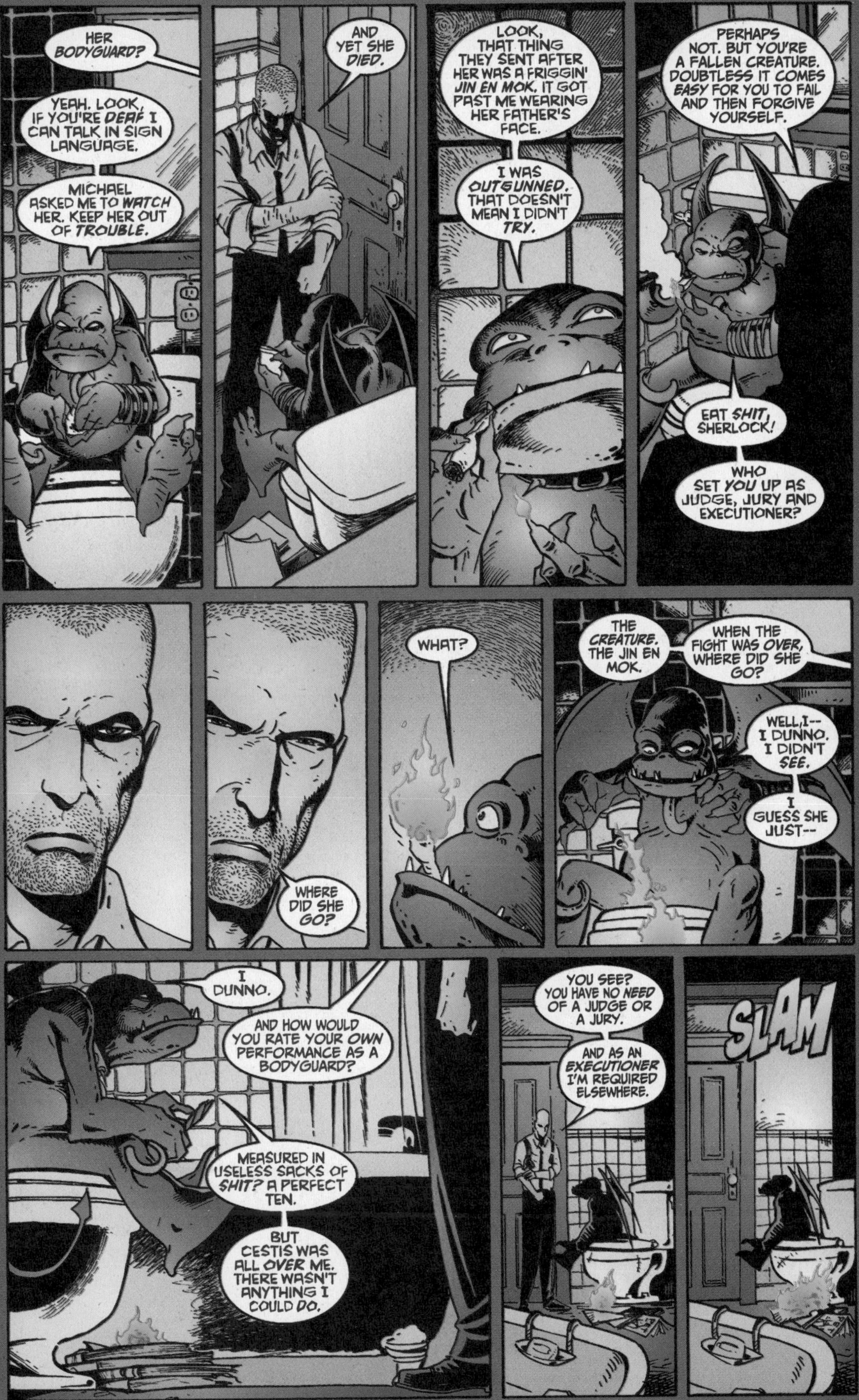
HER BODYGUARD?
YEAH. LOOK, IF YOU'RE DEAF I CAN TALK IN SIGN LANGUAGE.
MICHAEL ASKED ME TO WATCH HER. KEEP HER OUT OF TROUBLE.
AND YET SHE DIED.
LOOK, THAT THING THEY SENT AFTER HER WAS A FRIGGIN' JIN EN MOK. IT GOT PAST ME WEARING HER FATHER'S FACE.
I WAS OUTGUNNED. THAT DOESN'T MEAN I DIDN'T TRY.
PERHAPS NOT. BUT YOU'RE A FALLEN CREATURE. DOUBTLESS IT COMES EASY FOR YOU TO FAIL AND THEN FORGIVE YOURSELF.
EAT SHIT, SHERLOCK!
WHO SET YOU UP AS JUDGE, JURY AND EXECUTIONER?
WHERE DID SHE GO?
WHAT?
THE CREATURE. THE JIN EN MOK.
WHEN THE FIGHT WAS OVER, WHERE DID SHE GO?
WELL, I-- I DUNNO. I DIDN'T SEE.
I GUESS SHE JUST--
I DUNNO.
AND HOW WOULD YOU RATE YOUR OWN PERFORMANCE AS A BODYGUARD?
MEASURED IN USELESS SACKS OF SHIT? A PERFECT TEN.
BUT CESTIS WAS ALL OVER ME. THERE WASN'T ANYTHING I COULD DO.
YOU SEE? YOU HAVE NO NEED OF A JUDGE OR A JURY.
AND AS AN EXECUTIONER I'M REQUIRED ELSEWHERE.
SLAM

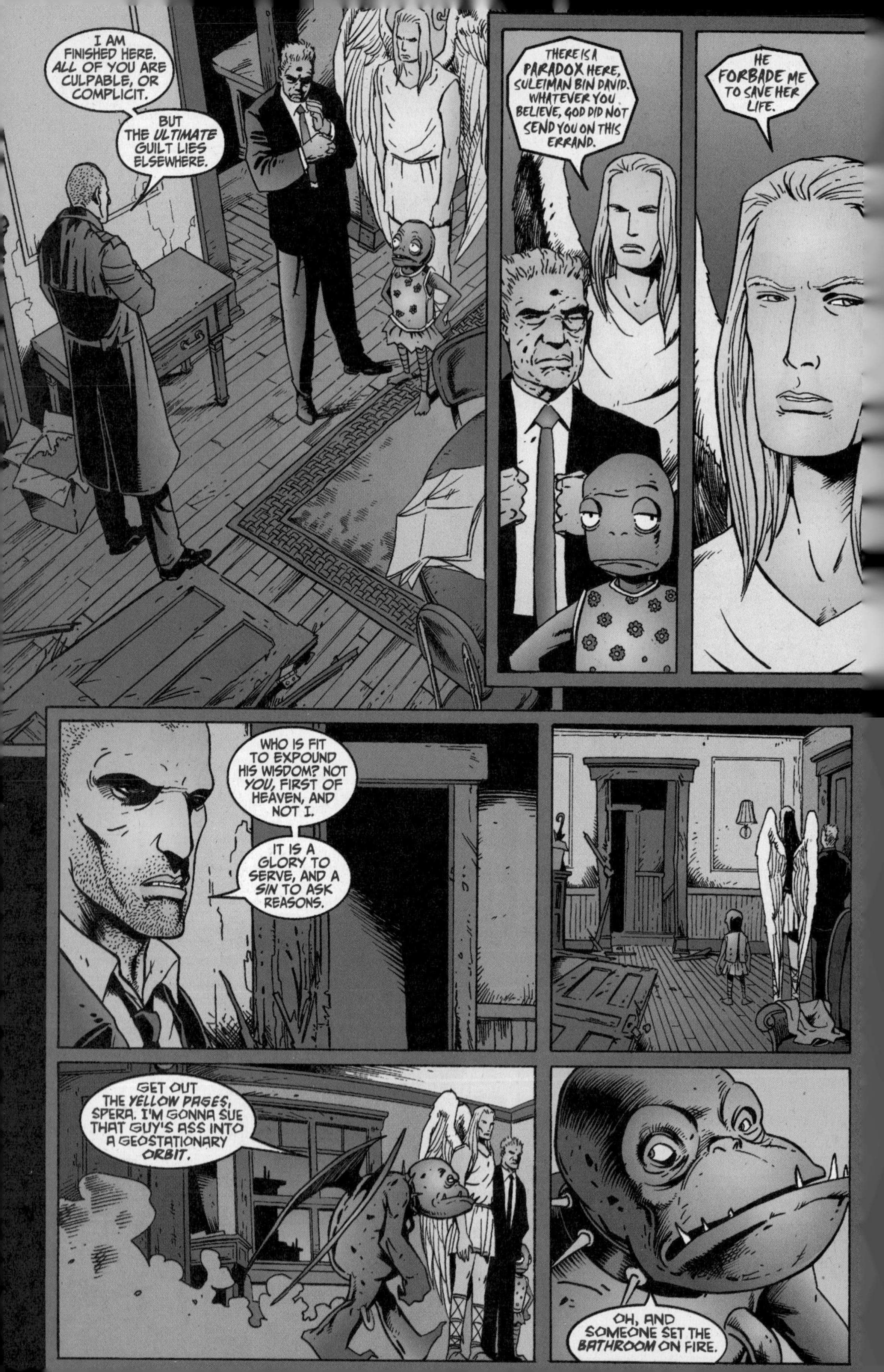
I AM FINISHED HERE. ALL OF YOU ARE CULPABLE, OR COMPLICIT.
BUT THE ULTIMATE GUILT LIES ELSEWHERE.
THERE IS A PARADOX HERE, SULEIMAN BIN DAVID. WHATEVER YOU BELIEVE, GOD DID NOT SEND YOU ON THIS ERRAND.
HE FORBADE ME TO SAVE HER LIFE.
WHO IS FIT TO EXPOUND HIS WISDOM? NOT YOU, FIRST OF HEAVEN, AND NOT I.
IT IS A GLORY TO SERVE, AND A SIN TO ASK REASONS.
GET OUT THE YELLOW PAGES, SPERA. I'M GONNA SUE THAT GUY'S ASS INTO A GEOSTATIONARY ORBIT.
OH, AND SOMEONE SET THE BATHROOM ON FIRE.

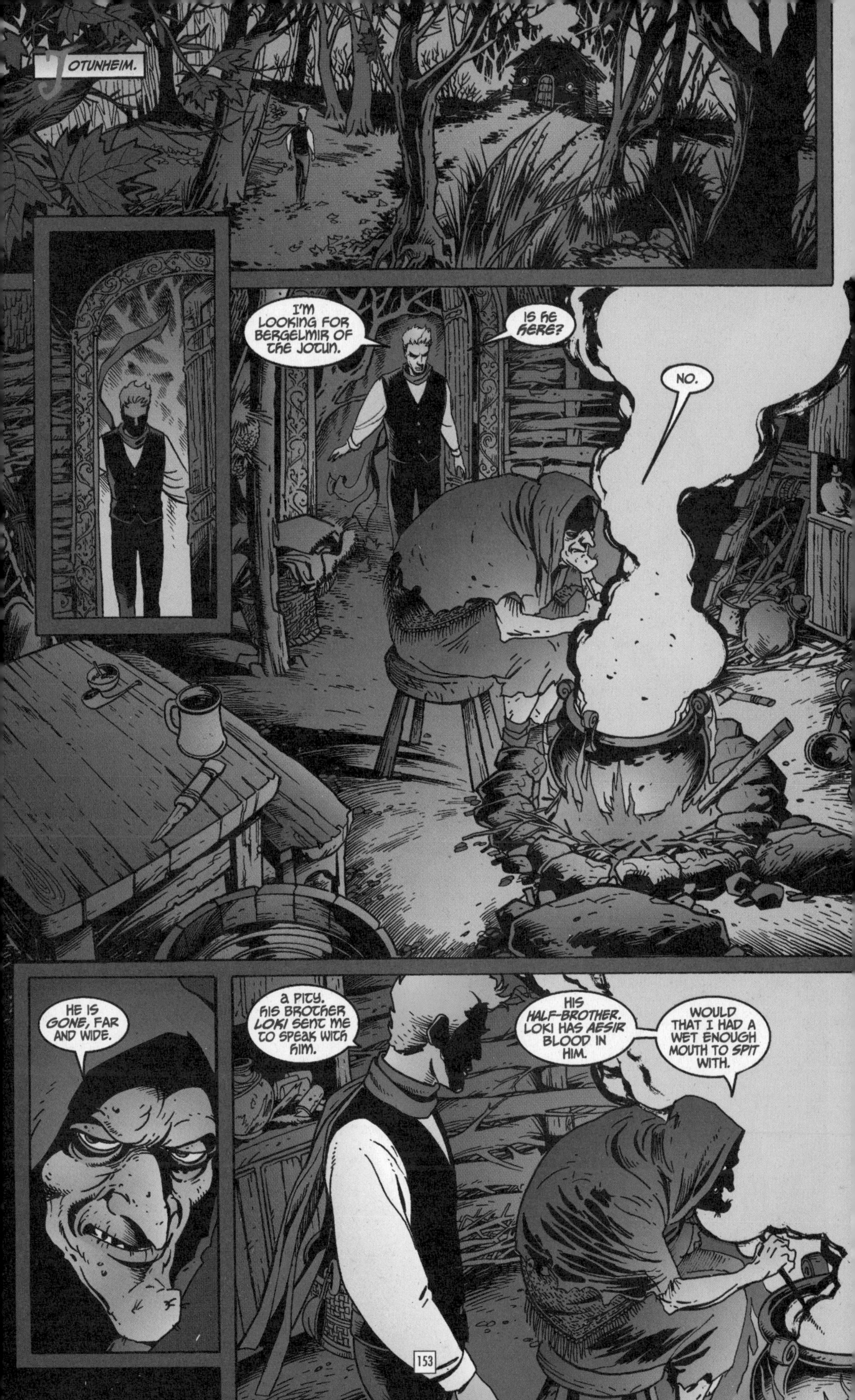
JOTUNHEIM.
I'M LOOKING FOR BERGELMIR OF THE JOTUN.
IS HE HERE?
NO.
HE IS GONE, FAR AND WIDE.
A PITY. HIS BROTHER LOKI SENT ME TO SPEAK WITH HIM.
HIS HALF-BROTHER. LOKI HAS AESIR BLOOD IN HIM.
WOULD THAT I HAD A WET ENOUGH MOUTH TO SPIT WITH.

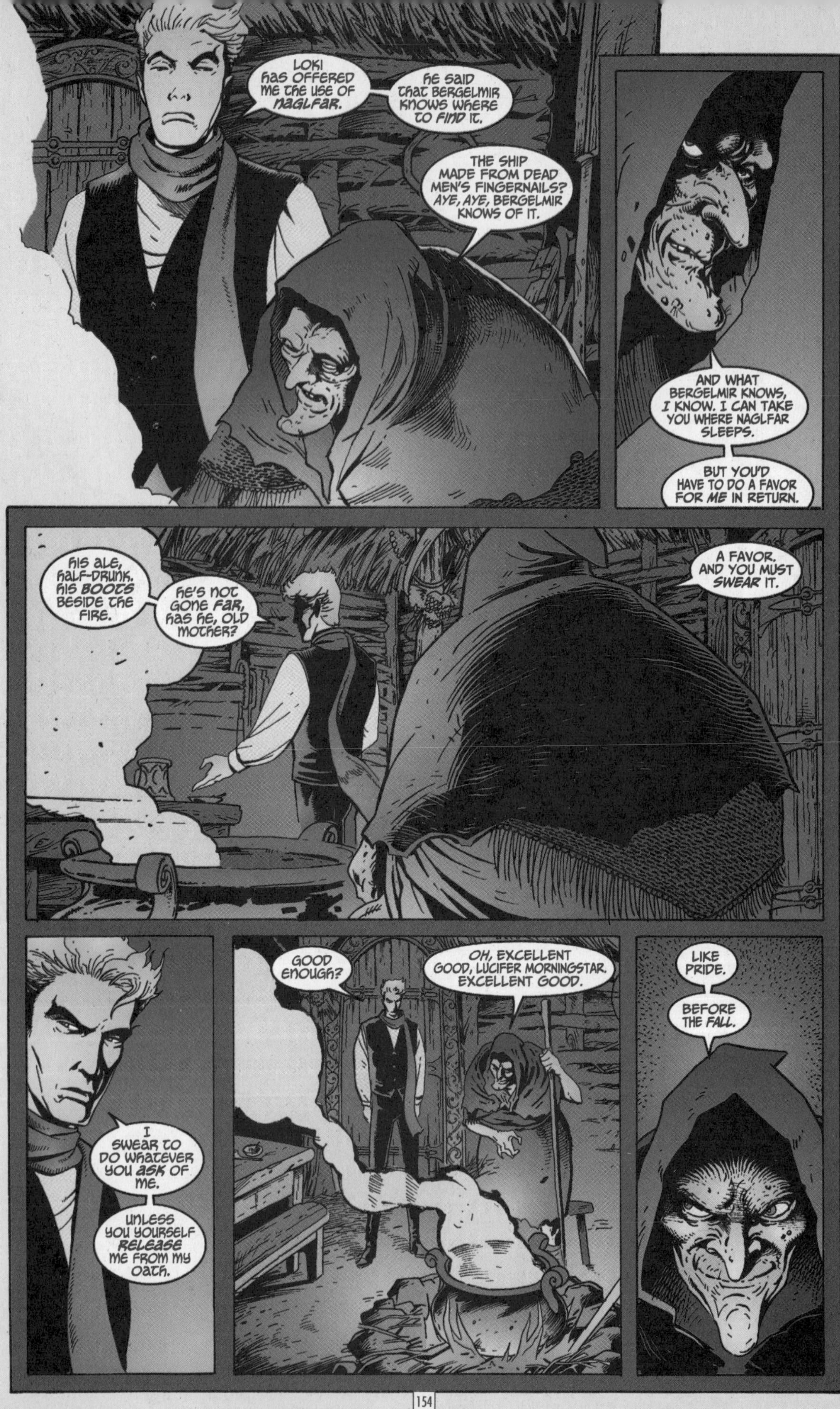
LOKI HAS OFFERED ME THE USE OF NAGLFAR.
HE SAID THAT BERGELMIR KNOWS WHERE TO FIND IT.
THE SHIP MADE FROM DEAD MEN'S FINGERNAILS? AYE, AYE, BERGELMIR KNOWS OF IT.
AND WHAT BERGELMIR KNOWS, I KNOW. I CAN TAKE YOU WHERE NAGLFAR SLEEPS.
BUT YOU'D HAVE TO DO A FAVOR FOR ME IN RETURN.
HIS ALE, HALF-DRUNK. HIS BOOTS BESIDE THE FIRE.
HE'S NOT GONE FAR, HAS HE, OLD MOTHER?
A FAVOR. AND YOU MUST SWEAR IT.
I SWEAR TO DO WHATEVER YOU ASK OF ME.
UNLESS YOU YOURSELF RELEASE ME FROM MY OATH.
GOOD ENOUGH?
OH, EXCELLENT GOOD, LUCIFER MORNINGSTAR. EXCELLENT GOOD.
LIKE PRIDE.
BEFORE THE FALL.

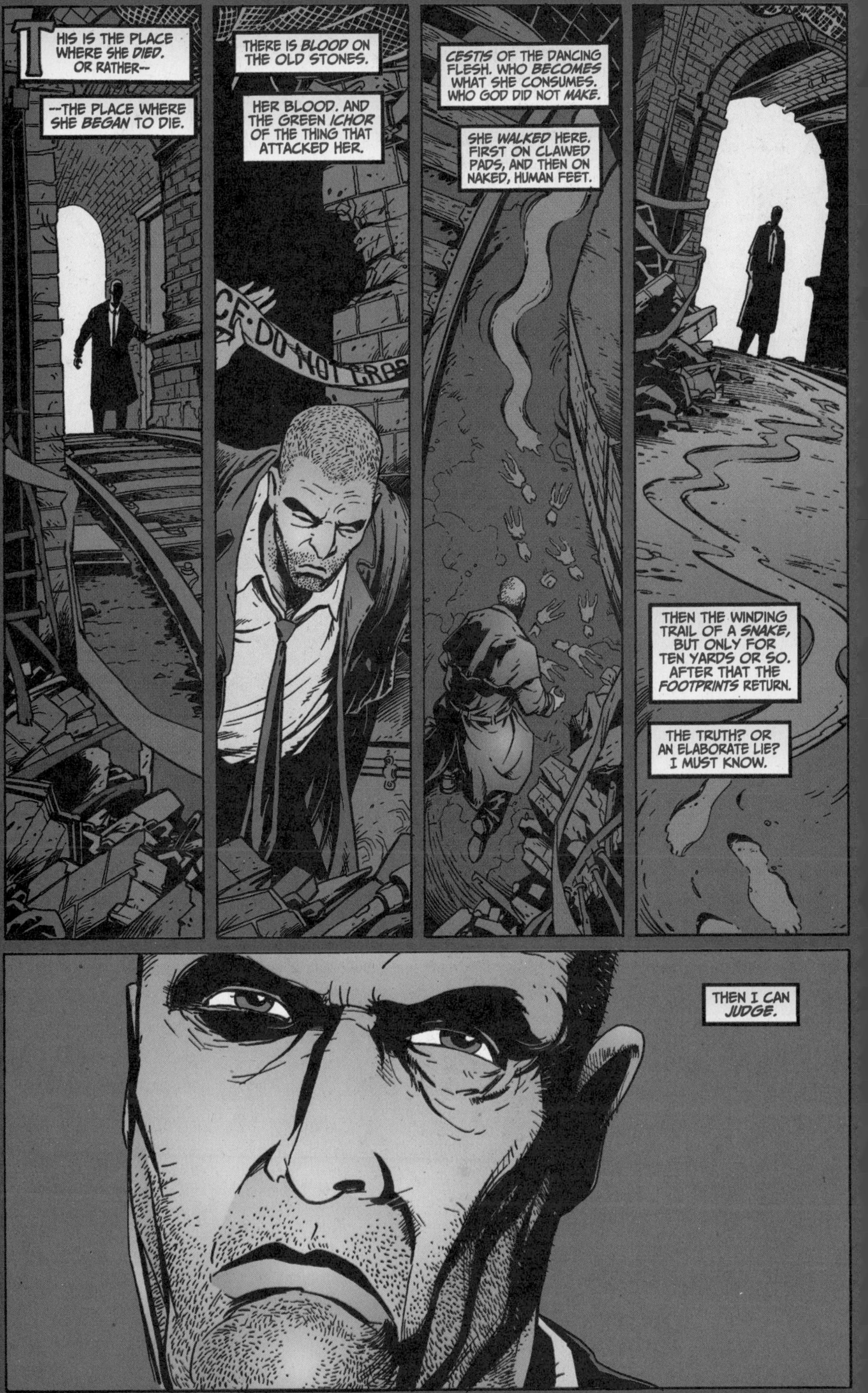
THIS IS THE PLACE WHERE SHE *DIED.* OR RATHER--
--THE PLACE WHERE SHE *BEGAN* TO DIE.
THERE IS *BLOOD* ON THE OLD STONES.
HER BLOOD. AND THE GREEN *ICHOR* OF THE THING THAT ATTACKED HER.
CF DO NOT CROS
CESTIS OF THE DANCING FLESH. WHO *BECOMES* WHAT SHE CONSUMES. WHO GOD DID NOT *MAKE.*
SHE *WALKED* HERE. FIRST ON CLAWED PADS, AND THEN ON NAKED, HUMAN FEET.
THEN THE WINDING TRAIL OF A *SNAKE,* BUT ONLY FOR TEN YARDS OR SO. AFTER THAT THE *FOOTPRINTS* RETURN.
THE TRUTH? OR AN ELABORATE LIE? I MUST KNOW.
THEN I CAN *JUDGE.*

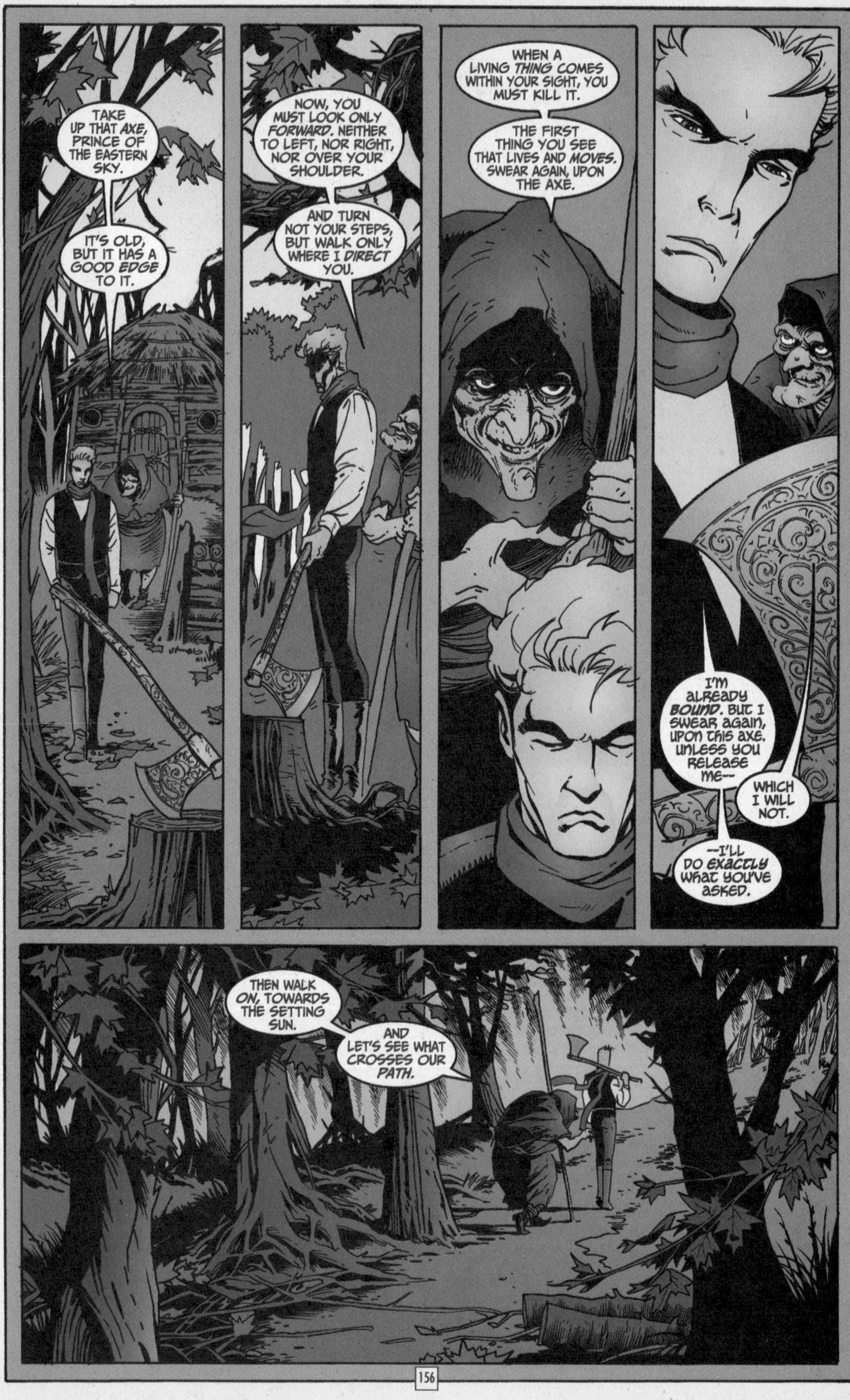
TAKE UP THAT AXE, PRINCE OF THE EASTERN SKY.
IT'S OLD, BUT IT HAS A GOOD EDGE TO IT.
NOW, YOU MUST LOOK ONLY FORWARD. NEITHER TO LEFT, NOR RIGHT, NOR OVER YOUR SHOULDER.
AND TURN NOT YOUR STEPS, BUT WALK ONLY WHERE I DIRECT YOU.
WHEN A LIVING THING COMES WITHIN YOUR SIGHT, YOU MUST KILL IT.
THE FIRST THING YOU SEE THAT LIVES AND MOVES. SWEAR AGAIN, UPON THE AXE.
I'M ALREADY BOUND. BUT I SWEAR AGAIN, UPON THIS AXE. UNLESS YOU RELEASE ME--
WHICH I WILL NOT.
--I'LL DO EXACTLY WHAT YOU'VE ASKED.
THEN WALK ON, TOWARDS THE SETTING SUN.
AND LET'S SEE WHAT CROSSES OUR PATH.

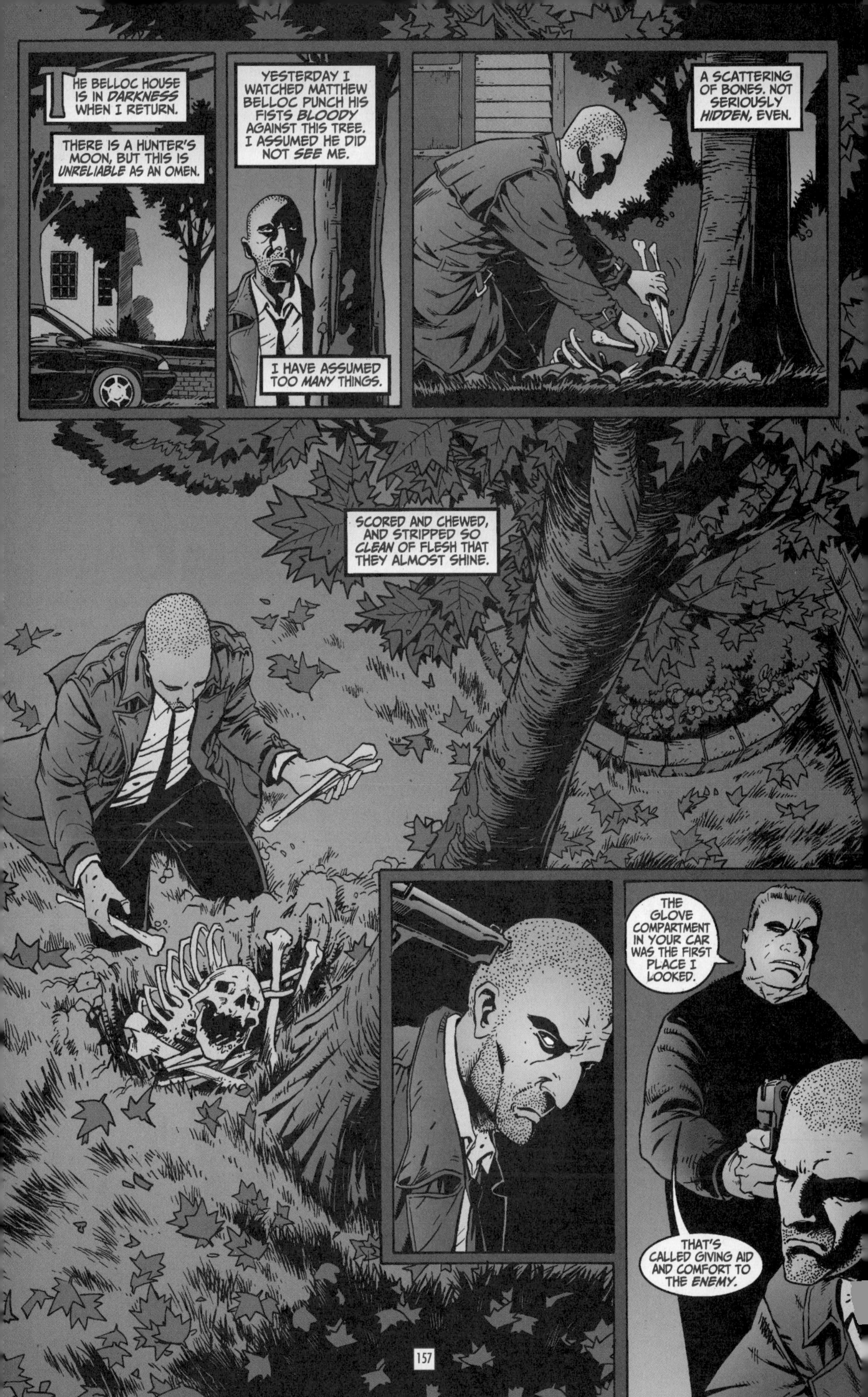
THE BELLOC HOUSE IS IN DARKNESS WHEN I RETURN.
THERE IS A HUNTER'S MOON, BUT THIS IS UNRELIABLE AS AN OMEN.
YESTERDAY I WATCHED MATTHEW BELLOC PUNCH HIS FISTS BLOODY AGAINST THIS TREE. I ASSUMED HE DID NOT SEE ME.
I HAVE ASSUMED TOO MANY THINGS.
A SCATTERING OF BONES. NOT SERIOUSLY HIDDEN, EVEN.
SCORED AND CHEWED, AND STRIPPED SO CLEAN OF FLESH THAT THEY ALMOST SHINE.
THE GLOVE COMPARTMENT IN YOUR CAR WAS THE FIRST PLACE I LOOKED.
THAT'S CALLED GIVING AID AND COMFORT TO THE ENEMY.

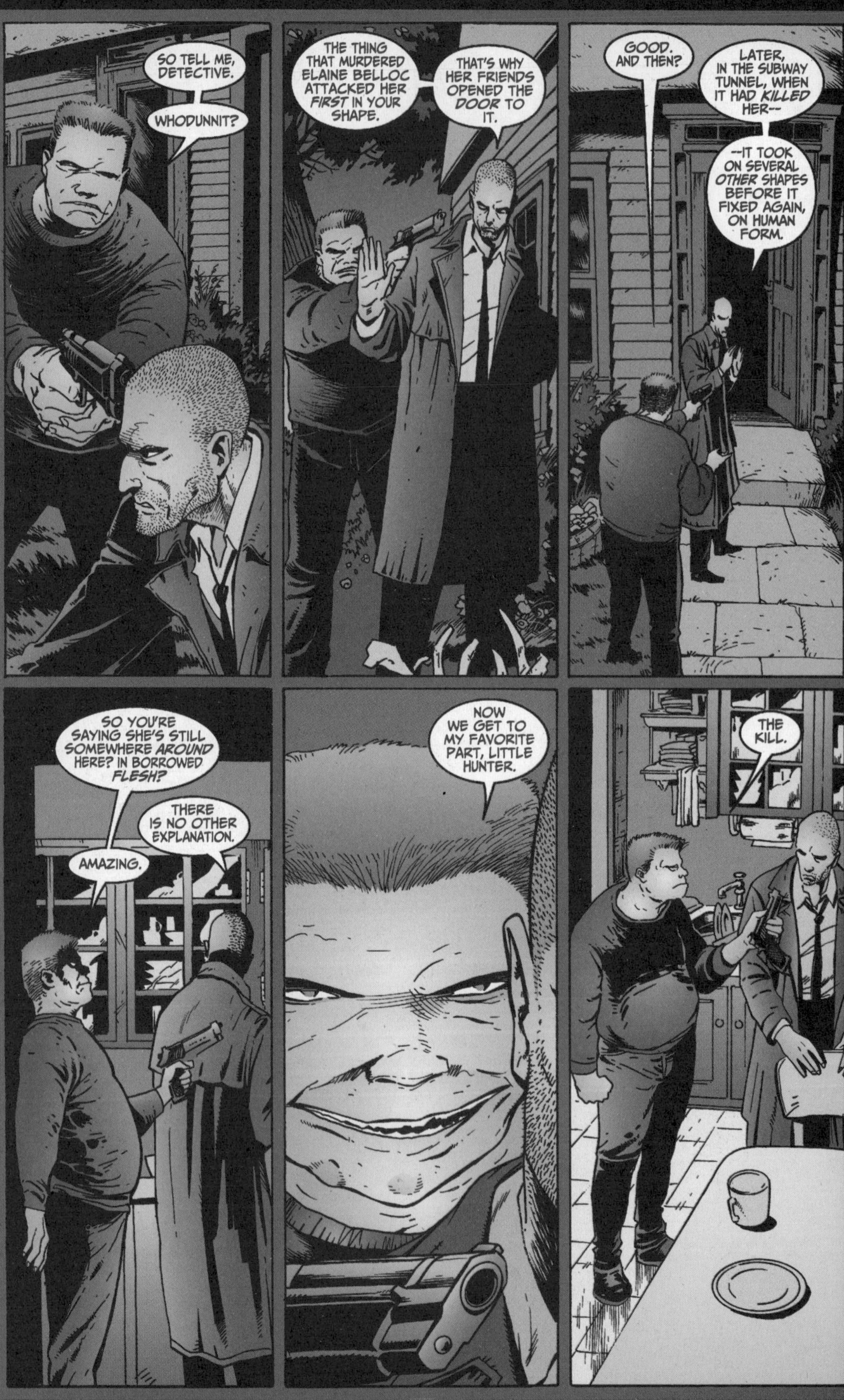
SO TELL ME, DETECTIVE.
WHODUNNIT?
THE THING THAT MURDERED ELAINE BELLOC ATTACKED HER *FIRST* IN YOUR SHAPE.
THAT'S WHY HER FRIENDS OPENED THE *DOOR* TO IT.
GOOD. AND THEN?
LATER, IN THE SUBWAY TUNNEL, WHEN IT HAD *KILLED* HER--
--IT TOOK ON SEVERAL *OTHER* SHAPES BEFORE IT FIXED AGAIN, ON HUMAN FORM.
SO YOU'RE SAYING SHE'S STILL SOMEWHERE *AROUND* HERE? IN BORROWED *FLESH?*
THERE IS NO OTHER EXPLANATION.
AMAZING.
NOW WE GET TO MY FAVORITE PART, LITTLE HUNTER.
THE KILL.

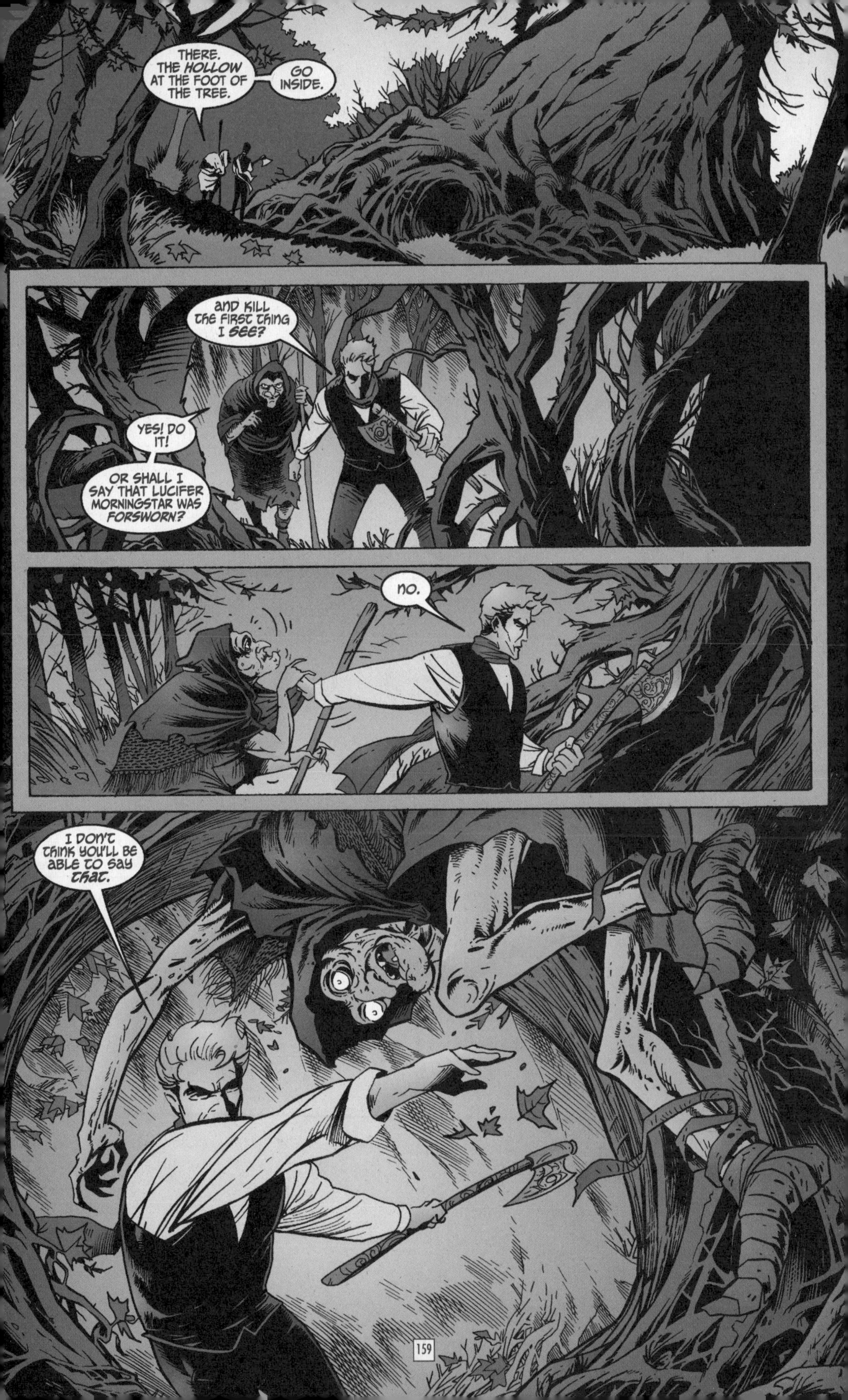

THERE. THE *HOLLOW* AT THE FOOT OF THE TREE.
GO INSIDE.
AND KILL THE FIRST THING I *SEE?*
YES! DO IT!
OR SHALL I SAY THAT LUCIFER MORNINGSTAR WAS *FORSWORN?*
NO.
I DON'T THINK YOU'LL BE ABLE TO SAY *THAT.*

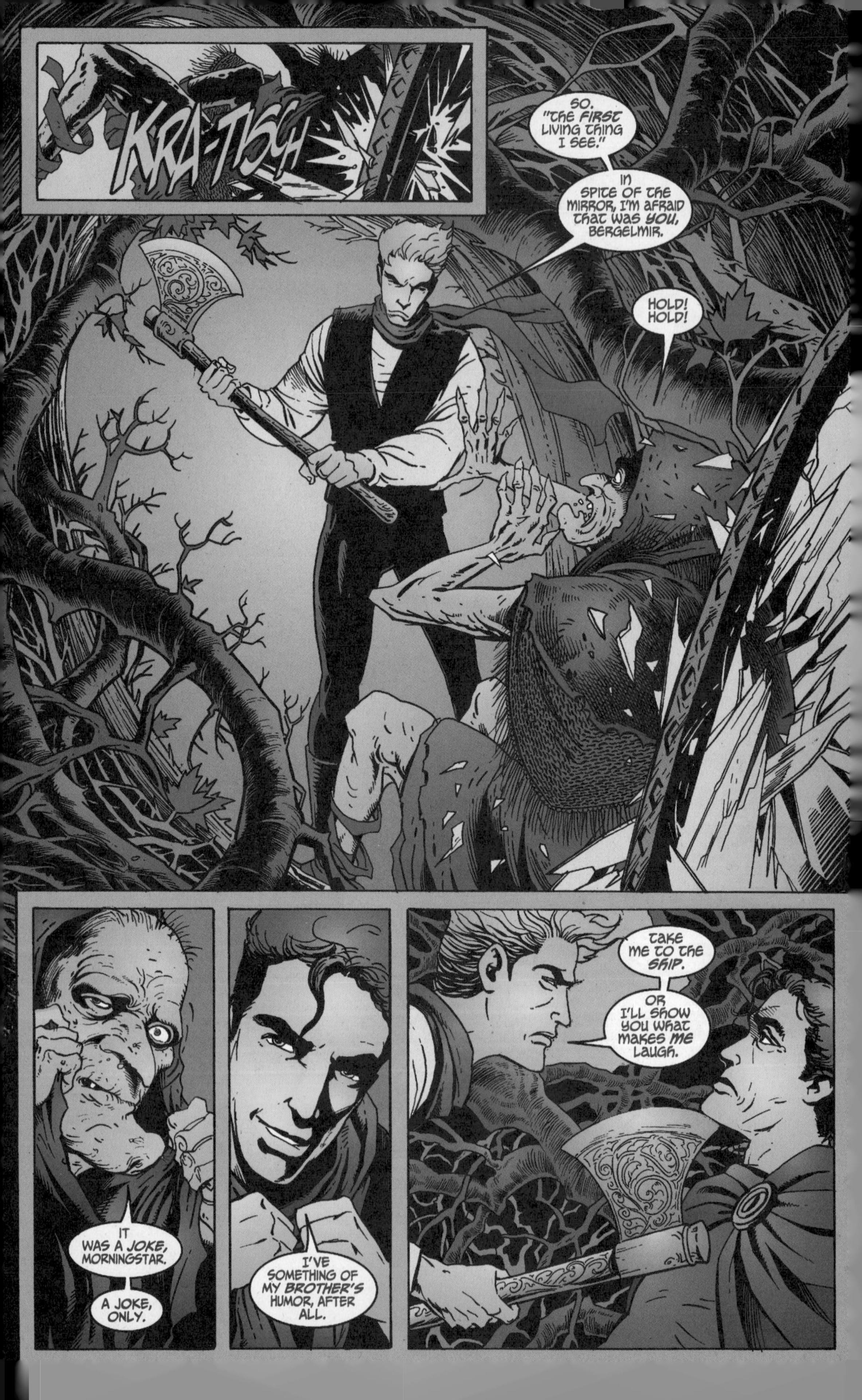
KRA-TISCH
SO. "THE FIRST LIVING THING I SEE."
IN SPITE OF THE MIRROR, I'M AFRAID THAT WAS YOU, BERGELMIR.
HOLD! HOLD!
IT WAS A JOKE, MORNINGSTAR.
A JOKE, ONLY.
I'VE SOMETHING OF MY BROTHER'S HUMOR, AFTER ALL.
TAKE ME TO THE SHIP.
OR I'LL SHOW YOU WHAT MAKES ME LAUGH.

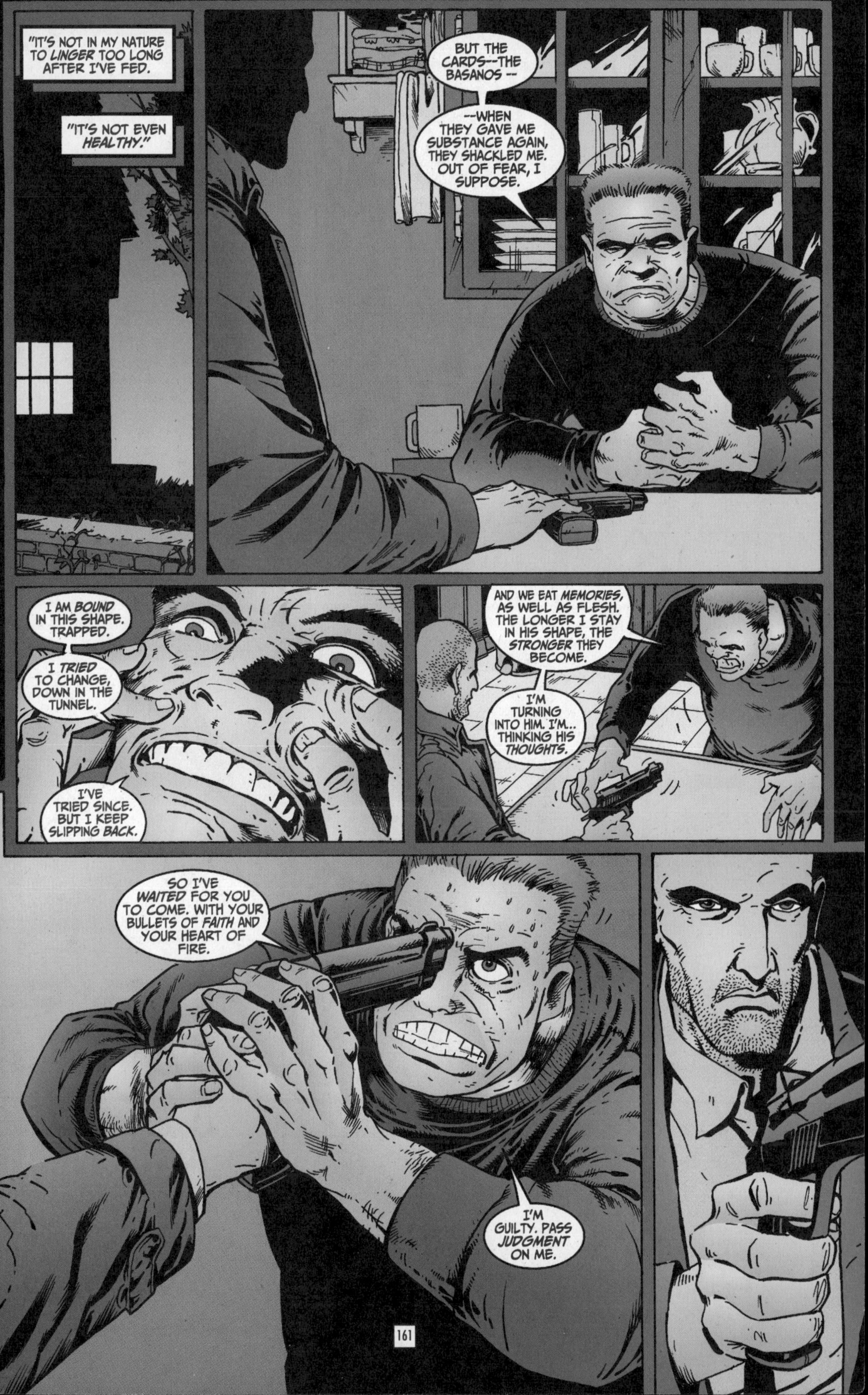
"IT'S NOT IN MY NATURE TO LINGER TOO LONG AFTER I'VE FED.
"IT'S NOT EVEN HEALTHY."
BUT THE CARDS--THE BASANOS --
--WHEN THEY GAVE ME SUBSTANCE AGAIN, THEY SHACKLED ME. OUT OF FEAR, I SUPPOSE.
I AM BOUND IN THIS SHAPE. TRAPPED.
I TRIED TO CHANGE, DOWN IN THE TUNNEL.
I'VE TRIED SINCE. BUT I KEEP SLIPPING BACK.
AND WE EAT MEMORIES, AS WELL AS FLESH. THE LONGER I STAY IN HIS SHAPE, THE STRONGER THEY BECOME.
I'M TURNING INTO HIM. I'M... THINKING HIS THOUGHTS.
SO I'VE WAITED FOR YOU TO COME. WITH YOUR BULLETS OF FAITH AND YOUR HEART OF FIRE.
I'M GUILTY. PASS JUDGMENT ON ME.

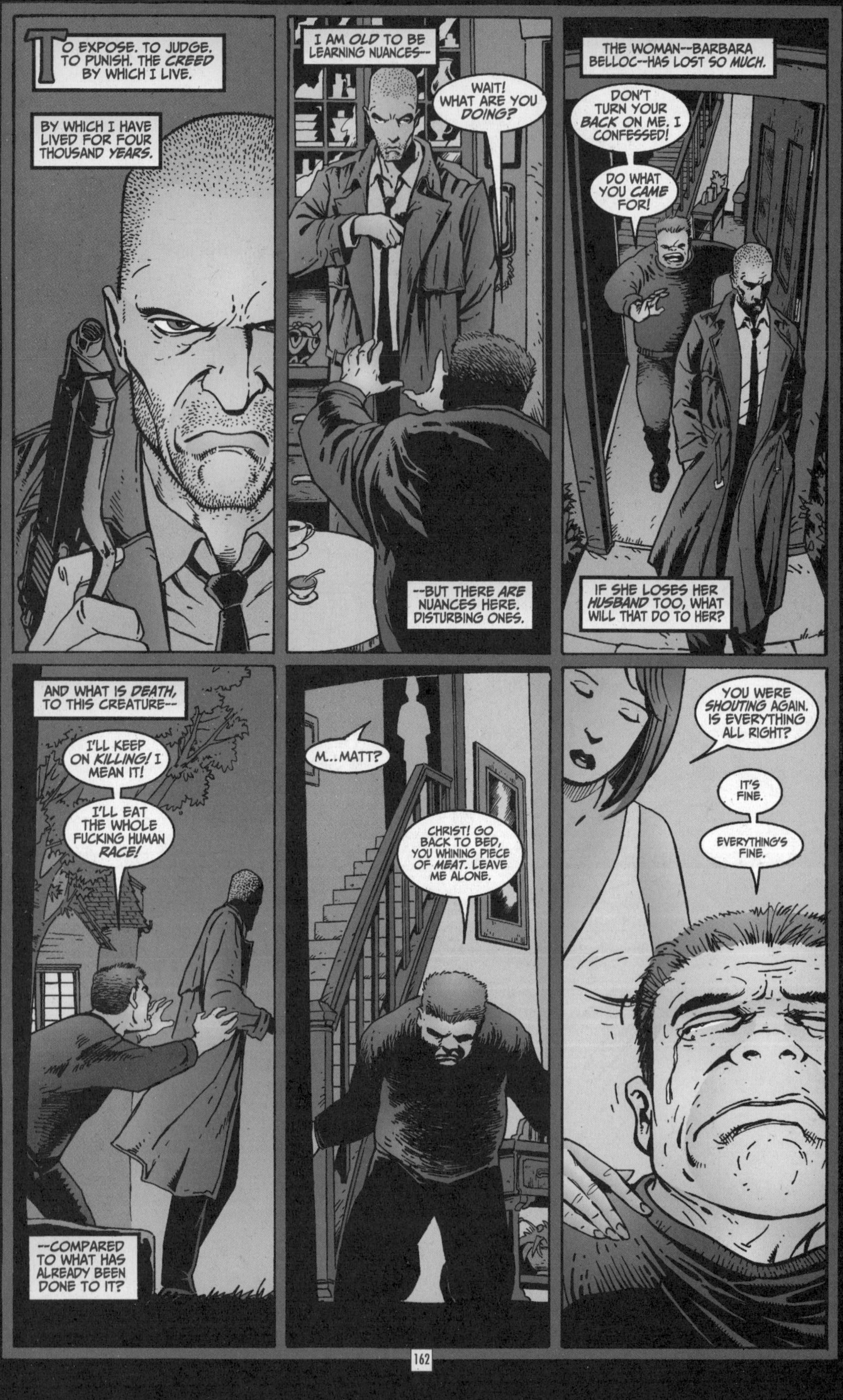
TO EXPOSE. TO JUDGE. TO PUNISH. THE CREED BY WHICH I LIVE.
BY WHICH I HAVE LIVED FOR FOUR THOUSAND YEARS.
I AM OLD TO BE LEARNING NUANCES--
WAIT! WHAT ARE YOU DOING?
--BUT THERE ARE NUANCES HERE. DISTURBING ONES.
THE WOMAN--BARBARA BELLOC--HAS LOST SO MUCH.
DON'T TURN YOUR BACK ON ME. I CONFESSED!
DO WHAT YOU CAME FOR!
IF SHE LOSES HER HUSBAND TOO, WHAT WILL THAT DO TO HER?
AND WHAT IS DEATH, TO THIS CREATURE--
I'LL KEEP ON KILLING! I MEAN IT!
I'LL EAT THE WHOLE FUCKING HUMAN RACE!
--COMPARED TO WHAT HAS ALREADY BEEN DONE TO IT?
M...MATT?
CHRIST! GO BACK TO BED, YOU WHINING PIECE OF MEAT. LEAVE ME ALONE.
YOU WERE SHOUTING AGAIN. IS EVERYTHING ALL RIGHT?
IT'S FINE.
EVERYTHING'S FINE.

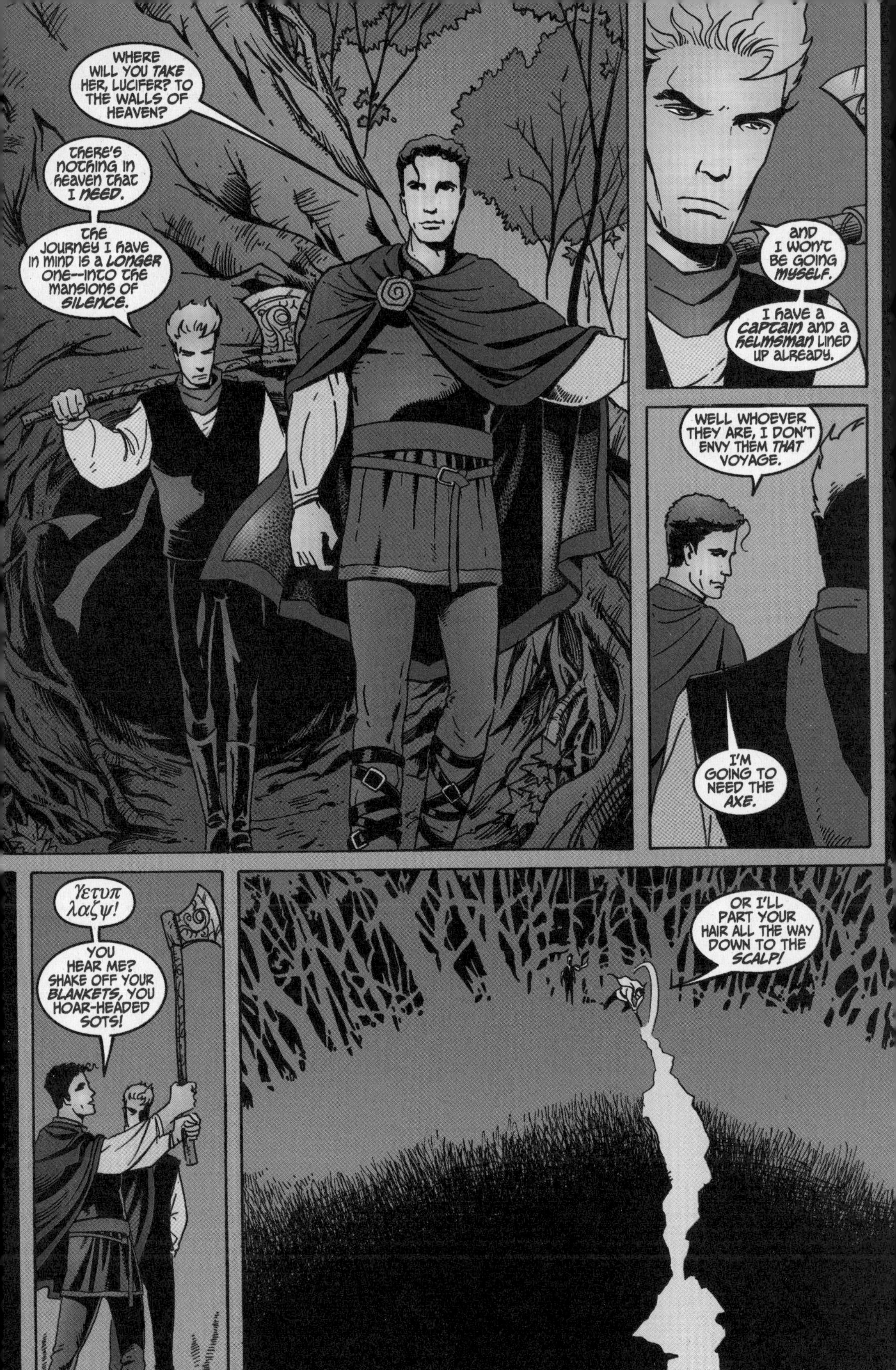
WHERE WILL YOU TAKE HER, LUCIFER? TO THE WALLS OF HEAVEN?
THERE'S NOTHING IN HEAVEN THAT I NEED.
THE JOURNEY I HAVE IN MIND IS A LONGER ONE--INTO THE MANSIONS OF SILENCE.
AND I WON'T BE GOING MYSELF.
I HAVE A CAPTAIN AND A HELMSMAN LINED UP ALREADY.
WELL WHOEVER THEY ARE, I DON'T ENVY THEM THAT VOYAGE.
I'M GOING TO NEED THE AXE.
γετυπ λαζψ!
YOU HEAR ME? SHAKE OFF YOUR BLANKETS, YOU HOAR-HEADED SOTS!
OR I'LL PART YOUR HAIR ALL THE WAY DOWN TO THE SCALP!

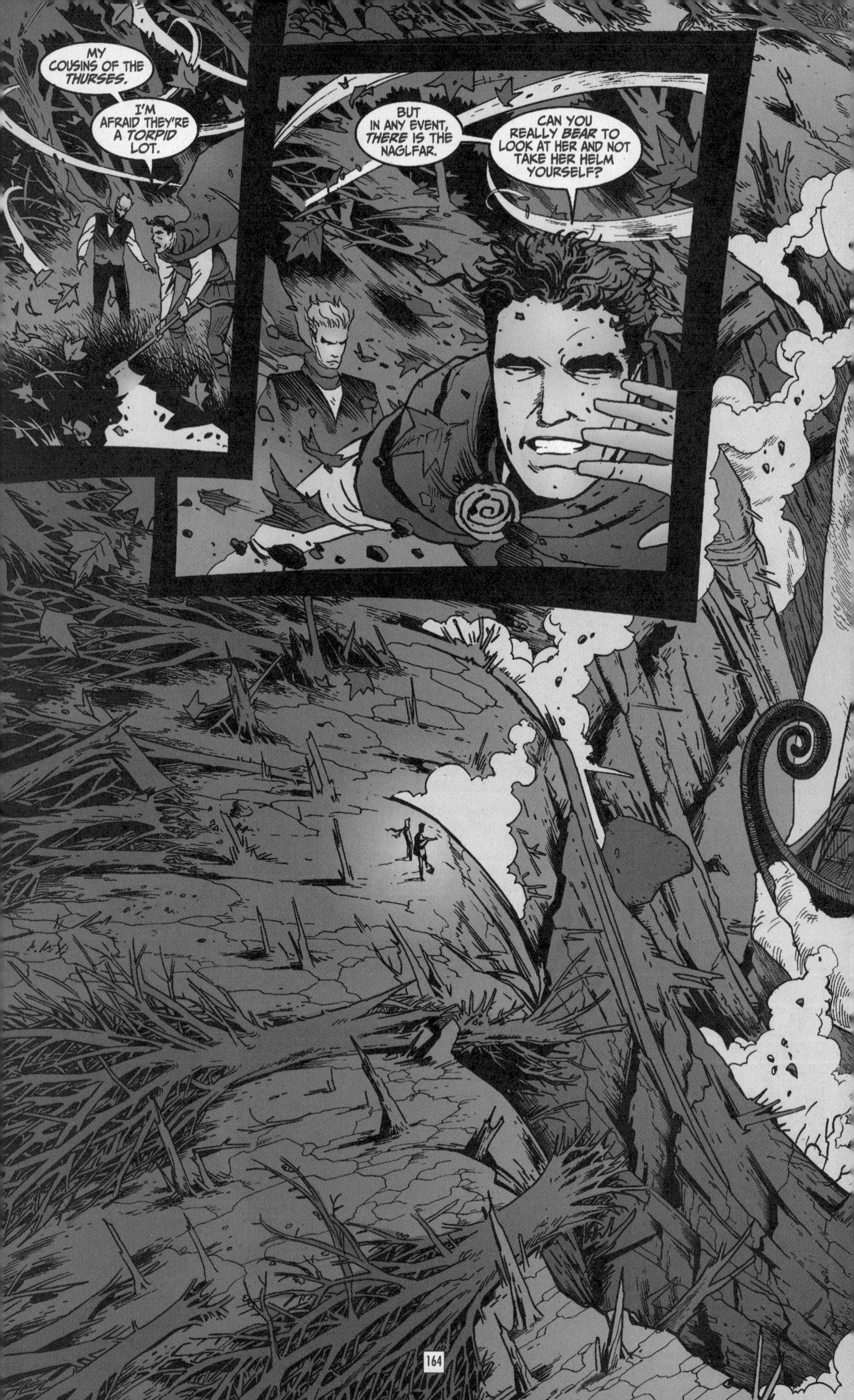
MY COUSINS OF THE *THURSES.*
I'M AFRAID THEY'RE A *TORPID* LOT.
BUT IN ANY EVENT, *THERE* IS THE NAGLFAR.
CAN YOU REALLY *BEAR* TO LOOK AT HER AND NOT TAKE HER HELM YOURSELF?